STUDIES IN
CHRONOLOGY AND
HISTORY

STUDIES IN
CHRONOLOGY AND
HISTORY

BY

REGINALD L. POOLE

COLLECTED AND EDITED
BY
AUSTIN LANE POOLE

OXFORD
AT THE CLARENDON PRESS

Oxford University Press, Ely House, London W. 1

GLASGOW NEW YORK TORONTO MELBOURNE WELLINGTON
CAPE TOWN SALISBURY IBADAN NAIROBI LUSAKA ADDIS ABABA
BOMBAY CALCUTTA MADRAS KARACHI LAHORE DACCA
KUALA LUMPUR SINGAPORE HONG KONG TOKYO

FIRST PUBLISHED 1934

REPRINTED LITHOGRAPHICALLY IN GREAT BRITAIN
AT THE UNIVERSITY PRESS, OXFORD
BY VIVIAN RIDLER
PRINTER TO THE UNIVERSITY
1969

PREFACE

THE papers collected in this volume were mainly written between the years 1916 and 1928. They have been chosen for republication partly on account of their historical value, partly because, having some point of common interest, they fall into three or four distinct groups within each of which the articles are interdependent. Ill health, unfortunately, has prevented my father from undertaking any editorial work. For any mistakes that have crept in, therefore, in the process of preparing the book for the press, I am alone responsible.

I gladly avail myself of this opportunity to express my grateful thanks to several friends of my father and of myself for their kind help, and especially to Dr. C. C. J. Webb who revised the four articles relating to John of Salisbury; to Dr. J. K. Fotheringham for his help in those concerned with early chronology; and to Dr. C. W. Previté-Orton for advice on the essays dealing with Burgundian history.

Lastly thanks are due to the publishers of the periodicals in which the articles originally appeared for their graciously allowing them to be republished: to Messrs. Longmans, Green & Co. for the papers reprinted from the *English Historical Review*; to the Council of the British Academy for those which appeared among their *Proceedings*; to the Medieval Academy of America for the paper first published in *Speculum*; and to the Trustees of the T. F. Tout Memorial Publication Fund for the article contributed to the volume of Essays presented to the late Professor Tout.

A. L. P.

29 March 1934.

CONTENTS

THE BEGINNING OF THE YEAR IN THE MIDDLE AGES[1]

FEW questions of detail give the student of medieval history more trouble than that which concerns the date at which the year is reckoned to begin in the chronicles and charters of Western Europe, and few have given rise to so many wrong statements. Dr. E. A. Abbott, in his work on *St. Thomas of Canterbury, his Death and Miracles*, asks:

Why do all our authorities, except Benedict and Garnier, either omit the date [of the archbishop's murder], or give it incorrectly, as 1171 instead of 1170? Perhaps the fact that, in most parts of England and Europe, the death (occurring on 29 Dec. 1170) would not be known till 1171, and would be associated with 1171, may have contributed to the error.[2]

But the error is Dr. Abbott's, who composed two volumes of elaborate criticism of twelfth-century evidence without informing himself of the elementary point, from what date it was then customary to begin the year. In England, of course, the established practice was to begin on Christmas Day, and the 29th of December was quite correctly placed in 1171. But another mode of reckoning was coming into fashion; and this began the year, not, as Dr. Abbott seems to suppose, on 1 January, but on 25 March. Even in modern times it is often difficult to persuade well-educated people that the Revolution of 1688 means, in our present way of speaking, 1689, since that event took place on 13 February of that year. If mistakes like this can be made in matters which can be easily ascertained, it is not surprising that they should occur when the facts are not so simple. Indeed, in the Middle Ages they are very far from simple. Chroniclers seldom explained the system which they followed: they took a knowledge of it for granted; and any one who explores the mass of evidence as to the various usages prevalent, especially in France, which has been assembled by Ducange and the authors of the *Art de vérifier les Dates*,[3] and repeated with some

[1] Reprinted from the *Proceedings of the British Academy*, vol. x (1921).
[2] Vol. i. 190 (1898); so too '1171, an error for 1170', '1171 (wrongly)', in footnotes to pp. 176, 177, 181, 183 (twice), 185.
[3] In an immense footnote which extends from p. 21 to p. 31 of the first volume of the second series in the octavo edition of 1818.

additions and a few corrections by Arthur Giry, may be apt to
think that the confusion is so great and the alternatives offered
are so many that it must frequently be impossible to decide
whether a particular date belongs to the calendar year named or
to that which precedes or follows it. But these lists do not
profess to do more than register recorded dates. They hardly
distinguish between the evidence of a charter and that of a
chronicler. Valuable as they are, they need at every point
analysis and criticism.

When we are told that in the province of Rheims the year was
computed as beginning at Easter in the ninth century, at
Christmas in the eleventh, on 25 March in the thirteenth, and in
the fifteenth on 25 March in the year preceding the current
year, the series of variations at once provokes suspicion; and
it is hardly doubtful that the first and fourth of these modes of
dating depend upon records in which the year is miswritten.
The second and third, on the other hand, reflect a gradual
change which was introduced from the eleventh century onwards.
Another cause of confusion arises from the statement that a
particular practice prevailed at a certain place *down to* a given
date, when the evidence only informs us that it prevailed there
at that date, and it can be shown that a different practice was
in use at that place some time earlier. Here there is no contradiction; it is only that one system superseded another. In
France, as we shall see, there is a uniform sequence from the
eighth century onwards: first, Christmas; then Lady Day;
lastly, Easter. We shall hardly find an instance in which this
order is disturbed.

In many books we find the different ways of beginning the
year arranged according to the almanack: 1 January, 1 March,
25 March, Easter, 1 September, Christmas. This may be convenient for reference, but it entirely obscures the process by
which these various dates came into currency. If we are to
interpret dates correctly, we must follow the evidence for their
use in the order of time; and for this purpose we must distinguish
between the practices which prevailed before and after the
introduction of the Year of the Incarnation, or as we call it
shortly, the Year of Grace, in the seventh century. The earlier
modes of reckoning are in origin pagan; the later ones are
strictly Christian, until in modern times there was a reversion
to the pagan beginning of the year on 1 January.

I. ANCIENT RECKONINGS

For our present purpose it is not necessary to go further back than the time when Julius Caesar established or revised the calendar. Thenceforward the Civil Year always began on 1 January. But the older system according to which the year began on 1 March, of which we are still reminded in the names of the last four months of the year, was still, as it seems, retained for the computation of the terms of military service,[1] and it seems to me not unlikely that to this usage we may trace the fact that the Franks are found to have begun their year on 1 March. It must be borne in mind that the Franks passed into Gaul probably as opponents of the new dynasty set up by Odoacer and as adherents of the Empire. There are signs that Chlodovech did not disdain appointment to a military command in Belgica Secunda,[2] and he accepted the proconsular dignity from the Emperor Anastasius.[3] Hence it would not be surprising if the Frankish 'March day' as the beginning of the year were derived from the Roman military system. In the eighth century, however, the solemn assembly which was wont to be held on that day was transferred to 1 May, and there was no longer any question of connecting it with the beginning of the year.

At Rome, as I have said, the civil year began on 1 January, and though in later times it was made to begin at other dates —days of Christian observance—the term New Year always meant 1 January. For instance, late in the seventeenth century, Mr. Pepys altered the number of his year on 25 March, but on 1 January he marked his Diary 'New Year', or at any rate made mention of the New Year. It is a striking testimony to the persistence of Roman usage. Even for Church purposes, though the date was condemned on account of its association with pagan festivities,[4] the Golden Number and the Sunday Letter were always changed on 1 January.

But in the Middle Ages it was only in the regions subject to Visigothic rule that the year was regularly counted from that day. This was due to the introduction, in the fifth century, of

[1] See Mommsen, *Gesammelte Schriften*, iv (1906) 102–9.
[2] See the letter of Bishop Remigius of Rheims, in *Epistolae Merowingici et Karolini aevi*, i (ed. W. Gundlach, 1892), 113.
[3] Gregory of Tours, *Historia Francorum*, ii. 28 [38].
[4] See below, p. 10.

the Spanish Era, reckoned from 38 B.C. Thenceforward, for eight hundred years and more, the Spanish peninsula alone in Western Europe possessed a chronological system which could not possibly be misunderstood. But the Era was abrogated in Aragon[1] in 1349, in Castile in 1383, and in Portugal in 1420 ; and it was ordered that the year should be reckoned from Christmas, a date which at that time had become almost obsolete as a chronological starting-point.

The simplicity of the calendar was disturbed towards the end of the third century after Christ by the adoption of a cycle which in its origin was designed not for chronological but for fiscal purposes. It was a series of fifteen years used in Egypt for reckoning a period of taxation,[2] just as in England new assessments for local rates are made at certain intervals of time. This Indiction, as it is called, became generally accepted in the Empire, and the Paschal Chronicle at the end of its record for what we know as the year 312 notes 'the beginning of the Constantinian Indictions'.[3] The Egyptian date for its commencement, 29 August, was altered to 1 September; and thenceforward the Byzantine year was reckoned from this day.

Meanwhile Christianity had introduced a mode of counting the months which we find mentioned in a religious or ecclesiastical connexion. According to this, March ranked as the first month, and the others were numbered conformably. Its origin must be sought very far back. The Mosaic ordinance for keeping the Passover was constantly repeated: *This month shall be unto you the beginning of months; it shall be the first month of the year to you.*[4] To Christians March continued to be 'the first month', because in it appeared the moon which became full at Eastertide, the date from which the Paschal Full Moon was reckoned. But this mode of statement, which found a place in the records of Church Councils and in the Lives of Saints,[5] stood out of relation with the common usage as to the beginning of the year. We may say nowadays that the ecclesiastical year begins with Advent, but

---

[1] This included the country of Roussillon beyond the Pyrenees, which since 1258 had been subject to Aragon.

[2] See U. Wilcken, *Grundzüge der Papyruskunde*, i (1912), pp. lix ff., 222 ff.

[3] Vol. i. 522, ed. L. Dindorf, Bonn, 1832. The Indiction in fact began fifteen years earlier: see Wilcken, p. 223.

[4] Exodus xii. 2.

[5] See the references in F. K. Ginzel, *Handbuch der mathematischen und technischen Chronologie*, iii. 159 f., 1914.

no one computes the year from that fluctuating date. It was natural, however, that the date from 1 March should take a permanent place in Easter Tables, which were constructed for the purpose of ascertaining the day on which Easter should be observed in any particular year. Among the elements contained in such tables were the Concurrents or numbers giving the week-day of 24 March; by adding to these the number of the Solar Regulars, which gave the relative week-days of the different months, for a given month one obtained the week-day of the first of that month in a particular year. These Solar Regulars were computed from 1 March right through the Middle Ages. *Habent enim ortum regulares a Martio*, said Bishop Durandus[1] in the thirteenth century; and the memorial distich which he quotes reappears in an Oxford manual printed in 1520.[2] But it would be idle to suggest that these writers reckoned the year from 1 March for other purposes.

A misunderstanding of this matter has led M. Charles Pfister[3] to lay down that it was the practice at Chartres to date the year from 1 March in the time of Bishop Fulbert, who died in 1028. We possess in fact a set of verses *de Signis et Mensibus* attributed to Fulbert,[4] which include an enumeration of the Solar Regulars in the usual arrangement; but this does not mean that Fulbert, any more than Durandus or the Oxford computist of 1520, began the year with 1 March. But M. Pfister, having fallen into this error, goes on to claim 1 March to have been the first day of the year not only at Chartres but also elsewhere in France, and indeed in the contemporary chancery of King Robert II. He finds a charter of Brioude in Auvergne, the date of which is given as 26 February 1011, *anno iam pene finito*,[5] which he takes as evidence of this mode of reckoning. If there were other examples of it, we might accept the charter as adding confirmation of the practice; but as it stands by itself, it is not sufficiently precise to establish it, and we may more reasonably follow Mabillon[6] in understanding that the year was to end shortly,

---

[1] *Rationale Divinorum Officiorum*, VIII. v. 5, fo. 476b, ed. Lyons 1584. A page earlier Durandus provides for convenience an alternative couplet with the months arranged from January.

[2] *Compotus manualis ad usum Oxoniensium*, 1519–20, reprinted by Christopher Wordsworth, *The Ancient Kalendar of the University of Oxford*, p. 163, 1904.

[3] *Études sur le Règne de Robert le Pieux*, pp. xxxvii f., 1885.

[4] Migne, *Patrologia Latina*, cxli. 348.

[5] D'Achery, *Spicilegium*, iii. 386a, ed. 1723.

[6] *De Re Diplomatica*, p. 173, ed. 1709.

that is on 24 March. For the usage in the chancery of Robert
II, M. Pfister[1] adduces three documents which, he says, oblige
us to place the beginning of the year on 1 March. One of these
is dated at Sens on 24 February 1118 (=1119); the others have
no month: they are all compatible with a reckoning from Lady
Day. Moreover the charter of 24 February is taken from a
chartulary of Lagny,[2] which was written in 1513,[3] and the
regnal year *xxxii* may well be a slip for *xxxi*. But even if the
year is correctly transcribed, we have to remember that Robert's
chancery was in extreme confusion. The dates of his documents
present frequent difficulties, so that the authors of the *Art de
vérifier les Dates*[4] were led, on insufficient grounds, to believe
that he computed the year by the Pisan style.[5] He is known to
have reckoned his regnal years from three different epochs. In
some instances there is an error either in the regnal year or in
the Indiction. For example, a document bears the date of
27 February a. 30, Indiction 1; but the king's thirtieth year
began on 30 December 1016, so that February would fall in 1017,
whereas the Indiction denotes 1018.[6] It may be said with
confidence that M. Pfister would never have propounded his
theory about the practice of this king's chancery had he not
stumbled into a mistake as to the meaning of the Solar Regulars.[7]

The reckoning of the year from 1 March is found, I believe,
with a single exception, in only one place in the west, namely
in Venice, where it held its ground until the fall of the republic
in 1797. How it came to be used there, and at what time the
practice began,[8] are questions which have not been satisfactorily

---

[1] p. xl. [2] Mabillon, p. 581.

[3] See H. Stein, *Bibliographie des Cartulaires Français*, p. 246, 1907.

[4] Vol. i. 11. [5] Cf. Pfister, p. xxxv.

[6] M. Pfister unaccountably says 1019 (p. xlii); but in another place (p. xl) he
states that Robert's thirty-second year began in December 1018. His calculations indeed cannot always be relied on. He assigns, for instance, a document of
26 October a. 12, Indiction XII, correctly to 999 on p. xxxv, but on p. lxvi he
takes it as 998. A charter of a. 39 (where the regnal year is reckoned from
29 March 991) he places before 1 March 1031 (pp. xl, lxxii), but as Sackur points
out (*Die Cluniazenser*, ii. 34, 1894) it must be earlier than 29 March 1030.

[7] Late in the thirteenth century the reckoning of the year from 1 March does
in fact appear in one single town of France. A notary of Figeac in the territory
of Cahors adopts this computation for the years 1289 and 1290. See Noël
Valois in the *Bibliothèque de l'École des Chartes*, xl (1879), 422 f. This looks like
the caprice of an individual scribe, who had possibly been trained in Venice.

[8] It is found in original diplomas in the Venetian archives from the middle of
the eleventh century; see V. Lazzarini, 'Originali antichissimi della Cancellaria
Veneziana', in the *Nuovo Archivio Veneto*, new series, viii (1904), 202.

explained and need not be discussed here. It has indeed been asserted by M. Georges de Manteyer[1] that the system was employed in the chancery of the Emperor Lewis III while he was in Italy from 901 to 902. This opinion is based solely on a diploma for Nonantola, dated 11 February 901 [= 902], in the fifth Indiction;[2] and almost at the same time as M. de Manteyer wrote it was shown by Signor Schiaparelli to be a forgery.[3] It is in fact constructed out of a diploma of Berengar I of 19 August 899,[4] which is likewise spurious. Both documents have their earliest witness in transcripts of the end of the fifteenth century. The single exception to which I have referred is formed by Falco, the chronicler, who wrote towards the middle of the twelfth century. He was a notary of the holy palace at Benevento, and judge of that city. Nothing appears to connect him with Venice; and as he was a layman, he can hardly be supposed to have brought into practice that old reckoning of the months from March, which we have seen to be limited to the dating of strictly religious transactions. The origin of Falco's plan of beginning his record of each year with the 1st of March is unexplained.[5] The supposition that, with this isolated exception, the style of 1 March was used in France or Italy, outside Venice, may then be rejected: it rests for the one country on a simple mistake, and for the other on an undoubted forgery. It is to be regretted that both errors have been incorporated in standard works.[6]

II. RECKONINGS BY THE YEAR OF GRACE

Down to the seventh century after Christ we find the old Roman reckoning of the year from 1 January and the Byzantine reckoning from 1 September, besides the religious reckoning from 1 March, which hardly comes into account as a chronological element. The revolution which introduced more than one new mode of dating was immediately derived from the use of the Easter Table of Dionysius Exiguus. This table was

---

[1] *La Provence*, p. 465, 1908.

[2] Printed by L. Schiaparelli, *I Diplomi di Lodovico III*, pp. 76 ff., 1910; and by A. Gaudenzi, in the *Bullettino dell' Istituto storico Italiano*, XXXVI (1916), pp. 99 ff.   [3] *Bullettino*, XXIX (1908), 185-8.

[4] Printed by Schiaparelli, *I Diplomi di Berengario I*, pp. 373 ff., 1903.

[5] See Muratori, *Rerum Italicarum Scriptores*, V (1724), 82, and the note of Camillo Peregrini there.

[6] The one in Giry, *Manuel de Diplomatique*, pp. 116 f., 1894; the other in Ginzel, iii. 166. Both M. Luchaire and M. R. de Lasteyrie concern themselves unnecessarily with M. Pfister's hypothesis, though neither of them accepts it.

constructed at Rome in 525, but there is no certain trace of its use until nearly a century and a half later. Some indications lead me to conjecture that it was preserved in the monastery founded by Cassiodorus at Squillace and that, when the famous library collected there was dispersed towards the middle of the seventh century, the manuscript passed back to Rome, where St. Wilfrid made acquaintance with it. The rules which Dionysius laid down for the date of Easter were first brought forward when Wilfrid expounded them at the synod of Whitby in 664.[1] Now Dionysius had accompanied his list of the various elements necessary for the finding of Easter year by year with a series of years reckoned from the Incarnation of our Lord. His intention was, of course, simply practical; he had no historical object in mind. But his reckoning from the Incarnation was almost immediately accepted in England as establishing an Era for chronological use. This application of it is generally supposed to be due to the Venerable Bede, who treated of the subject in his work *de Temporum Ratione* published in 725. But it did not need a book to evolve an Era from a collection of Easter Tables. The earlier cycle of Victorius, in which the years were computed from the Passion, was on the way to found an Era[2] when historical writing died out in the darkness of the seventh century. In like manner there is no difficulty in believing that the Table of Dionysius, as continued by Abbot Felix, was at once interpreted as furnishing an Era. And there are in fact a few charters which bear the date from the Incarnation earlier than the time when Bede wrote, though it is true that they are only preserved in transcripts and some of them have been considered to be of doubtful genuineness.

1. *The Reckoning from Christmas*

It now becomes important to inquire at what point in the solar year the year reckoned from the Incarnation was deemed to begin. Bede in his theoretical work *de Temporum Ratione* states, as a matter which needs no explanation, that it began on Christmas Day; but when some time later he came to write his Ecclesiastical History he found himself confronted with the fact that the Acts of Councils and other documents which he cited

---

[1] See my notes on 'The Earliest Use of the Easter Cycle of Dionysius', below, pp. 28 ff.

[2] See the 'Paschale Campanum', in Mommsen's *Chronica Minora*, i. 744 ff.

all bore dates reckoned from the Indiction of September; and the same rule persisted for long after Bede's time in the dating of charters. The Indiction was the old, established, official date, and could not be interfered with. The Year of the Incarnation, on the other hand, was a quite new invention, and it was natural that its definition should give way to the old. Consequently throughout his History Bede made his Year of Grace begin in September.[1] An examination of a large number of chronological statements in that work has convinced me that this was the plan he adopted. It was by no mistake that he dated the synod of Hertford 24 September, Ind. I, in 673, or the synod of Hatfield, 17 September, Ind. VIII, in 680;[2] though these assemblies were held in what we call 672 and 679; and his dating of the comet observed in the autumn of 676 as appearing in 677 is decisive. The conclusion in this matter which I published in October 1918[3] has not, to my knowledge, been impugned. While I was at work on the subject another writer gave reasons for believing that the same practice was continued down to the tenth century;[4] and a long time earlier Sir James Ramsay suggested that it was dispossessed in favour of a reckoning from Christmas in the reign of King Edred, for his death on 23 November 955 is recorded under that year in the Anglo-Saxon Chronicle.[5] The fact that the Canterbury and Abingdon manuscripts of that work (B and C) enter the king's death under 956 seems to show that the usage had not yet become regular.

The Year of Grace passed to the Continent with the English missionaries; but they, it would seem, had learned the system from Bede's chronological treatise, before he came to adopt the reckoning from the Indiction in his History. Thus St. Willibrord,

---

[1] The beginning of the Indiction was shifted, apparently by Bede himself, from 1 to 24 September, and it has been suggested by Mr. A. Anscombe that, when Bede was not citing from documents but giving dates of his own, he reckoned from the later date. See the *Athenaeum*, 3804, p. 380, 22 September 1900. But Mr. Anscombe is in error in quoting the *Hist. eccles.* v. 15 in support of this opinion. Bede says that St. Adamnan converted the Irish to the correct date for the observance of Easter and kept it on that date. Then he returned to Iona and hoped to persuade the monks to adopt the same usage, but was unable to carry out his intention because he died before a year was out; *contigit eum ante expletum anni circulum migrasse de saeculo*. Adamnan died on 23 September and therefore had not another opportunity of keeping another Easter. There is no reference here to the date when the year ended.

[2] *Hist. eccles.* iv. 5, v. 24.   [3] Below, pp. 38 ff.

[4] See the late Mr. M. L. R. Beaven's paper in the *English Historical Review*, xxxii (1917), 516–31.   [5] *Athenaeum*, 3810, p. 511, 3 November 1900.

in a note written with his own hand in 728, says that he was consecrated on St. Cecilia's Day, 22 November 695,[1] while Bede, meaning the same date, says 696.[2] St. Boniface in 742 speaks with horror of the heathen rites with which, as he heard, it was customary at Rome to celebrate the New Year on 1 January[3]; and Pope Zachary joined in his condemnation of these customs.[4] Hence it was natural to choose for the beginning of the year a day which was associated only with Christian observances. But the holiday season of Christmas lasted at least through the eight days following the principal feast. Not much business was transacted in that week, and we have not many documents dated in its course. It is indeed likely that, as a date, Christmas was not infrequently equated with the beginning of the old Roman civil year on 1 January. If one used a calendar, one was apt to look to that date rather than a week earlier. But if in this way some confusion arose,[5] there is no doubt that in theory the reckoning from Christmas became the established system among the Frankish Emperors, at least from the last quarter of the ninth century. It was specifically the Imperial reckoning, and it prevailed wherever the Emperors held rule or exerted influence. From the Empire it passed to the Papacy after the Roman coronation of Otto the Great in 962, and it was regularly employed by the Popes from John XIII to 1098. After that time, though other dates were used in the more solemn documents (*Privilegia*), the style of Christmas continued in the Pope's ordinary correspondence. In the chancery of the French kings it was not abandoned until after 1111,[6] and generally in Western

---

[1] Or the Eve of St. Cecilia, 21 November. The note in the margin of his Calendar is not in line with the indication of St. Cecilia's Day but seems rather to be so placed as to point to 21 November. See the facsimile in *Calendar of St. Willibrord*, ed. H. A. Wilson, 1918, and the editor's note on p. 43.

[2] *Hist. eccles.* v. 11. Yet there are signs that the reckoning from September was still advocated at the Palace School of Charles the Great at the end of the eighth century. Alcuin reproves the practice, *Epist.* xcviii (Jaffé's *Monumenta Alcuiniana*, p. 403, 1873), now numbered cxlv (*Epist. Karol.* ii. 231 f.). It is of course possible, as Dr. Bresslau thinks, *Archiv für Urkundenforschung*, vi (1916), 23, that we have here to do with Byzantine influence.

[3] *Epist.* xlii, in Jaffé's *Monumenta Moguntina*, p. 115, 1866.

[4] *Epist.* xliii, pp. 120 f.

[5] Occasionally, even in originals, we may find the number of the past year entered by inadvertence in the course of January. Thus a charter of Lewis III, which certainly belongs to 19 January 901, bears the date 900: Schiaparelli, *I Diploma di Lodovico III*, p. 18; cf. *Bullettino dell' Istituto Italiano*, xxix. 126.

[6] An instance of the Christmas dating is quoted from Soissons in the year 1135: *Art de vérifier les Dates*, i, note on p. 28. See also below, p. 19.

Europe, outside Spain, it kept its supremacy until the twelfth century. At Narbonne it persisted until the thirteenth. In England it was used in great Benedictine houses down to the beginning of the fourteenth; and an instance has been cited from Newcastle-upon-Tyne as late as 1404.[1]

2. *Reckonings from the Annunciation*

(*a*) This paramount date was soon threatened by a mode of computation which began the year nine months before Christmas. Bede himself had observed that the reckoning from the Incarnation, according to Dionysius's table, started from the year 1 B.C. For the first year of his cycle of five hundred and thirty-two years was A.D. 532, and consequently the cycle which preceded it began in 1 B.C.: the calendar notes of Dionysius's second year all correspond with those proper to A.D. 1.[2] His choice of the term *ab incarnatione* also favoured the interpretation that his years should be reckoned as beginning not on 25 December but on 25 March, 1 B.C. But when this theory was turned into practice has never been determined. Writers on chronology content themselves with the vaguest statements, and generally abstain from expressing a definite opinion. I venture to think that it originated in the kingdom of Burgundy towards the end of the ninth century. It was a time when men in that region were actively engaged in critical work, in manipulating texts, and forging documents.[3] An acuteness which was exercised in these ways would be not unlikely to lay stress on the precise meaning of the chronological term employed by Dionysius and

[1] H. Grotefend, *Zeitrechnung des Deutschen Mittelalters*, i (1891), 206*b* (where the year is misprinted 1407).

[2] Bede says, *de Temporum Ratione*, xlvii [olim xlv], that Dionysius, 'in primo suo circulo quingentesimum tricesimum secundum dominicae incarnationis annum in capite ponendo, manifeste docuit secundum sui circuli annum ipsum esse, quo eiusdem sacrosanctae incarnationis mysterium coepit. . . . Quia ergo secundo anno circuli, quem primum Dionysius scripsit, quinquagesimus tricesimus tertius ab incarnatione Domini completus est annus, ipse est nimirum iuxta concursus siderum ille in quo incarnari dignatus est; quia hic secundus annus decennovenalis octavusdecimus est cycli lunaris, xi habens epactas, v concurrentes septimanae dies, lunam paschae decimamquartam viii Calendas Apriles: omnia tunc fuere simillima, et si esset qui tunc Pascha more nunc ecclesiis usitata die dominica faceret, ipsa nimirum dies, quo modo hic adnotatum est, vi Calendas Apriles veniret, ac lunam haberet decimam-sextam.'

[3] Compare my paper on 'The See of Maurienne and the Valley of Susa, below, pp. 123 ff.

B

Bede. At all events, the first known instance of the reckoning from 25 March before the current year, distinguished from its later prevalence at Pisa as the *calculus Pisanus*, is traced to Arles. It does not appear in an award of Archbishop Rostang of that see in 874;[1] but it is manifest in the archbishop's will, dated Sunday, 6 June 897, in the 14th Indiction, which can only mean 896.[2] Probably it is found also in precepts of Lewis III, when he was king of Lower Burgundy and Archbishop Barnoin of Vienne was chancellor, between 891 and 898. But there are discrepancies in the dates, and M. de Manteyer[3] has been obliged to assume that the Indictions were also anticipated by a year in order to range with the Pisan style. Of such a practice there is, I believe, no other example. It must be observed that of the seven documents[4] upon which M. de Manteyer bases his theory only two give the month and day, and they are preserved only in modern copies. Rather than believe that the Indictions were designedly altered, I would suggest either that there are errors of transcription or else that in the table of Indictions used in the chancery the regnal years were accidentally inserted a year too late.

When Lewis III went into Italy in order to be elected Emperor, he naturally adopted the Imperial style and reckoned from Christmas; but some time after his return to Burgundy the Pisan dating is found once more, though documents are sparse and often badly drawn up.[5] There is, however, no certain evidence of its use in Italy[6] until Hugh of Arles became king of Lombardy in 926. The circumstances of his rule made it impossible for his chancery to be properly organized, and there are frequent irregularities in the dates of his documents. But it is worth noticing that the first definite instance of a charter bearing the Pisan date is also the first which was granted when

---

[1] *Gallia Christiana novissima*, Arles, p. 89, 1900.

[2] This fact escaped the editors, *ibid.*, p. 96.

[3] *La Provence*, pp. 456–9.

[4] Six are printed in Bouquet's *Recueil des Historiens de la France*, ix (1757), 674–80, and one by M. Poupardin, *Le Royaume de Provence*, pp. 406 f., 1901.

[5] See Manteyer, p. 501. I have already corrected this writer's mistake that his year in Italy was taken from 1 March, above, p. 7. His other hypothesis that when he went back to Burgundy he for a while dated from Easter Monday will be mentioned hereafter, p. 22.

[6] The documents of Berengar I are so full of discordant and contradictory dates that it is best to leave them out of consideration. See Schiaparelli, in the *Bullettino dell' Istituto storico Italiano*, xxiii (1902), 81 f.

Gerlannus was chancellor;[1] and Gerlannus is recorded to have been brought in by Hugh's queen Alda.[2] Therefore he was not a native official, but a man who no doubt came from Burgundy. It is probable, therefore, that it was Hugh's clerks who transplanted the reckoning into Italy. But in the royal chancery it did not survive the fall of his dynasty. It became a local style which held its ground in the districts where Hugh's authority had chiefly prevailed. We find it at Pisa and Lucca, but seldom anywhere else. It is said to have been in use at Siena,[3] but this was only for a short time; it has been observed in a document of that town in 947, but from about 1070 it was superseded by the Florentine reckoning.[4] Probably through the employment of scribes from the region of Pisa this style made its way into the Papal chancery under Urban II;[5] but his successors used it more and more rarely, and it is not found after Adrian IV. Its persistence at Pisa down to 1750 is a remarkable fact, which justifies the name of *calculus Pisanus* given to this mode of reckoning, though it did not originate at Pisa. It was a very inconvenient style when it came to be twelve months in advance of that used at Florence; but its use never extended over a very large area. I once noticed it in a charter of Richard I of England; but this was in favour of the Pisan merchants at Acre, and was no doubt drawn up by a Pisan clerk there.[6] There is an isolated specimen of the date in a council held at Florence in 1455, where the year is given as 1456.[7] Whether the Acts were written by a notary from Pisa or there is an error in printing, I am unable to say.

(b) Of far greater importance is the reckoning of the year from

[1] Two documents granted under his hand in February 927 bear dates compatible with the Pisan style, and this is found unmistakably in May 928. After this time it appears more and more frequently down to 939. From 939 onwards the chancery falls into confusion. See Schiaparelli's tables in the *Bullettino dell' Istituto storico Italiano*, xxxiv (1914), 236–55.

[2] 'Miracula s. Columbani', viii, in Mabillon, *Acta Sanctorum O.S.B.* ii. 44, 1669; and in C. Cipolla's *Codice diplomatico del Monasterio di San Columbano di Bobbio*, i (1918), 296.   [3] Grotefend, i. 9.

[4] F. Schneider, *Regestum Senense*, i. 5 and p. lxxviii (1911); cf. A. Luschin von Ebengreuth, in the *Mittheilungen für Oesterreichische Geschichtsforschung*, suppl. vol. vi (1901), 333–6.

[5] Hence no doubt the reckoning was used by Bishop Obert of Liége on 14 June 1095; see A. Wauters, *Table chronologique des Chartes concernant l'Histoire de la Belgique*, i (1866), p. lvii. But this seems to be a solitary example in the north.   [6] *Proceedings of the British Academy*, 1911–12, p. 220.

[7] Labbe and Coleti, *Concilia*, xix (1732), 182b.

25 March after Christmas. This became famous as the *stylus Florentinus*, but it was no more invented at Florence than the Pisan use was at Pisa. The two modes originated in different centuries and sprang from different sources. The earlier one was based on a chronological interpretation; the later had a definitely religious motive. Both alike may be called reckonings from Lady Day, but in view of the wide diffusion of the Florentine mode I propose to reserve this name to it alone. The style of Lady Day became accepted in England in the latter part of the twelfth century and continued to be the official mode of reckoning down to 1752. It has been traced to the influence of the Cistercian movement, but there is no doubt that it was employed long before the foundation of the abbey of Cîteaux. When it first came into use has not been explained. Pagi is cited[1] for the statement that the practice of beginning the year at Lady Day or Easter—which are not at all the same thing—was first used in Aquitaine under Duke William I Tow-head, who died in 963. It is not unlikely that this is an inference from the charter of 1011 which speaks of 26 February as near the end of the year.[2] This charter relates to the abbey of St. Julian at Brioude in Auvergne, which had been presided over by William the Pious, duke of Aquitaine, the founder of Cluny, who died in 918.[3] His line died out ten years later, and Auvergne passed to the father of William Tow-head, who after an interval himself acquired the county in 951. Now Odilo, who became abbot of Cluny in 994, was brought up at St. Julian's, near his birthplace.[4] One might be tempted to suppose that the reckoning from Lady Day came directly or indirectly from Cluny. But the charters of that house, which are often insufficiently and often wrongly dated, will hardly support this view. In 1004 the year was then reckoned from Christmas.[5] But in 1023 and 1029 the dates are interpreted by the editor of the charters, who disregards the Indictions, as calculated by the Florentine style.[6] If this be so, the approximation of date with that which we have noticed in Aquitaine is remarkable. Cluny at this time was active in bringing its influence to bear upon the monastic life of Aquitaine.

---

[1] *Art de vérifier les Dates*, x. 95. No reference is given. If it is to his *Critica in Baronii Annales*, a. 964, v, vol. xvi. 146, ed. Lucca 1744, Pagi speaks only of Easter.   [2] See above, p. 5.

[3] *Gallia Christiana*, ii. 472 f.   [4] Sackur, *Die Cluniazenser*, i. 301 ff.

[5] *Chartes de Cluny*, iii. 643, no. 2588, ed. A. Breul.

[6] *Ibid.*, pp. 799 ff., no. 2777; vol. iv. 17 f., no. 2814.

St. Cyprian's at Poitiers, where William Tow-head became a monk not long before his death, was placed under Odilo's authority.[1] But he was also energetic in other parts, for example, in promoting the reform of Fleury, in the diocese of Orleans. We have therefore to consider the possibility that the Lady Day reckoning was adopted from Fleury, when the great basilica was dedicated to Our Lady. Gilbert, a kinsman of Abbot Abbo of Fleury, was abbot of St. Cyprian at Poitiers about 1004.[2] We find the Lady Day style in use at Fleury in 1030. A comparison of these facts raises a presumption that the reckoning was introduced through the Cluniac reform, and that it may have been connected with some special observance at Fleury.

It has been supposed that this reckoning can be found at Poitiers a few years earlier. A charter granted at that place for the building of the church of our Lady at Lusignan is dated on 6 March 1024 in the seventh Indiction.[3] The Indiction points to 1024, but M. Pfister explains the date as meaning 1025. For, he says, we know that William duke of Aquitaine, who attests the document, was not in France at that time; he had gone to Italy: and another witness, Bishop Jordan of Limoges, was not yet consecrated.[4] As a matter of fact, the year of Jordan's consecration is quite uncertain. His predecessor, Gerald, died in November 1020; but the Benedictine authors of *Gallia Christiana*[5] prudently abstain from fixing the year of Jordan's election. The particulars are recorded only by Ademar of Chabannes, whose editors, both before and after M. Pfister wrote, give the year as 1021.[6] Ademar says that the election took place in January, and that then, as Lent was approaching and the duke was about to depart for Italy, he enjoined his son to take charge of the consecration, which was performed at Mid-lent.[7] There had been, however, some trouble about the election, and one may doubt whether it was made so early as January 1021. The facts that there was a dispute and that there was a popular movement to hasten the election suggest that a

---

[1] See Abbo of Fleury's letter to Odilo, in Mabillon's *Annales O.S.B.* iv (1707), 171.   [2] *Ibid.*

[3] Cousseau, 'Mémoire sur l'église de Notre-Dame de Lusignan', in *Mémoires de la Société des Antiquaires de l'Ouest*, 1844, pp. 291 ff., 397 f.

[4] *Études sur le Règne de Robert le Pieux*, p. xxxviii.   [5] ii. 514.

[6] Waitz, in *Monumenta Germaniae historica, Script.* iv (1842), 142, and J. Chavanon, *Adémar de Chabannes*, p. 182 (1897).

[7] Ademar, iii, 57, pp. 182 f., ed. Chavanon.

longer interval than two months elapsed after the death of Bishop Gerald. It is therefore more likely that Jordan was elected in 1022 or even 1023; but for M. Pfister's assertion that he was not yet consecrated in March 1024 there is no evidence whatever. Even if it were correct, we cannot say that it was impossible for Duke William to have been at Poitiers on 6 March 1024 and to have visited Rome about Easter, 5 April, in the same year, supposing indeed that he was at Rome by Easter.[1] He went to Rome most years, but we are not informed positively that he did so in 1024. He was invited to accept the kingdom of Italy after the death of the Emperor Henry II in 1024; but that event occurred in July, and it was some time later that Duke William visited the country and found reason to abandon the proposed enterprise. We have not therefore sufficient materials for deciding whether the charter of 6 March 1024 belongs to that year or to 1025.[2]

Yet in spite of the Indiction I am disposed to think that the date for which M. Pfister contends is the right one. The church at Lusignan was dedicated in honour of our Lady, and there are many signs that the devotion to the Blessed Virgin was greatly stimulated by the religious movement which is connected with Cluny and Fleury. One cannot miss the significance of the fact, lately brought out by the Dean of Wells, that when St. Oswald returned to England from his training at Fleury and became bishop of Worcester, he rebuilt the cathedral church of St. Peter and dedicated it anew in honour of St. Mary.[3] This was in 983. In the following century this dedication, from a rare one in England, became the most frequent. The feast of the Annunciation thus assumed a greater prominence, and it is not an unlikely supposition that this led to the day being taken to begin the year. The primary meaning of the *annus ab incarnatione* was recalled, and the fact that the date was twelve months late was unheeded. It was the day, not the year, that men considered. A singular parallel to such inconsistency may be noticed in the use of the year *a passione Domini*. It was an ancient belief that

----

[1] If the election was in 1023 there would have been abundance of time, for Easter in that year fell on 14 April.

[2] Cousseau, who edited the charter, gives its date as 1024, but speaks of Bishop Jordan as having been consecrated on the Sunday before. This implies that he took the year to be 1022, when Mid-Lent Sunday fell on 4 March.

[3] J. Armitage Robinson, 'St. Oswald and the Church of Worcester', *British Academy, Supplementary Papers*, v, s.a.

the Annunciation and the Passion both took place on 25 March,[1] and so we find charters of St. Maixent (dio. Poitiers) in which a date given *a passione* is synonymous with one *ab incarnatione*.[2] The day was the important matter, and the difference of some thirty years between the two eras was disregarded.[3]

The increasing use of the Lady Day style as we advance in the eleventh century may be illustrated by a few examples. Richard III, the short-lived duke of Normandy, succeeded his father in August 1026; but there exists a charter granted by him which is dated in January 1026,[4] in the ninth Indiction, where, though the Indiction denotes 1026, the year can only be 1027. In Andrew of Fleury's Life of Gauzlin we have a mention of Mid-Lent Sunday, 8 March 1029,[5] which means 1030. Another monk of Fleury, who passed to the monastery of St. Peter's at Sens, shows how the reckoning which I have connected with Fleury became diffused in other parts of France. This writer, Clarius, gives an account of the translation of the reliques of St. Benedict to the reconstructed choir of the abbey church at Fleury on 20 March 1107. He has already recorded the events of 1108, and then proceeds with remarkable precision:

> Verum ut ad quaedam quae de praeterito anno, incarnationis scilicet Dominicae millesimo centesimo septimo, quatuor diebus ante praesentem annum de quo agitur, meminisse decet.

After narrating the proceedings at the translation he concludes:

> Hoc totum factum est XIII Kal. Aprilis.[6]

The high altar, it may be noted, was then dedicated in honour of St. Mary.

While the reckoning from Lady Day was gradually becoming accepted in France, the old Christmas style held its ground in some religious houses. Thus in the monastery of St. Maixent charters of January 1099, March 1110, and February 1114 are

---

[1] Augustin, *de Trinitate*, iv. 5. 9.

[2] See A. Richard, 'Chartes et Documents pour servir à l'histoire de l'Abbaye de Saint-Maixent', in *Archives historiques du Poitou*, xvi (1886), 168 ff.

[3] This mode of dating is unrelated to the early reckoning from the historical year of the Passion, supposed to be A.D. 28, of which there are traces in the chronicle of Victor Tunnunensis and which was derived from the Paschal Cycle of Victorius of Aquitaine.

[4] D'Achery, *Spicilegium*, iii. 390, ed. 1723.

[5] *Gallia Christiana*, viii. 1552; *Neues Archiv*, iii. 383. The manuscripts give two discrepant Indictions, both wrong.

[6] D'Achery, *Spicilegium*, ii. 478 f.

unquestionably dated from Christmas. It is true that an original charter of that house of 24 February 1080 [=1081] appears to be dated from Lady Day,[1] because it mentions Ansegisus as abbot, and he was elected on 29 September 1080 ;[2] but probably here the word *primo* was accidentally omitted in the year. Moreover, when Aquitaine passed under the rule of an English king the Christmas reckoning seems to have been revived. There is a definite example of this in a charter of 29 December 1198 (=1197) ;[3] and two other instances have been cited from texts in chartularies dated so late as 1260 and 1290.[4] But Giry's statement[5] that it prevailed in Poitou *à l'exclusion de tout autre* down to 1225 needs considerable qualification.

This mode of reckoning the year was slow in penetrating into the chancery of the French kings. The evidence drawn from the charters of Robert II is, as we have seen,[6] too insecure to establish his system. It is probable that a close examination of the documents of his successors would show that most of them bearing a date with a year reckoned from Lady Day were drawn up in the religious house to which they were granted and were dated in accordance with the practice of that house. Henry I at Tours writes 19 January 1056, when we should write 1057 ; but not many weeks later at Angers on 1 March, he reverts to the traditional Christmas style,[7] which in fact continued to prevail in Anjou all through the eleventh century.[8] It was held by Natalis de Wailly[9] that in one document Philip I reckoned the year from Easter, but the charter cited contains such discordant dates that it cannot warrant any positive conclusion.[10] That the Christmas style was that which was regularly employed in the royal chancery down to 1111 has been abundantly proved by the evidence collected by MM. Robert de Lasteyrie[11] and

---

[1] See Richard, *op. cit.*, pp. xxxiii, xxxiv.

[2] *Chroniques des églises d'Anjou*, ed. P. Marchegay and E. Mabille, p. 407, 1869.   [3] Giry, p. 115, n. 4.

[4] Richard, p. xxxv.   [5] p. 115.   [6] Above, p. 5 f.

[7] *Recueil des historiens de la France*, xi (1767), 592 f.

[8] An exception is quoted from a document of St. Florent at Saumur, where 21 January 1075 means 1076. But slips about the year were apt to occur in January, and moreover the charter is preserved only in a transcript. Another document relating to the same monastery, of 30 December 1093 (=1092), is definitely dated from Christmas Day. See Giry, p. 115, nn. 2 and 3.

[9] *Éléments de Paléographie*, i. 350, 1838.

[10] The charter bears the date of 24 February 1100; but the Indiction and concurrent are those of 1099, and the epacts and the *luna* are of 1101.

[11] *Cartulaire général de Paris*, i, pp. xxxi, xxxii, 1887.

Achille Luchaire.[1] Two documents a little before the year just
named contain indeed a date reckoned from Lady Day; but one
of these is an act executed in 1104 in the chapter house of
Beauvais,[2] where that style undoubtedly prevailed, and the
other is a private document recording an agreement made in
1110 between the church of St. Geneviève and the monastery
of Bec.[3] From 1112 the Lady Day reckoning becomes normal
in the French chancery.

About a century later it is certain that Philip Augustus began
the year not from Lady Day but from Easter, and it has therefore naturally been disputed whether the dates which I have
counted as from Lady Day were not really counted from Easter.
It is agreed, however, that all the examples cited are equally
consistent with either reckoning, and it seems more probable
that a style was employed which is known to have been extensively used, rather than one of which there is no clear proof
before 1215. But this, of course, is a matter of opinion. The
difficulty in arriving at a certain conclusion with regard to the
documents of Louis VII arises from the fact that his letters
patent bore no date of month and day, and his royal charters
bore them only exceptionally. One single document with the
Christmas reckoning has been brought forward; but this is
clearly not a production of the king's chancery; it was drawn
up by an official of the church of Montpellier after an approved
ecclesiastical pattern. Against this Luchaire[4] is able to set six
charters in which the old year is continued into the early months
of the new. One of these, a charter for the church of St. Benignus
at Dijon, is dated in the year 1146, and we know that the king
was at Dijon on 30 March 1147 and was present at the consecration of the church on the following day. This might be taken as
proof that the year was reckoned from Easter; but M. Robert
de Lasteyrie[5] points out that we cannot tell that the king was
not at Dijon a week earlier, so that the charter may have been
drawn up before 25 March.

The reckoning from Lady Day seems not to have travelled far
into the regions eastward of France, parts of the old duchy of
Lorraine. Here it is found in the province of Treves, where it

[1] *Louis VI le Gros*, pp. 296 f., 1890.
[2] Luchaire, no. 28.   [3] *Ibid.*, no. 94.
[4] *Étude sur les Actes de Louis VII*, pp. 25 ff., 1885.
[5] *Cartulaire général de Paris*, i, p. xxxiii.

persisted down to the seventeenth century ;[1] and in the university
of Cologne, a foundation of Urban VI. That it sometimes
appears in the Imperial chancery from Philip of Swabia to
Frederick II was probably due to Italian influence, but it was
never a serious rival to the time-honoured Christmas style. In
the south-east, in the old kingdom of Burgundy, it was probably
used at Lyons in 1201 and at Arles in 1249.[2] In the Papal
chancery, where chronology had become disturbed from the
time of Urban II, this reckoning was frequently adopted, until
in the thirteenth century there was a reaction to the date of
Christmas.

3. *The Reckoning from Easter*

There was an ancient usage of appending to the candle which
was lit on Easter Eve a label, *indiculus*, recording the chronological notes of the year. In the later centuries of the Middle
Ages these included the Epacts, the Concurrent, the year of the
Lunar and Solar Cycles, the day of Easter, and other data. In
700 the monks of Jarrow found such a label at Rome, which
gave the number of years from the Passion of our Lord.[3] It
implied a mode of reckoning, from A.D. 33, which nowhere
obtained currency, though it is mentioned in order to draw
attention to certain portents in 1033 by a nearly contemporary
writer, Rodulf Glaber.[4] It might naturally be supposed that
these inscriptions would lead to a computation of the year from
Easter. But when this was done the Era was still that of the
Incarnation. It was an attempt to combine two inconsistent
systems. Nor has any sufficient evidence been brought forward
to show that the year was in fact reckoned from Easter until
about 1200, when Gervase of Canterbury, enumerating the
various ways in which historians began the year, says *quidam
vero a Passione*.[5] For a much earlier time a document of Adalard,
abbot of St. Bertin, has often been cited which bears the
following date:

Actum Aria monasterio, VI kalendas Aprilis, anno incarnationis
Domini dccclvi et bissextili ascensu I, indictione v ac embolismo,

---

[1] Grotefend, i. 8. See also below, p. 24.
[2] *Mémoires de la Société des Antiquaires de France*, 3rd series, ii (1855),
244 f.   [3] Bede, *de Temporum Ratione*, xlvii [olim xlv].
[4] *Hist.* iv. 1, 4, 5, 9, ed. M. Prou, 1886.
[5] *Opera historica*, i. 88, ed. Stubbs, 1879.

sabbato ante medium Quadragesimae, anno XVII regnante Karolo cum fratre Hludovico ac nepote Hlotario.[1]

All these notes of time, except the year 856, agree with 857. The authors of the *Art de vérifier les Dates*[2] indeed thought that *ascensu I* gave the Paschal regular for 856, but Auguste Bernard showed that it goes with *bissextili* and means the first year of the *bissextus*, that is, of the leap-year period; in other words, the first year after leap-year.[3] In the same way Bede speaks of the *crementum bissextile*.[4] We need not doubt that the year of Grace is miswritten. Folquin, the compiler of the chartulary a century later, was careless in matters of chronology. He almost always made blunders in adjusting regnal years to the years of Grace.[5] His inaccuracy may be shown by his notice of the death of his namesake Bishop Folquin of Térouanne, which he places on Tuesday, 15 December 855 in the third Indiction and the 15th year of Charles the Bald: 15 December fell on a Tuesday in 856, which was not in the third Indiction. The same writer composed a Life of Bishop Folquin in which he said that he died on a Saturday.[6] The bishop's epitaph places his death on 14 December, which was a Saturday in 855.[7] We cannot found the use of the Easter dating in the ninth century upon such an authority.[8]

A second piece of evidence for its early use was suggested by Dr. W. Levison in 1919. The biographer of Archbishop Rigobert of Rheims mentions an event of 15 January 894 as occurring in the twelfth year of Archbishop Fulk of Rheims; so that, as Fulk was consecrated on 7 March 883,[9] either the bishop's year is wrong or else perhaps it was reckoned from Easter.[10] It would be simple to propose an emendation of XII into XI; but if the date is correctly given we have not a few examples of regnal and pontifical years being adjusted to the year reckoned from

---

[1] *Cartulaire de l'Abbaye de Saint-Bertin*, p. 162, ed. B. Guérard, 1840. The text is quoted inaccurately by Giry, p. 113, n. 4.   [2] Vol. i. 27 note.

[3] *Mémoires de la Société des Antiquaires de France*, 3rd series, ii (1855), 252 f.

[4] *De Temporum Ratione*, xxxix [olim xxxvii].

[5] See Guérard, *Cartulaire*, notes on pp. 17, 20, 28, 31.

[6] *Monumenta Germaniae historica, Script.* xv. i (1887), 429.

[7] L. Duchesne, *Fastes épiscopaux de l'ancienne Gaule*, iii (1915), 135, n. 9.

[8] It may be added that Folquin, in the *Cartulaire*, p. 138, says that Charles the Simple died before Robert I. Charles died in September 939; Robert in January 936.

[9] Flodoard, *Historia Ecclesiae Remensis*, iv. 10.

[10] *Scriptores Rerum Merovingicarum*, vii. 78.

Christmas; so that if a bishop were consecrated in March, his second year would be counted as beginning on 25 December. Another example has been quoted from Rheims by a mere mistake. Archbishop Arnulf, says A. Wauters,[1] promised fealty to Hugh Capet in 989, in the second Indiction; and he was not made archbishop until after 23 January 990. But this latter date is an inference from a somewhat confused statement in Richer's History; and the year of his appointment is proved by letters of Gerbert to have been 989 [2]

It is contended by M. de Manteyer[3] that when the Emperor Lewis III departed homewards from Italy, disgraced and blinded, in 902, he adopted a computus beginning with Easter Monday. This he infers from a charter dated 17 April 902,[4] which indubitably means 903. But the dating clause is incomplete: it omits the Indiction and leaves a gap for the Imperial year. The charter, moreover, is preserved only in a modern copy taken from a chartulary. It would be more natural to emend *dccccii* into *dcccciii* than to postulate the use of a style which is otherwise completely unknown.[5] But M. de Manteyer finds no difficulty in his hypothesis, and explains by its help a charter of 900[6] which but for this assumption would have seemed manifestly dated according to the Christmas reckoning. What is more likely than that Lewis should have made use of this—the Imperial—style in September 900 in anticipation of his quest for the Imperial crown?

Again, that the Easter reckoning appears in the Abingdon text of the Anglo-Saxon Chronicle from 1044 to 1053 was maintained by Henry Petrie,[7] who was followed by Mr. Plummer; but this opinion seems to me quite erroneous.[8] It would indeed

---

[1] *Table chronologique des Chartes concernant l'Histoire de Belgique*, i, p. lxiii (1866).　　[2] See Julien Havet's note to the *Lettres de Gerbert*, p. 105, 1889.

[3] *La Provence*, pp. 462–5.

[4] U. Chevalier, *Cartulaire de l'Abbaye de Saint-André-le-Bas de Vienne*, pp. 219 ff., 1869.

[5] There are signs that in France, long after the Easter reckoning was accepted, the year might be deemed to begin on the Monday following; but this was not for dating charters but for keeping accounts. Giry (p. 111, n. 3) quotes from a register of the Cour des Monnaies an entry *jusques au samedi, veille de Pasques l'an* [m]*cccxiii, dont l'incarnation se mua le lundi ensuivant*. No business was transacted on Easter day, and therefore the accounts started a new year on the Monday.

[6] p. 469. See the text in Bouquet, *Recueil des Historiens*, ix. 680.

[7] *Monumenta Britannica historica*, i. 435, n. *a*.

[8] See my note in the *English Historical Review*, xvi (1901), 719 ff.

be strange if an English monastery at that time employed a mode of dating more than a century and a half before it was used anywhere else.[1]

In the thirteenth century, certainly from 1215, the reckoning of the year from Easter became the established rule in the French chancery. The reasons which induced Philip Augustus to adopt a new and extremely inconvenient system of chronology have never been explained. I can only conjecture that he desired to mark his conquest of the English possessions in France by the use of a style different from those which had been current in them. The reckoning of the year from Lady Day was steadily gaining ground in the dominions of the English king, and Philip may very well have chosen a style distinct from it and yet so much like it that its adoption would not affect more than a small number of dates during a limited period of the year. Anyhow, from this time the date from Easter became specifically the style of the court of France. It gradually prevailed not merely in the kingdom itself, but also in regions beyond where the French court had influence.

We have then to proceed by citing instances where this style was not observed. It is perhaps immaterial to mention that in a record of councils held at Beauvais in 1232 and 1233 we read: *Notandum quod more Gallicano mutatur annus in Domini annuntiatione dominica;*[2] for the dates are not long after the new reckoning was introduced. Besides, Beauvais lay in the province of Rheims, which was largely contiguous to the Imperial territory, and indeed in parts extended into it. Hence it was desirable to make it clear that the Imperial style of Christmas was not intended: by 1310 the court style was in use at Rheims.[3] Of greater significance is the fact that by the end of the thirteenth century the Easter date was so well established at Limoges and found so inconvenient that it was ordered that the year 1301 should begin with Lady Day.[4] The court style seems never to have penetrated into Cahors, Rodez, or Angoulême;[5] and it is more than doubtful whether it did into Poitou.[6] But it is found

---

[1] Giry indeed states, p. 123, that it was in use in Béarn in the eleventh century, and cites the *Cartulaire de Sainte Foi de Morlaas*, ed. L. Cadier, p. xviii, 1884. The book does not seem to be found in England, and I can only presume that here as in other instances the reckoning is in fact from Lady Day.

[2] Martene and Durand, *Thesaurus novus Anecdotorum*, iv. 182 (1717).

[3] Grotefend, i. 141b.   [4] Giry, p. 116, nn. 1 and 2.

[5] Giry, p. 115, n. 7.   [6] Richard, *op. cit.*, pp. xxxiv–xxxvi.

in Toulouse when that county passed into the hands of Alfonse of Poitiers towards the middle of the thirteenth century.[1] In Auvergne the reckoning from Lady Day was still current in 1478.[2]

The statement that the court style prevailed in the region of Lyons from the twelfth century is unproved and improbable. It is possible that that reckoning was adopted there from the time when Philip IV took the city under his protection in 1292 ;[3] but the documents bear a date which is equally compatible with a calculation from Easter and from Lady Day.[4] The earliest document which is indubitably dated according to the Easter style was produced in April 1310 on the eve of the French king's annexation of Lyons in the following July.[5] In Dauphiné, however, which became a French possession in 1343, the reckoning from Lady Day still continued. In other parts of the Burgundian kingdom we find the survival of the old reckoning from Christmas at Avignon in 1215.

When we pass to the eastern districts of what is now French territory, a clear distinction has to be drawn between the lands which were Imperial and those which were subject to the crown of France. In the former we should expect the Christmas reckoning to prevail, and this was so in Alsace and the County of Burgundy (Franche-Comté). But the date from Lady Day penetrated into Lorraine and the County of Bar. Finally, in the thirteenth and fourteenth centuries, the French court style of Easter was extensively adopted. It is found in Franche-Comté as early as 1246. When in 1301 the count of Bar did homage to the French king for his dominions west of the Meuse, this territory (known as *Barrois mouvant*) naturally reckoned the year from Easter; but the rest of the county held to Lady Day. The Three Bishoprics were suffragans of Treves, where the year was reckoned from Lady Day ;[6] but Toul and Verdun in time accepted the French style from Easter; Metz, however, which

---

[1] Giry, p. 122, n. 6. [2] Giry, p. 117, n. 6.

[3] See A. Leroux, *Les Relations politiques de la France avec l'Allemagne de 1292 à 1378*, p. 144 (1882).

[4] See the *Cartulaire municipal de la Ville de Lyon*, ed. M. C. Guigue, pp. 416 f., 35, 36, 108 f., 424, 110 f. (1876).

[5] The date is given as Saturday before Palm Sunday 1309. But there was no Palm Sunday in 1309 according to the Lady Day reckoning. In 1308–9 it fell on 23 March 1309; and in 1310 on 12 April. If, therefore, the year is correctly given it can only be reckoned from Easter.

[6] See above, p. 19.

as late as the beginning of the thirteenth century had not altogether abandoned the older reckoning from Christmas, adopted that from Lady Day and maintained it until modern times.

Farther north, especially in the Low Countries, the chronology was complicated by the varieties of ecclesiastical and temporal relations. Indeed, the dynastic changes in these regions led to such frequent disturbance of practice that in a short survey like the present it is impossible to attempt more than a general statement which must be subject to revision at many points. Beyond the French border the reckoning from Christmas was retained in Hainault; it is not until 1431 that we find the Easter date there. But as in the thirteenth century the province of Rheims began the year on Lady Day, we find this system in use at Ghent as late as 1308. In the thirteenth century, however, the church of Cologne accepted the French style of Easter, and this therefore makes its appearance at Liège and Utrecht. It was powerfully stimulated when step by step the dukes of Burgundy acquired the greater part of the Low Countries in the fifteenth century It is, however, to be observed that here the Easter date was constantly noted as the style of the court, to distinguish it from the popular usages which were maintained in different places. Thus in the town of Rotterdam the reckoning from Christmas held its ground down to the fourteenth and fifteenth centuries. Meanwhile in the latter part of the thirteenth century this Christmas style was more and more commonly used by the Popes, and in 1310 a council at Cologne ordered its adoption;[1] and this led to its reappearance at Liège in 1333; but even at Cologne itself the municipality adhered to the Easter reckoning.[2]

In a very different region, the County of Vienne, the Christmas date was established, in place of that of Lady Day, in 1292; but as the Dauphin had done homage to Rudolf of Hapsburg in the preceding year, this would seem to mean the acceptance of the Imperial reckoning, which agreed with that known as the usage of the Papal court. To distinguish it from the French practice it was called 'le style Delphinal'. In 1305 it was introduced into Geneva,[3] which thus fell into line with the lands of Switzerland proper.

[1] Hartzheim, *Concilia Germaniae*, iv. 125a (1761).
[2] *Art de vérifier les Dates*, i, note on p. 22.
[3] F. Rühl, *Chronologie des Mittelalters und der Neuzeit*, p. 38, 1897.

III. THE RESTORATION OF THE ANCIENT RECKONING

We have seen that the Church steadily opposed the observance of 1 January as the beginning of the year. That date was indeed accepted for calendar purposes, and the Golden Number and the Sunday Letter were reckoned from it. By the sixth century at least it was also established as a festival, the feast of the Circumcision; but it was hardly ever employed as a chronological landmark, though its closeness to Christmas appears occasionally to have led to confusion between the two dates.[1] Towards the middle of the thirteenth century, however, there are definite symptoms of a return to the ancient pagan system. This was perhaps partly due to an increasing use of almanacks, which were naturally constructed from 1 January. Probably it was also influenced by the study of Roman law. The restoration is said to be traceable in the chancery of William of Holland,[2] the rival of the Emperor Frederick II, and of Rudolf of Hapsburg. It is attested at Münster in Westphalia in 1313, and is frequently found in the documents of the Emperor Lewis the Bavarian and sometimes in those of Charles IV. At Frankfort-on-the-Main it prevailed from 1338 to 1484, when it was abandoned. At Mainz it gradually won ground in the fifteenth century.

This revival seems to have been almost entirely limited to Germany. It is noticeable that when in the latter part of the fourteenth century the Spanish Era was discontinued in the Peninsula the reckoning of the year from 1 January which went with it was also ordered to be given up, and the reckoning from Christmas took its place. Late in the fifteenth century the college of the Sorbonne at Paris used a different system from that of the French court; but whether it reckoned from Christmas or from 1 January has not been determined.

Here our inquiry properly ends, but it may be well to add a short statement of the dates at which the older systems were officially abolished.[3] The orders usually provided that the year following their issue should begin on 1 January, but sometimes

---

[1] This confusion has been observed in the documents of Charles I of Anjou, king of Naples, and his successors, from 1265 to 1343.

[2] I take this and the following statements from Rühl, p. 25.

[3] The list printed in J. J. Bond's *Handy-Book for verifying Dates*, pp. 91–101 (4th ed., 1889), needs a great deal of correction.

their execution was delayed. When the order was confirmed after an interval of years, I give both years.

Estates of Holland . . .	1532
Spain	1556
The Empire	1558
France	1564–7
Franche-Comté . .	1566–75
Geneva	1575
Lorraine	1579

The reform of the calendar effected by the bull of Gregory XIII of 24 February 1581–2 enacted that thenceforth the year should begin on 1 January; and this change became operative in countries of the Roman obedience in 1583, but in Austria twelve months later. Scotland followed their example in 1599. It is said that, in spite of the reform which they had brought about, the Popes did not adopt 1 January as the day at which they began the year until 1621 for briefs, and 1691 for bulls. Some time between these dates the new practice was adopted at Treves. From 1700 it received a further extension and was ordered at the following dates in

Protestant states of Germany .	1700
Guelderland	1700
Utrecht	1700
Grisons	1717
Protestant cantons of Switzerland	1739
Florence and Pisa . . .	1749
England and Ireland . . .	1751[1]
Venice	1797.

[1] This change involved several anomalies in 1752. See J. E. W. Wallis, *English Time-Books*, i (1921) 45 note, and the Special Table for 1752 in E. A. Fry's *Almanacks for Students of English History*, 1915.

THE EARLIEST USE OF THE EASTER CYCLE
OF DIONYSIUS[1]

I

THE question which I propose to examine is the earliest date at which the Easter cycle of Dionysius Exiguus can be proved to have been in use. This cycle, it is well known, was a continuation of that attributed to Cyril of Alexandria[2], and was drawn up in A.D. 525, for a period of five lunar cycles or ninety-five years. But whereas Cyril accompanied his Easter tables with a consecutive series of years beginning with the Emperor Diocletian, Dionysius, as he says, preferred to date his years not from the rule of a persecutor of the Christians but with the Incarnation of our Lord. There is no hint that he intended to establish an era for ordinary historical purposes; he only gave the years for reference, in order to identify the dates assigned to Easter.

The chief competitor of the system which Dionysius introduced into the West was that constructed in the fifth century by Victorius of Aquitaine, which held its ground in Gaul for nearly three hundred years. Both were based on the lunar cycle of nineteen years, but they differed in four points: the earliest permissible date of the vernal new moon, the earliest day after this on which Easter could be kept, the latest day on which Easter could fall, and the place in each cycle in which the lunar year should be shortened by one day (the *saltus lunae*). For my present inquiry it is only necessary to speak of the second of these points of difference. If we read that Easter might be observed on the day after the full moon, on the fifteenth moon as it was called, this was understood to mean the oriental reckoning adopted by Dionysius; if, on the other hand, we are told that Easter must not be kept until the sixteenth moon, then the cycle is definitely not that of Dionysius.[3] An older practice

[1] Reprinted with corrections from *The English Historical Review*, vol. xxxiii (1918).

[2] Dr. E. Schwarz traces it not to Alexandria but to Constantinople: see 'Christliche und Jüdische Ostertafeln', in *Abhandl. der kön. Gesellsch. der Wissensch. zu Göttingen, philol.-hist.* Klasse. N.F. viii (1905), 22 f.

[3] Though Victorius in his letter (*Chronica minora*, ed. Mommsen, i. 679 f., 1892) admits both the alternatives, his rule seems to have been interpreted as excluding *luna xv*, and thus maintaining the definition which had previously prevailed at Rome. Cf. L. Ideler, *Handbuch der mathem. und techn. Chronologie*, ii (1826), 283; F. K. Ginzel, *Handbuch der mathem. und techn. Chronologie*, iii (1914), 245.

of permitting Easter Sunday to fall as early as the fourteenth moon—the discussion of which played a great part in controversy with the Celtic churches of the British Isles—does not concern us. We have only to do with the question as between *luna quintadecima* and *luna sextadecima*.

Now, although Dionysius composed his cycle in 525, there is no trace of its having been immediately adopted by any one. Cassiodorus, indeed, who was personally acquainted with him, may have known of the cycle;[1] but there is no sign that he himself made use of it. Nor do any Roman inscriptions of the sixth century supply evidence of its employment.[2] In the discussion concerning the right date of Easter in 550, Bishop Victor of Capua opposed the system of Victorius; but Dr. Bruno Krusch, a most accomplished computist, has shown that he based his arguments not on Dionysius but directly upon his Greek authorities, and he has also made it probable that the cycle inscribed on the great monument in the sacristy of the cathedral at Ravenna is in like manner derived immediately from the East.[3] It has indeed been supposed that a table of Easter days written in the last quarter of the sixth century gives evidence not only of the use of the cycle of Dionysius but also of its employment for historical purposes, for the insertion of annalistic notices. This is a mistake. The table contains the cycle of Victorius, and the years are reckoned, as Victorius reckoned them, not from the Incarnation but from the Passion.

[1] The Pinax referred to by Cassiodorus, 'Deinde Pinacem Dionysii discite breviter comprehensum, ut quod auribus in supradicto libro [*sc.* Marcellini] percipitis pene oculis intuentibus videre possitis': *De Institutione Divinarum Litterarum*, xxv, in Migne's *Patrol. Lat.* lxx. 1140, was identified with the tract of Dionysius Exiguus by Adolf Franz (*Cassiodorus Senator*, p. 83, 1872) and by Bruno Krusch, who added the precise comment, 'So werden Ostertafeln schon vom 3. Jahrh. an genannt' (*Neues Archiv*, ix. 113). This statement appears to be without foundation. The context of Cassiodorus' words leaves no doubt that he is referring to the work of an earlier Dionysius, whose *Periegesis* is known to have been illustrated by a πίναξ or map, apparently by more than one. See the extracts from the scholia quoted by Carl Müller, proleg. to *Geographi Graeci minores*, ii (1861), p. xxiv. The presumption therefore that the Table of Dionysius was known to Cassiodorus can be inferred only from the friendly relations of the two men, from Cassiodorus' constant activity in increasing his library, and from the well-recognized tendency of literature to gravitate towards a great centre.

[2] G. B. de Rossi, *Inscr. Christ. Urbis Romae*, i (1857–61), proleg., p. xcvi.

[3] 'Die Einführung des griechischen Paschalritus im Abendlande', in *Neues Archiv der Gesellschaft für ältere deutsche Geschichtskunde*, ix (1884), 111–14. For the inscription formerly at Périgueux (Gruter, *Inscr. Antiq.*, p. 1161, no. 5, 1707) see *ibid.*, pp. 129 ff.

It is now distinguished as the *Paschale Campanum*, because it was written in the region of Naples.[1] While, however, Dr. Krusch is persuaded that there is no trace of the use of the Dionysian reckoning until the very end of the sixth century, he contends that under Gregory the Great it was the accepted system at Rome. It is true, he says, that this cannot be discovered from the Roman sources, but it follows without doubt from the history of the conversion of Britain by Augustine.[2] This conclusion appears to me to be unproved.

Before turning to the English evidence it should be noticed that St. Columbanus in a letter to Pope Gregory, written between 595 and 600, looks on the Easter controversy as one between the Celtic practice and the rule of Victorius; of Dionysius he says not a word, and he 'can hardly believe' that Gregory approves the cycle of Victorius.[3] For the facts of the mission of St. Augustine and its results we are almost entirely dependent upon Bede; and it is remarkable that in all the earlier part of his History, while he is precise in defining the limits within which the Celts allowed the observance of Easter, he never, except on one single occasion, states what the catholic rule was. This may be, of course, because it was obvious and well known, and there was no reason to explain it. But there may be another reason, namely, that the Roman Church still adhered to the reckoning of Victorius. The following considerations lead me to think that this was the truth. Honorius I, who was Pope from 625 to 638, wrote to the Irish warning them not to persist in a practice which cut them off from the rest of Christendom.[4] The sequel is told in a long letter by Cummian, an Irishman who had abandoned the Celtic rule about Easter.[5] From this we learn that the cycle introduced into Ireland in consequence of the Pope's advice was a cycle of 532 years, and this can only be that of Victorius.[6] In the following year, probably in 638,[7] a synod was held near Tullamore, at which the southern Irish yielded to the Pope's directions. But some resisted, and it was agreed to send a mission to Rome to obtain a definitive ruling.[8]

---

[1] It is printed by Mommsen, *Chronica minora*, i. 744 f.; see the description of the manuscript on pp. 371 f. [2] *Op. cit.*, p. 114.

[3] Epist. i, in *Epist. Merowingici Aevi*, i (1892), 156–8: 'Vix credere possum dum illum [*sc.* Galliae errorem] constat a te non fuisse emendatum, a te esse probatum', p. 157. [4] Bede, *Hist. eccl.* ii. 19.

[5] Printed in Ussher's *Vet. Epist. Hibern. Sylloge* (1632), pp. 25–35.

[6] Krusch, *op. cit.*, pp. 150 f. [7] *Ibid.*, p. 149. [8] Cummian, *op. cit.*, p. 34.

The answer is recorded by Bede in the one instance in which he defines the Roman practice. Pope John IV, he says, sent a letter full of authority and learning to correct the Irish error, *evidenter astruens quia dominicum paschae diem a xvᵃ luna usque ad xxiᵃᵐ . . . oportet inquiri*. This looks like Bede's own explanation of what he presumed the letter to direct: for when he sets out the text of the letter, which was written in the names of the chief officers of the Roman Church, the Pope having not yet been consecrated, he gives only the beginning as far as the statement of the Irish practice, and then summarizes, *exposita autem ratione paschalis observantiae*; after which he gives the rest of the letter, dealing with the Pelagian heresy, in full.[1] There are three possibilities: Bede may have had an incomplete copy of the letter before him; or he may have omitted the definition of the correct limits of Easter, because he had already mentioned that the letter dealt with it; or he may have found that it disagreed with what he had laid down, and in fact prescribed not *luna xv* but *luna xvi*. This last suggestion is confirmed by what Cummian says; for besides referring, as we have seen, to the cycle of Victorius, he accepts *luna xvi* as the earliest day of the *resurrectio*.[2]

Dr. Krusch, believing that the Dionysian reckoning was at that time adopted at Rome, thinks that the Irish emissaries may have picked up a Victorian calculus in Gaul on their way home.[3] But it is hardly conceivable that people should go to Rome in order to obtain a decision on a contested point, and then bring back to Ireland a calculus which differed from it. The natural inference from Cummian's letter is that Rome still adhered to the system of Victorius. It should be noticed that though the difference between this and the oriental system assumed importance when it was attempted to bring the date of Easter into harmony with the historical events recorded in the Gospels, yet as a matter of fact it did not often lead to actual disagreement as to the day on which Easter should be observed: in the seventh century the only absolute discrepancy occurred in 672; but it is true that in 645, 665, 685, and 689, and possibly in four other years, alternative dates were also admitted. Probably, therefore, the two systems were not generally distinguished.[4]

---

[1] *Hist. eccl.* ii. 19.
[2] *Op. cit.*, p. 27; cf. Krusch, pp. 150 f.   [3] p. 152.
[4] It has been generally held that a continuation of the Dionysian cycle is

It is at the synod of Whitby in 664 that we first find the Dionysian calculus formally brought forward by Wilfrid. His biographer Eddi,[1] or Stephen, says that at that council

De paschali ratione conquirebant, quid esset rectissimum, utrum more Bryttonum et Scottorum omnisque aquilonalis partis a xiiii luna, dominica die veniente, usque ad xxii [sic] pascha agendum, an melius sit ratione sedis apostolicae a xv luna[2] usque in xxi paschalem dominicam celebrandum.

He states the arguments shortly and gives the Northumbrian king's decision. Bede has a much fuller narrative of the proceedings and agrees on the essential point.[3] The details do not concern us[4], all that we need to know is that the Dionysian computation was definitely advocated and accepted at Whitby in 664.

It may be observed that the name of Dionysius is not mentioned; it was the 'Roman' or 'catholic' use of which Wilfrid was the champion.[5] By this time indeed the actual table of Dionysius had long expired, for his ninety-five years ran from 532 to 626. Ten years before it ended a continuation was drawn up for the years 627 to 721. This was the work of a writer who is called in the manuscripts *Felix abbas Cyrillitanus, Chyllitanus,*

found in the *Etymologiae* of Isidore of Seville, vi. 17; but Dr. Krusch has proved (pp. 117 ff.) that this is in fact a continuation of the Alexandrian table of Cyril, and is calculated for the ninety-five years from 532, not from 627; only the Easters (but not the *lunae*) have been altered in the first nineteen years. Mr. W. M. Lindsay in his edition of the *Etymologiae* (1911) gives no various readings for the Paschal table, but simply reprints Arevalo's text.

[1] *Vita Wilfridi*, x, in J. Raine's *Historians of the Church of York*, i (1879), 14; also in *Script. Rerum Merovingicarum*, vi (1913), 203, ed. W. Levison.

[2] The Fell MS. 3 (formerly 1) in the Bodleian Library, by an obvious homoeoteleuton, omits the words from the first *usque* to *xv luna*. It may be well to state that there is absolutely no doubt that this manuscript is in fact the Salisbury manuscript, as to the identification of which the editors express different opinions: see Raine, pref., p. xxxviii; Levison, pp. 184 f. Cf. W. D. Macray, *Annals of the Bodleian Library* (2nd ed., 1890), p. 155.

[3] *Hist. eccl.* iii. 25.

[4] Dr. J. K. Fotheringham has pointed out that in practice the difference between the Roman and Celtic Easters was due to the Roman placing of the new moon about five days later than the Celtic. This made far more difference than the question on which the discussion turned, whether the earliest date was *luna xiv* or *luna xv*. In 664 the Celtic new moon was five days before the Victorian and six days before the Alexandrian.

[5] When Colman includes Dionysius in a confused list of authorities, genuine and spurious, for the Easter cycle, he no doubt refers to Dionysius of Alexandria, whose cycle is mentioned by Eusebius, *Hist. eccl.* vii. 20.

or *Ghyllitanus*.[1] These variants show that the scribes from whom
these texts proceed had difficulty in reading the name, and
modern scholars have been content to repeat it without explanation. But it can hardly be doubted the word which the scribe
had in his exemplar was *Scyllitanus*, which is found in a letter
of St. Gregory the Great as the adjective from Squillace.[2] No
other name of a monastery at all resembling that given in the
manuscripts has been discovered; and no place more probable
than this for the construction of this cycle can be suggested.

We have presumed that Cassiodorus in the *Monasterium
Vivariense* at Squillace knew of the cycle of Dionysius.[3] We
have found no trace of its use until 664, when that cycle had
been continued by an abbot, as I suggest, of the same house.
The monastery appears to have been destroyed or abandoned
not many years after 634, and its books were dispersed throughout Italy. I venture to claim the manuscript containing this
cycle as one of the books which had belonged to the library of
Cassiodorus as increased by his successors, of which the recovery
of the scattered relics is one of the most striking achievements
of recent palaeographical study. Whether it was brought back
to England by Benedict Biscop on his return from his first
Italian visit, which began in 653, or whether Wilfrid learned its
contents during the time that he spent at Rome in the study
of catholic observances, must be left undetermined. I should
like to add that I had arrived at this conclusion as to the source
from which the manuscript was derived before I hit upon the
identification of Felix of Squillace.

So soon as the cycle of Dionysius gained currency, it was not
unnatural that the series of years, reckoned from the era of the
Incarnation which accompanied it, should be made use of for
the indication of historical dates. There is indeed evidence that
this era was known in Spain as early as 672;[4] but it is not until

[1] The preface and prologue to this table are printed from a Bobbio manuscript, cod. H. 150 (formerly S. 70) in the Ambrosian Library at Milan, by
Muratori, *Anecdota*, iii (1713), 168 f., and by Krusch, *Der 84-jährige Ostercyclus
und seine Quellen* (1880), pp. 207 f. In a manuscript of St. Remigius at Rheims,
no. 298, the name is given as *Gillitanus*: see J. G. Janus, *Hist. Cycli Dionys.*
(1718), p. 51.

[2] Reg. viii, ed. L. M. Hartmann, 1893. Various readings are *Scillitanus* and
Sillitanus. On the forms assumed by Scylaceum ($\Sigma\kappa\upsilon\lambda\lambda\acute{\eta}\tau\iota\upsilon\nu$) or Scolacium see
Mommsen's note in *Corp. Inscr. Lat.* x. i (1883), 12.   [3] Above, p. 29, n. 1.

[4] 'Ab incarnatione domini nostri Iesu Christi usque in praesentem primum
gloriosi principis Bambani, qui est era 740, sunt anni 672': Krusch, p. 121. The

the production of the Church History of Bede that we find an historical work in which it is inserted. It has commonly been held that it was brought into use by Bede's treatise *de Temporum Ratione*, which was written in 725, and consequently not a few Anglo-Saxon charters which contain the date from the Incarnation have been condemned as spurious or corrupt. There seems, however, to be no reason to suppose that the adoption of this era was originated by the treatise of Bede. It is much more likely that it was derived from the Easter tables. We have seen that late in the sixth century the cycle of Victorius was used, in a continuation, at Naples for the insertion of annalistic notices;[1] and in like manner the era of the Incarnation may have been adopted at any time after the middle of the seventh century, that is to say, at any time after the Dionysian cycle in its extended form became diffused. It was Easter tables that formed the basis of the numerous Frankish Annals, the model of which certainly came from England;[2] and the employment of them for this purpose was maintained until the tenth and eleventh centuries and even later.[3]

II

In the first part of this paper I endeavoured to ascertain the time at which the cycle of Dionysius first became current in the west. I mentioned that it was presumably known to Cassiodorus, but I did not refer to the little tract entitled *Computus Paschalis* which is printed among his works, because its authorship has been commonly denied. Mommsen pointed out that there was no good evidence for attributing it to him. Moreover, as the tract was written in 562, he thought it unlikely that Cassiodorus could have been still working at so late a date.[4] Krusch knew

manuscript, Madrid T. 10, is a modern copy, and the Spanish era is wrongly written 740 instead of 710. Cf. *Pertz's Archiv*, viii. 121.   [1] Above, p. 29 f.

[2] The earliest example known to be preserved is the beginning of the Annals of Fulda, which have been proved to have been written between 741 and 759: see Sickel, in *Forschungen zur Deutschen Geschichte*, iv (1864), 457. The era is mentioned in a Frankish manual of 737: see Krusch, in *Mélanges Chatelain* (1910), pp. 232–42.

[3] I have to thank my friend Dr. J. K. Fotheringham for much expert advice and criticism, but he must not be taken to be responsible for my statements of facts or for the conclusions at which I have arrived in this paper.

[4] *Abhandlungen der Kön. Sächsischen Gesellschaft*, philol.-hist. Classe, iii. 572, 1861. Mommsen then assigned the *Computus* to the compiler who continued the *Chronica* to 559, but afterwards he regarded this continuation as attached to the *Cursus Paschalis* of Victorius: *Chronica minora*, i (1892), 675.

of no earlier authority for attributing it to Cassiodorus than a modern note in the Cottonian MS. Caligula A. xv, fo. 71.[1] The source from which the annotator derived his information appears to be unknown. But Mommsen's argument from the date can hardly be maintained; for Cassiodorus tells us that he was still writing in his ninety-third year, and even if he was born as early as 480[2] there need be no difficulty in ascribing to him a tract composed in 562. The tract, it may be added, is simply a new edition of a work by Dionysius, adapted to the later date. The most recent writer on technical chronology, Dr. Ginzel, accepts it as the work of Cassiodorus and infers from it that he was the first person who applied the computus of Dionysius to the purpose of establishing the date from the Incarnation as an Era.[3] If the attribution be accepted it furnishes additional evidence for the knowledge of the cycle of Dionysius at Squillace,[4] and corrects my statement that Cassiodorus did not make use of it.

Mommsen[5] was of opinion that a chronological note at the end of the Chronicle of Victor Tunnunensis,[6] which was written in the latter part of the sixth century, was based on the table of Dionysius. This note states that the years from Adam to the Nativity are 5199 and the years from the Nativity to the first years of Justin II are 567. Had it been derived from Dionysius we should have expected the writer to speak not of the Nativity but of the Incarnation, for the terms are not synonymous. But in fact the calculation is evidently taken from St. Jerome's translation of the Chronicle of Eusebius, according to which the creation was placed 5201 B.C. and the Nativity 2 B.C.; so that 567 years from this date bring us to A.D. 565, the year of the accession of Justin. Moreover, it cannot be said that Victor made use of an era.[7] In his Chronicle he reckons by consular, and at the end by Imperial, years. In the last few years the

---

[1] *Neues Archiv der Gesellschaft für ältere deutsche Geschichtskunde*, ix (1884), 113 f.

[2] Cf. Chapman, *Notes on the Early History of the Vulgate Gospels* (1908), p. 36 and n. 3.

[3] *Handbuch der mathem. und techn. Chronol.* iii (1914), 180.

[4] There is nothing to indicate any connexion with Rome, as Ideler supposed: see his *Handbuch der mathem. und techn. Chronol.* ii (1826), 375.

[5] *Chron. min.* ii (1894), 181.

[6] Vict. Tonnennensis [so Mommsen spells the word], *Chron.*, *ibid.*, p. 206.

[7] Cf. J. G. Janus, *Hist. Aerae Christ.*, p. 25 (Wittenberg, 1714); and W. H. Stevenson, in *Notes and Queries*, 9th ser., i (1898), 232.

chronology becomes confused:[1] he makes Justinian reign on
into an imaginary fortieth year; and he places the first year of
Justin in the fifteenth indiction, i.e. in A.D. 567, an error which
was repeated by John of Biclar. The note and the chronological
scheme of the Chronicle thus appear to be drawn from independent sources, and the note is merely a chronological statement
of a type of which there are numerous examples.

It has lately been suggested that there is evidence of the use
of the Era in Spain nearly thirty years before the synod of
Whitby. In 1811 Jaime Villanueva described a Visigothic
manuscript of the eighth century (not earlier than 773) in the
monastery of Ripoll in Catalonia (cod. 62), which gave a table
of ancient eras, and included the following notice:

Ab incarnatione autem Domini Iesu Christi usque in presentem
primum Quintiliani principis annum, qui est Era lxx quarta sunt
anni DCCXXXVI.

Villanueva thought that DCC was omitted in the Spanish Era,
and interpreted the date as referring to A.D. 736 and to a
Chintila otherwise unknown.[2] The manuscript has disappeared
and we can only take the text as it is printed. But it is evident
that a writer who was capable of omitting the hundreds in the
Era might also insert a hundred too many in the years of the
Incarnation, especially since by so doing he gave the century in
which he lived. Rudolf Beer therefore proposed to read the Era
as 674 and the Year of Grace as 636, which was in fact the first
year of the Visigothic King Chintila.[3] The emendation seems
convincing, but it does not follow that the original from which
the manuscript is taken actually contained a mention of the
year of the Incarnation. There are other instances in which
writers of the eighth century inserted that year with an equation
with the Spanish Era.[4]

When I discussed the place with which *Felix abbas Cyrillitanus, Chyllitanus*, or *Ghyllitanus*, the continuator of the cycle
of Dionysius, was connected, I ought to have mentioned that he
had a namesake sixty years earlier who bore a similar appella-
tion. Pope Vigilius speaks of him as *monachum Afrum qui*

---

[1] Cf. Mommsen, *Chron. min.* ii. 180.

[2] *Viage literario a las Iglesias de España*, viii (Valencia, 1811), 45–50.

[3] 'Die Handschriften des Klosters Santa Maria de Ripoll', in *Sitzungsberichte
der kais. Akad. der Wiss. in Wien*, philos.-hist. Klasse, CLV. iii (1907), 25–8.

[4] Cf. above, p. 33, n. 4.

Gillitano monasterio dicitur praefuisse.[1] He is twice mentioned by Victor Tunnunensis: once under the year 553 as *Felix Gillensis monasterii provinciae Africanae hegumenus*, with a variant *Guillensis*; the other time under 557 as *Felix hegumenus monasterii Gillitani* or *Gallitani*.[2] In the former passage Mommsen suggested that *Cillensis* was meant, a name which might indicate several places in Africa. I was not aware that in 1899 Father Delattre published some inscriptions which had then been recently found at Henchir el Fras, near Thibar, some seventy miles west of Tunis, and which contain dedications by the *decuriones Gillitani*; one of them bears a date corresponding to A.D. 229.[3] These, he believes, establish the fact that the Felix of the sixth century belonged to a monastery at this place, Gillium. He adds that he was informed by Monsignor Toulotte that the monastery was founded by monks who came from Saint Sabas in the Holy Land after the Byzantine conquest: these Greek monks quitted Africa on the Arab invasion and went to Rome, where they settled themselves on the Palatine, and there their name of Saint Sabas remains to this day. I have not examined this statement, and will only note that the accuracy of a writer who places the monastery of St. Saba on the Palatine, whereas it lies to the south-east of the Aventine, is not above suspicion.

While, however, I do not dispute the identification of the monastery over which this Felix presided, I hesitate to accept it for that of his later namesake, whose denomination appears in various forms and in only one manuscript is given as Gillitanus.[4] If he came from Gillium, he wrote at a date earlier than the Arab invasion, and it would not be easy to show how his cycle travelled into western Europe. If on the other hand, as I have suggested, he belonged to Squillace, the transmission of his manuscript would be readily intelligible.

[1] See his letter in the 7th collation of the Fifth General Council: Labbe and Cossart, *Concilia*, v (1671), 556 D; Mansi, *Concil. Collect. ampliss.* ix. 359 A.

[2] *Chron. min.* ii. 203, 204.

[3] *Comptes rendus de l'Académie des Inscriptions et Belles-Lettres*, 4th ser., xxvii. 16–19.

[4] MS. 298 of St. Remi at Rheims, according to Janus, *Hist. Cycli Dionysiani* (Wittenberg, 1718), p. 51.

THE CHRONOLOGY OF BEDE'S *HISTORIA ECCLESIASTICA* AND THE COUNCILS OF 679-680[1]

I

IN considering difficulties about dates in the latter part of the seventh century it may be taken for granted that Bede, the greatest master of chronology in the Middle Ages, did not make mistakes. If he went wrong, it would be in consequence of imperfect information as to the time when a particular king succeeded to his throne or matters of that sort. We may presume that his Indictions are correct, and his years of the Incarnation are nearly always computed by himself. But at the outset we are confronted by a difference of opinion as to what kind of Indiction was used in the texts of the Acts of Councils which Bede inserts in his history.

The oldest mode of reckoning the Indiction was the Greek one beginning with 1 September; but in Bede's time the starting-point is found shifted to the 24th of that month. These two are the only forms of the Indiction with which we have to concern ourselves. It has, however, been often asserted that the so-called Pontifical Indiction—which I prefer to distinguish as the Roman Indiction—beginning on 25 December or 1 January has also to be taken into account. This is the more important because in Haddan and Stubbs's edition of the Councils the Roman Indiction is sometimes admitted as an alternative, and even as a preferable alternative, to the others. It is necessary, therefore, to give reasons for excluding it.

According to Franz Rühl[2] this Indiction of the New Year has been noticed as early as the sixth and seventh centuries; it would be more correct to say that evidence for its use has been cited from about the middle of the sixth century until A.D. 619, for it does not appear again until the ninth century. Rühl says that this reckoning of the Indiction was adopted by Dionysius Exiguus. This is not so. Dionysius deals with the Indiction only in his *Argumenta Paschalia*, chapter ii,[3] where he gives the familiar rule for computing it. But he says nothing about the day on which it began, for this was irrelevant to the

---

[1] Reprinted from the *Journal of Theological Studies*, vol. xx (1918).

[2] *Chronologie des Mittelalters und der Neuzeit*, p. 173.

[3] Migne, *P. L.* lxvii. 499.

subject of his tract, the chronological elements connected with Easter. There are, however, undoubtedly some inscriptions at Rome which seem to imply a New Year's Indiction. The most famous example is an epitaph to one Theodorus and his son Theodoracius in the church of St. Cecilia, of which an engraving is given by Antonio Maria Lapi.[1] The date of their interment is recorded as follows:

DEPOSITVSQVIN

TADECIMAM̄AVGVSTIINDSEPTIMAETFILIVSEIVSTHEODORACIQVII
BIXITM̄VIIDEPOSITVSIDVSOCTORISIIMP̄PDDN̄N̄PIISSIMISAVḠGHERACLI
OANNONONOP̄CEIVSDEMD̄N̄ANNOOCTABOATQHERACLIOCONS
TANTINONOVOFILIOIPSIVSANNOSEPTIMOINDICTSEPTIMA

Lapi proposed to emend the last word into *octavo*; Clinton[2] thought that *idus octorisi* (for *idibus Octobribus*) was a blunder for *ii. K. Septembris*. The former correction is probably right; the engraver having accidentally repeated the *septimo* just before, or else having been supplied with a text of the inscription in which the word was written indistinctly in numerals VIII[a]. De Rossi,[3] however, accepts the epitaph as definite proof of the use of the Roman Indiction, though elsewhere he draws attention to the frequency of errors in numerals in inscriptions of about this date.[4]

This is the only example of it which is free from ambiguity. In others cited by Gaetano Marini[5] an uncertainty arises from the employment of the Post-Consular date. Mommsen,[6] writing with reference to the time immediately preceding that to which these inscriptions belong, remarks that the dates on Christian inscriptions do not always agree with the official Post-Consular year: the masons must as a rule have trusted to memory for their dates, or else have used lists at hand which had not received the latest revision. Besides this, it should be added that the apparent use of the Roman Indiction has been in some cases inferred from inscriptions of which the dates are in fact compatible with the Greek style. There are indeed some specimens at Lyons which may possibly, as De Rossi thinks,[7] bear witness to the employment of the Roman Indiction; but it is

[1] *Dissertatio ad Severae Martyris Monumentum*, Palermo, 1734, p. 25.
[2] *Fasti Romani*, iii. 165.
[3] *Inscriptiones Christianae Urbis Romae*, i (1857–61), proleg, p. c.
[4] P. 502; cf. proleg., p. xlviii.   [5] *Papiri Diplomatici*, pp. 260, 308.
[6] 'Ostgothische Studien', i, in *Neues Archiv der Gesellschaft für ältere deutsche Geschichtskunde*, xiv (1889), 237 f.   [7] Proleg., p. xlviii.

not clear that the ambiguity in these instances is not due to an error in the calculus of Victorius which was current in Gaul. The specimens are so few, and most of them so doubtful, that they do not appear to furnish any sufficient evidence for the belief that in the sixth or seventh century the Indiction was reckoned from the New Year. Private persons may conceivably have adjusted the beginning of the Indiction to that of the civil year; but to grant this is very different from supposing that this alteration was permitted in the official Acts of Councils.

In dealing, therefore, with the chronological data supplied by Bede, we may leave the Roman Indiction altogether out of account. We have a choice only between the Indictions beginning on the 1st and the 24th September, the Greek and the Caesarean. Now there is, as we shall see, good reason for holding that it was the Greek Indiction which was in use in the time of Archbishop Theodore, even as it continued to be the only one employed in the papal chancery down to 1087. The Caesarean Indiction is first mentioned by Bede himself, in a treatise which he wrote in 725. He speaks of it without comment, as the accepted reckoning, but it seems most likely that it was his own invention designed to bring the Indiction into accord with the autumnal equinox.

The importance of establishing the type of Indiction in use becomes evident when we remember that the Indiction was the one stable element in the date of a document. The *annus Domini* was a recent importation. It was not intended to provide an era for historical purposes; its object was merely to serve as a reference in Easter tables. Naturally therefore it was taken as running on the same lines as the Indiction; and as the Indiction began four months before what we call the current year, so was the Year of Grace reckoned. The acceptance of this principle for the period with which we are concerned will, I believe, produce harmony between a number of dates which are regarded as discrepant. It will also have the result of fixing a good many events a year earlier than they are placed by modern scholars, though not always by their predecessors in the seventeenth century.

Next to the Indiction the most stable chronological elements in the History of Bede appear to be the Regnal Years, primarily of the Northumbrian kings, but hardly less definitely of the kings of Kent. The Year of Grace has only indirect value for

the purpose of determining dates. It was no part of the chronological tradition but was added by means of calculation. It does
not therefore stand on the same footing as a date transcribed
from an older text. Moreover, the Year of Grace and the
Regnal Year began at different periods, and it was inevitable
that in reckoning the former from the latter an error should
frequently creep in. I write these words for instance in the 9th
year of King George V, but that year began on 10 May 1918; the
first four months of the calendar year belong to his 8th year.
The common opinion is that these Years of Grace are Bede's own
calculations, but Pagi's suggestion[1] that some of them were
added by transcribers is worthy of notice.

In order to test the positions I have laid down, I may avail
myself of a summary of chronological difficulties brought together
by Mr. Plummer in a note to the *Historia Ecclesiastica* iv. 5.[2]

1. Bede names 15 February 670, as the date of the death of
Oswy, *qui est annus secundus ex quo Britanniam venit Theodorus.*
Mr. Plummer comments, 'February 15 670, is within the first
year of Theodore's arrival, seeing that he did not reach England
until May 669'. But in strictness there is no discrepancy. Bede
does not say that a full year had elapsed, but merely that 670 was
the second year after that in which Theodore reached England.

2. Mr. Plummer cites book v. 24, where 'Bede says distinctly
that the Council of Hertford was held on September 24 673, in
the third year of Egfrid. But if Egfrid's accession was in
February 670, this would be his fourth year'. The mentions
of the regnal year and of the month come in fact from book iv.
5; book v. 24 gives only the Year of Grace. Now in the former
reference Bede says that the Council was held in the first
Indiction, and this began in September 672. Mr. Plummer
writes, 'If Theodore (like Bede himself) used the Caesarean
Indiction, this day, September 24, 673, was the very first day of
the first Indiction.'[3] It was not: 24 September 673, whether the
Indiction be Greek or Caesarean, was in the second Indiction.
Since then Bede reckons 24 September in the first Indiction as
falling within the year 673, it follows that he began his year
with the Indiction. This date for the Council of Hertford,
24 September 672, corresponds with Egfrid's third year.[4]

---

[1] *Crit. in Baronii Annales* (ed. Lucca, 1742), xi. 609.
[2] *Opera Historica*, ii. 211.   [3] Vol. ii, 212.
[4] The correct date was pointed out by Mr. Alfred Anscombe, in the

3. 'In C. 12 Bede says that the comet of August 678 was in Egfrid's eighth year; but August 678 is in the ninth year from February 670.' The comet was a famous phenomenon, but it was observed not in 678 but in 676. It appeared at the time of the election of Pope Donus, who was ordained on 2 November 676. About this date no doubt is possible: the entries in the *Liber Pontificalis* are contemporaneous and the records of the duration of each Pontificate are precisely stated. More than this, Bede's account of the comet was manifestly written with the description in the Lives of the Popes before him:

Liber Pontificalis lxxx. 3	Bede, iv. 12
Hic dum esset electus, per Augusto mense, apparuit stella a parte orientis a gallo canto usque mane per menses tres, cuius radia coelos penetravit.	Apparuit mense Augusto stella quae dicitur cometa; et tribus mensibus permanens, matutinis horis oriebatur, excelsam radiantis flammae quasi columnam praeferens.

That the year given in the *Liber Pontificalis* is correct is proved by other evidence. A comet was observed in China at a time corresponding to the autumn of A.D. 676. It appeared in the East in the morning. On 4 September it was near the head of Gemini, and on 1 November it was no longer seen. Pingré,[1] from whom I learn these particulars, says that it might have been visible in Europe some days earlier. It should be mentioned that Pingré's dates are in disaccord with those given in the more modern work on the subject by John Williams,[2] where the comet is said to have been observed from 7 July to 3 September. But this discrepancy, as Mr. E. B. Knobel has pointed out,[3] is due to the fact that Williams forgot that the year 676 had an intercalary month beginning on 20 March.[4] The month in

Athenaeum, no. 3804, p. 380 (22 September 1900). He also amended the years of death of King Edwin and of Paulinus in the same way as I have done. These results were at once accepted by Sir James Ramsay: *ibid.*, no. 3810, p. 579 (3 November 1900). [Since this paper was written I have noticed that the true date of the Council of Hertford was given by Bruno Krusch in the *Neues Archiv*, ix. 160, so long ago as 1884.]

[1] *Cométographie*, 1783, i. 332 f.

[2] *Observations of Comets from B.C. 611 to A.D. 1640*, 1871, p. 41.

[3] 'On the Astronomical Observations recorded in the Nihongi', published in the *Monthly Notices* of the Royal Astronomical Society, lxvi (1906), 72.

[4] See W. Bramsen, 'Japanese Chronology and Calendars', in the supplement to the *Transactions of the Asiatic Society of Japan*, xxxvii (1910), p. 53. The rule for the intercalations is explained on pp. 18 ff.

which the comet appeared began on 15 August. Consequently, Pingré's chronology is correct. The identity of the comet seen by the Chinese in 676 with that mentioned by the Papal biographer and by Bede is beyond dispute; and we need not take refuge in Pagi's argument that, since Donus's pontificate lasted one year, five months, and ten days from 2 November 676, the only August which it included was in 677, and that this therefore must have been the year of the comet.[1] Still less will it do to speak with Mr. Plummer of 'the comet of August 678'.

Nor is it even certain that Bede assigned it to this year. The next preceding year mentioned in the same chapter is 676, and in the summary at the end of the History[2] the number DCLXXVIII appears to have been altered from DCLXXVII in the Moore MS. which is regarded as the best authority for the text. Besides this, the year is given as 677 in a manuscript of the ninth or tenth century formerly at St. Maximin's at Treves, from which Pierre François Chifflet printed the History in 1681.[3] It is also recorded under this year by Florence of Worcester and a number of later chroniclers. Unless, therefore, Bede made a bad chronological mistake, which is unlikely, it is plain that the year given in most of his manuscripts is erroneous and that the reading 677 is the correct one. Reckoning that year from the Indiction of 1 September, his date included almost the whole of the time during which the comet was visible. It was also the year in the course of which the eighth year of Egfrid began, though this did not in fact begin until the following February. We must remember that if Bede wrote *anno dominicae incarnationis* DCLXXVII, *qui est annus imperii regis Ecqfridi* VIII, he was bound to be inexact in one of his numerals, unless the king chanced to come to the throne on the first day of the year. Bede, I take it, described the comet on the basis of the *Liber Pontificalis* and prefixed the *annus Domini* according to his mode of reckoning the year, from September to September. Having then supplied the year as 677, he not unnaturally equated it with the eighth year of Egfrid. If this explanation be rejected, the alternative is to suppose that Bede's information

---

[1] *Crit. in Baronii Ann.* xi. 608 b.   [2] *H.E.* v. 24.

[3] *Bedae Presbyteri et Fredegarii Scholastici Concordia*, pp. 210, 313. Chifflet discusses the date in an appended dissertation 'de Annis Dagoberti', p. 392. The Treves manuscript passed in turn to the College of Clermont, to the libraries of Meerman and of Sir Thomas Phillipps, and ultimately to Berlin, where it is now Cod. Phillipp. 133.

was incorrect and that he really understood the comet to have been seen in the autumn of 677 instead of 676.

4. Mr. Plummer proceeds: 'In c. 17 Bede says that the Council of Hatfield, which was held September 17, 680, was in the tenth year of Egfrid; but September 680 is in the eleventh year from February 670.' Now the Acts of this Council, set out by Bede, have an extremely precise date: in the 10th year of Egfrid, the 15th of the calends of October, in the 8th Indiction, the 6th year of Ethelred king of the Mercians, the 17th of Aldwulf king of the East Anglians, and the 7th of Lothair king of the Kentishmen. Bede has not here inserted the year of the Incarnation, but in the summary (v. 24) he places the Council under 680. The 8th Indiction, however, ran from September 679 to 680, and if the Greek Indiction was used the Council was held in 679. Mr. Plummer says[1] that 680 'agrees best with the regnal years of the kings mentioned'. These years must there-fore be examined. Now 679 is in the 10th year from the date assigned by Bede to the accession of Egfrid; it is in the 7th year of Lothair, whose accession in the summer of 673[2] is not disputed. The date when Aldwulf came to the throne is inferred only from the regnal year in the document which we are dis-cussing. The 6th year of Ethelred of Mercia calls for closer inquiry.

There is no doubt that Bede in his summary (v. 24) enters the death of Wulfhere and the accession of Ethelred under 675, that is, as I have argued, in the year beginning in September 674. If those events took place near the beginning of that period, then a Council held on 17 September 679, might fall within Ethelred's sixth year. It has been attempted to fix the year 675 as that of the death of Wulfhere by citing the statement that he reigned seventeen years[3] and presuming that these years are reckoned from 658. But this date is only obtained by inference from another which is not secure. *Completis autem tribus annis post interfectionem Pendan regis* Wulfhere was raised to the throne.[4] But when was Penda killed? The battle of the Winwaed was fought on 15 November in the 13th year of Oswy. We have then to find out when Oswy became king. Bede says that Bishop Paulinus died on 10 October 644, in Oswy's 2nd year.[5] This date, according to the mode of computation

---

[1] Vol. ii. 231.   [2] *H.E.* iv. 5.   [3] *H.E.* iii. 24 *sub fin.*   [4] *Ibid.*
[5] *Ibid.* iii. 14.

which we have seen established in other examples, means October 643.[1] Hence Oswy became king in 642 or towards the end of 641,[2] and the battle of the Winwaed in his 13th year was fought in November 654. Three years afterwards, that is in 657, Wulfhere was made king; and seventeen years later, in 674, he died and was succeeded by Ethelred. Ethelred's sixth year therefore ran from 679 to 680.

If it be objected that the year in which I place the death of Bishop Paulinus disagrees with the recorded length of his pontificate, *x et viiii annos, menses duos, dies xxi*, where it is admitted that, since Paulinus was consecrated on Sunday 21 July 625,[3] the days should be xx, I reply that there is no more violence in subtracting one from the years than in adding one to the days: the information which Bede received was inexact, and a number like *uiiii*, when the *i* was not dotted, was constantly liable to be miswritten.

5. 'Again,' says Mr. Plummer, 'in c. 26 Bede says that Egfrid was slain in May 685, in the fifteenth year of his reign; but if he came to the throne in February 670, this would be his sixteenth year.' This is perfectly true. Egfrid died on 20 May[4] 685, which, as the Ulster Annals correctly state, was a Saturday. But the Ulster Annals also record the date as *anno xu regni sui consummata* [sic], which may mean a short time after the completion of his fifteenth year. Either then Bede was for once in error, or, as I would rather believe, *xu* is a slip in transcription for *xui*.

6. 'Further, in iii 14, *ad init.*, Bede says that Oswy, coming to the throne in August 642, held it *per annos uiginti octo*. But if he died in February 670 he only reigned twenty-seven years and a half.' In order to arrive at the date of Oswy's accession we have again to go back to the death of Edwin, which Bede places on 12 October 633,[5] that is 632. His successor Oswald reigned nine years, i.e. until 641, when he was slain at the battle of Maserfield on 5 August; so that Bede's words *quo completo annorum curriculo*[6] are not quite exact. Now we have seen already that 10 October 643, was reckoned to fall in Oswy's

---

[1] The date given in the Chronicle MSS. B.C.E.

[2] The acceptance of this date removes the difficulty which Mr. Plummer noted as to the death of Paulinus (vol. ii. 162) that it 'falls in Oswy's third year'.   [3] *H.E.* ii. 9.

[4] Mr. Plummer in his margin, i. 267, like Moberly before him, has inadvertently translated *die xiii Kalendarum Iuniarum*, 'May 21'.

[5] *H.E.* ii. 20.   [6] *Ibid.* iii. 9.

2nd year; it must therefore be presumed that in the confusion following the defeat at Maserfield some time elapsed before Oswy was able to secure the throne, and his accession may be dated soon after 15 November, 641. This would make the reckoning of his twenty-eight years of reign correct.

Mr. Plummer concludes his careful statement of the evidence by saying, 'All these independent indications seem to shew that . . . Bede or his copyists have written 670 for 671; and that Oswy's death and Egfrid's accession ought to be placed in 671.'[1] To me, on the contrary, the dates supplied by the Indictions and by the comet of 676 appear decisive in favour of the date as it stands. In support of this I may turn to the chronology of Benedict Biscop in connexion with the history of the two monasteries about which Bede was specially well informed. Wearmouth was founded in the 2nd Indiction and the 4th year of Egfrid, between September 673 and February 674; Jarrow was founded eight years later. The anonymous author of the *Lives of the Abbots*, whose statement is followed by Bede, says that Benedict ruled Wearmouth for eight years by himself and Jarrow for another eight (*alios totidem*) by the means of Ceolfrid; in the first four of which he had Eosterwine as his helper at Wearmouth, in the next three Sigfrid, and in the last Ceolfrid.[2] Bede adds the figures together and says that Benedict ruled the monastery for sixteen years. But it is manifest that we have to do with round numbers; for Eosterwine died on 7 March, Sigfrid on 22 August, and Benedict on 12 January. The one precise and indisputable date in this course of years is furnished by the appointment of Ceolfrid as abbot of both monasteries on 12 May in the 3rd year of Aldfrid in the 1st Indiction.[3] Whatever form of Indiction we adopt, this can only mean A.D. 688. Sigfrid's death followed on 22 August, and Benedict's on 12 January, that is, in 689. Reckoning therefore from the autumn or winter of 673–4, the first eight years end in 681–2. Then Eosterwine was appointed, and he died on 7

---

[1] Mr. Plummer cites in confirmation the brief Annals of Fulda printed in the *Monum. Germ. Hist., Script.* ii. 237 and iii. 116*. These are not really helpful. The one, which dates Egfrid's accession 671, places the eclipse of 1 May 664 under 663 and makes St. Colman die in 664 instead of 666. The other is printed in parallel columns with a St. Emmeram MS at Munich which makes Egfrid succeed in 670.

[2] Anon. Hist. Abbat., § 18, in Bedae, *Opp. Hist.* i 394; Bede, *Hist. Abbat.*, § 14, *ibid.* p. 379.

[3] Anon. Hist. Abbat., § 17.

March in his fourth year,[1] that is, in 685. Sigfrid, who succeeded, held the abbacy for three years (in fact, nearly three years and a half), dying in August 688. The last year is necessarily a short one, ending in January 689. Mr. Plummer, on the contrary, calculating a full sixteen years from the foundation of Wearmouth, which he places in 674, inclines to remove Benedict's death to 690 and make Ceolfrid's appointment, regardless of the Indiction, fall in 689.[2] This, he points out, is supported by the statement of the anonymous biographer that Ceolfrid ruled the two houses for 27 years,[3] for he certainly resigned on 4 June, 716. But this number is a manifest slip, which Bede, with the text before him, silently corrected into 28.[4] With the exception of this single number there is no discrepancy between the chronology of the two Lives, and Benedict's death may be fixed without hesitation in January 689.

It has been thought that light might be thrown on the supposed difficulty by examining the liturgical rites which were performed at the time of Benedict's death. Mention is made of the recitation of Psalm lxxxii (lxxxiii). Mr. Plummer writes, 'In the Roman use the Psalm *Deus quis similis* occurs at matins on Friday; in the Benedictine use, which would be that of Wearmouth, it occurs at matins on Thursday. January 12 was not a Thursday or a Friday in either 689 or 690, though it was a Thursday in 691.'[5] I do not think this argument can be pressed. Bede tells us that when Benedict was dying the brethren assembled in the church and spent the night in devotion: *insomnes orationibus et psalmis transigunt umbras noctis.* Then after mentioning the abbot's death, he resumes: *Namque fratres ad ecclesiam principio noctis concurrentes, psalterium ex ordine decantantes, ad octogesimum tunc et secundum cantando pervenerant psalmum, qui habet in capite, Deus quis similis erit tibi?* The monks, it would appear, had been engaged in the recitation of the entire Psalter and had reached Psalm lxxxii when Benedict died. In like manner, when St. Wilfrid was dying, the brethren *in choro die noctuque indesinenter Psalmos canentes et cum fletu miscentes usque dum in Psalmo centesimo tertio ad versiculum illum pervenerunt in quo dicitur, Emitte spiritum tuum, et creabuntur, et renovabis faciem terrae. Tunc sanctus pontifex noster emisit spiritum suum.*[6] The practice of such a

---

[1] Anon. Hist. Abbat., § 13. [2] Vol. ii, 364. [3] Anon. Hist. Abbat. § 19.
[4] Bede, *Hist. Abbat.*, § 15. [5] Vol. ii, 364. [6] *Vit. Wilfridi*, 64.

recitation at a deathbed is found in Archbishop Lanfranc's constitutions for Canterbury.¹ These constitutions were indeed of foreign origin, having been introduced from Bec²; but in this particular they seem to represent a long current monastic custom, of which Bede and Eddi give examples in the passages quoted above.

II

The comet of the autumn of 676 enables us to fix the time when Wilfrid left England to prosecute his first appeal to Rome. Bede³ says that he departed in the same year, that is, in the twelvemonth following September 676. According to Eddi⁴ the battle of the Trent was fought just a year afterwards; and this was in the 9th year of King Egfrid, who began to reign in February 670 and whose 9th year therefore ran from February 678 to February 679. Consequently Wilfrid went abroad between February and September 677. He spent the winter in the Netherlands, and in the following spring resumed his journey. But he was wont to be a leisurely traveller. On the present occasion he stopped for a time with the Austrasian king Dagobert II, whom he had assisted some years before to recover his throne; and he was also entertained by the Lombard king Perctarit,⁵ who had himself spent a period of exile in Frankland.⁶ He reached Rome to find a new Pope, Agatho, in office, and an English envoy present with letters from Archbishop Theodore. A synod was then convened, and Wilfrid's appeal was heard. Eddi sets out the parts of the proceedings which concerned this business,⁷ but he gives no dates. Only in a different connexion he mentions that Wilfrid took part in a Roman synod against the heretics, manifestly the Monothelites, on Tuesday in Easter week.⁸ He made, indeed, a long stay at Rome after his appeal was settled,⁹ and then returned homeward. When he passed through Gaul he found that King Dagobert was dead, and Dagobert was murdered on 23 December 679.¹⁰

---

¹ Cap. xxiii, in Migne, *P.L.*, cl. 508 ff.
² See J. Armitage Robinson, in the *Journal of Theological Studies*, x (1909), 375–88.   ³ *H. E.* iv. 12.
⁴ *V. Wilfr.* 24. It is not impossible, however, that Pagi is right in understanding Eddi to mean merely the same day of the year, not necessarily in the next year: *Crit. in Baronii Ann.* xi. 610 b.   ⁵ Eddi, 28.
⁶ Paul. Diac. *Hist. Langob.* v. 2, 33.   ⁷ *V. Wilfr.* 29–32.
⁸ c. 53.   ⁹ 'Transactis ibi multis diebus', c. 33.
¹⁰ See the texts cited by M. L. Levillain, 'La Succession d'Austrasie au VIIᵉ siècle', in the *Revue Historique*, cxii (1913), 86, note 6.

We thus get the outside limits of Wilfrid's peregrination from about the middle of 677 to 680. In order to arrange the events within these limits it is necessary to inquire into the antecedents of the Sixth General Council held at Constantinople in November 680.

1. As early as 12 August 678, the Emperor Constantine Pogonatus had addressed a letter to Pope Donus asking him to send representatives.[1] But Donus was then already dead, and his successor Agatho had been elected in June. The new Pope, it seems, at once exerted himself to procure official declarations of adhesion to the Catholic faith. To England he sent John, the archchanter of St. Peter's, who was instructed to ascertain the opinion of the English Church and to report it to Rome. John therefore attended the synod of Hatfield, which is expressly said to have been called for this purpose, and took his report with him abroad; but he died on the way in Gaul, and the Acts of the synod[2] were taken on to Rome by other hands. It necessarily follows that the synod of Hatfield was held on 17 September 679, not 680. I have already contended for the earlier year simply from an examination of the chronological data presented by the Acts as recorded by Bede.[3] The course of events indicated by it appears to me to place the conclusion beyond doubt; for it would be manifestly absurd to assemble a synod in England in the middle of September with a view to its resolutions being reported to Rome and then sent on to Constantinople for presentation at a Council in the following November. The Roman envoys were already at Constantinople a week before the day when (on this assumption) the Hatfield synod met.[4]

Nevertheless, almost all modern writers, with the exception of Baronius,[5] agree in placing that synod on 17 September 680. The alteration was made by Pagi on the ground that Pope Agatho's bull for Peterborough was confirmed by King Ethelred in a document which bears the subscriptions both of Wilfrid and of John *Romanus legatus*,[6] and was presented at the synod of Hatfield; Wilfrid could not have been back in England until 680, and as John was present at Hatfield the synod must have

---

[1] Mansi, *Concil.* xi. 195 ff.
[2] 'Exemplum catholicae fidei Anglorum', Bede, *H. E.* iv. 18.
[3] Above, pp 44 f.
[4] See the Emperor's sacra of 10 September 680, in Mansi, xi. 202 f.
[5] *Ann.* xi, 623 ff.   [6] Haddan and Stubbs, iii. 156.

been in that year. Pagi saw that the document was open to suspicion, but believed it had a genuine basis.[1] But apart from the fact that Wilfrid certainly did not return to England until 681, the document is so glaring a forgery that we need not further consider it. It is in fact an improved version of one of a series of entries which were inserted in the Peterborough text of the Anglo-Saxon Chronicle, including the forged charters of King Wulfhere and Popes Vitalian and Agatho. The first and third of these are stated in that text to have been found in the old wall at Peterborough in 963, and the manuscript in which they appear was not written until the twelfth century. But although the foundation of Pagi's argument has been unanimously rejected by scholars, his date has been upheld on the supposition that the Indiction is reckoned not in the old way from 1 September, but from 24 September. Until, however, any evidence is produced to show that the latter form of Indiction was used before Bede's time, I must maintain that the Greek Indiction of 1 September is here used.

2. The opinion, then, of the English Church having been declared on 17 September 679, it was transmitted, as we have seen, to Rome; and there, as Eddi tells us,[2] Wilfrid subscribed a declaration of faith together with a hundred and twenty-five bishops on Tuesday in Easter week, plainly 27 March 680, in preparation for the great Council of the following November. The letter which bears these subscriptions is included in the Acts of the Council, and for reasons which will appear later it is desirable to quote the names at length. It is evident, though the fact has not, I think, been observed, that the subscriptions were written in five columns. Such an arrangement, though not common, may be found in Anglo-Saxon charters which unquestionably derived their forms from Italian models. In the Roman letter the first, second, and fourth columns are headed by bishops of Roman sees; the third by the bishop of Milan and his suffragans; and the fifth is reserved for the bishop of Ravenna and his suffragans. The bishops are ordered regularly under provinces, and only in two instances (Crescens of Vivonia and Mauricius of Tibur) have names been inserted altogether out of place. But no provinces are named in the cases of the sees immediately dependent upon Rome, Milan, and Ravenna, and it is not easy to explain why the province of Tuscia is uniformly

---

[1] *Critica in Baronii Ann.* xi. 623–5.   [2] *V. Wilfr.* 53.

mentioned in column 4, though it is omitted after the names occupying the lower part of column 3. The list is of remarkable interest as furnishing a Directory, not very far from complete, of the Italian bishoprics in 680, and as giving a large number of names otherwise unknown.[1]

3. The Acts of a Roman synod held in October 679 were printed by Sir Henry Spelman in 1639[2] from a manuscript of which no trace now remains. It is not to be found among Joscelyn's transcripts in the British Museum; nor is there any indication of it in Dr. Macray's Report for the Historical Manuscripts Commission on the Gurney collection at Keswick Hall, Norfolk,[3] which contains fourteen volumes of Spelman's papers. We have, therefore, only Spelman's printed text to go upon, and from this it is apparent that his original was a late and blundering copy. John Johnson, who translated the *Laws and Canons of the Church of England* in 1720, truly remarked, 'Never any synod, or consistory, met with a more ignorant transcriber of its acts, than he was who wrote the copy published by Sir H. Spelman.'[4] There are features in the document which raise the suspicion that it was produced, together with a number of admitted forgeries, in order to support Archbishop Lanfranc's claim to the primacy of Canterbury. On the other hand, it includes an element which I cannot but believe to be genuine in its enumeration of the bishops who attended the synod. 'The names of the Bishops', as Haddan and Stubbs pointed out,[5] 'with the single exception of George of Catania, are consistent with the signatures attached to the letter' which we have spoken of above. This one exception need not cause difficulty, for it can hardly be doubted[6] that the copyist has carelessly thrown two Sicilian bishops into one, and written *Georgio Catanensi* instead of *Georgio Triocalitano, Iuliano Catanensi*, who appear side by side in the Roman letter (nos. 46, 47). The question then arises, Can Spelman's document have been

---

[1] I print the list below, p. 54 f. from Mansi, xi. 298–315. The subscriptions are given both in Greek and Latin. I have followed the Latin, occasionally emending, in square brackets, from the Greek. I omit the word *episcopus* and the formulae connected with it throughout, and I abbreviate in other ways.

[2] *Concilia*, i. 158–60.

[3] Twelfth Report, Appendix ix (1891), 116–64.

[4] p. 100, n. d, in the edition by John Baron, 1850. The Latin text has been amended by a succession of editors, whose corrections have been silently accepted by Haddan and Stubbs.   [5] *Councils*, iii. 135, n. *b*.

[6] This suggestion is due to Dr. Levison.

forged with the help of the Roman letter? Twelve years ago, in the hope of obtaining an answer, I examined the Cottonian MS. Claudius B. v, fo. 30–1, which contains the Acts of the Sixth General Council. The manuscript is assigned to the tenth century, and is supposed to have come to England as a present from Otto the Great; it was long preserved at the abbey of Bath. The order of the subscriptions agrees almost entirely with that given in Mansi's edition of the Councils. Now it appeared to me incredible that a forger should have selected eighteen names[1] (I assume the one emendation suggested above) out of this list and arranged them in the following order: nos. 40, 2, 25, 51, 110, 42, 41, 112, 27, 28, 109, 26, 88, 48, 24, 46, 47, and 49. I inferred, therefore, that Spelman's document in its opening paragraph was derived from an independent and genuine source. The acceptance of this paragraph may reasonably be held to include the protocol which gives the date in full. Unluckily the dates it records are mutually incompatible, and we have to adopt the least violent correction of them that we can find. If we accept the Imperial year as correct and emend the Indiction VII into VIII, we obtain the date October 679, which is on all grounds the probable one. The Post-Consular date (x for xi) and the years of the Imperial colleagues (xxii for xxi) must be neglected. But when I had satisfied myself that Spelman's document contained a genuine beginning, I found myself unable to reconcile this with the manifest fabrication which appears in the course of the text.

The solution of the problem has since been satisfactorily accomplished by Dr. Wilhelm Levison, of Bonn, in a paper on *Die Akten der römischen Synode von 679* which appeared in 1912.[2] By an acute analysis of the text he showed that only the last part of the document, beginning with the eighth clause,[3] is an unmistakable product of the factory from which Lanfranc's evidence for the primacy of Canterbury issued. The earlier

---

[1] It will be noticed that eleven of the eighteen held sees in the vicinity of Rome. One came from Calabria, five from Sicily, and one (who, Eddi tells us, c. 28, accompanied Wilfrid) from Toul, 'ecclesia Leucorum'. Dr. Levison thinks that the order in Spelman's document is that of the bishop's seniority in consecration, and this is favoured by the prominent place taken in the proceedings by the bishop of Vivona, whose name stands first in the enumeration.

[2] *Zeitschrift der Savigny-Stiftung für Rechtsgeschichte*, xxxiii (Kanonistische Abteilung ii), 249–82.

[3] In Haddan and Stubbs, iii. 133 middle. Dr. Levison, contrary to the accepted usage, includes the protocol in his numbering of the clauses.

part may be most of it genuine—Dr. Levison goes farther on this side than I should myself be disposed to go—but, what is of chief importance for my present purpose, he appears to me to have proved that the initial protocol is in truth the opening of the genuine Acts of the synod from which Eddi excerpted the clauses which dealt with Wilfrid's appeal. Eddi, as has been mentioned above, says that the synod which heard Wilfrid was attended by more than fifty bishops and priests and was held at the Lateran:[1] our document gives the same place, and the number as fifty-three.[2] The first speech of Pope Agatho begins both in Eddi and in Spelman's text in the same terms, though the composer of the latter has interpolated some words in it from Bede and has altered the end of it. I suspect he has played more tricks with the document than Dr. Levison will allow; but I am persuaded that we have here the genuine framework of the instrument of which Eddi supplies some of the contents, and that the two Councils distinguished by Haddan and Stubbs as the one 'in the cause of the English Church [irrespective of Wilfrid, although after he had reached Rome]',[3] and the other 'to decide upon Wilfrid's appeal',[4] are really parts of a single council, though the former can only be accepted with a liberal use of the obelus. We can assign it to the definite date of October 679, and we have the list of bishops and priests who were actually present.

[1] Cap. 29.
[2] This is assuming the one emendation proposed above.
[3] Vol. iii. 131.   [4] Vol. iii. 136.

[I]

Agatho episcopus sanctae Dei catholicae atque apostolicae ecclesiae urbis Romae

Andreas s. Ostiensis eccl.

Agnellus s. eccl. Tarracinensis provinciae Campaniae

Agnellus s. Fundanae eccl. prov. Camp.

5 Adeodatus s. Formianae[1] eccl. prov. Camp.

Petrus s. Cumanae eccl. prov. Camp.

Agnellus s. eccl. Misenatis prov. Camp.

Gaudiosus s. Puteolanae eccl. prov. Camp.

Stephanus s. Locrensis eccl. [prov. Calabriae[2]]

10 Agnellus s. Neapolitanae eccl. prov. Camp.

Aureli[an]us s. Nolanae eccl. prov. Camp.

Barbatus s. Beneventanae eccl. prov. Camp.

Decorosus s. eccl. Capuanae prov. Camp.

Iulianus s. Consentinae eccl. prov. Brutiorum

15 Ioannes s. Hydruntinae eccl. prov. Brut.[3]

Germanus s. Tarentinae eccl. prov. Calabriae

Theophanes s. Thurinae eccl. prov. Calabriae

Petrus s. Crotonensis eccl. prov. Brutiorum

Paulus s. Scylletiensis eccl. prov. Brut.

20 Georgius s. Taurianae eccl. prov. Calabr.

Theodorus s. Tropeianae eccl. prov. Calabr.

Abundantius Tempsanae eccl. prov. Brut.

Hyacinthus s. Surrentinae eccl. prov. Camp.

Placentius s. Veliternensis eccl. prov. Camp.

[II]

25 Iuvenalis s. Albanensis eccl.

Vitus s. eccl. Silvae candidae

Paulus s. Nomentanae eccl.

Ioannes s. eccl. Portuensis

Stephanus s. Praenestinae eccl.

30 Felix s. Spoletanae eccl.

Honestus s. Esinatis[4] eccl.

Felix s. Camerinae eccl.

Florus s. Fulginatis eccl.

Decentius s. Foroflaminiensis eccl.

35 Ioannes s. Nursinae eccl.

Felix s. eccl. Asculanensis

Hadrianus s. Reatinae eccl.

Florus s. Furconiensis eccl.

Clarentius s. eccl. Balnensis

40 Crescens[5] s. eccl. Vibonensis [prov. Calabr.]

Theodosius s. eccl. Syracusanae prov. Sicil.

Benedictus s. eccl. Messanensis prov. Sic.

Ioannes s. eccl. Thermitanae prov. Sic.

Ioannes s. eccl. Mylanae prov. Sic.

45 Petrus s. eccl. Tauromenitanae prov. Sic.

Iulianus s. eccl. Catanensis prov. Sic.

Georgius s. eccl. Trioclitanae prov. Sic.

Georgius s. Agrigentinae eccl. prov. Sic.

Adeodatus s. eccl. Leucorum legatus venerabilis synodi per Galliarum provincias constitutae

50 Wilfridus s. eccl. Eboracenae insulae Britanniae legatus venerabilis synodi per Britanniam constitutae

Mauricius s. Tiburtinae eccl.

Felix Arelatensis eccl. legatus venerabilis synodi per Galliarum provincias constitutae

Taurinus diaconus s. eccl. Telonensis legatus venerabilis synodi per Galliarum provincias constitutae

---

[1] i.e. *Firmanae*.   [2] For *Brutiorum*.   [3] For *Calabriae*.

[4] From Aesium (mod. Iesi).

[5] Κρέσης, Lat. *Orestes*, but *Crescis* in Cotton MS.

[6] *Vadensis* in Cotton MS.   [7] Probably a mistake for *Soranae*.

[8] For *Vicentianae*.

[9] In this and the two following sees I take the names from the Greek: the Latin has *Paduanae, Patavinae*, and *Altinensis*. The first probably designates not Padua but Pedena.   [10] Greek Φαλάρεως; Lat. *Salernitanae* vel *Sarnensis*.

[11] v. l. *Caesenatis*; Greek Σανσινάτης. The see is Sarsina.

[12] Greek Βικοαβεντίνης, that is, Ferraria.

[III]

Mansuetus s. Mediolanensis eccl.
55 Ioannes s. eccl. Bergomatis
Donatus s. eccl. Laudensis
Anastasius s. eccl. Ticinensis
Valentinus s. eccl. Aquensis
Desiderius s. eccl. Cremonensis
60 Gratianus s. eccl. Novariensis
Desiderius s. eccl. Eporediensis
Ioannes s. eccl. Genuensis
Deusdedit s. eccl. Brixianensis
Audacis s. eccl. Dertonensis
65 Benenatus s. eccl. Astensis
Benedictus s. eccl. Valvensis[6]
Bonus s. eccl. Albiganensis
Theodorus s. eccl. Vercellensis
Rusticus s. eccl. Taurinatis
70 Ioannes s. eccl. Vintimiliensis
Severus s. eccl. Lunensis
Eleutherius s. eccl. Lucensis
Maurianus s. eccl. Pisanae
Serenus s. eccl. Populoniensis
75 Reparatus s. eccl. Florentinae
Valerianus s. eccl. Rosellensis
Cyprianus s. eccl. Aretinae
Vitalianus s. eccl. Senensis
Marcianus s. eccl. Volaterranae
80 Mauricius s. eccl. Suanensis
Agnellus s. eccl. Vulsiniensis
Theodorus s. eccl. Clusinae
Custoditus s. eccl. [Valentinocastri]

[IV]

Vitalianus s. eccl. Tusculanensis
85 Mauriciuss. eccl. Anagninae
Saturninus s. eccl. Aletrinae
Valerianus s. Rosanae[7] eccl.
Gaudiosus s. eccl. Signinae
Agatho s. eccl. Aquileiensis prov. Istriae
90 Cyriacus s. eccl. Polensis Istriae
Aurelianus s. eccl. Parentinae prov. Istriae
Ursinus s. eccl. Cenetensis prov. Istriae
Andreas s. eccl. Veientanae[8] prov. Istriae
Gaudentius s. eccl. Tergestinae prov. Istriae
95 Benenatus s. eccl. Opitergiensis prov. Istriae
Ursinianus s. eccl. Patavinae[9] prov. Istriae
Paulus s. eccl. Altinensis prov. Istriae
Paulus s. eccl. Ariminensis prov. Pentapolis
Beatus s. eccl. Pisaurensis
100 prov. Pentapolis
Dominicus s. Fanensis eccl. prov. Pentapolis
Hadrianus s. eccl. Numanatis prov. Pentapolis
Ioannes s. eccl. Auximatis prov. Pentapolis
Ioannes s. eccl. Anconitanae prov. Pentapolis
Benenatus s. eccl. Perusinae prov. Tusciae
105 Bonifacius s. eccl. Tudertinae prov. Tusciae
Exhilaratus s. eccl. Metuarensis prov. Tusciae
Amator s. eccl. Bleranae prov. Tusciae
Gratiosus s. eccl. Sutrinae prov. Tusciae
Theodorus s. eccl. Nepesinae prov. Tusciae
110 Ioannes s. eccl. Falaritanae[10] prov. Tusciae
Theodorus s. eccl. Amerianae prov. Tusciae
Barbatianus s. eccl. Polymartiensis prov. Tusciae
Deusdedit s. eccl. Narniensis prov. Tusciae

[V]

Theodorus s. eccl. Ravennatis
115 Stephanus s. eccl. Saranatis[11]
Barbatus s. eccl. Corneliensis
Victor s. eccl. Bononiensis
Florus s. eccl. Cesenatis
Vitalis s. eccl. Faventinae
120 Iustinus s. eccl. Fidentinensis[12]
Vincentius s. eccl. Liviensis
Placentius s. eccl. Placentinae
Mauricius s. eccl. Regiensis
Petrus s. eccl. Mutinensis
125 Gratiosus s. eccl. Parmensis
Magnus s. eccl. Pupilensis

ST. WILFRID AND THE SEE OF RIPON[1]

THE career of Wilfrid, bishop in turn at Ripon, York, Selsey, Leicester, and Hexham, is so remarkable, and the narratives of it which have come down to us contain so many discrepancies and even contradictions, that it may be permitted to make yet another attempt to examine the value of our materials in the hope of ascertaining what actually happened. In pursuing this inquiry we leave on one side most of the features which give interest to the bishop's activity. We are told that when he was threatened with humiliation in his old age, he made a speech in which he set forth his merits: he had uprooted the pestilent growth of the Scottish teaching, had established the true observance of Easter, and the right fashion of the tonsure; he had brought in the primitive use of chant and the rule of St. Benedict.[2] These matters lie beyond our present province. Nor are we concerned with his work in introducing, chiefly as I believe from Italy, new patterns in church building and new forms of art, a subject on which much light has been thrown by scholars in our own time.[3] My task is limited to the claims which he made, or which he is said to have made, for himself as bishop, and to the see which he held for most of his life in Northumbria.

Wilfrid had the advantage of having his Life written by two younger contemporaries. One of them, Stephen, is better known as Eddius or Eddi, because it has almost universally been agreed that he is the *Aeddi cognomento Stephanus* who was taken by Wilfrid from Kent some time between 665 and 668, to teach the art of chant in the Northumbrian churches.[4] He accompanied Wilfrid during his stay in the Netherlands in 677–8,[5] and doubt-

[1] Reprinted from the *English Historical Review*, vol. xxxiv (1919).

[2] Eddi, *Vita Wilfridi*, 47.

[3] Cf. G. T. Rivoira, *Le Origini della Architettura Lombarda*, ii (1907), 254–70; and Bishop G. F. Browne, *The Ancient Cross Shafts at Bewcastle and Ruthwell* (1916), *passim*. Mr. G. Baldwin Brown would lay more stress on Romanized lands, especially Gaul, as furnishing Wilfrid's models: *The Arts in Early England*, ii (1903), 320–3.

[4] Bede, *H. E.* v. 2; Eddi, 14. The argument adduced by Levison, *Scriptores Rerum Merovingicarum*, vi (1913), 180, that he cannot be the same man as the biographer because the latter speaks of him in the third person can hardly be pressed; for in ch. 53 in like manner he mentions in the third person Wilfrid and his companions, *venerabiles presbyteri et diacones eius*, being presented before the Pope in council, though he had already in ch. 52 spoken of them as going to 'our lodgings', *habitacula nostra*.   [5] Eddi, 27.

less went with him to Rome; he also attended him on his second appeal there more than twenty years later,[1] and was with him in France on his return homewards.[2] There are abundant indications throughout his book that he was a monk of Wilfrid's own house at Ripon.[3] He wrote his Life not long after, certainly between 711 and 731, and in all probability much nearer the first than the last of these years. Bede, our other authority, was a good deal younger, but he was in middle life at the time of Wilfrid's death, and therefore in a position to know much about him from direct information, and to form an independent judgement on the account given by Eddi. I do not propose to contest the accepted opinion that Bede wrote with Eddi's book before him, but I am not at all sure that the book he read was that which we now possess. Eddi's Life is preserved in no manuscript earlier than the twelfth century, and there are indications in it that it has received later additions. But until further criticism has been supplied I accept the current view. It is agreed then that Eddi was the earlier writer and that Bede wrote at least his biographical chapter with the help of Eddi's Life. It therefore follows that, when Bede differs from Eddi, he differs intentionally, and the question is, which of the two writers deserves the more confidence. Now Bede has the fullest credentials, and no one who has studied his voluminous works is likely to disagree with the judgement of Mommsen, that he is 'first and foremost a man of integrity and a faithful witness. He calls himself a *verax historicus* and he has a right to the title: all who have followed in his track will testify that few writers have treated matters of fact with such, and often with such laborious, accuracy'.[4] There is therefore a presumption that, when Bede alters or contradicts a statement by Eddi, he does so because he knows that it is incorrect, and in some cases because, to speak plainly, he knows that Eddi is not telling the truth.

Bede's account of Wilfrid in book v, ch. 19 of the History[5]

---

[1] Allusions of a general kind to Eddi's personal recollections of Wilfrid occur in the prologue and in ch. 11.

[2] ch. 57. [3] See ch. 17, 45, 61–3, 65, 67.

[4] *Neues Archiv der Gesellschaft für ältere Deutsche Geschichtskunde*, xvii (1892), 389.

[5] References to the *Historia Ecclesiastica* are to the books and chapters in the edition by the Rev. C. Plummer, 1896; where chapters have a double numbering the higher number is cited. In translating I have sometimes used the excellent version by Miss A. M. Sellar, as reissued in 1912.

is often cited as though it were a regular Life of the saint. This is not so: when Bede in the course of his narrative comes to the death of Wilfrid, he takes occasion to write what may be called an obituary notice; but he avoids repeating—as he explains once and might have explained more often—what he has already said earlier in his work. The scattered notices which are found elsewhere in the History form an important supplement to that chapter, all the more since, as it has been acutely observed,[1] Bede is here more independent of Eddi than in book v. 19. It is indeed not unlikely that he did not get access to Eddi's work until he was near the end of his History. In addition to these materials we have the summary Annals given in book v. 24. These consist almost entirely of notices of natural phenomena (eclipses, comets, plague), accessions, abdications, and deaths of kings, conversions of tribes, synods, and appointments and deaths of bishops. Wilfrid's expulsion in 677[2] is the only event of the sort recorded, the reason why it is noted is in order to explain the appointment of three bishops in his stead. There is, therefore, nothing strange in the omission of any later facts in Wilfrid's life; but copyists, nevertheless, endeavoured to supply the missing events. All the important insertions in the manuscripts of the Annals for this time relate to Wilfrid. One of them is a stupid repetition of the event of 677 entered ten years too late; a second contains a singularly confused summary of Wilfrid's doings for the eleven years from 692;[3] the rest record correctly essential facts in his life, which the transcribers considered ought to have been inserted. But to have inserted them would have been foreign to the scheme of the Annals.

While we have the fullest materials for judging the good faith and scrupulous exactness of Bede's writings, we have no such advantage in forming a preliminary estimate of Eddi's Life of

[1] By Dr. Wells in the paper mentioned below, p. 59.

[2] With regard to the dates found in Bede I may refer to my paper on *The Chronology of Bede's Historia Ecclesiastica*, above pp. 38 ff, where I have given reasons for believing that his *annus Domini* was reckoned from the Indiction of the preceding September.

[3] This is found in the Winchester MS. 3, of the late tenth century, and in the Durham MS. B. ii. 35, and the Balliol College MS. 176, of the twelfth. It runs substantially as follows: 'Anno DCXCII ab Alfrido rege iterum expulsus est, et primo Romam adiit, et inde rediit et in Mediterraneorum Anglorum regione morabatur: multaque diu loca pervagatus Romam adiit et Britaniam rediit; divertens ad Australes Saxones paganae adhuc culturae deditos, illis in illa patria per v annos docebat evangelium.' See the variants in Plummer, i. 355, n. 11.

Wilfrid,[1] for we possess no other book by him. It is plain first of all that Eddi was not composing a history but a work of edification. His task was to display the merits of the saint, and he yielded to the temptation which has commonly beset hagiographers of making too much of his hero's importance, and of treating any opposition which he suffered as due to jealousy, malice, or some other evil cause. He puts in the lights and shades too heavily. But how far these characteristics have affected the veracity of his Life must be decided by detailed criticism of his statements, and by comparison with the parallel statements of Bede. Many years ago its character was examined in an able paper in the *English Historical Review*[2] by Dr. Benjamin W. Wells, who arrived at the conclusion that Eddi

was not a conscientious historian. He did not hesitate to suppress and to distort inconvenient facts. . . . Throughout he is advocate, not judge, and pleads his patron's cause with more zeal than discretion.[3]

Dr. Levison, who more recently edited the Life, thought Dr. Wells too severe,[4] but it deserves attention that on some of the vital points in which Eddi and Bede disagree, he accepts the evidence of Bede.[5] Dr. Wells sought, as far as possible, to avoid the controversial features in the discussion: in the present article I do not propose to shirk them, and while in many particulars I am unable to follow Dr. Wells, I think his judgement errs on the side of leniency. But before coming to the more difficult questions I will take a couple of examples to illustrate Eddi's mode of treatment in regions unconnected with the crucial problems in Wilfrid's biography.

I take first a series of notices relative to the contemporary history of Gaul, which are the more interesting since they furnish almost the sole existing evidence for the restoration of Dagobert II to the Austrasian throne after his banishment to Ireland. The time is one of extreme obscurity in Merovingian history, and we get but little light from charters and a few Lives

---

[1] I have used indifferently the text edited by James Raine, in *The Historians of the Church of York and its Archbishops*, vol. i (1879), and that by W. Levison in the *Scriptores Rerum Merovingicarum*, vol. vi (1913).

[2] vi. 535–50, 1891. [3] p. 550.

[4] *Scriptores Rerum Merovingicarum*, vi. 182, n. 6.

[5] e.g., pp. 169, 205, n. 5, p. 208, n. 6.

of Frankish bishops.[1] What Eddi therefore tells us is the more welcome, and the information he gives has the merit that it is in almost all points[2] consistent with what we have from those meagre sources. But he plainly magnifies the importance of the part which Wilfrid played in the matter. He says that Dagobert when a youth was driven away into exile and took refuge in Ireland. After a time his friends learned from some seafaring folk that he was still alive, and they sent to Wilfrid asking him to bring him over from Ireland and send him to be their king. This Wilfrid did: he fetched him back, supplied him with arms, and restored him to his throne.[3] It is not easy to understand why the Franks should have applied to the Northumbrian bishop, and it would seem more natural that they should have entrusted the mariners from whom they had the news with a message inviting him to return to Gaul. Possibly the suggestion came from one of the bishops who assisted at Wilfrid's consecration at Compiègne more than eleven years before, and Dagobert, passing through England between April and July 676, may well have had a friendly reception from him, and this would explain the favour which he showed him when he was on the Continent in 677 and 678.

Eddi, however, thinks his share in Dagobert's restoration so important that the king's enemies, headed by Ebroin, the mayor of the palace, had the coast watched in order to capture him when he went abroad, and by a mistake in the name—*errore bono unius syllabae*—imprisoned Winfrid, the deposed bishop of Lichfield.[4] This looks like a good story which easily passed current. According to Bede,[5] Winfrid, who was deprived probably several years earlier, retired to his monastery and died there. But Eddi tells us that Wilfrid avoided danger by making for the east—Bede says it was the wind that took him—and landed in the Netherlands.[6] When he was there Ebroin sought to induce the Frisian chief, in whose land he was staying, to hand the bishop over to him alive or dead.[7] Then again, when Wilfrid travelled homewards from Rome in 680, after Dagobert's death, he was met by an immense army, whose commander

---

[1] Full references to these materials and to recent publications on the subject will be found in an article by M. L. Levillain on *La Succession d'Austrasie au VIIe Siècle*, in the *Revue historique*, cxii (1913), 62–93.

[2] Perhaps the one exception is his denunciation of Queen Balthildis in ch. 6.

[3] Eddi, 28.   [4] ch. 25.   [5] *H.E.* iv. 6.

[6] Eddi, 26.   [7] ch. 27.

threatened to enslave or kill him, or at least to bring him to Ebroin for judgement, because he had fetched the king back from exile.[1] But Ebroin was no longer living. Wilfrid was present at a council in Rome on 27 March 680, and he did not return to England at once.[2] Ebroin, however, was murdered some time before 15 May, for a charter quoted in the *Vita Condedi anachoretae Belcinnacensis*[3] bears date in the seventh year of Theodoric III,[4] and is subscribed by Waratto, who was Ebroin's successor as mayor.[5] It is therefore hardly possible that Wilfrid should have reached Gaul during Ebroin's lifetime. But, apart from this, the whole account of Wilfrid's relations to the rulers of Frankland is so much exaggerated as to lead one to distrust Eddi's fidelity. The foundation of his story is true, but the superstructure is fiction.

As a second test of Eddi's trustworthiness I take his account of Wilfrid's life in Sussex in the years following his return from Rome in 680. For this we have the advantage of a particularly full narrative in Bede,[6] which deserves the more confidence because for part of it he expressly vouches the authority of Acca, the future bishop of Hexham, who was Wilfrid's companion at the time, and we shall not be far wrong if we take the whole to represent substantially what Acca told him. From this I take only the points which challenge comparison with the facts as recorded by Eddi. According to Bede, when Wilfrid arrived in Sussex, its king Ethelwalch had been lately baptized in Mercia, and his queen was a Christian from the land of the Hwiccas; we may presume that, as in other cases at this time, his baptism was connected with his marriage. There was also a Scottish monastery at Bosham, a few miles west of Chichester. But the mass of the people were still heathen, and Wilfrid spent five years in preaching and baptizing. Ethelwalch granted him land at Selsey where he founded a monastery. Eddi, on the

---

[1] ch. 33.   [2] ch. 34.

[3] ch. 8, *Scriptores Rerum Merovingicarum*, v (1910), 649.

[4] The view maintained by Julien Havet and formerly by Krusch that Theodoric's years are reckoned not from 673 but from 675 was silently abandoned by Krusch himself in the *Neues Archiv*, xvi (1891), 579, n. It was demolished by Vacandard in the *Revue des Questions Historiques*, lix (1896), 491–506.

[5] The only reason which has led Krusch and Levison to doubt the evidence of the charter in the *Vita Condedi* is derived from the unsupported statement by Eddi: see *Scriptores Rerum Merovingicarum*, v. 320, n., and 649, n. 5.

[6] *H.E.* iv. 13–16.

other hand, makes Wilfrid convert not only the people but also both the king and queen: he is not contented with Ethelwalch's grant to him of Selsey, but makes him give his own *vill* as a bishop's see.[1]

A more serious difference arises in what we are told about Caedwalla, who afterwards became king of Wessex. Bede says that this *iuvenis strenuissimus* had been banished from his country, and went with an army into Sussex where he killed Ethelwalch, but was soon driven out. If we believe Eddi, Caedwalla, when living as an exile in some wild district, apparently in Sussex, desired the friendship of Wilfrid, and promised to be obedient to him as a son. So Wilfrid became devoted to him.[2] Eddi omits to mention that Caedwalla slew his patron and ravaged the country. When Caedwalla became king of Wessex, he continues,

> he humbly called Wilfrid, his honoured father and dearest above all men, to come to him. And when our holy father came, King Caedwalla soon established him as his high counsellor in all his kingdom, as the king of Egypt appointed Joseph. Then indeed King Caedwalla in his triumph granted our holy bishop innumerable tracts of land and presents of gifts and honoured him gloriously.[3]

Now it is true, as Bede informs us,[4] that Caedwalla made Wilfrid a large grant of land in the Isle of Wight, but he notes that the king was still unbaptized.[5] This is very different from the intimate association which Eddi describes. We may blame Wilfrid, if we like, for accepting gifts from the murderer of his first protector; but we need not charge him with close friendship with him. Nor is there the smallest reason for believing that Wilfrid was given any position in Wessex except in the newly conquered Isle of Wight. Thus Eddi's desire to magnify the greatness of the saint leads him to make Ethelwalch a heathen in order that he may convert him, and Caedwalla a Christian in order that he may be closely attached to him, and to suppress the fact that one of his patrons was murdered by the other. If it be maintained that Eddi was ignorant of the truth, it is remarkable that he should not have known just those facts which were fatal to his story.

---

[1] ch. 41.   [2] ch. 42.
[3] I abbreviate the text slightly.   [4] *H.E.* iv. 16.
[5] He was, indeed, not baptized until he had abdicated and gone to Rome in 688–9, *H.E.* iv. 7.

I now proceed to the questions relating to Wilfrid's bishopric.

1. The first important difference between our authorities relates to the appointment to the Northumbrian diocese when Colman withdrew at the synod of Whitby in 664 and retired to Ireland. It should be observed that Bede almost always speaks of a bishop by his territorial style; he is bishop of a kingdom or under-kingdom: or more exactly his title is gentilic; he is bishop of the Northumbrians, or the Middle English, or the Gewissas, or the like. It is only in regard to the most ancient bishoprics, Canterbury, Rochester, London, and York, that he designates a bishop by his 'see' or place of residence. Elsewhere he may mention the see as an historical description, but we shall not find him speaking of the bishop of Winchester, of Lichfield, or of Worcester. If we read that a bishop was granted a monastery, this often means that the monastery became his see. When there were more than one bishop in a kingdom, they might be removed from one diocese to another within its limits. Thus, when Lindsey was conquered from Northumbria by Mercia, Egfrid translated its bishop Eadhed to Ripon; and when Cuthbert was chosen bishop of Hexham, the bishop of Lindisfarne proposed to him to exchange sees, and this was done.[1] If a bishop was deprived of his see, he continued to rank as a bishop in the kingdom to which he belonged; for when Chad was removed from York, Oswy's permission was asked before he was appointed bishop for the Mercians.[2] Wilfrid for a course of years held the bishopric of the Middle English (*episcopatum gerebat*),[3] but the see vanished when he returned to Northumbria; Bede does not include it in his list of bishoprics existing in 731,[4] and it does not reappear until 737. It may be noticed that in this list he does mention Selsey, though for some years past the see had had no occupant.[5] It has sometimes been attempted to draw a distinction between the statements that a man was bishop of a particular diocese and that he administered a bishopric during a vacancy. I am not sure that this can be made out. It is true that Bede says[6] that Wilfrid kept (*servabat*) the bishopric of Lindisfarne until a successor could be appointed in the place of St. Cuthbert; but he speaks of Wilfrid as *administrante episcopatum Eboracensis ecclesiae nec non et omnium*

[1] *H.E.* iv. 28.
[2] *Ibid.* iv. 3.
[3] *Ibid.* iv. 23.
[4] *Ibid.* v. 23.
[5] *Ibid.* v. 19.
[6] *Ibid.* iv. 29.

Nordanhymbrorum[1] at the only time when beyond all dispute he was bishop of the undivided diocese.

The missionaries of Northumbria, coming from Scotland, settled themselves for security on an island off the extreme north coast, at Lindisfarne. This was the 'see' of Aidan, and in it he was succeeded by Colman. It was the diocese from which Colman retired at the synod of Whitby, and to which Tuda was then appointed. Tuda died almost immediately, but he had no direct successor in the entire diocese. Oswy's son Alchfrid held a *provincia*, or under-kingdom, in what we may roughly describe as the West Riding of Yorkshire, and there he desired to have a bishop of his own, *pro se et suis*. He therefore asked his father's leave to appoint Wilfrid bishop of that district; and so, according to the modern way of speaking, Wilfrid was made bishop of Ripon: that is to say, he was consecrated bishop, and on his return from abroad went back to live in his old monastery. But the larger part of the Northumbrian kingdom was for the moment unprovided for, and Oswy, following the example of his son's zeal,[2] caused Chad to be appointed bishop of York. It is clear that in Bede's view the two rulers acted in agreement: the part of Northumbria which was not assigned to Wilfrid was entrusted to Chad, but his see was removed from the Scottish influences of Lindisfarne and placed in the city which had long before been designated by Gregory the Great. Thus the Roman victory at Whitby was almost immediately followed by the erection of a definite see at the place chosen by the Pope.

Wilfrid at the time was still abroad; he had gone to Compiègne to be consecrated, and he was always leisurely in his movements: but the supposition that Oswy took advantage of his absence to oust him from the bishopric which had been conferred upon him receives no support from Bede's narrative. In his Annals he notes concisely, *Ceadda ac Vilfrid Nordanhymbrorum ordinantur episcopi*.[3] When Wilfrid returned he went quietly to his see at Ripon and continued to dwell there[4] until he was called upon to act in a larger sphere. This happened when Archbishop Theodore in 669 visited the north and took objection to Chad's orders.[5] Chad ceased to be bishop of York

---

[1] *H.E.* iv. 3.   [2] *Imitatus industriam filii*: *H.E.* iii. 28.

[3] *H.E.* v. 24.

[4] Eddi, 14, says for three years: Bede apparently by inadvertence takes these three years to limit Chad's tenure of the see of York, *H.E.* v. 19.

[5] *H.E.* iv. 2.

and Wilfrid occupied his place,[1] thus becoming for the first time—as Aidan, Colman, and Tuda had been—bishop of all Northumbria.

This story is too simple to please Eddi: it does not sufficiently illustrate the grandeur of Wilfrid or the persecution which he endured. Hence on the retirement of Colman he makes Wilfrid immediately to be acclaimed as his successor.[2] He may have been ignorant of the short pontificate of Tuda. But he has to reconcile the position which he assigns to Wilfrid with the fact that Chad was made bishop of York. Consequently he says that during Wilfrid's absence abroad Chad was set up in his place, *male suadente invidia*, by his enemies.[3] But he gives no indication that Wilfrid considered himself ill-treated or that he attempted to gain possession of York. Theodore, he says,[4] deposed Chad not on account of his Scottish orders but because he was an intruder. Now Bede wrote with Eddi's book before him: he supplements it from his own information and he corrects it where it is wrong.

2. We come next to the question of the partition of the great Northumbrian diocese. In 672[5] Archbishop Theodore proposed at the synod of Hertford that the number of bishops should be increased, but this was not accepted, and the matter was for the time passed over.[6] The plan remained however a leading feature of the archbishop's policy, and in 677 he took steps to carry it into effect in Northumbria. The opportunity arose out of a quarrel between Wilfrid and King Egfrid, in consequence of which Wilfrid 'was expelled from the seat of his bishopric and two bishops substituted in his place; namely, Bosa who should govern the province of the Deirans and Eata that of the Bernicians, the one having his episcopal chair in the city of York, the other in the church of Hexham or of Lindisfarne'. In addition to these, Eadhed was made bishop in Lindsey which Egfrid had lately conquered from Wulfhere of Mercia. All the three were consecrated at York by Archbishop Theodore.[7]

The account given by Eddi[8] does not differ in substance from that of Bede, but he gives it a different colouring. The dispute between Wilfrid and Egfrid, he says, arose from the envy

---

[1] *H.E.* iv. 3. In October 679 Wilfrid speaks of having held the see for ten years and more: Eddi 30. [2] ch. 11.
[3] ch. 14. [4] ch. 15. [5] See above p. 41 and n. 4.
[6] *H.E.* iv. 5. [7] *Ibid.* iv. 12. [8] ch. 24.

of Queen Iurminburg, who was jealous of his magnificence and wealth. Eddi does not here mention, what did not escape the attention of later writers, that Egfrid had another wife living,[1] so that Wilfrid had good cause for displeasure. Eddi says that Egfrid and his queen bribed Archbishop Theodore to take their part; he went to the north and, in Wilfrid's absence, set up three bishops, imported from without (*aliunde inventos*) and not belonging to his diocese, in the places of his bishopric. This statement is untrue, for all the three were Northumbrians; and Eddi cannot be acquitted of falsehood, because one of them, Eata, had been abbot of his own monastery of Ripon. When Wilfrid learned what had been done, he approached the king and the archbishop, and asked what offence he had committed. They replied that they charged him with no crime, but would not alter their decision.

Before passing on to Wilfrid's appeal to Rome against his deprivation, the question may be asked whether he was in fact deposed from his bishopric, or whether he was removed from York and limited to the smaller diocese which he had at first held, at Ripon. This is much how William of Malmesbury understood the matter. He follows Eddi closely until he comes to explain Theodore's action, then he says,

Praetendebat tamen causam iustitiae, ut inde tres alerentur episcopi, unde unus tumebat: sufficere tantos sumptus tantaeque diocesis circuitum quattuor episcopis.[2]

Such a proceeding would suit well with the archbishop's scheme of breaking up dioceses, and the interpretation is not absolutely excluded by the words of Eddi and Bede—for Wilfrid would have been deprived of his see of York even if he had been permitted to keep one at Ripon;—but it must be said that they give no hint that Wilfrid retained anything, and certainly leave the impression that he was expelled from Northumbria. Dr. William Bright not only follows the explanation of William of Malmesbury, but supposes that the plan of establishing four bishoprics, of which Wilfrid was to have one, namely York, was altered into a resolution to supersede him altogether in consequence of his announcement that he would appeal to Rome.[3]

---

[1] William of Malmesbury, *Gesta Pontificum*, p. 219.

[2] *Ibid.*, p. 220.

[3] *Chapters in Early English Church History*, pp. 322, 413 f., 3rd ed., 1897.

But there is not a word of any such change either in Eddi's narrative or in Wilfrid's own petition which he presented at Rome. Still, from several indications which appear later on, I am led to believe that Malmesbury's account of what Archbishop Theodore proposed to do is substantially true; only I hold that the see which Wilfrid was to retain was not York but Ripon. This would agree with what Eddi relates about Egfrid's offer to Wilfrid, after his return from Rome, to give him *episcopatum ex parte quem prius possidebat* if he would deny the authenticity of the decree he brought back with him.[1] This arrangement would at the same time have carried out the archbishop's policy, and would have so far satisfied the king that it would remove Wilfrid from his immediate neighbourhood.

3. Wilfrid's first appeal is related in full by Eddi, who accompanied him on the journey and who gives us a large part of the Acts of the synod which inquired into the case. Unfortunately he omits some portions which appeared to him unnecessary or perhaps inconvenient. The decree prescribes that Wilfrid *episcopatum quem nuper habuerat recipiat, salva diffinitione superius ordinata*—but Eddi has left out the clause containing the qualifying terms of the bishop's restoration:—*et quos cum consensu concilii ibidem congregandi elegerit sibi adiutores episcopos, cum quibus debeat pacifice conversari, secundum regulam superius constitutam*—again the defining provision has been omitted—*a serenissimo archiepiscopo promoti ordinentur episcopi, expulsis proculdubio eis qui in eius absentia in episcopatum innormiter missi sunt.*[2] Thus we are not informed as to the limitations which the synod imposed on Wilfrid's restoration and on his subsequent procedure. But it seems to have acted with the moderation and common sense which Roman councils had learned from long experience. It accepted Archbishop Theodore's plan of increasing the number of Northumbrian bishops, but conciliated Wilfrid by providing that the particular people whom he had appointed should be removed. Wilfrid was to regain his see and to nominate the new bishops; but this was to be done subject to the consent of a Northumbrian council, and the new bishops were to be consecrated by Theodore. So much we are told: we do not know in what way the omitted parts of the decree modified the terms of Wilfrid's restoration or the conditions under which the new bishops were to be appointed.

[1] ch. 36.　　　　　　　　　　　　[2] ch. 32.

Dr. Levison[1] has endeavoured to extract them from a document preserved in a very bad copy which has certainly suffered later manipulation, and it seems unsafe to rely upon this for the particulars of the decree.[2] Besides this decree it appears from a later reference in Eddi[3] that Wilfrid obtained a privilege or bull confirming him in the possession of the monasteries of Ripon and Hexham. These two documents must be carefully kept distinct.

4. On Wilfrid's return to England in 680 Eddi seems to have parted company with him, and there is no express indication of any personal relations between them during the following twenty-two years. Indeed, for the period from 691 to 702 he has absolutely nothing to relate. For all this time, therefore, Eddi's Life has not the same claim to first-hand knowledge as it has for the years down to 680. He tells us such facts or stories as he heard at Ripon, possibly long after the dates at which they occurred or were reported to have occurred.

His description of Wilfrid's reception at the Northumbrian court when he arrived with the papal decree is famous. The bishop produced before the king 'the judgements of the apostolic see with the consent and subscription of the whole synod' authenticated 'with bulls and seals'.[4] This statement needs examination. The use of the plural should indicate that Wilfrid brought with him the *constitutum* of the synod as well as the Pope's rescript embodying the decree. But it is altogether improbable that he was supplied with both documents. Secondly, if he had the synodal Act, it would bear no seals of the prelates, for it was not then the practice at Rome to authenticate subscriptions by means of seals. Possibly Eddi had seen documents written in Gaul which bore bishops' seals. Thirdly, in any case the original would be preserved at Rome and only a copy sent out.[5] But it is far from likely that Wilfrid was furnished with a single authoritative document, namely the Pope's rescript; and this in the nature of things could only bear one *bulla*. The plural may mean that Wilfrid also produced the

---

[1] *Zeitschrift der Savigny-Stiftung für Rechtsgeschichte*, xxxiii (Kanonistische Abteilung, ii), 249–82.

[2] Compare my paper above, p. 52 f.

[3] ch. 51. In ch. 47 a privilege for Ripon only is mentioned.

[4] ch. 34.

[5] This was done after the Roman synod of 745. See the letter of Pope Zachary printed in *S. Bonifacii Epistolae*, li (*Monumenta Moguntina*, p. 151).

privilege for Hexham and Ripon, but his claim to these properties was not at the time contested. In any case the mention of the seals as well as the *bullae* raises grave suspicion as to the veracity of Eddi's story. He goes on to say that a council was then held and the documents read; whereupon some contumaciously rejected them and some even declared that the judgement was obtained by bribery. It was decided by the king and his counsellors, with the agreement of the bishops who occupied Wilfrid's see, to place him in confinement for nine months. This time of durance is illuminated in Eddi's narrative by several hagiological features, which probably formed the basis on which the rest of the story was built up. When at last Wilfrid was set free, he sought refuge with a nephew of the king of Mercia and then with the king of Wessex; but the persecution of his enemies drove him from both, and he found his way to the remote country of the South Saxons, where he stayed for a long time.[1] Now there is not room for all these doings, least of all for the nine months' captivity; for Bede says precisely that Wilfrid stayed in Sussex for five years, *hoc est usque ad mortem Ecgfridi*,[2] and Egfrid died on 20 May 685.[3] It is only from incidental references made by Eddi later on in his book[4] that we gather that during this period Wilfrid again invoked the support of the Holy See, and that a rescript was sent in his favour by Benedict II in 683 or 684. Not long after this he was enabled to go back to the North.

Archbishop Theodore, Eddi relates,[5] feeling his death approaching, invited Wilfrid to meet him and confessed his regret for what he had done to him. He adjured him to consent that he should appoint him as his successor in the archbishopric. This proposal Wilfrid modestly deferred for the consideration of a larger council. For the moment he asked only that Theodore would write letters to his friends to notify their reconciliation, so that they might acknowledge that they had despoiled him wrongfully, and might restore to him 'some part of his substance'. Theodore accordingly wrote letters to King Aldfrid of Northumbria, to his sister Alfleda, abbess of Whitby, and to Ethelred, king of Mercia. The letters were no doubt written *a pari*, as it is called; that is, their text was the same and only the addresses differed. Eddi gives that to Ethelred. It is a simple letter of recommendation, stating that the archbishop has made peace

---

[1] See above, pp. 61 f.   [2] *H.E.* iv. 13.
[3] *Ibid.* iv. 26.   [4] chs. 43, 46, 51, 52.   [5] ch. 43.

with Wilfred and desiring that Ethelred will do the like. Thus, when the opportunity presented itself for Wilfrid to claim his right to complete reinstatement, all he did was to ask that he might be allowed to go home and to recover some part of his property. It is a strange and (on Eddi's showing) an inexplicable anticlimax.

Eddi concludes the narrative by saying that Ethelred obeying the authority of Popes Agatho and Benedict and Sergius—the last of whom was not yet Pope—received Wilfrid with favour and bestowed upon him many monasteries and estates. In the next chapter he relates how Wilfrid went back to Northumbria. King Aldfrid, he says, invited him to return and granted him first the monastery of Hexham with its lands, and then after a space, in accordance with the judgement of Pope Agatho and the Roman synod, restored to him the see of York and the monastery of Ripon with its revenues. The intruded bishops were expelled.[1] These were Bosa of York and Eadhed of Ripon. There is no evidence other than Eddi's that either of them was removed. In later years Bosa was bishop of York and continued to be so until his death after 704; Eddi alone speaks of his position there having been interrupted. Moreover, we hardly find any definite trace in anything that Eddi says in the sequel that Wilfrid ever recovered York. The place is not named again until he was for the last time in Rome in 704, and then it is mentioned in terms which show that he had abandoned all hope of regaining the see.[2]

For the eleven chapters which Eddi devotes to the time between 680 and 686 Bede offers hardly as many lines, except when he describes Wilfrid's life in Sussex, about which, as we have seen,[3] he had particularly full information. He says that owing to the hostility of King Egfrid he could not be received in his country or diocese, and therefore turned aside to preach the Gospel to the South Saxons, among whom he stayed for five years until Egfrid's death.[4] Egfrid died in May 685, and a year later, in the summer of 686, Wilfred was invited back by his successor King Aldfrid, and recovered his see and bishopric, *sedem suam et episcopatum recepit*.[5] To what diocese then did he

[1] ch. 44. [2] ch. 51.
[3] Above, p. 61. [4] *H.E.* iv. 13.
[5] *Ibid.* v. 19. It may be observed that Florence of Worcester completes Bede's statement about Wilfrid's restoration by adding the name of Hexham (*Chronicon*, a. 686, in *Monumenta Historica Britannica*, p. 537). But the context

return? Not certainly to that of the entire Northumbrian kingdom, of which he had had charge before 677, for St. Cuthbert had been bishop of Lindisfarne since March 685, and held the see for all but two years. According to Eddi Wilfrid was given Hexham, which is not impossible, for its bishop Eata died at the beginning of Aldfrid's reign. Bede, however, says that he was succeeded by John,[1] known as St. John of Beverley, who was consecrated on 25 August 687;[2] and this was the tradition at Lindisfarne.[3] Meanwhile, when Cuthbert died on 20 March 687, Wilfrid occupied the bishopric of Lindisfarne until a new bishop should be appointed in his place,[4] and Eadbert was ordained a year later. So far then Wilfrid seems to have been employed merely to administer a diocese, or perhaps two dioceses, during a vacancy. But Bede says he regained his see and bishopric. What was this see? I submit, it can only have been Ripon. Whether Eadhed was removed or resigned may be left doubtful; it is just as likely that he died—he was a priest so long before as 664—and thus provided a convenient means of replacing Wilfrid in the monastery where he had first lived as bishop.

This supposition is confirmed by what we know of the lands which Wilfrid possessed. We have seen that Eddi makes him petition Archbishop Theodore for restoration to some part of his property. Now Eddi repeatedly speaks of the innumerable monasteries and lands which he was given in Northumbria and Mercia, but the only properties of which the names are recorded, except Hexham,[5] are connected with Ripon. The earliest mark of Alchfrid's favour to Wilfrid, before he was a bishop, was a grant of two estates to him, *terram decem tributariorum Æt Stanforda et post paululum coenobium in Hrypis, cum terra triginta mansionum.*[6] Bede repeats this statement in his biographical notice, but elsewhere speaks of the *monasterium xl familiarum in loco qui dicitur Inhrypum.*[7] From this Mr. W. H.

shows that he has misplaced a notice which belongs to 705, for he next speaks of John as succeeding Bosa at York on his death—an appointment which left Hexham open for Wilfrid (*H.E.* v. 3). In consequence of this error Florence calls Wilfrid bishop of Hexham under the years 687 and 691; and some of the lists of bishops printed at the end of his Chronicle (p. 625, n. 10) even make him consecrated bishop of Hexham, that is, in 664.

¹ *Ibid.* v. 2. ² See Bright, p. 397, n. 3.
³ *Annales Lindisfarnenses*, in Pertz's *Monumenta*, xix. 504.
⁴ *H.E.* iv. 29. ⁵ Eddi, 22.
⁶ ch. 8. ⁷ *H.E.* iii. 25.

Stevenson, who has printed a remarkable survey of the lands
of the church of York drawn up in the first half of the eleventh
century, infers with great cogency that 'he regarded Stanford
as merged in the grant of land at Ripon'.[1] The locality of
Stanford has never been settled except by vague conjecture,
but Mr. Stevenson's argument seems to fix it, though the name
has disappeared, as a part of the *leuga S. Wilfridi* surrounding
Ripon, which is mentioned in Domesday Book and there stated
to consist of forty-three carucates. It is however possible that
the forty carucates were made up by other grants, and that
Stanford may be sought elsewhere. For, when the church of
Ripon was built at the time of Wilfrid's greatest prosperity, he
received from King Egfrid and his young brother Alfwin a
grant *regionum iuxta Rippel et in Gaedyne et in regione Dunutinga
et in Caetlaevum.*[2] These names have been identified, but only
as a guess, with the tract of country running northward from
the Ribble to the borders of the modern Cumberland—the
western portion of the medieval archdeaconry of Richmond.[3]
Without taking so ambitious an interpretation, it may be
suggested that the land *Æt Stanforde* was at Stainforth on the
Ribble a short distance above Settle. But whatever may be
said about the outlying properties, there is no doubt that the
great nucleus was an estate comprising lands in seventeen
villages, of which the names are recorded in the eleventh-
century survey,[4] and extending some eight miles from north to
south and not much less from east to west. Near the middle
of this lay Ripon, the seat of Wilfrid's monastery. Hence, as
the church of his other possession, Hexham, was occupied by
Bishop John, Ripon was the only place where he could establish
himself when he left Lindisfarne in 688.

5. In 691, after there had been alternately peace and dissension
between Wilfrid and the king, Eddi says, with characteristic
exaggeration, for many years,[5] the bishop was at length expelled
from Northumbria. He enumerates three causes of dispute.
First, Wilfrid complained that the church of Ripon[6] had been

---

[1] *Eng. Hist. Rev.*, xxvii. 19, n. 149.

[2] Eddi, ch. 17.   [3] See Raine's notes to Eddi, ch. 17.

[4] See *Eng. Hist. Rev.*, xxvii. 18 f.   [5] ch. 45.

[6] Eddi says, the church of St. Peter, which might mean York equally with
Ripon; and Haddan and Stubbs, *Councils*, iii. 219, take it to mean York, but
the following sentence in which it is said that *monasterium supradictum* had
been changed into a bishop's see proves that it refers to Ripon.

deprived of its lands and possessions. About this we know nothing. The second ground was that Ripon had been made into a bishop's see. But it had had a bishop long before Wilfrid's return to the north in 686. Eadhed had been obliged to leave his see in Lindsey when that province was lost to Northumbria, as a consequence no doubt of the battle of the Trent in 678, and had been given Ripon instead.[1] Moreover, according to Eddi's own account, he was removed from his bishopric by Aldfrid in order to allow of the reinstatement of Wilfrid. Either then Eddi's statement that Eadhed was deprived is false; or else, if there was no bishop at Ripon, Wilfrid had no reason for complaint on this head. The third ground for disagreement was that the king urged him to obey the commands and decrees of Archbishop Theodore, apparently the very acts for which Eddi says[2] he had declared his repentance, and which on the same showing he may be presumed to have taken steps to modify. It will not escape notice that this third count is not given the prominent place we should have expected Eddi to give it: it is thrown in at the end, after the special injury of Ripon. For these reasons, we are told, Wilfrid was driven out. It is perhaps more likely.that, as he could not obtain redress for his grievances, he chose to leave the kingdom. He sought the hospitality of Ethelred of Mercia and was made by him bishop of the Middle English, it is supposed at Leicester. For the following years Bede has preserved a few scanty notices about Wilfrid. He held the bishopric of the Middle English when he consecrated Oftfor bishop of the Hwiccians during the interval between the death of Theodore and the ordination of Bertwald,[3] that is, between 691 and August 693. In the same interval, or more precisely between 1 July 692 and August 693, he consecrated Suidbert bishop for Frisia.[4] About 695, he appears to have been present at the translation of St. Etheldreda at Ely,[5] but this may have been ten years later.[6] In March 692 or 693 he subscribed a charter relative to lands in Essex in company with Bishops Erkenwald of London and Heddi of Winchester.[7]

But there are indications that during these years he again

---

[1] Florence of Worcester says in 681. [2] ch. 43.
[3] H. E. iv. 23. [4] Ibid. v. 11. [5] Ibid. iv. 19.
[6] According to the hymn in Bede, H. E. iv. 20 she was queen for twelve years, i.e. until 682. She lived eight years as a nun, and her body was translated after sixteen years. This seems to take us to 706.
[7] British Museum Facsimiles of Ancient Charters, i. 2.

brought his case before the Roman court. Eddi several times speaks of a bull in his favour having been granted by Sergius I, who was Pope from the end of 687 until September 701. Now we possess a letter addressed by Sergius to Ceolfrid, abbot of Wearmouth, thanking him for a letter which he had received by a messenger from him. In this, while speaking of his petitions in favourable terms he adds that, *quia exortis quibusdam ecclesiasticarum causarum capitulis non sine examinatione longius innotescendis, opus nobis sunt ad conferendum artium literatura imbuti,* he desires Ceolfrid to send a certain monk, *N.,* of his house to Rome to assist in the discussion.[1] William of Malmesbury, who quotes the substance of the letter, supplies the name of the monk, *Bedam presbyterum.* This may be a guess or a later tradition, but it is not impossible. It is true that Bede finished his Church History in 731,[2] and is commonly understood to place its completion in his fifty-ninth year. Hence, as he was ordained priest in his thirtieth year, his birth is placed in 672–3 and his ordination in 701–2. But what Bede in fact says is as follows:

Ex quo tempore accepti presbyteratus usque ad annum aetatis meae LVIIII haec in scripturam sanctam . . . ex opusculis venerabilium patrum breviter adnotare . . . curavi.[3]

Haec refers to his Commentaries on the Bible which he proceeds to enumerate. He then completes his catalogue by adding the rest of his writings, but this list stands apart from the chronological computation which he has just given. Now all the Commentaries were written earlier than the Church History, and thus the sentence quoted furnishes no evidence as to his age when he composed that work. We cannot therefore infer from it the date at which he was ordained. It may perfectly well have been before the close of the seventh century, and Malmesbury's statement need not be rejected on chronological grounds. Bede, however, it is known, never went to Rome, and his omission to carry out the Pope's wish—if he was really named—has been explained as due to the death of Sergius in September 701;[4] but the business on which the Wearmouth monk was to be consulted, if, as is presumed, it related to the case of Wilfrid, had been dealt with before this. For the probable date of the English monk's visit to Rome is supplied by a notice in Bede's

---

[1] Haddan and Stubbs, iii. 248 f.   [2] *H. E.* v. 23.
[3] *H. E.* v. 24.   [4] See Haddan and Stubbs, iii. 250, n.

book *de Temporum Ratione*.[1] He tells us that certain monks of his house were in Rome at Christmas 701, in the fourteenth Indiction, that is Christmas 700, as we should reckon it. They brought back with them a privilege for Wearmouth,[2] and also, I have little doubt, the bull relating to Wilfrid, the date of which is nowhere mentioned. It was in consequence of the arrival of this second bull, I venture to argue, that King Aldfrid was compelled to summon a council to go into Wilfrid's case once more.

6. For the eleven years after the dispute of 691 Eddi has nothing to record. He proceeds at once to narrate that King Aldfrid held a synod at Austerfield in the presence of Archbishop Bertwald and almost all the bishops of Britain, at which Wilfrid was invited to attend. This might have taken place any time after the archbishop's enthronement on 31 August 693; and Eddi clearly means us to understand that Aldfrid took the earliest steps he could to obtain ecclesiastical authority to terminate the dispute. He was in fact so understood by James Raine, the careful historian of Hexham, who says that Wilfrid went abroad in 692 and seems to have lived for thirteen years at Rome.[3] But Eddi lets out that Wilfrid protested that the Pope's decree had been set at nought for twenty-two years;[4] and as Wilfrid returned to England, after that decree was issued, in 680, this leads on to the year 702, which suits well with the return of the monks from Rome. This is not incompatible with the notice that Wilfrid had been a bishop for nigh upon forty years,[5] which gives an extreme date of 704, but is plainly a rough statement. But the hiatus in Eddi is remarkable. If it pointed merely to his ignorance of the particulars of this part of Wilfrid's life, it would not be of much significance. But what is important is that by Eddi's admission Wilfrid acquiesced in his exile from Northumbria for eleven years, and that when it was sought to redress his wrongs the overture came not from him but from Aldfrid. As a fact, it is evident that the synod was summoned in consequence of Pope Sergius's rescript.

At the synod the ordinances of Theodore were put forward on the one side and the Roman decree of 679 on the other.[6]

---

[1] ch. 47 [*al.* 45].
[2] *Vit. Ceolfr.* 20, in Plummer's edition of Bede, i. 394; Bede, *Hist. Abbat.* 15.
[3] *The Priory of Hexham*, i (1864), xxxi.
[4] ch. 46.   [5] ch. 47.   [6] ch. 46.

In the end it was proposed to offer Wilfrid the possession of the monastery of Ripon with its belongings, on the conditions that he should confine himself within its walls and abstain from the performance of episcopal functions; indeed, he was called upon to divest himself of his orders (*gradum honoris abiiceret*[1]). This is Eddi's account;[2] but we can hardly believe that the assembled bishops proceeded to this extreme of violence. It is more probable that the Pope ordered Wilfrid's restoration to his bishopric, and that the synod decided that his see should be Ripon. Moreover, the statement is irreconcilable with Eddi's own narrative. In 691 it was Wilfrid who was the complainant; there was no charge against him. Then for eleven years he lived with repute as a bishop in Mercia. What business had a Northumbrian synod in 703 to degrade him? I suspect that it was not without design that Eddi omitted this honourable period of eleven years; he wished us to believe that Aldfrid in 691 was determined to crush Wilfrid, and sought to carry out his intention at the earliest possible moment. Or are we to infer from Bede's omission of the whole transaction that the council of Austerfield never took place, and that we have here another example of Eddi's inventions? I think rather that Bede knew the account to be in part false and did not know how to correct it: he therefore observed silence.

The decision of the synod of Austerfield led to Wilfrid's second appeal to Rome. But he first went into Mercia and inquired of King Ethelred what action he proposed to take with regard to the lands which he had given him. Ethelred promised to secure the church of St. Peter, that is, as before, of Ripon, in its possession of them until the affair was settled at Rome.[3] Wilfrid then set out on his long journey. In this as on the former occasion he was accompanied by Eddi, who gives a full account of what happened, and again had the advantage of being furnished with some of the documents which were drawn up. Wilfrid must have started with unusual promptitude, for we read that he travelled the whole way from the French coast to his destination on foot,[4] and this would mean a walk of more than a thousand miles after crossing the Channel; and the proceedings were terminated under Pope John VI, who died at the beginning of 705. The appeal, therefore, cannot have

---

[1] The text has *abiecerit*.
[2] ch. 47.   [3] ch. 48.   [4] ch. 50.

been heard later than 704; and it was probably in the winter of
703-4. Moreover, Eddi says that Wilfrid's case was on the
agenda of seventy meetings extending over a period of four
months.[1] Wilfrid in his petition[2] asked for a confirmation of
the decrees of Popes Agatho, Benedict, and Sergius, that is no
doubt of the decree of 679, which had already been confirmed by
two Popes, and begged that any charges which might be brought
against him should be heard. He further asked that the Pope
should order Ethelred of Mercia to maintain him in the possession of the monasteries and lands which Ethelred and Wulfhere
before him had granted him; and should admonish Aldfrid of
Northumbria to execute the decrees of Pope Agatho. If this
should appear too hard for the king, Wilfrid would leave the
decision about the bishopric of York and the monasteries
dependent upon it to the Pope's judgement: only let him be
restored to the monasteries of Ripon and Hexham which were
granted to him by a bull of Pope Agatho. In other words, if he
cannot get the decree of 679 carried out, he is ready to fall back
on the other document relating to Ripon and Hexham. In the
last sentence of his petition, Wilfrid promises to observe canonical respect to Archbishop Bertwald, but only on the condition
that he carries out the decrees of Agatho and the other Popes;
so that if Wilfrid was granted only his second alternative, he
would not be bound to obey his archbishop.

We need not linger over the proceedings of the synod, for
according to Eddi,[3] who is followed by Bede, the decision was
arrived at for a reason wholly irrelevant to the case. It was
discovered that in 680 Wilfrid had subscribed a declaration of
orthodoxy, and the fact was testified to by some who had been
present on the occasion. Eddi professes to quote the terms of
the subscription, *in qua scriptura inventum erat, inter caetera:
Wilfridus Deo amabilis episcopus*, and so forth. He may be
giving the words which were read out before the synod. But
they are not the terms of the subscription. No bishop ever
wrote himself *Deo amabilis*: he would be *humilis* or *indignus*,
like the rest of the 125 bishops who subscribed the document;[4]
and it is inexplicable that Haddan and Stubbs should accept
the form here given and pointedly condemn that printed in the
editions of the Sixth General Council as 'the invention of the

---

[1] ch. 53.   [2] ch. 51.   [3] ch. 53.
[4] See the text in Mansi, *Conciliorum Collectio Amplissima*, xi. 292.

notary who drew up the acts of the council'.[1] The discovery
of this subscription settled the question. That Wilfrid had
professed his orthodoxy twenty-four years before was held a
sufficient warrant for his success in an appeal in which his
orthodoxy was not in any way impugned. So at least Eddi says,
and so Bede repeats after him. The Pope thereupon pronounced
Wilfrid innocent of any offence, and confirmed his predecessors'
decrees in the form of a rescript addressed to Ethelred and
Aldfrid, which Eddi sets out in full.[2] In this he recited the
course of Wilfrid's former appeal, and the fact that the sentence
given upon it by Agatho had been acted upon by the Popes
after him. He added that Archbishop Theodore was not known
to have opposed this sentence; he had not brought the matter
up again, but, on the contrary, had accepted the decision.
Et haec de praeteritis memoravimus: the Pope has rehearsed this
by way of record. Then he turns to the present dispute. The
facts have been most carefully examined, but as the principal
persons in the suit—clearly Archbishop Bertwald and the
Northumbrian bishops—had not appeared, the Pope admonishes
the archbishop to hold a synod in company with Wilfrid, to
cause Bishops Bosa and John to appear, and after hearing the
parties to determine the dispute. If they cannot arrive at a
decision they are to have recourse again to the apostolic see.
The Pope ends by calling on the king to remember what Agatho
and the others *consona voce nobiscum* have ordered. The letter
is a masterly production, and illustrates well the skill with which
the trained experience of the Papal officials could deal with
a difficult situation. The Pope, it will be observed, recites what
his predecessors had done in the case, but avoids confirming in
terms the decree of 679. That decree had restored Wilfrid to
York and left the question of new bishoprics to be settled in
England. This second part John repeats, but he could not
decree Wilfrid's restoration to York because since 679 fresh
charges had been made against him, and the Pope was not
satisfied with the evidence brought forward in Rome. Consequently he referred the matter also to the decision of a synod to
be held in England.

7. Wilfrid then returned homewards and sent messengers to
Archbishop Bertwald to apprize him of the result of his appeal.
On his way northward he visited Ethelred, who, after he had

[1] *Councils*, iii. 141.   [2] ch. 54.

reigned thirty-one, or according to another reading thirty, years, had become a monk at Bardney.[1] The date of his retirement is given as 704, and as he came to the throne in 674, this supports the variant reading. In this same year Wilfrid must have visited him. He is next found living at Ripon.[2] He sent two friends to King Aldfrid to prepare for an interview, but the king refused to alter the previous arrangements. He was in fact very near his end, for he died on 14 December 704.[3] His successor Eadwulf reigned but a short time. After two months he was driven out and Aldfrid's son Osred, a boy of eight years, set up in his stead. A synod was held in his first year, between February 705 and February 706, at a place by the river Nidd. There the archbishop proposed that effect should be given to the Pope's judgement. Peace was made between Wilfrid and the other bishops, and he was restored to Ripon and Hexham, *duo optima coenobia, quae [sunt] in Hripis et in Agustaldesie cum omnibus redditibus suis.*[4] From the language in which Eddi describes the settlement it appears that Wilfrid got at least as much as he expected. There is no hint of any proposal that he should be given York. He was secured in Ripon, which apparently he had already. But he did not perhaps at once obtain Hexham. The way was opened by the death of Bosa. John of Beverley was removed from Hexham to York, and Hexham left free for Wilfrid. The dates of these events are uncertain, and indeed we only know of them from an incidental notice of Bede, who relates an occurrence as happening *cum reverentissimus vir Vilfrid post longum exilium in episcopatum esset Hagustaldensis ecclesiae receptus, et idem Iohannes, defuncto Bosa viro multae sanctitatis et humilitatis, episcopus pro eo Eboraci substitutus.*[5] The accepted date for the death of Bosa is 705. From this time, until he also died in 709, Wilfrid had no more troubles. He possessed the two monasteries confirmed to him by the privilege of 679 and made no claim to anything further. If Eddi tells us more particulars about his doings at Ripon[6] than at Hexham, this may be because he was a monk at the former place. But Ripon, at the end as at the beginning of his life, was still his home, and when he died at Oundle in the land of the Middle English it was to Ripon that his body was taken for burial.[7]

---

[1] Eddi, 57.
[2] This appears from Eddi, 59.
[3] See appendix, below, pp. 80 f.
[4] Eddi, 60.
[5] *H. E.* v. 3.
[6] chs. 62, 63.
[7] ch. 65.

When we have removed the element of fiction in Eddi, the main course of Wilfrid's episcopate seems to become clear. He was consecrated bishop of Ripon in 664, and his diocese was extended to the whole of Northumbria, with his see at York, in 669. From 669 to 677, and for those years only, he was bishop of York. Nine years of exile follow, during part of which he was bishop of Selsey. Then not long after 686 he was once more bishop of Ripon. In 691 he was again driven away and became bishop of the Middle English, with his see, according to Florence of Worcester, at Leicester. At last, after about thirteen years, he was restored not only to Ripon but also to Hexham.

APPENDIX

The Date of Wilfrid's Death

In order to ascertain the year when Wilfrid died, it is necessary first to fix the date when King Aldfrid of Northumbria died. This date, about which a doubt has been expressed,[1] is clearly given by Bede. Aldfrid succeeded his brother Egfrid, who was killed on 20 May 685,[2] and died *anno regni sui xx° nondum completo*, that is, in the course of the year beginning in May 704; the day is given as 14 December in the two texts of the Anglo-Saxon Chronicle known as those of Worcester (D) and Peterborough (E), and the year according to Bede's mode of reckoning is given as 705. But Osred did not succeed immediately; according to Eddi[3] two months elapsed before he obtained the throne. His reign may therefore be taken to begin about the middle of February 705. In his fourth year, February 708 —February 709, Coenred of Mercia abdicated.[4] This is stated to have happened in 709, that is, later than September 708.[5] Coenred became a monk and proceeded to Rome. 'In the same year that he left Britain,' not necessarily in the fourth year of Osred, Wilfrid died. Coenred's preparations would take some time, and he would not naturally leave England until early in the year, that is, in 709. It need not therefore be questioned that Wilfrid's death occurred some time in the course of this year, presumably before the September Indiction of 710 (=709). This agrees with the statement that after the synod on the Nidd, which for other reasons we incline to place in the spring of 705, Wilfrid *iiii annis, id est usque ad diem obitus sui, vitam duxit in pace.*[6] Again, Bede says that he died *post XL et V*[7]

---

[1] Plummer, ii. 305 f., 329.   [2] *H. E.* iv. 26.   [3] ch. 59.

[4] *H. E.* v. 19.   [5] *Ibid.* v. 24.   [6] *Ibid.* v. 19.

[7] Bede here, *H. E.* v. 19, silently corrects Eddi's statement, ch. 65, that he was bishop for forty-six years.

annos accepti episcopatus, and as he was consecrated almost certainly late in 664 or early in 665, his forty-fifth year began late in 708 or early in 709. This date may be confirmed from the statement of Eddi that when Wilfrid lay sick at Meaux on his return from Rome, he had a vision of St. Michael, who promised to appear to him again after four years. Now Wilfrid was back in England some time before the death of Aldfrid in December 704; his illness at Meaux may therefore be placed in the previous summer. Four years from that take us to the summer of 708; and after the archangel's renewed visitation Wilfrid lived on for a year and a half, that is, to about the end of 709. The calculation is necessarily a rough one, as we have no means of fixing the exact time when Wilfrid was at Meaux; nor can we presume that the four years and the year and a half indicate exact dates.

As for the day on which Wilfrid died, in view of the two different observances, it will be best to cite the opinion of a most learned liturgical scholar, the late Edmund Bishop, who places with confidence 'the primitive feast of St. Wilfrid on 24 April', . . . but adds that 'in the event St. Wilfrid on 24 April fell out of consideration in the calendars, except that of York . . .; and 12 October was universally received as the day of Saint Wilfrid's *depositio*. . . . The 24th of April in 709 fell on a Wednesday; and if St. Wilfrid died in the later part of the day, it is easy to understand how and why "the abbat" (as recorded by Wilfrid's friend and biographer Eddius in the *Life*, c. 61) regularly said mass for him on Thursdays'.[1] I venture to suggest that both days may be right: that the *depositio* of the saint was not the day of his death at Oundle but that of his burial at Ripon. If this was made in a temporary tomb on 12 October, a long time would be needed for the construction of a permanent resting-place worthy of his eminence. This, it seems, was done in the course of the winter, and the monks waited until after Easter, 20 April 710, to carry out his solemn sepulture on 24 April. If such is the correct interpretation of the observances, no difficulty arises from the Thursday, which was the day of Wilfrid's death.

It is the mention of Thursday alone that has induced Dr. Levison[2] to advocate 710 as the year. Had he read on to the next chapter in Bede's History, he would have seen that his proposed date is incompatible with the statement that Abbot Hadrian died in the year after Wilfrid, in the fifth year of Osred, 'which year is the 41st year' after he was sent to England by the Pope.[3] The fifth year of Osred ran from about February 709 to about February 710, it began in the forty-first year from May 668: Bede does not say that Hadrian died in the forty-first year, that is, before May 709; had he done so Wilfrid's death would have occurred in 708, which is against all the evidence.

[1] *The Bosworth Psalter*, p. 159, 1908.   [2] p. 179.   [3] *H. E.* v. 20.

MONASTERIUM NIRIDANUM [1]

ABBOT HADRIAN, the companion of Archbishop Theodore, is said by Bede to have resided *in monasterio Niridano, quod est non longe a Neapoli Campaniae*.[2] The name was given in two of the oldest manuscripts as *Hiridano*, but John Smith made a note in the passage that other copies had *Niridano* and that this was correct: it is in fact the reading found in the great majority of manuscripts. Smith added that the place was near Monte Cassino;[3] but no such place is known to exist. Bede's later editors either repeat Smith's statement[4] or leave the name unexplained.[5]

1. At one time it occurred to me that *Niridano* might stand for *Neritino* (more properly *Neritio*), from Neritum (now Nardò) in Calabria. If this were so, it would be necessary to assume that Bede's informant described the locality in the most general terms and thought that to an Englishman any place in the south of Italy might be called 'not far from Naples'. There is in fact evidence of a flourishing school at Nardò at a later date, but I am afraid there is nothing to show that it was there in the seventh century. Antonio Ferrari, or Antonius Galateus (1444–1517), speaks of it as formerly (*quondam*) having been famous for its Greek studies, and in particular for the beauty of its Greek handwriting. He adds that after the province passed from the Greeks to the Latins the school enjoyed great celebrity.[6]

---

[1] Reprinted from the *English Historical Review*, vol. xxxvi (1921).

[2] *H. E.* iv. 1.

[3] *Codices primaevae auctoritatis in hac voce differunt. Alii enim habent* Niridano, *et quidem recte. Locus est iuxta* Montem Cassinum: adnot. ad *H. E.* iv. 1, p. 141, Cambridge 1722.

[4] So J. E. B. Mayor and J. R. Lumby, *Ven. Bedae Hist. eccles. gentis Angl. libr. iii, iv.* 292 (3rd ed. Cambridge, 1881), and C. Plummer, *Baedae Opera hist.* ii. 202 (Oxford, 1896).

[5] Thus G. H. Moberly, *Ven. Baedae Hist. eccles.*, p. 212 (Oxford, 1869), leaves the place unidentified. The suggestions he quotes of Aretiano and Hadriano are unsupported conjectures.

[6] 'In hac urbe de qua nunc eloquimur, et gymnasium quondam fuit Gręcarum disciplinarum tale, ut cum Mesapii Graeci laudare Graecas literas uolunt, Neritinas esse dicunt. Sunt enim hae literae perpulchrae, et castigatae, et iis quibus nunc utuntur impressores Orientalibus ad legendum aptiores. Inclinante Graecorum fortuna, postquam a Graecis prouincia ad Latinos transmigrauit, celeberrima Neriti hoc toto regno fuere literarum studia. Hanc urbem San-seuerinorum familia armis et literis illustrauit. Temporibus patris mei ab omnibus huius regni prouinciis ad accipiendum ingenii cultum Neritum confluebat. Omnis, si qua est in toto terrarum angulo disciplina, a Nerito ortum

The statements about the time at which the school first flourished are too vague to support any definite conclusion; very likely it was not older than the fifteenth century.

The early history of the church of Nardò is very obscure. It is said that there were Greek bishops, whose succession was interrupted, and that in the middle of the eighth century the church was occupied by Basilian monks who were expelled from Constantinople by the iconoclastic Emperor, Constantine V. The only authority cited is a bull of Paul I preserved in the original in the archives of the see, dated on 4 September in the Fifteenth Indiction, that is in 761.[1] An original bull of that date would be a unique discovery, and until it is produced I must decline to accept it. On the other hand, there is an antecedent probability that a monastery would be founded at a place of some consideration like Nardò, and if monks there were, we need not doubt that they belonged to the eastern rite. It is said that in 1090 Urban II substituted Benedictine monks for them, but no precise reference is given for the statement.[2] In any case no evidence has been brought forward which would authorize us in carrying back the monastery at Nardò into the seventh century.

2. Leaving therefore Nardò out of account, I turn to a suggestion which has been favoured by many writers that the *monasterium Niridanum* was at Nisida, the 'little island' in the Bay of Naples, nearly over against Pozzuoli. This identification presumes that the information on which Bede relied was written in an insular handwriting, in which *s* and *r* are easily confounded; so that *Nisidanum* was read *Niridanum*. The itacism in the first syllable is too familiar to call for comment, and the name has for centuries been spelled *Nisida* or *Nisita*. A change of accent has shortened the *i* in the second syllable. Nesis is known

habuit. Hic literas didicere illa duo nostri seculi lumina, Robertus Lupiensis et Franciscus Neritinus: alter ecclesiasticorum declamatorum, omnium qui fuerunt, quique futuri sunt praestantissimus, alter Patauinę Academię pater. Hic et ego prima literarum fundamenta hausi.' Antonii Galatei Liciensis [of Lecce], *Liber de Situ Iapygiae* (Basle, 1558), pp. 122 f.

[1] See N. Coleti's addition to Ughelli, *Italia sacra*, i. 1039 (ed. Venice, 1717). Pietro Pompilio Rodota dates the Greek immigration from 741: *Dell' Origine, Progresso e Stato presente del Rito Greco in Italia*, i. 388–96 (Rome, 1758). He supposes that the school mentioned by Galateus arose subsequently to the time of Paul I, and that the monks supplied the citizens of Nardò with an *accademia delle greche discipline*. All this seems to be purely conjectural.

[2] See G. Cappelletti, *Le Chiese d'Italia*, xxi. 463–9 (Venice, 1870).

in classical times; Cicero wrote one of his letters upon it,[1] and Pliny commends its asparagus.[2] It has been by a mistaken identification supposed to be the island which Constantine the Great is said to have granted to the church of Naples, and local writers assure us that Nisida belonged to the archbishop down to the sixteenth century.[3] But Bede speaks not only of a monastery in which Hadrian dwelt, but also of a convent of nuns in the neighbourhood.[4] Neither of these houses is certainly attested, and the evidence which has been drawn from the Lives of two saints in all probability has no relation to Nisida.

The Life of St. Patricia, a lady of Constantinople who lived in the middle of the seventh century under Constans II, has come down to us in two forms, and the age of neither has been ascertained.[5] One is said to be a translation from the Greek preserved in an imperfect Latin text;[6] the other was written by Leo, priest of the church of SS. Nicander and Marcian at Naples.[7] The manuscripts of both are of modern date. The 'Greek' Life relates that the saint when on a voyage was carried *ad Neapolitanas oras*, and as her death was approaching was taken 'to a certain little island' where the Body of our Lord was and is honoured, so that the place has taken from the church the name of Salvator.[8] The virgins who are mentioned appear to have been her attendants and do not necessarily imply the existence of a religious house. Leo in his Life speaks of the monastery of the Saviour and mentions the *fratres* but not the virgins.[9] All this story is extremely unsatisfactory. If there be any truth in it, it must refer, as we shall see and as the Bollandists long ago noted, not to Nisida but to the island of Megaris, afterwards made into a fortress by the Normans and now known as the Castello dell' Ovo, which has become a part of the city of Naples.

The second saint to whom I have alluded is Athanasius,

---

[1] *Ad Atticum Epist.* xvi. 1.   [2] *Hist. Nat.* xix. 8, § 146.

[3] Bart. Chioccarelli, *Antistitum Neapol. Eccl. Catal.*, p. 322, Naples [1643]; A. S. Mazochius, *Dissert. hist. de Cathedr. Eccl. Neapol. variis Vicibus*, pp. 5, 216, Naples, 1751.

[4] 'De vicino virginum monasterio': *Hist. Eccl.* iv. 1.

[5] *Acta Sanctorum, Aug.* v. 201 E; see the Life by Leo, § 3, *ibid.*, p. 216 A. Older writers, as Chioccarelli, pp. 36 f., placed the saint in the fourth century.

[6] *Act. SS., Aug.* v. 210–15; cf. p. 200 C, D.

[7] *Ibid.*, pp. 215–19; cf. p. 200 D.

[8] 'Fertur itaque in parvam quamdam insulam in qua venerabile corpus Domini nostri Iesu Christi Salvatoris colebatur et colitur, sumens ipse locus denominationem ab ecclesia, Salvator nomine proprio appellatur:' § 7, p. 212 D, E.   [9] § 7, p. 216 E.

archbishop of Naples, who lived in the ninth century. Of him also there are two biographies. The earlier one, by John the Deacon, forms a continuation of the Lives of the archbishops of Naples, which are contained in a fine uncial manuscript of about A.D. 800 in the Vatican Library (cod. 5007); John's part being written in a Beneventan hand of the first half of the tenth century.[1] It is the antiquity of the manuscript which gives interest to the reference in it to the monks of the island of the Saviour.[2] The other Life, which is anonymous and perhaps not much later in date,[3] and is preserved in a thirteenth-century manuscript in the Corsini Library at Rome (cod. 777), adds the statement that the island was hardly twelve stadia distant from Naples.[4] The importance of this latter notice is that it shows that in the language of a writer of the ninth or tenth century, whose work at any rate is preserved in a manuscript of the twelfth, the island of the Saviour was described as situate rather less than a mile and a half from Naples. This can only be the Castello dell' Ovo.[5]

Now Mazzochi, whose opinion was repeated by Waitz,[6] endeavoured to prove that the island of the Saviour was Nisida and was so named because it was the property of the cathedral church of the Saviour at Naples. It was necessary therefore to suppose either that the *stadium* as a measure of length had changed its meaning, or else that *xii* was a corruption for *xxii*.[7] He had, however, to admit that in later times, from the twelfth century onwards, the island of the Saviour was unquestionably the Castello dell' Ovo.[8] Consequently he produced a theory that the original monastery at Nisida had sent an offshoot to the Castello some time earlier, and that this had appropriated

---

[1] See G. Waitz's preface to the work, *Scriptores Rerum Langobard.* (Monum. Germ. hist.), p. 399 (1878), and E. A. Loew, *The Beneventan Script*, pp. 53, 74, 364 (Oxford, 1914).

[2] *Quasi convivium monachis insulae Salvatoris exhibiturus. . . In eandem ascendit insulam*: lxv. 435, ed. Waitz; *Acta Sanctorum, Iulii*, iv. 76 c, § 8.

[3] Mazzochi erroneously held that this Life was not written until the eleventh century or later: see p. 36, n. 29, and p. 218, n. 27.

[4] p. 444, ed. Waitz; *Acta Sanctorum, Iulii*, iv. 81 c, § 14 (from another manuscript at Monte Cassino).

[5] Cf. *Napoli e i Luoghi celebri delle sue Vicinanze*, i. 482 f. (Naples, 1845).

[6] p. 444, n. 1.   [7] *Dissert. hist.*, p. 221.

[8] *Ibid.*, pp. 221 ff. Mazzochi quotes Peter of Eboli, who died probably between 1212 and 1220: see G. B. Siragusa's preface to his *Liber ad honorem Augusti*, p. xviii (Rome, 1906). Peter's verses, i. 945–56, state clearly that the Castello dell' Ovo *nomen Salvator habet*: p. 69.

the name of the parent house. When he found an abbot of the monastery of the Saviour *insulae maioris de Neapoli* mentioned in a charter of 1202 cited by Capaccio,[1] he maintained that he belonged to Nisida. Mazzochi's course of argument, it is clear, involves a series of unproved assertions. Not merely from the twelfth century, but as early as 937 the *monasterium insule Salvatoris*[2] or *monasterium sancti Salvatoris in insula maris* means a building on the island called the Castello dell' Ovo and no other building.[3]

3. In the *Liber Pontificalis*[4] the Emperor Constantine is recorded to have conferred *insula cum castro* upon the church of Naples. That the *insula* was Nisida was maintained with confidence by Mazzochi,[5] who on this point is followed by Monsignor Duchesne.[6] But the *castrum* is undoubtedly the *castrum Lucullanum*, and this was formerly identified with the Castello dell' Ovo.[7] It was a natural inference that the *insula* was the island on which the castle stood. Mazzochi successfully contested this opinion and placed the *castrum* on the mainland, only by a wild conjecture he transplanted it to the neighbourhood of Pozzuoli.[8] This conjecture has long been abandoned.[9] The *castrum* of Lucullus was a short distance to the north of the island, on the hill called Pizzofalcone between the coast and the Strada di Chiaja. It was to this castle or *oppidum* that the body of St. Severinus was taken in the fifth century,[10] and a

---

[1] J. C. Capacius, *Neapolitana historia*, p. 408 (Naples, 1607).

[2] *Regii Neapolitani Archivi Monumenta*, i (Naples, 1845), 101; B. Capasso, *Monum. ad Neapolit. Ducatus Historiam pertinentia*, ii. i, no. 38 (Naples, 1885).

[3] Under the Norman kings the monastery was removed to St. Peter's ad Castellum: see Capasso, ii. ii (1892), 172.

[4] xxxiv. 32, vol. i. 186, ed. L. Duchesne, Paris, 1886.

[5] *Dissert. hist.*, pp. 199–227. In his later work, *De sanctorum Neapolitanae Ecclesiae Episcoporum Cultu*, pp. 445–51 (Naples, 1753), Mazzochi discusses the passage in Bede, but does not add materially to what he had published in his *Dissertatio*.

[6] *Lib. pontif.* i. 200, n. 118.

[7] Capaccio, p. 405; Chioccarelli, p. 87.

[8] *Dissert. hist.*, pp. 207–15.

[9] It was demolished by Chiarito in a work which I have been unable to consult. See *Napoli e i Luoghi celebri delle sue Vicinanze*, i. 483; and Capasso, ii. ii. 171 f.

[10] In castello Lucullano: see Eugippius, *Vita S. Severini*, xlvi. 2, p. 65, ed. P. Knöll, Vienna, 1886. Eugippius is described by Isidore, *de Viris illustr.* xxxiv, as *abbas Lucullanensis oppidi*. The mistake that the monastery was on the island was repeated by Leimbach in Herzog and Hauck's *Realencyklopädie*, v. (1898) 591, and by the Rev. John Chapman, *Notes on the Early History of the Vulgate Gospels*, pp. 41, 44, Oxford, 1908.

monastery certainly existed there, as well as several churches, in the time of Gregory the Great.[1]

4. The attempt to prove that Nisida was the Insula Salvatoris has in fact been given up, and its failure has left the place from which Abbot Hadrian came unidentified.[2] But although the discussion has been confused by a great deal of irrelevant topography, I incline to believe that Bede's words do in fact refer to the island of Nisida. It is true that no monastery can be proved to have existed there,[3] but the documentary materials relative to the district in the earlier middle ages are extremely scanty. There are, however, grounds for believing that Nisida with a monastery on it came to be known by another name. Capasso, the leading authority on medieval Naples, found record of a monastery *sancti Archangeli de insula Gipei* in the eleventh century for which he could assign no place except on Nisida,[4] and the *ecclesia sancti Angeli de Zippio* is mentioned as a property of the archbishop of Naples in a writ of the Emperor Frederick II of the year 1240.[5] If this identification is correct we must suppose that Nisida acquired a new name some time after the seventh or eighth century. But whether this represents a place, Gipeum, as Capasso thought, or is taken from a person (as we find a Eugippius on the mainland near by), must be left undecided. It would be satisfactory if the home of the abbot who was the learned man of Archbishop Theodore's mission, and the founder of the Greek tradition of the school of Canterbury, could be discovered with certainty in the Bay of Naples.

[1] *Reg.* i. 23 [24], iii. 1, x. 7 [19]. Cf. Capasso, II. ii. 172.

[2] Cf. Luigi Parascandolo, *Memorie storiche-critiche-diplomatiche della Chiesa di Napoli*, ii. 23 (Naples, 1848).

[3] Dom G. Morin is perhaps alone in following Mazzochi in the assertion that 'il y a eu effectivement dans cette île un monastère qui a laissé çà et là quelques traces dans l'histoire, du septième au treizième siècle': *Revue Bénédictine*, viii (1892), 482. [4] *Monum.* II. ii. 183.

[5] Huillard-Bréholles, *Cod. dipl. Frid. II.* v (1859), 960; cf. Capasso, II. ii. 159, n. 4.

A STAGE IN THE HISTORY OF THE LAUDIAN
MS. OF ACTS[1]

MR. E. A. LOWE contributes to the January number of *Speculum* a welcome note on the later history of the famous Laudian manuscript of the Acts (Bodl. Libr., MS. Laud. Gr. 35). That this book was used by the Venerable Bede for his commentary is generally acknowledged; but what happened to the manuscript after it left Bede's hands and before it was acquired by Archbishop Laud is not clearly ascertained. About twelve years ago I noticed three lines written with a dry point on fol. 226*b*. These lines are read by Mr. Lowe as

MARIAE UIR[GINIS]

GAMUNDUM

I tried without success to explain this last word, and abandoned the inquiry. But I mentioned to Dr. Craster the fact that these scratches could be discerned, and he wrote a short paper on the history of the manuscript in the *Bodleian Quarterly Record*, ii. 288–90 (1919). He was of opinion that the word in the last line 'is apparently a variant of Gimmund or Gaemmunt, a name of common occurrence in Germany in the eighth and ninth centuries, and found at Lauresheim, Fulda, and St. Gall. Inasmuch as the connexion of the manuscript with Bede and even with the Anglo-Saxon world rests wholly on internal evidence it is important to find a Teutonic name inscribed on its pages'.

Mr. Lowe, on the other hand, takes the word to indicate the name, not of a person, but of a place: 'Gamundum, Gamundium, Gamundiae, can be no other than Hornbach, situated in the diocese of Metz.' It may now be added that the *Monasterium Hornbah* is glossed *sive Gamundias* in the ninth-century confraternity book of St. Gall.[2] This identification is beyond dispute. If any question arise about the termination of the word, it may be added that both forms Gamundium and Gamundum are found in the two earliest manuscripts of the Life of St. Pirminius,[3]

---

[1] Reprinted from the *Journal of Theological Studies*, vol. xxix (1928).

[2] P. Piper, *Libri Confraternitatum* (Berlin, 1884), p. 42.

[3] Ch. vi, ed. O. Holder-Egger, 1887, in *Monumenta Germaniae Historica, Scriptores* xv, p. 27.

which was composed in the beginning of the ninth century,[1] and in which it is said that Pirminius died there[2] (about 753). Walahfrid Strabo, in verses written about 826, speaks of the saint as buried at Hornbach,[3] a place which lies in what is now the Palatinate, about four miles south of Zweibrücken (Deux-Ponts).

The fact thus established that the Laudian manuscript was at some time in the eighth century preserved at Hornbach is of remarkable interest. St. Pirminius is known as the founder of the famous monastery of Reichenau on the Lower Lake of Constance. He used to be taken for a Frank, but Hrabanus Maurus says expressly that he left his native land and settled in the Frankish territory.[4] He was not an Irishman, and Hauck thought that he was perhaps an Anglo-Saxon.[5] In 724 he founded the monastery at Reichenau, but after three years was obliged to depart. He made his way into Alsatia, and there took part in erecting a monastery at Murbach in the Vosges. Before many years Murbach became the home of the compilers of the earliest Annals drawn up on a definitely Anglo-Saxon model, reckoned by the years of the Incarnation, and in part written in an Insular hand. These Annals enjoyed a very wide diffusion. They passed in course of time down the Rhine to Cologne, across France into Normandy, and from Rouen into England, where they formed the basis of many sets of Annals; but these belong to a later stage. All that concerns us here is that the Laudian manuscript was at Hornbach at a time when that monastery was closely affected by Anglo-Saxon influences.

[1] The editor, Holder-Egger, explains the word 'Gemünd, ahd. "Gamundi, gemundi," est confluentia'. [2] p. 30.
[3] *Poetae Aevi Carolini*, ii. 304, ed. E. Dümmler, Berlin, 1884.
[4] *Ibid.*, p. 224. [5] *Kirchengeschichte Deutschlands*, i (3rd ed., 1904), 347.

SEALS AND DOCUMENTS[1]

I

THE study of seals belongs in part to archaeology, in part to the history of art; it only in a secondary degree falls within the province of diplomatic. In its earlier ranges it includes the clay seals of the East; in Europe seals are either of metal or wax, rarely of clay, and it is with these alone that I am concerned. As the skill of the engraver advanced, the designs upon them become of great interest; and these designs, with the inscriptions either on the field of the seal or running round the circumference, have mainly occupied the attention of the archaeologists who have dealt with the subject. It is only incidentally that they mention the purpose for which seals were used, and even then they seldom tell us more than that they were employed to seal up a document so as to protect it from being read by any one except the person to whom it was addressed, and that they served to identify and authenticate the document.

That this should have been so was inevitable from the fact that all the earliest specimens have been found detached from documents and hardly ever present any evidence that they were once affixed to them. This is true not only of early seals, but even not unfrequently of much later examples. For instance, in 1913 I described the one single preserved original of Henry III's first confirmation of Magna Charta in the Bodleian Library. I mentioned the two seals, of the Legate and of the Earl Marshal, as still appended to it.[2] My statement is now no longer true. The seals have since been cut off by the direction of Mr. Falconer Madan, when he was Bodley's Librarian, and this unique document has been irreparably mutilated. But usually the detachment of seals is due simply to the ravages of time, and it is not surprising that they should have fallen off a brittle substance like papyrus, when we remember that no single papal document written on that material is preserved in the original until late in the eighth century and only twenty-seven in the three following centuries.[3]

---

[1] Reprinted with corrections from the *Proceedings of the British Academy*, vol. ix (1919).

[2] 'The Publication of Great Charters by the English Kings', below, p. 316.

[3] See my *Lectures on the History of the Papal Chancery* (1915), p. 197.

Diplomatic scholars, on their side, have been usually too much preoccupied by the important questions as to the legal significance of the seal to pay much attention to the manner in which the seal was attached to the document. The classification of seals too, according as they are attached to public or private documents, or used by secular or ecclesiastical persons, does not become really helpful for discriminating their use until late in the Middle Ages. A seal may be affixed in various ways, and these various modes are found at times far removed from one another. The study of the different modes assists us to trace the history of the document itself and is of more value than might appear at first sight. But the inquiry is a difficult one; there is always a risk of being misled by fallacious resemblances; and above all there is the problem, which cannot be said to have been successfully solved, how to bridge over the gap between the ancient and the medieval.

It must be borne in mind that for the purpose of the present inquiry the design on the seal is of subordinate interest. The seal might be taken from a gem, or a seal of any sort might be taken to represent the portrait of the owner. What is important for us is that the seal was the one thing which identified a man; it was known to be his seal and could be sworn to by witnesses. It therefore served as a means of authentication.

In what I have to say I shall use the word seal to indicate not the seal ring or other instrument—the matrix, punch, or die—by which the seal was impressed, but always as meaning the impression; and I shall begin with the clay or wax seal. But here I must make a distinction. A seal was employed to close up a document and to authenticate it, or else it was employed merely to authenticate a document which was not closed. The Germans have adopted the word *versiegeln* for the one method, and *untersiegeln* for the other. In English we have not the same facility of inventing new terms, and it is with hesitation that I propose in the present paper to call the closing external seal the *affixed* seal, and the internal seal, which only authenticates, the *impressed* seal. The *pendent* seal belongs to a different class from either, and will come under discussion later. For the present I am concerned only with the affixed and the impressed seal. I should be glad if more appropriate names could be suggested, for those which I have chosen are no doubt arbitrary.

Both uses of the seal can be traced back in Babylonia to

G

remote antiquity, but it would take me far beyond my range if I were to attempt to trace any connexion between such seals and those of Rome. All I need say is that the Roman opinion was that the seal ring was introduced from Greece[1] and that there are indications that it may have come from Asia Minor. At all events the clay or wax seal is first found in Italy in the southern parts which were colonized from the East. In order to understand the manner in which seals were used in Rome we must remember that waxed tablets with two or three leaves —diptychs or triptychs—were the ordinary materials for everyday writing, and these might bear seals either on the outside or within. The latter mode, that of the impressed seal, appears on tablets of the first and second century brought to light in modern times in Dacia and at Pompeii.[2] A receipt for money paid was witnessed by several persons whose seals were impressed on the tablet side by side with the subscriptions identifying them.[3] There are also examples of such seals serving a double purpose. The record of the transaction was written on the first leaf and on the face of the second: these were pierced and a string passed through them. The string was then fixed on the back of the second leaf by the witnesses' seals, and the remaining space occupied by a transcript for reference. Thus the outsides of the exterior leaves of the triptych were left plain, and the interior was half sealed up, half open. In a diptych the record in the interior was entirely closed by a string passing round the tablet, on which the seals of the witnesses were imposed.[4] A similar method was employed in the military diplomas or metal tablets conferred on discharged veterans.[5] Seals were also impressed on the passes for the use of the imperial post. But these passes, it has been pointed out, must have been issued open, for had they been sealed up they would not have served for more

---

[1] Pliny, *Nat. Hist.* xxxiii. 1, § 4.

[2] See *Corpus Inscriptionum Latinarum*, iii (1873), 938; iv. Suppl., pp. 277b, &c.

[3] See C. G. Bruns, 'Die Unterschriften in den Römischen Rechtsurkunden', in the *Philologische und Historische Abhandlungen* of the Berlin Academy for 1876, p. 46.

[4] A remarkably perfect specimen of a deed of A.D. 199 has recently been presented to the Bodleian Library, Lat. Inscr. 10, 11. A full description of it by Dr. B. P. Grenfell appears in the *Bodleian Quarterly Record*, ii (1919), 258 ff.

[5] See B. Faass, 'Studien zur Ueberlieferungsgeschichte der Römischen Kaiserurkunde', in the *Archiv für Urkundenforschung*, i (1908), 185 ff.

than the first stage of a journey.[1] In like manner we find seals
impressed on the face of papyrus deeds written in Egypt in
the early centuries of our era.[2]

The more common use of the seal among the Romans was to
secure a document. Private letters, wills, and contracts were
regularly written on tablets, which were pierced with two or
three holes. Through these a string was drawn, and its ends
were fastened with a seal, most often of wax, but sometimes of
clay.[3] We are told of a man breaking the seal in order to read
a letter, and this fact explains why only the pierced tablets and
hardly any reliques of the seals are preserved.[4]

Tablets continued to be used for accounts, school-exercises,
and the like—much as we use slates—until modern times; but
for other purposes[5] they were gradually almost entirely superseded by the use of papyrus rolls. A material like papyrus
would perhaps hardly bear the affixion of a closing seal, so that
this had to be attached to the loose ends of the strings. But
this must not be confused with what we know as the pendent
seal; for its purpose was to secure a closed document, whereas
the pendent seal served merely as a means of authentication.
Moreover, it was always a single seal, taken from a ring or
similar matrix, and presented but one face, whereas the pendent
wax seal when it first appears is double, with a design on the
back, and such a seal is unknown in Roman times. It needs
two matrixes, which are never identical; and it does not make
its appearance until the eleventh century. The problem is, on
what model it was formed.

When parchment came to take the place of papyrus, there is
no reason to suppose that letters or wills were sealed in any
other manner than that which I have described. But the nature
of the new material enabled the writer to dispense with strings

---

[1] See H. Erman, in the *Zeitschrift der Savigny-Stiftung*, xx (1899), 186 ff. of
the Romanistic section.

[2] Mr. E. O. Winstedt has kindly shown me several specimens from the rich
collection of the Bodleian Library.

[3] Suetonius, *Nero*, xvii, cites a law of Nero, *ne tabulae nisi pertusae ac ter lino
per foramina traiecto obsignarentur*.

[4] St. Augustine, who habitually used tablets, mentions the design on his
seal: *Epist.* lix (*al.* ccxvii) ad Victorinum, *sub fin.*

[5] In 613 Queen Brunichildis sent an order on a *tabula cera linita*: Fredegar,
Chron. xl.; and as late as 1075 Archbishop Anno of Cologne wrote a letter on
tablets *propter maiorem secreti cautelam*; Lambert of Hersfeld, *Chron.*, p. 247,
ed. O. Holder-Egger, 1894.

and construct the tie out of the parchment itself. A strip was cut from the lower margin nearly to the left edge; the document was folded small, the strip folded round it, and the seal imposed upon this. The fact that the strip had to be cut before the document was read explains why the seal has been lost and no specimen preserved. This mode of sealing is that which the French call *sur simple queue*. But its origin has never, to my knowledge, been carried back to early times. It is spoken of as a variation of the pendent seal,[1] which is not found until the eleventh century; and we are told that it was frequently employed about the middle of the thirteenth century.[2] But there are plain traces of its use on documents of the ninth century[3] in England, where there are a good many specimens preserved of the eleventh; and Giry has called attention to its appearance on a little mandate of Philip I of France issued between 1104 and 1108.[4] I believe it to be a direct continuation of the ancient method by which letters were sealed up. There is evidence also that letters in the eighth century might be closed by means of strings passing through four holes.[5]

The use of seals went out of fashion in Italy. To wills indeed they continued to be affixed,[6] and the rule *agnitis signis, rupto lino aperiatur et recitetur*,[7] was repeated in Frankish formularies down to the eighth century and later.[8] But in other documents their place was taken by autograph subscriptions. If a man was unable to write, he marked a cross, his *signum manus* or sign manual; and from the time of Justinian the certificate of a notary was required. The seal thus came to be unnecessary for the legal validity of a document.[9] But the period at which the

---

[1] W. Ewald, *Siegelkunde* (1914), p. 170.

[2] *Nouveau Traité de Diplomatique*, iv (1759), 405. So too Bresslau, *Handbuch der Urkundenlehre* (1st ed., 1889), p. 957 (2nd ed., 1931, ii. 590).

[3] See below, pp. 106 f.

[4] *Manuel de Diplomatique* (1894), p. 640.

[5] See W. Diekamp's notes on the Vienna MS. 751 of the Letters of St. Boniface, transcribed in the ninth century: *Neues Archiv der Gesellschaft für ältere deutsche Geschichtskunde*, ix (1884), 26.

[6] See Ulpian, in 43 *Digest*. v. 3, § 9; and Gaius, in 29 *Digest*. iii. 7.

[7] *Pauli Sent*. iv. 6. A well-known example of the procedure at Ravenna in 474 is printed from the papyrus original in Bruns's *Fontes Iuris Romani antiqui* (6th ed., 1893), pp. 280 ff.

[8] Marculf, Form. ii. 17, in Zeumer's *Formulae* (1886); *Collect. Flaviniac.* viii, *ibid.*, p. 476.

[9] It is said that the last traces of the use of seals to witness documents found in the *Corpus Iuris Civilis* are of the third century: 8 *Cod*. xli. 6 (A.D. 214), 11 *Cod*. xxxix (A.D. 230), and 5 *Cod*. xxxvii. 15 (A.D. 287).

seal lost its importance corresponded with the time when a new influx of Greek practices began, and the Greek metal seal or bull (*bulla*) was introduced.

II

Now the bull has two faces, an obverse and a reverse, or (as they are called) a seal and a counterseal; it was, as the Germans say, a 'coin-seal', a seal like a piece of money. It was generally made of lead, though specimens in gold and other metals are also known. It was a product of warm countries, in which an impression in wax would not retain its distinctness. Hence we find that its home was in the Eastern Empire, whither it was probably imported from Asia. It passed into the parts of Italy which were connected with the Empire. We shall even find it in England. From its nature the bull could not be impressed on a document; it could only be appended on strings. If it was desired to close the document, the strings must be tied round it and the bull fixed on them so that the document could not be opened without cutting them.

It is true that a leaden seal may be found in Italy from the early days of the Empire, but this was a counter or *jeton*, which was not intended to be attached to anything. Such specimens are taken to be the *tesserae* which served as tokens for the distribution of corn or as tickets for admission to the theatre.[1] Some have a hole pierced through them and were evidently worn as ornaments. These must be distinguished from the seals which were employed as marks to identify pieces of marble[2] or to consign merchandise.[3] Both types are of Greek derivation, but neither seems to stand in direct relation to the bull applied to documents.[4]

How early this bull makes its appearance has not been established. It is undoubtedly found under Justinian,[5] and may have been used earlier. After the Imperial restoration in Italy

[1] See M. Rostovtzeff, 'Römische Bleitesserae', in *Beiträge zur alten Geschichte*, 3tes Beiheft (1905), pp. 4–10. There is a large collection of examples figured by F. Ficoroni, *de Plumbeis Antiquorum Numismatibus* (1750).

[2] Ficoroni, pp. 1–9. [3] Cf. Liudprand, *Legatio*, liii.

[4] A. Eitel's contention, *Ueber Blei- und Goldbullen im Mittelalter* (1912), p. 84, that the papal bull was of native Italian origin, is based on a confusion between its type and that of the tokens or marks which I have just mentioned.

[5] G. Schlumberger, *Sigillographie de l'Empire Byzantin* (1884), p. 418, note 3. In the fifteenth century it was said by Codinus, *de Officialibus*, p. 64 A (p. 34, ed. Bekker 1839), that the Emperors used a wax seal for familiar correspondence.

it was employed by the Exarchs and other high officials. But the most remarkable fact is that this leaden seal was adopted by the Popes and has been used by them for rescripts in solemn form down to modern times; and that they employed it not, as had always been the practice, for the purpose of securing a closed document, but in order to authenticate a document which was issued open. No papal letter is known to have been sealed up before the twelfth century, but it must be presumed that secret correspondence was somehow protected from publicity. No specimen, however, is preserved in the original. All that we possess are the solemn grants of privileges, and these are invariably open documents.

A great deal of uncertainty prevails as to the correct attribution of many of the earliest preserved papal bulls.[1] No specimen exists actually appended to a document until a relatively late time, for the statement made by Giry that Pope Zachary's seal is found on a privilege for Monte Cassino is based on a misunderstanding: the original of that document is not extant.[2] Moreover, no Pope before Leo IX in the middle of the eleventh century gave his number on the seal,[3] and there were very many Popes of the same name. But there are two criteria which help us in determining the dates of doubtful bulls. One is based on the grammatical form in which the name is written. With the single definite exception of Agapetus II in the tenth century,[4] every Pope wrote it in the genitive until Urban II (1088) introduced the nominative. But if this test enables us to exclude some, it does not go far in settling the attribution of the numerous uncertain bulls ranging from the seventh to the tenth century. There is, however, another guide which reduces the margin of doubt. This is the fact that all the Popes down to Benedict III (855–8) wrote their names not round the circumference of the seal, but across the field.[5] Benedict made several experi-

[1] See Camillo Serafini's careful discrimination of the types of bulls earlier than Leo IX: *Le Monete e le Plombe del Medagliere Vaticano*, i (1910), pp. lxxxiv–lxxxviii.   [2] See below, appendix. pp. 110 f.

[3] The bull bearing the legend DAMASUS II, figured by Julius von Pflugk-Harttung, *Specimina selecta Chartarum Pontificum Romanorum*, iii (1887), plate vi. 10, is rightly condemned by Serafini, p. lxxxvii, n. 6, as a modern forgery.

[4] Benedict III's monogram is hardly an exception, because a monogram was constructed on different principles from a legend.

[5] The bull with the circular legend assigned by Mabillon, *de Re Diplomatica* (ed. 1709), p. 436, to John V (685–6), has been proved by Delisle to belong to John XV; see my *Papal Chancery*, pp. 177 f.

ments: he had a monogram of his name, and a cruciform arrangement

B

E

D I C $+$ T I

N

E

But as early as October 7, 855,[1] he introduced the circular plan, which was that used on coins, and this practice was maintained, except in the last twenty years of the ninth century —a time of great confusion and turbulence—until the pontificate of Urban II.

The most ancient bull now extant about which there is no dispute is that of Pope Deusdedit (615–18). It was discovered on the Coelian Hill in 1727,[2] and the attribution is free from ambiguity, because Deusdedit was alone of his name. His seal, moreover, is unique in its class. For his successors were content to give their names with no ornament but a cross or star; but Deusdedit has a pictorial design of the Apostle Peter feeding his lambs on the seal, and DEUSDEDIT PAPE on the counterseal.[3] Whether this represents a continuation of an earlier series it is impossible to say, but it is certain that in the twelfth century it was a fixed tradition that the leaden bull was in use in the time of Gregory the Great (590–604). By a curious chance the evidence for this tradition was alleged in two cases arising out of disputes about the genuineness of papal rescripts both preserved in England. They have been constantly cited from the time of Mabillon[4] downwards. The first was in an appeal from Archbishop Thurstan of York in 1123 against the claim of Canterbury to the primacy. A lively description of what happened at Rome is given by Hugh, the York chanter. The Canterbury documents, he says, were ordered to be read; and when certain documents, including one of Gregory the Great to Augustine, were produced, some of the Romans inquired whether they had seals (*bullae*). The monks replied that they had left the sealed originals behind and brought only transcripts. They were then asked whether they would swear that they possessed originals of them with

---

[1] In his immense privilege for Corbie, now preserved at Amiens. See the facsimile of a part of it in Mabillon, p. 439, plate xlviii.

[2] See Ficoroni, xxiii. 3.

[3] See the facsimile in Serafini, i, plate A. 1.

[4] *De Re Diplom.*, p. 128; *Nouveau Traité de Diplomatique*, iv. 24, n. 1.

seals. Upon this they withdrew to take counsel among themselves. At first they were disposed to affirm that the documents had no seals, but after this they decided to swear that the seals were perished or lost. The Romans were provoked to laughter, and observed that it was strange that the lead should have disappeared while the parchment remained. If we believe our informant, it was evidently not known that the Pope in Gregory's time wrote not on parchment but papyrus; and this ignorance of the older practice was in fact shared by Innocent III.[1] The monks then said that possibly in that age seals were not in use. 'But the Romans bore testimony that there were seals from the time of St. Gregory and that some sealed Privileges of his were still preserved in the Roman Church.'[2] This account, I have said, comes from York; but after making due allowance for its colouring we may, I think, take it as evidence that it was believed at Rome that bulls were in use in the time of Gregory the Great.

The second instance of an appeal being made to the fact that bulls were used in the time of Gregory the Great occurred in 1181, when a letter attributed to St. Augustine was impugned by the monks of Christ Church on the ground, among others, that it bore a bull. *Fuit etiam notatum, immo notorium et notabile, quod bulla ipsius plumbea fuit, cum non soleant cisalpini praesules vel primates scriptis suis authenticis bullas plumbeas apponere.*[3] Their opponents, according to a later authority,[4] maintained that St. Augustine merely followed the example of his master St. Gregory.

Nam cum idem Augustinus Romanus esset et legatione Anglorum apostolus, eundem potuit servare modum quantum ad personae suae dignitatem ratione legationis suae apostolicae in ecclesia Anglicana, quem modum servavit dominus apostolicus in ecclesia Romana.[5]

[1] See my *Papal Chancery*, pp. 148 f.

[2] Hugh's narrative is in the *Historians of the Church of York*, ed. J. Raine, ii. (1886) 204 ff. Its substance is repeated by Thomas Stubbs, *ibid.*, pp. 380 f.

[3] Gervase of Canterbury, *Opera Historica*, i. 296, ed. W. Stubbs, 1879.

[4] W. Thorne, in Twysden's *Scriptores Decem*, pp. 1764 f., 1652.

[5] Thorne's words are repeated by Thomas Elmham, *Historia Monasterii S. Augustini Cantuariensis* (ed. C. Hardwick, 1858), p. 122. The editor asserts (introd., p. xxxiii) that in the documents transcribed by Elmham it is narrated how the new pontiff Lucius III professed himself entirely satisfied by the production of the ancient bulls [of Boniface IV and Agatho] and the report which he at length received from the commissioners. But the Pope's rescripts there set out merely follow the rule of recognizing the *status quo* while the dispute was undecided. In letter 85, of May 21, 1182, he forbids the Archbishop

These are the only two examples which have been cited to prove that Gregory used a bull. They both come from a region where forgery was rife, but the statement of Hugh the chanter that the fact was well known in Rome has a certain weight. And as we still possess a bull of Pope Deusdedit a dozen years after Gregory's death, there is no inherent difficulty in believing that he also used one. Gregory lived several years in Constantinople, and he may very well have brought back the idea with him.

It has indeed been maintained that the bull was used a little before Gregory's time by John III (561–71) or even by Agapetus I (535–6); but the evidence for this opinion must be rejected. The seal of Agapetus may be dealt with shortly. It was until recently known only from a manuscript; and it bears the legends[1] on the two sides—

	•
+	PA
AGAP	• • •
ITVS	PAE
	•

Now the spelling of the name and the use of the nominative agree with the seal of Agapetus II, who, I have said, if we except the anomalous monogram of Benedict III, is the only Pope who wrote his name in the nominative before Urban II. But his name was engraved round the circumference, and it was therefore natural to suppose that the seal was that of the earlier Agapetus. The actual bull, however, has been discovered at Naples, and it is accepted as belonging to Agapetus II.[2]

The seal of the unknown John has been introduced into the question by mistake. As Serafini has observed,[3] it is not a bull which was meant to be appended to a document. There is no trace that it ever had a string, but there are notches on the rim made for the purpose of fixing it to a surface in which it was inserted. It is a seal which served as a mark for marble or for a package of merchandise. Nevertheless the design is so interesting that one wishes to establish its date, all the more since,

to interfere in regard to the matter in question, *lite pendente super privilegiis ipsis*; and in letter 86, of the same date, he orders the tenants of St. Augustine to pay no regard to any action of the Archbishop, if he should act contrary to the Pope's prohibition, *donec super privilegiis illis falsi quaestio terminetur.*

[1] Pflugk-Harttung, iii, plate xvii. 1.   [2] See Serafini, p. lxxxvii, n. 3.

[3] *Ibid.*, p. lxxxviii, n. 8, and p. 325, n. 45.

while Pflugk-Harttung[1] attributes it doubtfully to John III in the sixth century, its most recent editor places it as *incerto* among the bulls of the eleventh century.[2] It bears a Calvary cross potent, with the words IOHANNES PA written round the circumference.[3] The counterseal contains the XP monogram with the letters R and O in the side angles, and + ꞇ C ꞇ PETRVꞇ round it. Now the fact that the Pope's name is given in the nominative would imply that the seal was of very late date and therefore a forgery, or else that it was very early before the genitive was adopted. That it is written round the circumference suggests a date after 855–8. The other features lead to a more precise conclusion. The recumbent ꞇ is found on papal coins from the end of the eighth to the last quarter of the tenth century. The particular type of cross appears on seals rarely, and only, it is said, from the latter part of the seventh to the first half of the tenth century.[4] But Pope John's cross bears a close resemblance to that on a bull of Constantine, protospatharius and στρατηγός of Sicily, which is assigned to the eighth or ninth century.[5] This likeness suggests that it belongs to a Pope who was within the range of Byzantine influences, and I am inclined to attribute it to John X (914–28), who was a native of Ravenna and archbishop of that see before he was elected Pope, for at Ravenna Byzantine traditions were long maintained. We possess no seal which can be assigned with confidence to John X, for that which is given doubtfully under his name by Pflugk-Harttung[6] is carried back by Serafini to the time of John VIII. It need not, however, be inferred that the disputed seal was that used by John X for the authentication of documents; he may well have possessed a different seal for marking goods.

We conclude then that the evidence adduced to show that the Popes made use of the leaden bull before the pontificate of Deusdedit, or perhaps of Gregory the Great, is fallacious. At the same time we cannot exclude the possibility that the bull was introduced a little earlier, in fact any time after the recovery of Italy by Justinian. What is certain is that the mode of authenti-

---

[1] Plate i. 1.   [2] Serafini, p. 25 and plate G. 10.

[3] In Pflugk-Harttung's facsimile the name appears to be IOHANNIS, but the reproduction is blurred. It is clear in Serafini.

[4] Schlumberger, pp. 23, 81.

[5] It is preserved in the British Museum, No. 17527, and is figured by A. Salinas in the *Periodico di Numismatica e Sfragistica per la Storia d'Italia*, vi (1874), plate iv. 2, and by Schlumberger, p. 214.   [6] Plate v. 6.

cating the open document by means of a hanging seal has been used by the Popes from the first quarter of the seventh century. It is curious that the practice is not attested in the East until several hundred years later, when we find a certificate by the prefect of the Hippodrome recording that a rescript of Constantine Porphyrogenitus εἶχε καὶ βούλλαν κάτωθεν ἀπῃωρημένην.[1]

As my subject is limited to the employment of seals it would be out of place to comment on the series of attempts to make the bull more decorative which distinguish the generation following Leo IX, to the severe reaction to the plain horizontal legend under Urban II, or to the compromise which brought in the heads of the Apostles Peter and Paul under his successor Paschal II (1099–1118).[2] I will only note that the type of bull thus established has never been altered since, except only that the heads of the Apostles have been portrayed in a different style from the time of the Renaissance. But though the seal continued in principle unchanged, the open document was plainly not adapted for private correspondence, and it may be supposed that letters which were meant to be read only by the persons to whom they were addressed were first folded and then pierced through the folds with holes to receive the strings to which the bull was to be attached afterwards. We cannot tell when this plan of keeping their contents secret was first used, but specimens of such Letters Close are found from 1120 onwards.[3] It may be observed, as the matter has been disputed, that this plan of securing privacy is entirely different from the practice, which was adopted as early as the twelfth century, of leaving the ends of the strings after they had been attached to the bull protruding so that they could be tied round the document when folded.[4] This was done merely to protect the document in transit; it was a form of packing; but it did not

[1] Leunclavius, *Ius Graeco-Romanum*, p. 120 (1596). I owe the reference to the kindness of my friend Professor Bury. The date of the rescript, A.M. 6534 in the 9th Indiction (i.e. A.D. 1026), if correctly given, falls in the reign of Constantine VIII.

[2] The supposition that these heads are found on a bull of Paul I is erroneous. This bull, figured by Mabillon, suppl., p. 46, bears the name ΠΑΥΛΟΥ on the reverse. But it is the seal not of a Pope but of a member of the Roman clergy: see G. B. de Rossi, in the *Atti della R. Accademia dei Lincei*, 3rd ser., x (1882) 386, n. 5.

[3] See my *Papal Chancery*, p. 121 and n. 2. A facsimile of Calixtus II's letter of 25 June 1120 is given by A. Brackmann, *Papsturkunden*, plate vi. *a, b* (in Seeliger's *Urkunden und Siegel*, ii), 1914.

[4] *Papal Chancery*, p. 202 and n. 2.

prevent the document from being read by any one who chose to untie the strings.

The bull, however, was a clumsy contrivance which did not suit a time when the Pope's correspondence became heavy and needed dispatch. Hence even in the thirteenth century the Pope is found to have used his private seal-ring to close his letters, and in the fifteenth such letters assumed a particular type and were known as briefs. But the mode of sealing was not dissimilar to that which had become usual in the West of Europe and does not here call for further notice.[1]

III

We return now to the history of the wax seal. We have found it employed among the Romans chiefly for the purpose of closing documents; and from the fifth century it passed out of fashion in Italy except for wills and letters. Wills were tied up and sealed, but to open them it was only necessary to cut the string.[2] Letters on the other hand were so closed that they could not be read without breaking the seal. In 867 when Charles the Bald wished to ascertain the terms of a synodal letter he had to break the seal.[3] But an internal impressed seal was used, as we have seen, in connexion with commercial transactions in the first and second centuries, and this mode of sealing continued in practice at least down to the third century for military diplomas and passes for the post. Now the seals on these tablets were partially exposed, and it seems probable that when papyrus or parchment took the place of the wooden or metal tablet, the plan was adopted of impressing the seal on the open face of the document. We have no evidence of this in Italy, but it appears in Gaul in the fifth century; and the fact that the first example refers to ecclesiastical usage supports the conclusion that it was taken from a Roman source. This example occurs in the letter of Chlodovech, or Clovis, addressed to the bishops of Gaul between 507 and 511, and preserved in

---

[1] The *Recueil des Fac-similés de l'École des Chartes*, i, plate 69 *bis*, shows a specimen of a brief of Urban VIII (1626), in which the letter is folded and tied round, and the seal is impressed on the back.   [2] See above, p. 94.

[3] Hincmar, *Ann. Bertin.*, *s.a.* The king then had a new letter written, which he sealed *bulla sui nominis*. Mabillon, p. 132, misread this statement as referring to the seal of Archbishop Hincmar, and G. A. Seyler, *Geschichte der Siegel* [1894], p. 26, attributed it to Bishop Actard of Rheims. Actard was bishop of Nantes, and was merely the messenger.

a manuscript of not much later date, in which the king desires them to furnish *apostolia* or commendatory *epistulas de anulo vestro infra signatas*.[1] Not long afterwards the same practice is found among the Visigoths, and now it was employed for the authentication of a secular law. The fact was ascertained through the discovery at Leon of a palimpsest containing a constitution of King Theudis, of the year 546, which he promulgated *sigilli nostri adiectione firmatam*.[2] The law then undoubtedly bore the royal seal impressed on its face. No parallel exists for such a mode of sealing in Roman public documents, but there is no inherent improbability in its having been adopted from the usage of bishops' seals. However this may be, it is certain that the mode indicated in the law of the Visigothic king became the accepted practice in the precepts, or official documents, of the Frankish kings. Of this we have actual examples preserved from the last quarter of the seventh century, and one is found on a private deed, a sale to the abbey of St. Denis, in 766.[3] The affixed closing seal continued to be used for letters and wills, but the impressed seal was the mark of the more solemn document. The seal was a mark of office,[4] and it was natural that its impression should be given in some way on the document. When this was issued open, the obvious plan was to impress the seal on its face, for the notion of a hanging seal is not traceable in France until a much later time. The seal was not simply impressed: a cross-cut was made in the parchment and the wax was worked into it, so that part of it adhered to the back as well as to the face of the document;[5] but the seal had only one impression, on the face.

The double seal, with a counterseal, does not appear in France until the end of the eleventh century, and it is pendent upon strings or tags. Its origin we shall explore later on; for the present it is sufficient to note that it involved a vital change in the use of the seal; for the seal-ring could no longer be employed; it was necessary to have two dies or matrixes, and these bore different designs. But there has been a good deal of

---

[1] *Capitularia Regum Francorum*, i (ed. A. Boretius, 1882), 1 f.

[2] See Zeumer, in the *Neues Archiv*, xxiii (1898), 79.

[3] Mabillon, p. 146, saw a fragment of the seal; but this seems now to have disappeared: see Giry, p. 631, n. 2.

[4] Thus it was held by Syggo the referendary of Sigebert I († 575): Gregory of Tours, *Hist. Franc.* v. 3 (*olim* 1).

[5] The same method was adopted with the clay seals on papyrus deeds.

confusion as to the date when this pendent seal first appears in France. The Benedictine authors of the *Nouveau Traité de Diplomatique*, iv. 400, cite as an example a diploma of King Robert (1025); but it is now known that the seal was in fact impressed (*plaqué*).[1] There is also a charter of Fulk Nerra to St. Aubin at Angers, of about 1010, which bears the count's seal hanging on strings;[2] but Giry[3] is unable to affirm that this is not a later addition. It is not mentioned whether the seal had a counterseal. A third specimen is attached to a charter of Richard II of Normandy to Dudo of St. Quentin (1015). An engraving of it is given in the *Nouveau Traité*, iv. 226; and it is accepted by Giry[4] as genuine. But the long leather thongs described by the Benedictines as laced into the parchment were probably added later to preserve a seal, once impressed, which had fallen off the document. No example of a seal pendent to a document of a French king is known before 1113, when Louis VI granted a foundation charter to the abbey of St. Victor at Paris.[5]

It has been thought that the metal bull was used in Gaul at an early time, but no positive evidence for this practice has been adduced before the ninth century.[6] In 813 the Council of Chalon-sur-Saône enacted in its 41st canon that if a priest goes into a new diocese he must be provided with competent testimony: *litteras enim habebit in quibus sint nomina episcopi et civitatis plumbo impressa*;[7] where it is probable that *impressa* is mechanically reproduced from an older form which said *anulo impressa*, for a bull could not be impressed.[8] I take it that the bull was a recent device which was borrowed from the papal usage, for only three years earlier such a document was confirmed *impressione sigilli nostri*.[9] The time at which it appears suits this view, and there are good reasons for believing with

[1] Giry, p. 640, n. 1.

[2] Count Bertrand de Broussillon, *Cartulaire de l'Abbaye de Saint-Aubin d'Angers*, ii (1903), 10, n. 3.

[3] p. 641, n. 1.   [4] *Ibid.*, n. 2.   [5] *Ibid.*, p. 640.

[6] The supposition that it was used by the Vandal King Thrasamund (496–523) is based on a bull which bears the legend TRASEMVND with no title, and contains a Calvary cross potent—a type not found until late in the seventh century (see above, p. 100): Schlumberger, pp. 434, 735; Bresslau (2nd ed.), p. 514, n. 1.

[7] *Concil. Aevi Karol.* (1906), p. 282.

[8] Cf. *anulo ecclesiae nostrae bullare censuimus*, in *Form. extravag.* ii. 20, Zeumer's *Formulae*, p. 563.

[9] *Form. Senon. recent.* xiv, *ibid.*, p. 219; cf. *Form. extravag.* ii. 18, p. 561.

Mabillon[1] that the Emperor Charles the Great occasionally employed a bull. Theodor von Sickel indeed strenuously denied this,[2] and held that *bulla* in the precept of June 14, 811,[3] meant a wax seal. Giry,[4] however, maintained the contrary opinion, and his judgement has more recently been supported by Bresslau.[5] If Charles's employment of the bull is denied—for *bulla* is certainly sometimes used to denote a wax seal—still the recurrence of the word under Lewis the Pious adds weight to the view of Giry and Bresslau and favours the view that a practice which is proved to have been used by Lewis II of Italy was in fact a continuation of that of his Frankish ancestors nearly a century before him. Nor need we doubt that it, like the imperial monogram,[6] was derived from Byzantine usage.

IV

In England the bull makes its appearance earlier than the wax seal. It would not indeed be wise to lay too much stress upon the bull which St. Augustine was said to have used for his charter to the abbey at Canterbury, for that is undoubtedly a forgery of later date; but the fact that it was appealed to is evidence that long after the time when the practice of using bulls, if it ever existed, had been given up in England, they were believed to have been employed in the days of St. Augustine. The original document is unfortunately not preserved; but it is known that it had a bull, and a drawing of this is preserved in the manuscript of Elmham's History of the Abbey at Trinity Hall, Cambridge, which was written at the beginning of the fifteenth century. I should not be at all surprised if it were a genuine bull which was attached to a spurious document, for one cannot lay too much stress upon the details given by a late draughtsman.[7] It is said to have been of gold; if so, it was probably a leaden bull gilded.[8] No other instance of an English bull is known until nearly two hundred years later, when one

---

[1] *De Re Diplom.*, p. 141; cf. suppl., p. 47.
[2] *Acta Karolinorum*, i. 196 and note there.
[3] *Diplomata Karolinorum*, no. 211, p. 283.
[4] *Manuel de Diplom.*, p. 634, n. 3, and p. 720.
[5] 'Die Lehre von den Siegeln der Karolinger und Ottonen', in the *Archiv für Urkundenforschung*, i (1908), 255 ff.
[6] See my paper on the Seal and Monogram of Charles the Great below, pp. 112 f.
[7] See Spelman's engraving of it in Wilkins's *Concilia*, iv. 730.
[8] Of this type traces are conjectured by Eitel, pp. 13 ff.

bearing the name of King Kenulf of Mercia makes its appearance.[1] The reign of Kenulf's predecessor, Offa, who died in 796, was marked by its frequent relations with the Continent. Papal legates were in England in 786, and both Adrian I and Leo III were actively interested in its affairs. If the earlier use of the bull in England be discredited, or if it had passed into desuetude, it is not unlikely that this papal connexion suggested its introduction or revival. The size of Kenulf's bull, with an impression just an inch across, corresponds closely with that of the papal seals of the time. But the design cannot have been borrowed from them, because they had a horizontal legend while Kenulf's is circular. I suggest, therefore, that the idea of using a leaden bull comes from Rome, but that the engravers fell back upon a coin for a model of the lettering.

As for wax seals in England it has been an accepted doctrine, since George Hickes published his famous *Dissertatio Epistolaris* in 1703, that no royal charter or diploma had a seal until the time of Edward the Confessor. The statement is derived in fact from the forged History of Croyland attributed to Abbot Ingulph[2]; but Hickes supported it partly by the criticism of some Exeter charters which he proved to be forgeries, partly by the contention that *sigillum* in Anglo-Saxon charters means not a seal but a mark. This may be accepted as the common meaning, but he was in error in interpreting the Anglo-Saxon *insegl* in the same sense. The specimens which have been alleged against Hickes's opinion are preserved among the muniments of Saint Denis in French archives, and their spuriousness was proved beyond the possibility of doubt by Mr. W. H. Stevenson in 1891.[3] But this same scholar has more recently called attention to the rents appearing in a good many Anglo-Saxon charters 'at the left side at the foot of the document', which suggest that they once had seals imposed on them.[4] There is an example in a private charter at Canterbury of 860–6, which bears distinct evidence that it originally had a seal affixed to a strip cut from the lower margin, and one can even see how the document was folded and closed by the

[1] Where it was found is unknown. It had belonged to the Torlonia collection at Rome, and is said to have been brought from Italy some time before it was purchased for the British Museum in 1847. See *Archaeologia*, xxiii (1847), 449 f.

[2] Fulman's *Rerum Anglic. Script. vet.* i (1684), 70.

[3] *English Historical Review*, vi. 736–42.

[4] *Ibid.* xxvii (1912), 6 ff.

CHARTER (860–866) PRESERVED AT CANTERBURY

seal.[1] This is several centuries earlier than any specimen hitherto cited of sealing *sur simple queue.*

If England thus provides the first examples of this mode of sealing, it has also the distinction of inventing the double seal pendent, the prototype of the Great Seal of all the ages after. This is found under Edward the Confessor; the seal and counter-seal have different designs, and the seal is pendent upon strings. I have long been of opinion—and here, though I arrived at the conclusion independently, I am glad to find myself anticipated by Mr. Stevenson[2]—that this seal was not a new invention but merely a modification of the papal bull adapted to a different material. King Edward's seal, indeed, though very small, judged by the standard of later Great Seals—it had a diameter of less than three inches—was more than twice the size of the bull of that time, and unlike the bull it bore the royal effigy on both sides. But its origin is manifest, and it is strange that no one until Mr. Stevenson has drawn attention to its origin. The Benedictines, indeed, speak of the mode of hanging the seal as derived from the papal bull,[3] but they omit to notice the other important point about the seal itself, that, unlike previous wax seals, it had two sides; it was a 'coin seal'. Such a seal so used has no earlier example. It is true that, as Mabillon observed,[4] we find double seals in the Lombard principalities of Southern Italy from the end of the ninth century; these were evidently modelled on Byzantine bulls, which they resemble in size: but they were not pendent to the document, the two sides were impressed separately one above the other.[5] It is the hanging double seal which is the peculiar invention of Edward the Confessor.

Though I am not immediately concerned with the design on the seal, it may not be out of place to notice that Edward's seal

[1] See the accompanying plate showing both sides of the document, reproduced by permission of the Controller of His Majesty's Stationery Office from the *Ordnance Survey Facsimiles of Anglo-Saxon Manuscripts*, i (1878), plate ix. The original folding can be discerned by a comparison of the diamond-shaped hole where the seal was, with the holes through which the strip passed. The discoloured condition of the upper part of the parchment is due to a folding at a later time. In plate xviii, the will of the atheling Athelstan (1015), there is a small hole where the seal was torn off, and also a 'step' at the corner from which the strip once started. [2] l. c.

[3] *Nouveau Traité de Diplom.* iv. 399; cf. Bresslau (1st ed.), p. 954, n. 5 (2nd ed., 1931, ii. p. 586, n. 4). [4] *De Re Diplom.*, suppl., p. 49.

[5] See *Codex Diplomaticus Cavensis*, i (1873), no. cxi, where a facsimile is given of a document of Waimar I of Salerno of the year 899. This is a grant made under the authority of a golden bull of Leo the Philosopher.

is modelled upon the seal of majesty—a single seal—of the Emperors. The type is first found in the fifth seal of Otto III (997), which was closely followed on the second seal of Henry II (1013). Those of Conrad II have a remarkable resemblance to that of Edward the Confessor, and it cannot be forgotten that Edward's half-sister Gunhild married the son of Conrad, the future Emperor Henry III. There were frequent relations between England and the Empire about 1050,[1] and Edward's seal appears to have been in use not much later than 1051.

The example of Edward the Confessor was followed by William the Conqueror, but he appended the seal, not to a strip of the document, but on strings or on a tag or label of parchment. This practice was perpetuated in the more solemn charters of the English kings. Moreover, he wrote a different legend on the two faces of the seal, one declaring him king of the English, the other duke of the Normans; and the legends are composed of hexameter verses, just as other metrical forms were used on Byzantine bulls.[2]

+HOC NORMANNORUM WILLELMUM NOSCE PATRONUM SI
+HOC ANGLIS REGEM SIGNO FATEARIS EUNDEM

This type does not appear in France until the reign of Louis VII, who marked his kingship on the seal and his Aquitanian dukedom on the counterseal,[3] but the metrical element is absent. In the Empire, where the practice of appending seals is supposed to have been borrowed from France, the coin-seal is not found until the time of Sigismund (1435).[4] Before then the Emperors sometimes affixed their small *secretum*, or privy seal, on the back of the Great Seal; but this represents a different principle, derived from ecclesiastical usage, as when a bishop or abbot affixed his *secretum* on the back of the seal of his see or monastery.

---

[1] Cf. Stubbs, *The Foundation of Waltham Abbey* (1861), pp. ix, x; E. Steindorff, *Jahrbücher des Deutschen Reichs unter Heinrich III*, ii (1881), 67 ff.

[2] I may cite the lines appended to the certificate mentioned above, p. 11:

'Εκ τῆς σφραγῖδος ἴσθι τὸν γεγραφότα
Κριτὴν Πεκούλην ὃς θέλει γνωριζέτω. Leunclavius, p. 120.

[3] A. Luchaire, *Études sur les actes de Louis VII*, p. 80 and plate vi; Giry, p. 641.

[4] O. Posse, *Die Siegel der Deutschen Kaiser*, ii (1910), plate xv. 1, 2. The example of Alfonso X of Castile, *ibid*. i (1909), plate xxxix. 1, 2, is of course not relevant.

V

From the evidence which I have collected it appears that the mode of sealing *sur simple queue*, on a strip cut from the bottom of the parchment which was passed round the folded document so as to close it, represents a practice which goes back to Roman times. It was an adaptation of the mode of sealing tablets to a different material, namely parchment. If private letters were preserved in the originals, I believe we should find examples of it in continuous use; but I can only cite an English private document of the ninth century, English writs of the eleventh, and a French royal mandate of the beginning of the twelfth. It was the practice which became stereotyped as the form of the English royal letters close. Sometimes it was applied to a document which was issued open, and we may find as many as six strips cut parallel from the lower margin of the document and each provided with its separate seal.[1]

The seal impressed on the face of the document has also its witness in Roman times for commercial transactions. The break in its use is explained by the fact that seals ceased to be required as a means of validating legal deeds. But the barbarians, who might be expected to appropriate usages which were going out of fashion, adopted this manner of sealing not only for private certificates but also for public instruments. Of this we have evidence from the sixth century onwards. It became the regular mode of authenticating royal diplomas in France down to the twelfth century.[2]

The pendent seal is first found on the leaden bulls of the Popes, imported from the East. This is certainly attested in the early years of the seventh century; but the method is not known to have been applied to a wax seal, of a coin type, until the time of Edward the Confessor. Thenceforward it became more and more accepted as the regular mode of sealing solemn royal documents. In private deeds also the pendent seal came into general use in the twelfth century, and the impressed seal was given up except in the lands of the Empire. But this pendent seal on private deeds was single and it was held firm by a thick lump of wax; and it only became double when a bishop or abbot chose to affix his privy seal to the back. There is no trace here of the 'coin seal'. The attachment was made by a tag of parchment.

[1] Thus in an ecclesiastical writ of 1252: *Recueil de Fac-similés de l'École des Chartes*, i, plate 55.   [2] Cf. Giry, p. 641.

Several seals might be hung side by side. There is an instance in a will of a canon of Lyons of 1260, in which eight seals are arranged round the top and sides of the document and the testator's seal is hung on a tag passing through holes cut in its middle.[1]

In course of time, perhaps late in the thirteenth century, the old plan of closing letters and similar documents by means of a strip cut from the margin of the parchment was simplified. A separate band of parchment was passed round the folded document, or sometimes through cuts made in it, and the seal was imposed on this band on the back.[2] This method was adopted by the English king for business purposes. When he issued warrants to the chancellor or administrative orders without reference to the chancery, he used the privy seal, which was the instrument of the wardrobe, and later on the secret seal or signet which was in the keeping of his secretary. But if there was no need to close the warrant, he might impress the seal low down on the face of the document. This was done on bills of privy seal and letters of protection and the like.[3] This latter plan, which is found under Edward III, seems to have been borrowed from France; for there, though the seal *plaqué* had passed into desuetude in the twelfth century, it was revived before the end of the thirteenth, and became regular about the middle of the fourteenth for warrants of payment.[4] I incline to think that we learned the plan from France, because there is no sign of its earlier employment in England while it had old precedents in France. Very likely, as Giry suggests, it was adopted in consequence of the increasing use of paper for current correspondence, because paper would not bear the attachment of a seal pendent. But the employment of paper introduced so many changes in detail in the mode of sealing that they cannot be properly discussed here. They belong to the history not of the medieval but of the modern document.

APPENDIX

Giry says,[5] 'Les plus anciennes lettres apostoliques, revêtues de leur bulle, qui nous soient parvenues, ne sont pas, il est vrai, antérieures au milieu du VIIIe siècle;' and adds in a note, 'Je n'en connais

---

[1] *Recueil de Fac-similés*, i, plate 103.
[2] E. Déprez, *Études de Diplomatique Anglaise* (1908), pp. 52, 74.
[3] *Ibid.*, pp. 56, 59, 70. But the seal might also be impressed on the back of the letter, p. 56.   [4] Giry, pp. 655, 783 f.   [5] p. 633.

pas d'antérieure à la bulle du pape Zacharie pour l'abbaye du Mont-Cassin du 18 février 746 aux archives de l'abbaye,' with a reference to Pflugk-Harttung's *Specimina*, iii, plate ii. 8. Now the document which belongs to 748,[1] not 746, is very well known. It is preserved in two letters of inspeximus by Gregory IX and Urban V, and is unquestionably a production of the twelfth century; and the bull itself is judged to be without doubt a forgery.[2] The double dating of the document shows it to be not earlier than Adrian I. It may be observed that the fact of a privilege of exemption by Zachary to Monte Cassino having been confirmed by Adrian I is no argument, as has been asserted,[3] to decide the matter. We are not denying that Zachary made such a grant; all we maintain is that this particular document cannot possibly have been issued by him.

How loosely people have written on the subject may be illustrated from the remarks of Luigi Tosti in his *Storia della Badia di Monte-Cassino*, i (1842), p. 81. He says that the first mention of the Privilege of Zachary occurs in the precept of Charles the Great published by Muratori, *Antiquitates Italiae*, v. diss. 69, p. 837. The words he quotes will be found on p. 828 of the Milan edition of 1741. They are taken not from any precept of Charles the Great, but from a state-ment of the Frankish donations to the Papacy which Muratori says he cited from the manuscript of Cencius the chamberlain, that is, the Liber Censuum. In this statement we read that the monastery of Monte Cassino *habet privilegia suae tuitionis a Romanis pontificibus et Zacharia*, or in the edition of Paul Fabre, i. 346 b (1902), *a Romano Pontific[e] Zacharia*. The way in which Pope Zachary's name is tacked on may excite suspicion as to the fact; but whether Zachary granted a privilege or not, it supplies no argument—still less, as Tosti says, *bello argomento*—for the genuineness of the particular document certified in the thirteenth century. Moreover, neither in the genuine precept of Charles, of March 28, 787, nor in the spurious ones printed in Sickel's collection will any mention be found of Pope Zachary.[4] It is possible to maintain that the bull which is still preserved has been transferred from a genuine document, but I do not believe it, for the type differs in several respects from other bulls of this Pope.[5]

[1] Jaffé, *Regesta*, 2nd ed., No. 2281.
[2] See the description in Georg Pertz's *Italiänische Reise*, ii. 3, printed in the *Archiv der Gesellschaft für ältere Deutsche Geschichtskunde*, v (1824), 319 f.
[3] *Acta Sanctorum, Octobris*, viii. 152 A.
[4] *Diplomata Karolinorum*, i (1906) 213 ff., &c.
[5] The facsimile given by Pflugk-Harttung in plate ii. 8, should be compared with those in Nos. 4–7.

THE SEAL AND MONOGRAM OF CHARLES THE GREAT[1]

IN the documents of the Merovingian period the king's sub-scription is in a few instances accompanied not only by a seal but by a monogram in which the letters of his name were compressed. The seal presented a rude portrait of the sovereign, and the monogram had as its base a capital letter. When the Carolingian mayors succeeded to power they prefixed a simple cross, after the ecclesiastical manner, to the subscription which was written for them; but they used no monogram. Pippin, as king, did not alter this practice,[2] but his son Charles revived the monogram and introduced a new type of seal. The monogram, unlike that of the Merovingians, was constructed round a cross; and the seal was taken from an ancient gem, representing, it is said, the bust of Commodus[3] or of Antoninus Pius.[4] This was embedded in a metal frame on which the king's name was engraved. But it is not the name only that we read on the impression. It is written in the form of a prayer:

+ XPE PROTEGE CAROLVM REGEM FRANCORVM[5]

The origin of the monogram has been sought in various regions. Sickel compared it with that found on the coins of Theodoric the Ostrogoth.[6] G. Wolfram brought it into connexion with a design in a seventh-century manuscript which came into Gaul from Armenia, and thought that it was adopted through an unknown Syrian in Charles's employment.[7] J. Lechner, on the other hand, like Sichel remarked its similarity to those on Ostrogothic coins, but found its immediate pattern in the devices

---

[1] Reprinted from the *English Historical Review*, vol. xxxiv (1919).

[2] The seal attributed to him which bears a legend like that of Charles's comes from a drawing in a late Corbie chartulary and is no doubt imitated from it: see T. von Sickel, *Acta Karolinorum*, i (1867), 349, n. 4; ii. 219. Another specimen, figured in the *Nouveau Traité de Diplomatique*, iv (1759), 109, is an acknowledged forgery.

[3] Sickel, i. 349.

[4] Mühlbacher and Tangl, *Diplomata Karolinorum*, i (1906), 79.

[5] It is figured in O. Posse's *Die Siegel der Deutschen Kaiser*, i (1909), plate i, 4; and elsewhere. The engraving given by Mabillon, *de Re Diplomatica* (ed. 1709), p. 387, is taken from a document of which the authenticity is disputed (see Sickel, ii. 232 f., Mühlbacher, i. 102 f.), but the seal appears to be genuine.

[6] *Acta Karol.* i. 318.

[7] *Jahrbuch der Gesellschaft für lothringische Geschichte und Altertumskunde*, XVII. i (1905) 346–9.

found on coins of the Merovingian time.[1] Then Bresslau, in a notice of Wolfram's paper, maintained that there was no need to go so far afield as Armenia, since monograms resembling that of Charles were to be seen on Imperial coins of Justinian, and their use was general on Byzantine seals.[2] The reference to coins appears to me unnecessary and indeed irrelevant, because the monogram is an accompaniment of the seal and has nothing to do with a coin. It is, I believe, the Byzantine seal which tells us the history of the Carolingian monogram.

This seal, as is well known, was a *bulla*, a metal seal with two faces, like a piece of money. On it was shown a monogram which contained the letters, or some of the letters, of the words Θ ΕΟ ΤΟ Κ Ε ΒΟΗΘΕΙ, or less frequently ΚΥΡΙΕ ΒΟΗΘΕΙ, arranged round a cross. This is the normal type. In the angles of the cross was written ΤΩ CΩ ΔΟΛΩ or ΤΩ ΔΟΛΩ CΟ.[3] The owner's name, as ΘΕ|ΟΔ|ΩΡ|Ω, might take the place of these three words; but more commonly the sentence was completed on the reverse, or counterseal, which gave the name and title.[4] There are specimens of such seals used by the Exarchs of Ravenna. We may find the name and title written on straight lines across the counterseal; but there are examples in which this also contains a monogram formed round a cross. Thus the seal mentioned above, with ΘΕΟΔ ΩΡΩ on the face, has ΠΑΤΡΙΚΙΩ as a monogram on the counterseal, with ΚΑΙ[5] ΕΞΑΡΧΩ in the angles. But if the name is not given on the seal, it may be compressed into a monogram on the counterseal. This is found on a specimen in which ΘΕΟ-ΦΥΛΑΚΤΩ appears, greatly abbreviated, as a monogram,[6] with ΠΑΤΡΙΚ ΚΑΙ ΕΞΑΡ in the angles of the cross.

Now it is obvious that the legend on Charles's seal, XPE PROTEGE, is a translation of the words contained in the monogram on the Byzantine *bulla*; but as his seal was a single-faced wax seal, he could not insert in it the cross which was the

---

[1] *Neues Archiv der Gesellschaft für ältere Deutsche Geschichtskunde*, xxx (1905), 703 f.

[2] *Ibid.* xxxi (1906), 517; cf. *Archiv für Urkundenforschung*, i (1908), 360 n.

[3] See G. Schlumberger, *Sigillographie de l'Empire Byzantin* (1884), pp. 31, 211 ff.

[4] See A. Salinas, 'Sigilli Diplomatici Italo-Greci', in the *Periodico di Numismatica e Sfragistica per la Storia d'Italia*, iii (1871), 266, and plate xi. 2, 3; Schlumberger, p. 515.

[5] I write καί for the abbreviation S which appears on the seal.

[6] Salinas, plate xi. 4. Ficoroni, *de Plumbeis Antiquorum Numismatibus* (1750), cap. xiv. 3, read this monogram as ΘΕΟΤΟΚΟC.

characteristic feature of his original.[1] He therefore caused this
to be written alongside of the seal and made it the basis of a
monogram, arranging the letters of KAROLVS on the arms and in
the centre of the cross. Thus, it would seem, he took as his
model the seal of Theophylact, who was Exarch at the beginning
of the eighth century, or of some subsequent Exarch of whom
no seal is preserved. The employment of the letter K instead of C
is good evidence, as Wolfram observed,[2] that the design was
borrowed from a Greek model: whether, as is probable, that
model was ultimately derived from Asia is immaterial for our
present purpose.

[1] The fact that the cross was not retained in the monogram of Lewis the
Pious shows merely that its significance was forgotten; not, as Lechner thinks
(*op. cit.*, p. 704), that the design was unimportant.

[2] *Op. cit.*, p. 347. The opinion of Sickel, i. 264 n. 4, and Lechner, p. 706, that
the K was adopted because it was more convenient to attach to an arm of the
cross appears unlikely.

THE ALPINE SON-IN-LAW OF EDWARD
THE ELDER[1]

THE continental marriages of the daughters of Edward the Elder present difficulties which have not yet been satisfactorily explained. The earliest author who mentions more than one is Ethelwerd, who wrote in the last quarter of the tenth century and who claimed to be descended from the West Saxon royal line. The preface to his Chronicle is addressed to a certain Matilda, to whom he writes as his kinswoman. She cannot, therefore, be the abbess of Quedlinburg to whom Widukind dedicated his Saxon history, for she was the daughter of Otto the Great by his second marriage with Adelaide the Burgundian. The lady addressed was probably Matilda, abbess of Essen, daughter of Liudolf, Otto's son by his first marriage with Edith.[2] Ethelwerd brings together a string of facts relating to the foreign alliances of various members of the English reigning house. He begins with the marriage of Alfred's daughter Ælfthrythe to Baldwin of Flanders. Then he mentions the daughters of Edward the Elder: first, Eadgyfu married to Charles the Simple; secondly, Eadhild, wife to Hugh, son of Robert, the great duke. Next he says,

Alias vero duas Aedestanus rex tali ratione misit ad Oddonem, ut quae ab eis placuisset, sibi in matrimonium elegisset; cui visa est melior Eadgyde, ex qua tu principium tenes nativitatis; alteram vero subiunxit cuidam regi iuxta Iupitereos montes, de cuius prole nulla nobis notitia extet, tam pro extenso spatio, quam per obruptionem quodam modo temporum: sed vestrum hoc opus est innotescere auribus nostris.[3]

This account agrees with that of Hrotsvit, the nun of Gandersheim, who in her heroic *Gesta Ottonis*, finished in 967, tells us

---

[1] Reprinted from the *English Historical Review*, vol. xxvi (1911). I am greatly indebted to my friend the Rev. W. A. B. Coolidge for advice and for references; but he must not be taken as in any way responsible for my conclusions. The abundant stores of his library at Grindelwald have enabled me to consult works which would not otherwise have been at my disposal, but even with these advantages it is probable that I have overlooked some publications which have appeared since the paper was originally written several years ago.

[2] Dümmler, *Otto der Grosse*, p. 9, n. 2; p. 290, n. 2.

[3] *Monum. Hist. Brit.*, pp. 499 f.

how Henry the Saxon desired to provide a wife for his firstborn
son.

> Trans mare legatos sed transmisit bene cautos
> Gentis ad Anglorum terram sat deliciosam,
> Demandans ut continuo cum munere misso
> Aedwardi regis natam peterent Eaditham.[1]

The English king thereupon sent his sister:

> Necnon germanam secum transmisit Adivam,
> Quae fuit aetatis meriti pariterque minoris;
> Quo sic maiorem prorsus conferret honorem
> Oddoni, nato famosi regis amando,
> Egregiae binas stirpis mittendo puellas,
> Ut sibi quam vellet sponsam licito sociaret.[2]

Otto chose 'Eadit veneranda', but what became of her sister
is not stated. All we have learned from Hrotsvit is that she was
known to Germans, or at least to Germans who wrote Latin
verses, as Adiva.

For a full account of the alliances of the nine daughters of
Edward the Elder we have to pass on to the twelfth century and
the *Gesta Regum* of William of Malmesbury. William plainly
made use of the account given by Ethelwerd, but he seems also
in dealing with the reign of Athelstan to have incorporated a
good deal of what he found *in quodam volumine vetusto*.[3] Bishop
Stubbs takes this to be 'a poetical life or panegyric' on Athelstan,
of which no trace has since been discovered.[4] Whatever be his
authority, William's statements are unusually precise, although
it is manifest that he was ill informed as to the names and
relationships of some of the continental princes whom he
mentions. There are three passages in the *Gesta Regum* which
bear on the subject. Of these the first is introduced incidentally
in an account of the contemporary foreign history; the second
contains the genealogy of Edward's family by his second and
third wives; and the third forms part of the narrative of the
reign of Athelstan. I place the three accounts in parallel columns.

§ 112	§ 126	§ 135
Huic [Conrado] successit filius Henricus, qui misit ad Athelstanum regem Anglorum pro dua-	Tulit [Edwardus] ex illa [Elfleda] sex filias, Edfledam, Edgivam, Ethelhildam, Ethildam, Edgitham, Elfgivam. ... Edgifam dedit pater Carolo	[Edelstanus] perpenso consilio, quod quatuor sorores haberet, in quibus praeter aetatis discrimen

[1] *Gesta Ottonis*, 74–7, ed. P. von Winterfeld, 1902.   [2] *Ibid.*, pp. 112–17.
[3] *Gesta Regum*, § 132.   [4] *Ibid.*, ii. pref., p. lxi.

bus sororibus suis Aldgitha et Edgitha; quarum posteriorem filio suo Othoni collocavit, alteram cuidam duci iuxta Alpes nuptum dedit.

regi . . .; Ethildam frater Ethelstanus Hugoni, Edgitham et Elfgivam idem germanus misit Henrico Alamannorum imperatori, quarum secundam Othoni filio ille locavit, alteram cuidam duci iuxta Alpes. Suscepit etiam ex tertia uxore, Edgiva vocabulo, . . . filias duas, Edburgam et Edgivam. . . . Edgivam . . . coniunxit frater Ethelstanus Lodowico Aquitanorum principi.

nihil de formae gratia dissideret, duas postulanti Caesari misit . . . Tertiam legitima copula sortitus est comparem Lodovicus Aquitanorum princeps, de genere Caroli magni superstes. Quartam . . . Hugo rex Francorum per nuntios a germano expetiit.

It is important to notice that, in § 126, William of Malmesbury expressly assigns the marriage of the wife of Charles the Simple to the reign of Edward the Elder, and those of the four younger sisters to that of Athelstan, who came to the throne in 925. The correctness of the former statement is confirmed by the fact that Charles the Simple's first wife, Frederuna, died early in 916 or 917, and that Louis IV (d'Outremer), his son by Edgiva, was born in 920 or 921. That the marriage took place before 919 may be inferred from the silence of Flodoard, whose Annals begin in that year.[1] In like manner, the accuracy of William's date for the marriage of Edith with Otto the Great is certain, and we may not unreasonably accept his evidence on this point in regard to the other three marriages.[2] It is plain, however, that in § 126

[1] See A. Eckel, *Charles le Simple*, p. 104 (1899).

[2] Similarly the facts that William assigns the younger Edgiva to Edward's third marriage, and states that it was by Athelstan, that is, not before 925, that she was wedded to Lewis, prince of the Aquitanians, *de genere Caroli magni superstes*, hardly permit us to identify this prince with the deposed Emperor Lewis III, who died in 928, as Bishop Stubbs did (pref. to William of Malmesbury, *Gesta Regum*, ii, pp. lii, liii). But it is surely impossible to maintain that 'the king near the mountains of Jupiter' of Ethelwerd is a different person from 'the duke near the Alps' of William whom Dr. Stubbs accepted as Alberic. Nor does 'Lewis, prince of the Aquitanians' appear a likely designation for the Emperor Lewis, though the reference to Charles the Great may point to a confusion in William's mind of two distinct persons; in other words, he may have found authority for a marriage with a certain Lewis of Aquitaine, and have wrongly identified him with his namesake the ex-emperor. According to the *Art de vérifier les dates*, pt. 2, x. 93 (ed. 1818), Ebles Manzer, count of Poitou, married as his third wife Adèle or Alaine, daughter of Edward the Elder. There is a discrepancy in the account given by Ademar of Chabannes. In one place he says that Ebles married *Adelam, filiam Rosi Rotomagensis*, that is, the daughter of Rollo or Rolf the Norman (*Chron.*, pp. 143 f., ed. J. Chavanon, 1897); but in the earlier recension of his Chronicle, preserved only in a fragment, he makes Ebles's father, Ranulf II, marry Adelina, daughter of Ruinus, by whom he means Rollo (p. 198).

William has inadvertently transposed *Edgitham et Elfgivam*: there is no doubt about the name of Otto the Great's queen. In § 112, however, where her name is given correctly, her sister appears as *Aldgitha*. It must be left uncertain whether Hrotsvit's form *Adiva* represents Elfgiva or Aldgitha, or whether William became confused among the numerous similar names of the sisters, Elfleda, Ethelhilda, Ethilda, Edgitha, Elfgiva, Edburga, and Edgiva.

Adiva, if we may adopt this name for convenience, was sent with Edith to Germany in 928. Edith at once married Otto and bore him her only son in the following year. Adiva, the younger sister (as Hrotsvit expressly and Ethelwerd by implication describe her), may have been no older than thirteen or fourteen. Ethelwerd's language makes it clear that he never heard of her returning to England, and the presumption is that she stayed on at the German court until she found a husband. She was married, Ethelwerd says, *cuidam regi iuxta Iupitereos montes*, in other words, to a king whose dominions lay near the *mons Iovis*, or the Great St. Bernard. He appears as 'a duke near the Alps' twice over in William of Malmesbury. Who was this husband?

1. The English editor of Ethelwerd, following the *Art de vérifier les dates*,[1] made him the deposed Emperor Lewis III, the Blind,[2] and supposed Charles 'Constantinus' to be the issue of this marriage. Charles, however, was of an age to take part in legal business in 923,[3] and his father died in the summer of 928.[4] Waitz prudently rejected this identification, though he was unable to propose another with confidence.[5]

2. Dümmler believed that he had discovered the husband in a certain Burgundian Duke Alberic,[6] whom Bishop Stubbs thought to be a very obscure person.[7] His pedigree has since been worked out by M. Poupardin.[8] He was a son of Majolus,

[1] Pt. 2, x. 379, where the wife is called *Edgive*.

[2] Bishop Stubbs inclined to this identification of Ethelwerd's 'king near the mountains of Jupiter': pref. to William of Malmesbury, *Gesta Regum*, ii, p. liv, n. 2. But see above, p. 117, n. 2.

[3] *Chartes de Cluny*, 242, vol. i, 233 f. (1876).

[4] R. Poupardin, *Le Royaume de Provence*, p. 226 (1901).

[5] *Jahrbücher der deutschen Geschichte unter Heinrich I*, p. 135, n. 4 (ed. 3, 1885).

[6] *Otto der Grosse*, p. 9, n. 3.

[7] W. of Malmesbury, *Gesta Regum*, ii, pref., p. lii.

[8] *Le Royaume de Bourgogne*, pp. 213 ff. (1907).

viscount of Narbonne, and married Etola[1] the daughter of
Raculf, count of Mâcon, whom he succeeded in that office. The
document on which Dümmler relied was printed 'from the
original' by Mabillon[2] and is dated in 958. According to it
Burchardus miles, filius Alberici ducis, gave to the monastery
of Brai the body of St. Pavatius the Confessor, which *ex Anglia
attulit cum aliquibus religiosis quos avunculus eius rex Aedredus
ei dederat de coenobio de Persora*. Unfortunately the charter
must be rejected as a forgery.[3] In the final clauses there is no
separation of act and date; and the day of the month is given
in the modern way and not in accordance with the Roman
calendar. It would be interesting if we could trace the origin of
this Pershore legend. C. von Kalckstein wrote confidently in
support of the identification involved in it, but he had no
authority beyond the charter itself, and he took the name *Adiva*
which he assigned to Burchard's mother simply from Hrotsvit,
who does not mention the marriage at all.[4]

3. But even if we were to admit the genuineness of the charter,
the fact that Alberic held lands in the country of Besançon[5]
would not make him a duke near the Alps, far less a king near
the mountains of Jupiter. The only person who satisfies this
description is Conrad the Peaceable, king of Burgundy; and he
was actually resident at Otto the Great's court from about 937 to
942. He must have been some years younger than Adiva, since
he is called *filius parvus* by Flodoard in 937.[6] He cannot have
been born earlier than 922, and was probably not born until
some six years or more later,[7] while Adiva may have been more
than twenty-two or twenty-three years old in 937. Of few
sovereigns whose reigns cover a large number of years is the
personal history so obscure as that of Conrad of Burgundy, and
he was king for fifty-six years. According to the *Art de vérifier
les dates*[8] he was twice married, first to Adelana or Adela, whose

---

[1] The name appears in various forms: see Poupardin, *ibid.*, p. 213 n. One is
Tholosana, found in a Cluny document of 935 (*Chartes de Cluny*, 432, vol. i.
420 f.). The charter was wrongly assigned by Guichenon, *Bibl. Sebus.*, p. 168,
to 899: see the *Art de vérifier les dates*, pt. 2, xi. 13. A pedigree is given by H.
Bresslau, *Konrad II*, ii. 36, n. 5 (1884).

[2] *Acta Sanctorum O. S. B.*, saec. v. 245; Bouquet, *Recueil des Historiens*, ix.
622.   [3] So too F. Lot, *Les Derniers Carolingiens*, p. 59, n. 2.

[4] *Gesch. des französichen Königthums unter den ersten Capetingern*, i. 256, 298,
321 (1877).   [5] Poupardin, *Le Royaume de Bourgogne*, pp. 214 f.

[6] *Annales*, p. 68, ed. P. Lauer, 1906.

[7] Cf. Poupardin, *Le Royaume de Bourgogne*, p. 66 and n. 4.

[8] Pt. 2, x. 386.

origin is unknown, and secondly to Matilda, daughter of Louis IV of France. Now, since Matilda cannot have been born before 940, and was possibly not born until 948,[1] and since Conrad's daughter Gisela, who married Henry the Wrangler, duke of Bavaria, had herself a son in 973, it is evident that Matilda was not Gisela's mother.[2] ⸱The earlier marriage is attested by a charter for the monastery of Cluny, dated 23 March 963,[3] whereby Conrad grants lands to the abbey *pro remedio animę nostrae Adelane videlicet reginae et infantum nostrorum.*[4] Matilda must therefore have married him after this date and before 966, when she is definitely mentioned as his wife.[5] Hence it seems to follow that Gisela, the mother of the Emperor Henry II, and mother-in-law of King Stephen of Hungary, was Conrad's daughter by this Adelana.[6] Her name is known only through this single charter,[7] preserved in a relatively late copy; so that little stress can be laid on its precise form. But putting it side by side with the daughter of Edward the Elder who married the king near the mountains of Jupiter—the Elfgiva, or Aldgitha, who married the duke near the Alps—we can hardly be rash in venturing upon an identification; though of course the fact that Adelana is only known to us, as it were by chance, through a single incidental reference, leaves it possible that Conrad had yet an earlier wife, who died before his marriage with Adelana.

4. An alternative suggestion, which at first seemed tempting, I have been compelled after careful consideration to reject. There is evidence that Conrad had at one time a mistress, concerning whom there has been a good deal of discussion. For a long time it was maintained that she was Adelana herself, whom he subsequently married. But this has been shown to be impossible, because she afterwards entered lawful wedlock while Conrad was alive and married. It can be proved from a series of charters, first that she had a son by Conrad, Burchard, who became archbishop of Lyons, and secondly that she had several

---

[1] Poupardin, *Le Royaume de Bourgogne*, p. 384, n. 1, p. 386, n. 4.

[2] Siegfried Hirsch rightly saw that a previous marriage must be assumed, but thought there was no evidence of the fact or of the first wife's name: *Jahrbücher des Deutschen Reichs unter Heinrich II*, p. 87, n. 3 (1862).

[3] The twenty-sixth year of Conrad's reign.

[4] *Chartes de Cluny*, 1152, vol. ii. 242 (1880).

[5] *Historiae Patriae Monumenta*, Chart. i. 210.

[6] Poupardin, *Le Royaume de Bourgogne*, p. 385, n. 2; cf. p. 384, n. 2.

[7] The *Art de vérifier les dates, ubi supra*, also refers to Cluny charters of 937 and 944, but I have sought them in vain.

children by her husband Anselm, who was apparently count of Nyon.

a. Hugh of Flavigny, a writer of the beginning of the twelfth century, records the appointment to the archbishopric of Lyons of Burchard, *Rodulfi regis frater, Conradi ex concubina filius,* and adds that he obtained the see *in infantia.*[1] The date will be 978 or 979, since a document of 984, in the twelfth indiction, is in the archbishop's sixth year.[2] That Burchard was brother to Rodulf III is attested by several documents. One will suffice. On 28 July 1011, in a grant to the church of St. Maurice at Vienne, the king speaks of *Burchardo Lugdunensi archiepiscopo fratre nostro dilecto.*[3]

b. A document of 1005, preserved in a contemporary copy, contains a deed of exchange between Burchard, archbishop of Lyons, and Anselm, bishop of Aosta, wherein the latter grants to Burchard certain land at *Oponlongis infra comitatum Ottingin vocatum, hoc est quicquid inibi habere visus est ex parte matr*s̀ *sue Aldiud, quod rex Chuonradus ei prebuit.*[4] Another document was confirmed in 1002 at a *placitum* attended among others by *Anselmus pater Anselmi episcopi* and by *Anselmus episcopus. Augustiniensis;*[5] and a second document of 1002 bears the *signum donni archipresulis Burcardi et fratris sui Anselmi episcopi.*[6] Since, then, Burchard son of Conrad, and Anselm son of Anselm, were brothers, it follows that Aldiud was mother to both of them; and the deed of 1005 shows that she received property from Conrad. Now Bishop Anselm had also a brother, likewise named Burchard, who became archbishop of Vienne. There exists a grant by this Burchard and his brother Udolric, to the church of St. Peter without the Walls at Vienne, of certain vineyards in the territory of Geneva, *pro remedio animarum nostrarum vel pro genitore nostro Anselmo sive pro genitrice nostra Aaldui.*[7] The date is 19 August 1017.[8] From a

---

[1] *Chron. Virdun., Monum. Germ. hist.,* viii. 367.

[2] *Gall. Christ.* iv, instr. p. 6 (ed. 1876).

[3] *Cartul. de l'Abb. de Saint-André-le-Bas,* ed. U. Chevalier (Lyons, 1869), p. 251, app., no. 41*.   [4] *Hist. Patr. Monum.,* Chart. ii. 91 (1853).

[5] L. Cibrario and D. C. Promis, *Documenti, Sigilli, e Monete* (Turin, 1833), p. 7.   [6] *Hist. Patr. Monum.,* Chart. ii. 84. ·

[7] *Cartul. de Saint-André-le-Bas,* p. 256, app. no. 47*. In the document of 1011 cited above, n. 3, King Rodulf speaks of both Burchards as archbishops and as his brothers. Odolric also appears as brother of Burchard of Lyons in an undated charter printed in the *Hist. Patr. Monum.,* Chart. ii. 73.

[8] The twenty-fifth year of Rodulf.

combination of the evidence here given it results that Alduid or Aaldui was the mother by Conrad of Burchard of Lyons, and by Anselm of Burchard of Vienne, Ulric, and Anselm bishop of Aosta.[1] Her name has been modernized as Aldein by Carutti,[2] and as Aldvige by Gerbaix Sonnaz;[3] but neither of these forms is authorized by the documents from which our sole information is derived. Aldiud should probably be corrected into Alduid.[4] It is very tempting to see in Alduid or Aaldui a corruption of an Anglo-Saxon name, and to identify the bearer of it with the daughter of Edward the Elder. But chronological reasons forbid it. Burchard of Lyons lived on to 1031, his half-brother of Vienne to 1029, and Anselm to 1034. They cannot be supposed to be the children of a lady whose birth took place about 915, unless their longevity was, for the Middle Ages, quite unexampled; and if the elder Burchard was made archbishop *in infantia* in 978 the dates of birth of the whole family will hardly be reconcilable with the age of the presumed Anglo-Saxon mother. One regrets to abandon the identification, because, if correct, it would have led to an interesting genealogical consequence; for Ancilia, the daughter of Anselm and Aldiud, married Humbert aux Blanches-Mains, and was by him the ancestress of the house of Savoy, which would thus be descended in a left-handed manner from our Anglo-Saxon kings.

[1] So Cibrario, *Storia della Monarchia di Savoia*, i (Turin, 1840), p. 11, n. 2; G. de Manteyer, *Les Origines de la Maison de Savoie en Bourgogne (École Française de Rome, Mélanges d'Archéologie et d'Histoire*, xix. 465–84, 1899).

[2] *Il Conte Umberto I e il Re Ardoino* (ed. Turin, 1888), p. 301; *Regesta Comitum Sabaudorum* (Turin, 1889), p. 3.

[3] *Studi storici sul Contado di Savoia* (Turin, 1883), i. 113 note.

[4] G. de Manteyer, p. 540.

THE SEE OF MAURIENNE AND THE VALLEY OF SUSA[1]

I

THE history of the connexion between Maurienne and the valley of Susa is a good illustration of the tenacity with which the rulers north or west of the Alps endeavoured to maintain an outlet on the Italian side. And as ecclesiastical and civil boundaries in early times usually coincided, the history of the eastern limits of the diocese of St. John of Maurienne throws light also upon the history of that part of Burgundy which became in course of time the county of Savoy. Its investigation, however, is complicated by the fact that a large number of the documents upon which reliance has been placed are certainly spurious; and no single writer on the subject, so far as I am aware, has been on his guard against all the forged evidence that has accumulated round it. The influence of the fabrications of the church of Vienne has not been finally extirpated; the forged charter of King Boso (887) is still appealed to as an authority;[2] and the spuriousness of the diploma of the Emperor Conrad II (1038) has not yet everywhere been recognized.

In Roman times Maurienne and Susa, at the opposite ends of the pass of Mont Cenis, formed a single administrative unit, that of the Cottian Alps; and Susa, the residence of the prefect, was the chief town.[3] When, however, about 574 the Lombards ceded Susa to the Merovingian king Guntchramn, the whole district became Burgundian. This transference of government was accompanied by an ecclesiastical change, and the territory which had been dependent upon the see of Turin was made into a new diocese with a bishopric at St. John of Maurienne. The date of the foundation of the bishopric cannot be exactly fixed. Gregory of Tours appears to have been ignorant of its existence; for he tells us how a woman going forth (on a pilgrimage) from the city (*urbs*) of Maurienne obtained a thumb of St. John the

---

[1] Reprinted from the *English Historical Review*, vol. xxxi (1916).

[2] Duchesne, *Fastes épiscopaux de l'ancienne Gaule*, i. 242, 2nd ed., 1907.

[3] Gregory of Tours mentions that in 574 a 'magister militum a parte imperatoris in hac urbe residerit': *Hist. Franc.* iv. 44. Cf. A. Gros, in *Travaux de la Société d'Histoire et d'Archéologie de Maurienne*, 2nd ser., iv. 2 (1908), p. 290.

Baptist, and how afterwards Rufus, bishop of Turin, *quia locus ille Mauriennensis ad Taurinensem quondam urbem pertenebat*, was urged without success to make a claim on the relic.[1] Rufus, bishop of Turin, is otherwise unknown; but we must infer from the narrative that Maurienne had a church, though it may be too much to infer from the word *urbs* in the opening sentence that it had a bishop. The earliest evidence for the see is found in two letters of Gregory the Great written probably in July 599. In one of these, addressed to Bishop Syagrius of Autun,[2] he made mention of the loss which Ursicinus, bishop of Turin, had suffered *in parochiis suis* lying within the Frankish borders, and stated that another bishop had been set up there.[3] The second, dealing with the same matter, is addressed to Kings Theodebert and Theodoric.[4] In both the Pope desired that reparation should be made to Ursicinus. Nevertheless the new see continued undisturbed, but its ecclesiastical relations were not determined for a very long time.

In order to understand the subsequent history we must go back more than a century, to the time when Leo the Great in 450 attempted to settle an old dispute as to the respective jurisdictions of the metropolitical sees of Arles and Vienne.[5] Leo assigned to the latter the four bishoprics of Valence, Grenoble, Geneva, and Tarentaise;[6] and in 513 the decree was confirmed by Symmachus.[7] Notwithstanding this, in 517 Bishop Avitus of Vienne summoned to his council at Épaone a number of other bishops as well. A few years later a change in the political boundaries deprived Vienne of all the southern dioceses, and in 523 its province included only Die and Viviers besides the four authorized by Popes Leo and Symmachus; in other words, the province of Arles recovered an extension corresponding with

[1] *Liber in Gloria Martyrum*, xiii, ed. B. Krusch, 1885 [xiv, ed. Ruinart].

[2] Epist. ix. 214 [115], ed. L. M. Hartmann, 1899.

[3] The argument of Luigi Cibrario, in the *Memorie della Reale Accademia delle Scienze di Torino* (*Scienze Mor., Stor., e Filolog.*), ser. ii, tom. viii (1846), 2–6, that the Pope's protest did not relate to Maurienne itself but only to the Italian valleys of Susa and Lanzo, will not bear examination. Cf. F. Savio, *Gli antichi Vescovi d'Italia, Il Piemonte*, pp. 225–8 (Turin, 1898).

[4] Epist. ix. 226 [116].

[5] Compare for the following W. Gundlach's paper in the *Neues Archiv der Gesellschaft für ältere Deutsche Geschichtskunde*, xiv (1889), 330 ff.

[6] Epist. lxvi. 2, ed. Ballerini, in Migne's reprint (Epist. Arelat. xiii, in *Monum. Germ. hist., Epist.* iii (1892), 21) [Jaffé, *Reg.* no. 450].

[7] Epist. xiv. 2, in Thiel, *Epist. Roman. Pontif. genuinae*, i (1868), 723 (Epist. Arelat. xxv, p. 36) [Jaffé, no. 765].

the Roman Provincia as it was before its annexation to the Frankish kingdom.[1] When, however, the question of the limits of the two provinces was raised at the council of Frankfort in 794,[2] the letters of Leo and Symmachus with others were read, and Vienne was thus once more declared to possess four suffragans; Die and Viviers passed again to Arles. It was a matter, we should observe, solely between Arles and Vienne, and the evidence produced related strictly to the old controversy.[3] But a new subject of contention arose with respect to the claims raised by Tarentaise, Embrun, and Aix, which aspired to metropolitical rank. Of these we are only concerned with Tarentaise, which was one of the suffragans assigned to Vienne. It seems that the council had before it a copy of the *Notitia Galliarum*, originally drawn up about 400, in which Tarentaise and Sion were ranged outside the Viennensis, in the province of Alpes Graiae et Poeninae.[4] The matter was referred to Rome, and Tarentaise apparently secured the position at which it aimed, for it is mentioned as a *metropolis* in the will of Charles the Great.[5] In 867 Nicholas I, while declaring the bishop to be subject to the primate of Vienne, allowed him jurisdiction over three dioceses.[6] The names of these three are not given; they were Maurienne,[7] Aosta, and Sion. In 878 Maurienne was definitely recognized by John VIII as suffragan to Tarentaise.[8]

The bull of Nicholas I is generally understood to have directed a return to the arrangement laid down by Leo the Great,[9] but the provisions added with reference to Tarentaise appear to stand in unmistakable connexion with a text of the *Notitia Galliarum*, which has been further modified so as to rank the four sees of Tarentaise, Sion, Maurienne, and Aosta, as distinct from, and at the same time dependent upon, Vienne: *huic [provinciae Viennensi] sociata extitit provincia Alpium Graiarum*

---

[1] Duchesne, i. 135 ff.

[2] Concil. Francof. c. viii (*Monum. Germ. Hist. Concil.* ii (1904), 187).

[3] Maurienne therefore, it may be presumed, was not under discussion.

[4] Duchesne, i. 80; Mommsen, *Chron. min.* (*Monum. Germ. Hist.*), i (1892), 598 f.

[5] Einhard, *Vita Karoli*, xxxiii.

[6] Epist. cliii, *Monum. Germ. Hist., Epist.* vi (1912), 668 [Jaffé, no. 2876].

[7] In the *Neues Archiv*, xv (1890), 63 n., Gundlach says, 'Maurienne war nachweislich noch zu Nicolaus' I. Zeit der Vienner Kirche nicht unterworfen.' This is not true: it was subject, though not immediately.

[8] Epist. cxvii, *Monum. Germ. Hist., Epist.* vii (1912), 107 [Jaffé, no. 3150].

[9] Duchesne, i. 213.

et Penninarum.[1] For this reason it seems to me that the commencement of the first productive era—the manufacturing age —in the chancery of Vienne has been placed rather too late. Instead of being between 878 and 885,[2] the date should be a little before 867. The archbishops were resolved to establish their superiority to Arles, and incidentally to consolidate their jurisdiction in the eastern regions. They began by redacting the *Notitia.* The manuscript in which the sentence quoted occurs[3] contains Pope Adrian's collection of canons written in the ninth century. At least as early as 869 it belonged to the church of Vienne; not long after 915 it passed to Le-Puy-en-Velay in the time of Bishop Adalard, who occupied the see from 915 to 926; and before it left Vienne it received some additions.[4]

One of these new elements, which was inserted not earlier than 907, but before 15 January 915,[5] contained a narrative of the foundation of the see of Maurienne, in which the account given by Gregory of Tours was revised in such a manner as to show that that see was already in his time in the province of Vienne. This narrative is known as the *Auctoritas Moriensis.*[6] It tells how a woman named Tigris, *ex territorio Mauriginense orta*, discovered certain relics of St. John the Baptist in the East, and resolved to erect a church in his honour at Morienna. King Guntchramn then sent men to build the church and

---

[1] The sentence appears as a marginal insertion in a text of the *Notitia* added in a later hand in the Phillipps MS. 1745 (now at Berlin), which is of the eighth century: see Mommsen, *Chron. min.* (*Monum. Germ. Hist.*), i (1891–2), 580, 582. In the Paris MS., Lat. 1452, which is a copy of it, the words are, *Ad quam etiam provincia Alpium Graiarum et Penninarum pertinet: ibid.*, pp. 580, 599. Monsignor Duchesne, p. 214, prints the text of the latter more clearly than Mommsen.

[2] Georges de Manteyer, *La Provence du premier au douzième siècle*, 1908, p. 82.

[3] Bibl. Nat., MS. Lat. 1452.   [4] See Manteyer, pp. 487–98.

[5] *Ibid.*, p. 495. According to L. Cibrario and D. C. Promis, *Documenti, Sigilli e Monete*, Turin, 1835, pp. 323 f., a copy of the *Auctoritas*, written in the tenth century, is preserved in the bishop's archives at Maurienne: it is there preceded by a fragment entitled *carta de Maurienna et de Seusia*, which is substantially an abstract of those parts of it which describe the foundation of Maurienne, the annexation to it of Susa, and the subjection of the territory *ad ius Viennensis ecclesiae sicut in eiusdem auctoritatis scr[ipto] legitur.* It is also printed by Cardinal Billiet, *Chartes du Diocèse de Maurienne* (Chambéry, 1861), no. 2, pp. 7 ff. Cf. C. Troya, *Cod. dipl. Longobard.*, Naples, 1845, p. 39. Gundlach's suggestion (*Neues Archiv*, xv. 63 note) that the *Auctoritas* was composed towards the end of the eleventh century is on all grounds excluded.

[6] It has been frequently printed: e.g. in the appendix to Ruinart's edition of Gregory of Tours, p. 1342; in Billiet, pp. 8 f.; in *Gallia Christiana*, xvi (1865), 613 f.; and by B. Krusch, *Passiones Vitaeque Sanctorum Aevi Merovingici* (*Monum. Germ. Hist.*), 1896, pp. 533 f.

ordered the bishop of Vienne, *ad cuius diocesim pertinebat locus*, to consecrate it. This story combines the narrative of Gregory of Tours with a notice about St. John the Baptist taken from the Chronicle of Ado of Vienne,[1] and it makes several additions. First, it gives the name of the woman who brought the relics; and it is, as M. de Manteyer remarks,[2] hardly an accident that Tigris was a lady who effected an exchange of property with the bishop of Vienne in 910 (or perhaps 900).[3] Secondly, it makes the specific statement that Maurienne was situate in the diocese of Vienne, whereas Gregory tells the story in relation to Turin.[4] And thirdly, it states that King Guntchramn placed the city of Susa with all the inhabitants of the district under the jurisdiction of Maurienne.[5] Moreover, it names Ysicius (Hesychius) as bishop of Vienne, though this prelate's successor, Namatius, died in 559. The *Auctoritas* proceeds from the same mint which produced the earlier parts of the *Epistolae Viennenses*. We can trace these forgeries in the time of Otramnus, who was bishop of Vienne from 878 to 885; and they were completed in their first stage under Bishop Alexander, who was chancellor to the Emperor Lewis III about 912.[6] Among them is a spurious bull of Sergius III of 18 June 908, which subjects to Vienne not only Maurienne but also Susa and other places on the Italian side of the Alps.[7] Whether this is derived from the *Auctoritas*, or the *Auctoritas* made use of the bull, is immaterial for the present purpose; but it may be presumed that the bull was fabricated after the Pope's death on 23 May 911.

For a century after this the history of the see of Maurienne remains obscure; but in 1037 the influence of the forgeries becomes apparent.[8] Gundlach, whose critical work on the *Epistolae Viennenses* is of remarkable value, maintained that the entire series of letters was forged under the direction of

---

[1] Migne, cxxiii. 103.   [2] pp. 497 f.

[3] Monsignor Duchesne, however (p. 240 n.), thinks that it may represent a genuine local tradition.

[4] The late M. A. Longnon inadvertently attributed the name 'Tygris' to Gregory and spoke of the mention of Vienne as an 'inexactitude': *La Géographie de la Gaule au sixième siècle*, 1878, pp. 430 f. Both these statements conceal the real issue.

[5] 'Ad quam ecclesiam Maurigennensem . . . Seusiam civitatem iamdudum ab Italis acceptam cum omnibus pagensibus ipsius loci subiectam fecit.'

[6] Manteyer, p. 82.   [7] *Monum. Germ. Hist., Epist.* iii. 101 [Jaffé, no. 3544].

[8] See the charter of Archbishop Leger, in the *Cartulaire de Saint-Barnard-de-Romans*, 2nd ed., 1898, no. 79, pp. 89–94, where the bishops of Tarentaise, Sion, and Maurienne appear among the witnesses. Cf. Manteyer, p. 86.

Archbishop Guy (1088–1119), afterwards Pope Calixtus II ;[1] but we have seen that part of the collection is two centuries earlier. A further interesting trace of the process of manufacture was discovered recently in some notices relative to the archbishops of Vienne written on a blank page of a manuscript Bible now in the town library at Bern.[2] This has been minutely examined by M. de Manteyer, who gives reasons for dating the fragment about 1038 :[3] in any case, there can be little question that it was compiled under Leodegarius, or Leger, who was archbishop from 1030 to 1070 ; and a remarkable coincidence in a charter relating to St. Barnard of Romans, dated 1068, which speaks of Leger as the sixty-first bishop, makes it probable that the last notices in it were added in that year.[4] Very likely it was about the same time that a spurious bull of Leo IX was produced, giving Vienne authority over seven provinces of Gaul.[5] It may therefore be taken as proved that Gundlach was in error in maintaining that the whole series of Vienne forgeries was due to Archbishop Guy. What he did was to complete the collection, and then in 1119 and 1120, as Pope, to confirm all the privileges of Vienne vouched by these documents ; so that it was by his action that Die and Viviers were finally detached from Arles, and Maurienne from Tarentaise. Gundlach thought that these last bulls were also spurious ; but the originals of them are in fact preserved to this day in the archives at Grenoble.[6] Hence, although Archbishop Guy may not have been the actual fabricator of any documents in favour of his church, it was his authority as Pope which gave the province of Vienne the extended jurisdiction which it retained until modern times.

---

[1] *Neues Archiv*, xv. 101 f.

[2] MS. A. 9, fo. 321*b*–323. See Duchesne, i. 163–78.

[3] *Bulletin de la Société de Statistique de l'Isère*, 4th ser., vii (1903), 156–73, 188.

[4] *Cartul. de Saint-Barnard*, no. 148, p. 171.

[5] *Monum. Germ. Hist.*, *Epist.* iii (1892), 102 [Jaffé, no. 4285]; cf. Manteyer, *La Provence*, p. 86.

[6] The two privileges, of 28 June 1119 and 25 February 1120, are printed by M. U. Robert, *Le Bullaire de Calixte II*, i. 36 f., 214 f. (1891). They agree word for word, except that the later document omits the grant of rights 'in ecclesia beati Antonii' and adds an exemption from the authority of any legate except a cardinal or one sent *a latere*; it grants the archbishop the same rights over the churches consecrated by him after his election to the Papacy as in others ; and it forbids laymen to have houses or commit offences within the bounds of a monastery. Gundlach gives only the second bull [Jaffé, no. 6822], from printed sources, *Epistolae*, iii (*Monum. Germ. Hist.*), 108 f.: his volume is dated 1892, but the preface 1888. The varieties of reading are few and quite unimportant.

II

Hitherto we have considered only the ecclesiastical position of the see of St. John of Maurienne, as presumably separated from the diocese of Turin in the sixth century, subjected in course of time to the archbishop of Tarentaise, and ultimately placed by the help of forged documents in immediate dependence on Vienne. A distinct question is that of the relations of Maurienne towards the city and district of Susa on the Italian side of the Alps. There is no doubt that about the year 574 Susa passed from the Lombard to the Frankish kingdom and became a part of Burgundy. But how far down the valley of Susa the jurisdiction of Maurienne extended is not completely established. When the monastery of Novalesa on the Italian slope of Mont Cenis was founded in 726 by Abbo, son of Felix, a great Burgundian landowner, the grant was made with the consent of the clergy of Maurienne and Susa.[1] But in regard to the further parts of the valley, the rights of Maurienne had to be substantiated by means of forgery. A document was developed out of a probably genuine charter of King Boso, dated in 887, which conferred the village of Hermillon on the church of Maurienne: this modest text was interpolated by a clause declaring the church of St. Mary at Susa with the churches subject to it to be dependent on Maurienne; and mention was made of Asmund, *Secusinae civitatis vel Maurianorum episcopus*, and of his brother Leotman, bishop of Cremona. Why the forger should have given his bishops names which are not known in the sees referred to, or indeed in any other sees of Christendom, it is hard to understand.[2] Still, the charter, which is inserted at the end of a ninth-century Pontifical of the archbishop of Aix, in a hand of *c.* 1100, now preserved at

---

[1] The document even speaks of the *ecclesia Mauriennata et Segucina* in the singular: *Monumenta Novaliciensia vetustiora*, i. 7 (Turin, 1898). It mentions the 'counsel' of Bishop Walchunus, and if the Novalesa Chronicler be correct (*ibid.* ii (1901), 108, 223) in stating that he was archbishop of Embrun and uncle to Abbo, he may be named simply because he had a proprietary interest in some of the estates granted and took a personal share in the foundation of the monastery (see i. 34, 35). But it has also been conjectured that he was bishop of Maurienne. Other sees have been proposed for him: see Count Cipolla's note to i. 7.

[2] An imaginary Asmund, bishop of Ivrea, has found his way into Ughelli's list (*Italia sacra*, iv. 1066, ed. 1719) from the forged will of Bishop Atto of Vercelli, 945 (Migne, cxxxiv. 894): it does not appear in the genuine will of 948 (*ibid.*, pp. 22 ff.). I cannot explain Ughelli's date, 938.

Carpentras,[1] has been often printed,[2] and until lately never suspected.[3]

A more elaborate concoction is the Life of St. Tigris or Tigria, otherwise called St. Thecla, which is printed in the *Acta Sanctorum* under 25 June.[4] The greater part of this is compounded out of the account of the unnamed *mulier a Maurienna urbe progrediens*, given by Gregory of Tours,[5] and the more detailed narrative contained in the *Auctoritas Moriensis*, but the particulars are greatly embellished. Some of the changes are significant. We may note that where Gregory says,

Locus ille Mauriennensis ad Taurinensem quondam urbem pertenebat tempore illo quo Rufus erat episcopus,

the biographer writes,

Locus autem Maurianensis ad Viennensem[6] urbem pertinebat usque ad vallem quae dicitur Cottiana, in qua urbe domnus Rufus, vir religiosus, archiepiscopatus fungebatur officio.

After chapter x the writer deserts Gregory and follows the *Auctoritas* in chapter xi. The remaining three chapters are independent both of Gregory and of the *Auctoritas*. In chapter xiii we seem to be reading not a Life but a letter of edification, 'Haec, fratres carissimi, . . . scripsimus'; and chapter xiv contains an account of the saint's death awkwardly patched on. But chapter xii brings in matter which deserves attention.[7] It contains a record of the boundaries of the diocese of Maurienne, as they were fixed after a dispute between Bishop Leporius and the archbishop of Embrun. Now Leporius of Maurienne was present at the council of Chalon held somewhere between 639 and 654;[8] but the bishops of Embrun were suffragans of Arles, and made

[1] *Catal. des Manuscrits des Bibliothèques publiques*, Départements, Carpentras, i, no. 65, fo. 48*b* (1901). Cardinal Billiet states that the document is not to be found in the bishop's archives at Maurienne: *Chartes du Diocèse de Maurienne*, p. 5.   [2] Thus in the *Recueil des Historiens de la France*, ix. 672.

[3] M. Poupardin thinks it was fabricated in the eleventh century: *Le Royaume de Provence* (1901), p. 111, n. 2, and p. 138.

[4] *Acta Sanctorum, Jun.* v. 73 ff. ; where the Life is said to have been transcribed from a 'Gothic' Missal at Maurienne and sent in 1639 by Duverney, a canon of that church, to Ducange, who gave it to Bolland.

[5] *Liber in Gloria Martyrum*, xiii.

[6] The Bollandists (p. 75) have changed this word into *Taurinensem*, but left *archiepiscopatus* standing.

[7] Since I wrote this I have found that a variant text of chapters xii and xiii is found without the rest of the Life in a manuscript which Besson found among the bishop's archives at Maurienne. See Troya, *Cod. dipl. Longobard.*, p. 36.

[8] *Monum. Germ. Hist., Concilia*, i (ed. F. Maassen, 1893), 213.

no claim to the rank of metropolitan until the council of Frankfort in 794.[1] The delimitation itself, however, seems to be taken from a genuine text. M. de Manteyer thinks that the state of things represented by it agrees with a time subsequent to the will of Abbo of 739, which devised extensive lands to Novalesa,[2] because that document seems to imply that the territory of Briançon ran as far south as the Queyras valley,[3] whereas the Life places the southern border of the diocese of Maurienne 'uno miliario distante a civitatula nomen sibi impositum Rama', that is La Roche de Rame, near the confluence of the Biaysse with the Durance. As for the later limit of time, the eastern boundary is placed 'in loco qui dicitur Vologia', a considerable distance below Susa; this, in M. de Manteyer's opinion, points to a date before 774, because he holds that the region on the Italian side of Mont Cenis was transferred to the Lombard kingdom after its conquest by Charles the Great.[4] This, however, cannot be asserted without further inquiry. We shall see that the valley of Susa long continued, at least in its ecclesiastical aspect, a debatable territory.

The contents of the Life of St. Tigris raise a presumption that it was composed at a time when the rights of the primate of Vienne were endangered by a claim from the Italian side of the Alps. Such an occasion has generally been believed to have arisen when Conrad II, by his putative diploma of 1038, handed over the see of Maurienne bodily to Turin; but the document from which this has been inferred is, as will appear immediately, an unquestionable forgery. M. de Manteyer, not being aware of this, maintained that when in 1046 the bishop of Maurienne made a grant to his chapter, this implied a surrender of his newly-acquired rights by the bishop of Turin.[5] It was natural therefore that he should argue that the time after 1046 was a likely date for the assertion of the claims of Maurienne, and should connect the composition of the Life of St. Tigris with the activity of Archbishop Leger about 1060. This date, in

[1] *Ibid.* ii (1906), 167, c. 8; cf. Duchesne, i. 137.
[2] *Monum. Novalic.* i. 24.   [3] *La Provence*, pp. 172-81.
[4] That it was Frankish in 773 is shown by Charles's diploma of 25 March in that year, wherein he speaks of the valley of Susa as 'in regno nostro': *Diplom. Karolin.* (*Monum. Germ. Hist.*), i. 107 (1906).
[5] 'Les Origines de la Maison de Savoie en Bourgogne', in *Mélanges d'Archéologie et d'Histoire*, xix (1899), 402-5. Cf. Besson, *Mémoires pour l'Histoire ecclésiastique des Diocèses de Genève, Tarentaise, Aoste, Maurienne, et du Décanat de Savoie*, ed. Moutiers, 1871, p. 285.

fact, is perhaps on other grounds the most probable, though one cannot exclude the alternative possibility that the Life was an earlier improved and enlarged version of the *Auctoritas* of 912 which an ingenious redactor tried to amalgamate with the story in Gregory of Tours. A further suggestion was made by Father Fedele Savio[1] that this supposed restoration of the diocese of Maurienne was obtained at the price of the definitive transfer of the valley of Susa to Turin; and this conjecture was stated as an ascertained fact by M. de Manteyer.[2] But as the charter of Conrad is certainly forged, we need not speculate on its consequences.

The supposition that after the conquest of Lombardy by Charles the Great the monastery of Novalesa was incorporated in that kingdom and became at the same time dependent upon the see of Turin is based primarily on some lawsuits affecting that house which were heard at Turin or Pavia. The cases are of 827 and 880,[3] and the earlier of them refers back to an earlier suit (perhaps of 799) before Charles was crowned Emperor. They deal with complaints of certain tenants of Novalesa, but these were all resident at Oulx. The records prove that Oulx in the valley of Bardonnèche was subject to the jurisdiction of Turin,[4] but they say nothing of the ecclesiastical position of Novalesa. Early in the tenth century the monks of Novalesa were driven from their house by the Saracens, who burnt everything in the place,[5] and they took refuge near the church of St. Andrew in Turin. They then established themselves further east at Breme.[6] But when after nearly a hundred years some of them returned to Novalesa, it does not appear that they looked upon themselves as belonging to Turin.[7] On the contrary, the claims of Maurienne are at once reasserted. In 1081, in a docu-

---

[1] *Gli antichi Vescovi d'Italia, Il Piemonte*, pp. 231, 233.

[2] *Op. cit.*, p. 405. In his later work on *La Provence*, p. 182, he considers the valley of Susa to have been taken away from the diocese of Maurienne by Charles the Great.   [3] *Monum. Novalic.* i. 77–83, 90–4.

[4] It is too strong to assert with Dr. Bresslau, 'Zum Bezirk der Grafschaft von Turin gehört nun unzweifelhaft auch das Thal von Susa, die *vallis Segusina*': *Jahrbücher Konrads II*, i. 366 (1879).

[5] *Chron. Novalic.* iv. 24, in *Monum. Novalic.* ii. 236.

[6] See the charter of King Hugh, 929, in *Monum. Novalic.* i. 101 ff.

[7] They are said to have asked the bishop of Ventimiglia to consecrate their church: *Chron. Novalic.* v. 46, *Monum. Novalic.* ii. 279. The statement that in 1007 Bishop Gezo of Turin made a grant of tithes at Novalesa to S. Michele della Chiusa is known only from contradictory accounts in modern books, and need not be discussed: see Count Cipolla's observations, *ibid.* i. 131 f.

ment which Count Cipolla decided to be undoubtedly genuine, Humbert II of Savoy confirmed to the monastery of Novalesa a number of estates, including the valley of the Cinischia as far as Monpantero to the north-east of Susa.[1] The grant was made with the counsel of the bishop and canons of Maurienne; so that it is evident that that see did not consider its boundaries to be limited by the Alps. This claim was further extended by Calixtus II on 26 April 1123, when he issued a solemn privilege declaring that Susa, with the exception of the abbey of St. Justus, which was under the immediate jurisdiction of the Roman church, belonged to Maurienne. The confirmation addressed to the bishop of that see runs as follows:

Preposituram preterea Secusiensis ecclesie Beate Marie proprietario iure, atque ipsam civitatem Secusiensem cum omnibus appendiciis suis parochiali iure, tibi ac successoribus tuis et per vos Mauriannensi ecclesie confirmamus, salva dignitate abbacie Sancti Iusti, que sub Romane ecclesie iurisdictione consistit, et salva in omnibus obedientia et subiectione Viennensis ecclesie.[2]

It may be added that the series of Novalesa documents, though sound in most parts, is not free from the taint of forgery. There are a forged document of Charles the Great (774),[3] probably of the thirteenth century, which grants the monastery the third part of the valley of Susa; another of the Countess Adelaide (1039),[4] composed in the twelfth century or perhaps a little later; and in all probability one of Humbert II (1093),[5] which appears to have been written in connexion with the charter of Adelaide.[6] But they all seem to have been produced at a date subsequent to the bull of Calixtus II.

III

All the forgeries with which we have dealt—the charter of Boso and the Life of St. Tigris as well as the series which we have mentioned in our first section—were composed in the interest of the province of Vienne. In course of time they were met by reprisals from the side of Turin. The first example of a document fabricated for this purpose is the diploma of Conrad

---

[1] *Ibid.* i. 223 ff.

[2] Robert, *Le Bullaire de Calixte II*, no. 401, vol. ii, 198 f.; also in *Hist. Patr. Monum.* i. 751 f. (Turin, 1836). The original is not preserved, and the text is printed from a copy of the sixteenth century.

[3] *Monum. Novalic.* i. 57–60.   [4] i. 177 ff.   [5] i. 233 ff.

[6] See Count Cipolla's critical introductions to these three charters.

II of 1038, which conferred the bishopric of Maurienne on the bishop of Turin.[1] It was exposed by Dr. Bresslau[2] in 1884, but his argument has not received attention from the scholars who have dealt specially with the relations of Maurienne and Turin. More recently the charter has been brought into connexion with other forgeries, and traced to the hand of an unknown fabricator, probably a priest named Adam, at Turin.[3] The forgery is an early one, and was very likely made soon after the marriage of Odo of Maurienne with Adelaide, the heiress of Turin, some time between 1051 and 1057 ;[4] but the professing original, which has now disappeared, was written, according to the testimony of Bethmann, who examined it, in a hand of the thirteenth century.[5]

What actually took place as to the valley of Susa has to be collected from the documents of three religious houses, of Novalesa, of St. Justus at Susa, and of Oulx. Oulx, it may be explained, comes into our discussion because of the claims which it acquired on the church of St. Mary at Susa and which brought it into opposition with Maurienne. As it lay on the road giving access not directly to Mont Cenis but to a pass, Mont Genèvre, leading into a quite different territory, there is nothing to cause surprise in Turin's securing a hold upon it, though it was necessary to go through Susa in order to reach it. But it is singular that, with the exception of the forged charter of Cunibert, of which we shall speak shortly, no reference to Turin appears in any of the Oulx documents before 1095, and then only in a bull of Urban II, which in its present form is certainly not authentic.[6] The records of Novalesa form a remarkably fine series, and include few forgeries:[7] we have already quoted some evidence from them and shall return to them later on. It is far otherwise with the documents of the

[1] *Monum. Germ. Hist., Diplom.* iv (1909), 411 f.

[2] *Jahrbücher Konrads II*, ii. 475 f.

[3] See A. Hessel and H. Wibel, *Ein Turiner Urkundenfälscher des elften Jahrhunderts*, in *Neues Archiv*, xxxii (1907), 359 ff.

[4] For the date of the marriage see Bresslau, i. 377, and Carutti, *Regesta Comitum Sabaudiae* (1889), pp. 50–3; but it may be a few years earlier. The question is extremely obscure: see Count Cipolla's remarks in the *Bullettino dell' Istituto Storico Italiano*, xviii (1896), 23–32.

[5] See Bresslau, ii. 475.

[6] G. Collino, *Le Carte della Prevostura d'Oulx* (Pinerolo, 1908), no. xlvi [Jaffé, no. 5556]. The final protocol, however, which presents features incompatible with Urban's date, is not found in the earliest text of the chartulary.

[7] See above, p. 133.

other two houses. Of St. Justus we possess seven charters
earlier than the middle of the twelfth century. Four of them are
of the eleventh: of these, one, of 1029, is preserved in the original
and in two interpolated copies; the second (1033) has been
tampered with; the third (1034) is a pure forgery; and the fourth
(1037) is a forged original representing a genuine text which has
been contaminated. Two of the twelfth-century documents
(1134 and 1147) are genuine, but the third (also of 1147) is
suspicious.[1] The charters of Oulx have come down to us in still
more unsatisfactory condition. Out of 125 documents earlier
than the middle of the twelfth century, only two are preserved
in professing originals, and one of these—the charter of Bishop
Cunibert—is, as we shall see, a forgery of the most glaring type.
All the rest are contained in chartularies of the thirteenth
century and later.

To begin with the two originals, the foundation charter of
St. Justus was granted by members of the ruling family at Turin,
Alric, bishop of Asti, and his brother Odelric, otherwise Maginfred, marquess of Turin, and Bertha his wife, in 1029. The new
monastery was given a site and the third part of the city of
Susa and of its territory, with the exception of the castle, and
the third part of the valley of Susa, 'que iuris est nostri, tam
in montibus quam in planiciebus, sicut detinent montes qui
vocati sunt Genevi et Cinisi, usque in territorium et finem de
villa que vocatur Vaga', with other places named.[2] It is therefore evident that the lords of Turin claimed the whole valleys
of Susa and Bardonnèche as far as the passes of Mont Cenis
and Mont Genèvre. The second document is a charter of 1083,
whereby the Countess Adelaide, daughter of the above-named
Maginfred, and her daughter Agnes, grant to the house of canons
of St. Mary at Susa and to that of St. Lawrence at Oulx all
the tithes of the city of Susa and of its territory, excepting those
of the chapel in the castle.[3] It is curious that though mention is
made of the three persons who founded the monastery of St.
Justus, the rights of that monastery are not reserved.

We next come to the forged charter attributed to Bishop
Cunibert of Turin, which conferred great privileges on Oulx in

[1] See Cipolla, in the *Bullettino dell' Istituto Storico Italiano*, xviii. 7–59.
[2] *Ibid.*, pp. 69 ff.
[3] Collino, no. xxxvii. As the document is expressly stated to be an original,
it must be presumed that the statement that it is written in a hand 'del sec.
xii' is a misprint.

1065.[1] This charter has been relied on as a leading text by almost every writer on the subject;[2] but no one who reads the criticism of it made by Count Cipolla in 1899,[3] or even merely glances at the facsimiles he gives, can for a moment believe it to be genuine.[4] It is in fact a prodigious forgery, modelled on a papal bull of the middle of the twelfth century. That it has been so long accepted can only be due to the circumstance that it was known from copies in chartularies, and that no one before Count Cipolla had examined the pretended original.[5] After telling how the religious house at Oulx, which had long been desolate after the persecution of the heathen (evidently the Lombards),[6] was recently revived, the charter narrates that its provost went to Turin and made his profession to the bishop, and that Cunibert rewarded him by a grant of a long series of churches with all their tithes and other appurtenances. The charter proceeds:

Simili modo subdimus, conferimus, et damus huic sanctissimo loco beati Laurentii de Ultio et fratribus degentibus ibidem presentibus et futuris ęcclesiam, plebem, et penitentialem sanctę Marię quę sita est et ędificata infra civitatem Secusiam, cum omnibus pertinentiis et possessionibus suis, quę scilicet longeva matrix[7] et baptismalis ęcclesia quadam prerogativa et excellentia honoris nostram in omnibus quibus licitum est in suo plebanatu et assensu Taurinensis ęcclesię vicem gerit episcopalem et antiquitus multo iam tempore gerere consuevit. Quippe tam in urbe nobili Secusia quasi sedes est episcopalis antiqua, cuius plebanatus seu archipresbyteratus a palo Bonitionis ad pontem usque Volvutię fluminis extenditur, et a montium cacuminibus et infra hinc inde longe lateque comprehenditur et terminatur.

This church of St. Mary, with the whole parish of Susa, and a large number of other churches and the tithes of the entire

---

[1] Collino, no. xxi.　　[2] Even by M. de Manteyer, *La Provence*, p. 184.

[3] *Memorie della R. Accademia delle Scienze di Torino* (*Scienze Morali* ecc.), ser. ii, 1 (1901), pp. 103–26.

[4] Signor Collino, who prints the text of the document, no. xxi, does not attempt to defend it.

[5] He describes also a second supposed original, now in private hands, which is drawn on similar lines. This has been cited also by Father Savio, p. 349, n. 1; but he does not speak of having seen it.

[6] Possibly the author of the document took this statement from the Chronicle of Novalesa, ii. 14 (*Monum. Novalic.* ii. 158 f.), which states that in those early days Oulx was subject to Novalesa and explains its name Plebs Martyrum from the slaughter of the monks and nuns who sought refuge there 'a paganis Langobardi[s]'. The etymology is fictitious: see Collino, pp. v, vi.

[7] So Count Cipolla: Signor Collino has *matris*.

valley of Susa, excepting only one chapel in the town, Cunibert grants to the canons of Oulx. It is possible, as Count Cipolla suggested,[1] that the charter is developed out of a genuine document. Most of the grants contained in it are supported by other evidence. The passage which is quoted above appears to be the principal interpolation, and this explains the forgery. It not only confers upon Oulx the church of St. Mary at Susa, but claims for that church a quasi-episcopal position[2] and defines its jurisdiction as extending over the whole range of the valley of Susa. It was unmistakably composed with the design not only of establishing the position of Oulx with regard to Susa but also of resisting the claim of Maurienne to the Italian district.

IV

The history of these grants, as we read them in the Oulx chartularies, is as follows. In 1042 the Countess Adelaide granted to the church of Turin the church of St. Mary at Susa, with the tithes of the city and of the whole valley of Susa, 'sicuti detinent montes qui nuncupantur Genevus et Ciniso seu mons ille in quo Altareto dicitur',[3] as well as all the churches, save only the monastery of St. Justus, the chapel in the castle, and the church of St. Anthony.[4] It is this grant which Cunibert is claimed to have transferred to the house of Oulx. Then in 1083, as we have seen,[5] the Countess Adelaide confirmed substantially the same possessions to the churches of St. Mary at Susa and of

---

[1] pp. 113–18. Count Cipolla points out (pp. 115 f.) that the charter may have been composed between 1147 (Collino, no. cxvii), when such a document is only referred to, and 1149 (no. cxxv), when one is actually produced; but he inclines to think the forgery is a good deal later. My own suggestion is that it was concocted to make good the defect in the evidence in the former year.

[2] This looks like a retort to the 'Secusinae civitatis vel Maurianorum episcopus' in the forged charter of Boso; see above, p. 129. It may be remarked that Susa was not erected into a bishopric until 1772.

[3] We may note the use of the same formulary as in the foundation charter of St. Justus, above, p. 135. Whence the particular phrase is derived has not been ascertained: see W. A. B. Coolidge, *Entre Arc et Stura*, pp. 6 f. (extracted from the *Revue Alpine* for November 1908, xiv, pp. 384–5).   [4] Collino, no. i.

[5] Above, p. 135. An earlier charter attributed to Adelaide under the date 1057 (Collino, no. vii) confers upon Oulx not only several churches which were not granted to it until a later date, but also the church of St. Justus itself in direct contradiction to the genuine charters of that monastery. I am glad to find that in rejecting it I have the support of Count Cipolla, *Bullettino*, xviii, 8 note. The document, however, has been accepted as the foundation charter of Oulx: see Collino, p. 18, and L. Menabréa, *Des Origines féodales dans les Alpes occidentales* (Turin, 1865), pp. 238 f.

St. Lawrence at Oulx, the former being described as in the hands of the provost of the latter: in other words, St. Mary's was appropriated to Oulx. The transaction, however, was not free from suspicion of simony, and twelve years later, in the spring of 1095, when some important French prelates were passing through Susa on their return from the council of Piacenza, the opportunity was taken to have a suit on the matter solemnly heard. It was charged that Adelaide had received a sum of money for the grant of St. Mary's; evidence was received, and the charge was declared to be without foundation.[1] No record of the donation itself is preserved, and it is remarkable that, when in 1098 Bishop Guibert of Turin professed to confirm the grants made to Oulx by his predecessor Cunibert, one of the two copies of the document preserved in the chartulary altogether omits the words *ecclesiam sancte Marie de Secusia*, and in the other the order of the churches named is so deranged as to give the impression that it was sought to disguise an interpolation.[2] Much later, in 1172, Bishop Milo of Turin declared Adelaide's grant of St. Mary's to have been made *cum spontanea voluntate ac beneplacita permissione maioris Taurinensis ecclesie beati Iohannis Baptiste*,[3] and cited the forged charter of Bishop Cunibert and the confirmations of several Popes of which there is no trace elsewhere. We may notice that, though Adelaide's charter of 1083 was drawn up in Turin, no mention is made of any rights of the cathedral church.[4]

It may be inferred from the legal proceedings of 1095 and from the dubious testimony of the charter of Bishop Guibert that the canons of St. Mary at Susa were not well pleased with their dependence on Oulx. In 1116 an opportunity occurred for settling the question in favour of the latter. Two cardinals in succession passed through Oulx: one of them, we are informed, gave his presence and support to the investiture of the provost

---

[1] Collino, no. xlv. The document bears no date, but the names of the prelates are decisive. The accusation was revived in 1149: see no. cxxv.

[2] Collino, no. lxi, p. 69 and p. 71, n. 19. The document may refer to a lost charter of Cunibert on which the forged charter is partially based.

[3] Collino, no. clxii. This charter cites a number of documents of which there is no evidence elsewhere. See Collino's list on pp. xiii, xiv.

[4] The only reference to it in any charter bearing her name occurs in a grant of property said to have been made by her in 1075 to the chapel of Revello 'laude quoque et assensu Taurinensis ecclesie'; but the charter was impugned in 1252 on the ground that the copy then produced in a law-suit was interpolated. See Collino, no. xxvii.

of Oulx with the church of Susa by Bishop Mainard of Turin;[1] and the other confirmed to him the grant of that church which the bishop had made (*ecclesiam sancte Marie de Secusia quam . . . Mainardus Taurinensis episcopus ecclesie vestre concessit*),[2] the terms of the document appearing to indicate that it was a new grant by Bishop Mainard and not a confirmation of existing rights. I do not know how much credit is to be attached to this evidence; for a few years later a record was drawn up at Oulx which states that that church had formerly been despoiled of St. Mary's and had long been restrained by violence from entering again upon its possession. It goes on to say that Calixtus II heard the provost's complaint in the presence of the bishop of Maurienne and enjoined the latter, after taking counsel with his clergy, to restore St. Mary's to Oulx by the 1st of May. The bishop of Maurienne, however, interposed delays, and the provost followed him to Susa and showed him a mandate from the Pope requiring him to make restitution within forty days under pain of interdict. The Oulx chartulary contains this mandate, which is dated 28 March 1120.

Now on that same day Calixtus, who had been at Embrun on 15 March and no doubt stayed at Oulx on his journey into Italy, granted at Asti a privilege, of which the original is preserved, containing an ample confirmation of the possession of Oulx, but saying not a word about Susa.[3] The mandate to the bishop of Maurienne to which we have just referred is a demonstrable fabrication, composed in order to fill up this gap. In it the Pope recites that a complaint had been made by the provost of Oulx in the bishop's presence, and a term until the 1st of May had been prescribed *to the provost* within which the bishop was to do justice to him: as, however, the bishop had failed to carry out this injunction, the Pope commands him to restore the church to the provost, *salva Moriennensis ecclesie iusticia, si qua est*.[4] The absurdity of granting a term to the complainant is only equalled by the imposition of penalties for not doing what was not required to be done until a month after the date

[1] See the record of the investiture in Collino, no. xcv, p. 97.
[2] Collino, no. xcvi.   [3] Collino, no. ciii.
[4] Collino, no. civ. It is not, perhaps, irrelevant to observe that this dispute did not necessarily affect the jurisdiction of Maurienne. It was a question not between the sees of Maurienne and Turin, but between the churches of Oulx and Susa. It was perfectly possible for Oulx to possess a church in a different diocese.

of the mandate. The document is in fact a blundering reproduction of the statements contained in the earlier part of the Oulx record which we have just mentioned. Our rejection of it probably carries with it the mandate of the following December which answers to the latter part of that record.[1] But it must be said that this second mandate in itself presents no features of incongruity. It is discredited by its juxtaposition in the same chartulary. Both documents bore seals when they were laid before Eugenius III a quarter of a century later;[2] but this does not prove their genuineness, because it was a common practice to cut off seals from genuine bulls and attach them to forgeries.[3] We have to choose between two alternatives: either Calixtus II gave his support to Oulx in 1120, or else the charter which he granted to Maurienne in 1123, in which he confirmed to it the church of St. Mary and a great deal more,[4] is a forgery. What we know of the Pope's previous activity when he was archbishop of Vienne throws the balance of probability strongly in favour of the document of 1123. This conclusion is supported by the fact that in 1143 Bishop Obert of Turin confirmed the house of Oulx in the possession of its churches, but made no mention of Susa.[5]

But the canons of Oulx were not to be beaten, and when Eugenius III was on his way northward in the winter of 1146–7 he received a petition from the next bishop of Turin, Charles, in which he was prayed not to suffer the rights of Oulx to be impaired.[6] The Pope heard representatives of the parties, and delivered his decision in a bull dated at Lucca on 9 February 1147. From this document, which we know only from the Oulx chartulary, it appears that the provost brought forward the confirmation by Bishop Guibert of which the text has been tampered with,[7] the bull of Urban II which is not genuine in the form preserved to us,[8] and the two mandates of Calixtus II, one of which we have seen to be certainly spurious. The evidence produced by the clerks of Susa was no less unsatisfactory. They did not dispute these two mandates, but averred that they had been superseded by the judgement of a commission of four

---

[1] Collino, no. cvi.　　　　　　　　　　[2] Collino, no. cxvii.
[3] See my *Lectures on the History of the Papal Chancery* (1915), p. 155.
[4] See above, p. 133.　　　　　　　　　　[5] Collino, no. xcv.
[6] This document, which the chartulary describes as a 'charter of confirmation', is preserved in very inferior transcripts: Collino, no. cxvi.
[7] See above, pp. 138 f.　　　　　　　　　[8] See above, p. 134.

bishops (two of whose names are wrongly given) appointed by Calixtus,[1] which declared St. Mary's independent of Oulx; it was, however, admitted that only two of the four took part in the adjudication. On the other side it was maintained that no sentence had in fact been given, and letters were produced in which one of the commissioners, Peter, archbishop of Vienne, enjoined the clergy of Susa to restore their church to Oulx. Eugenius accepted the evidence given on the part of the petitioners and invested the provost of Oulx with the disputed church. The decision is stated to have been based principally on the two grounds that the clergy of Susa had not put in the alleged sentence and that, even if they had, a sentence delivered by two out of four commissioners was not valid.[2] In the twelfth, as in later centuries, a judgement was often given not on the whole facts of the case but on an irregularity in one of its last stages. But the sentence of Pope Eugenius settled the matter, at least for the time; and it is this, no doubt, which explains the statement of John of Salisbury about the petition made by the bishop of Maurienne at a council held by Eugenius at Cremona in July 1148:

Episcopus Maurianus adversus Mediolanensem questionem proposuit finium regundorum, rogans ut eum liceret egredi de cavernis montium sicut decessoribus suis antiquitus licitum fuerat.[3]

So long as he held jurisdiction over the valley of Susa, it was possible for him to escape from the mountain gorges; but when Susa was confirmed to Turin he was deprived of any outlet. He therefore raised his protest against the metropolitan of Milan.

It was not to be expected that the Pope would reverse his sentence of 1147. He had decided that Oulx was in the right, and on 14 May 1148, while he was at Lausanne on his road back to Italy, he granted a solemn privilege to Oulx in which he assured to it the possession of the church at Susa.[4] After this, it is not easy to understand why he should have thought it necessary to address another letter to Oulx on 15 January 1149, in which

---

[1] This mandate is not known to be in existence.

[2] Collino, no. cxvii.

[3] *Historia pontificalis*, xxi (ed. R. L. Poole, Oxford, 1927, p. 50).

[4] Collino, no. cxx. See also the subsequent confirmations by Adrian IV in 1158 (no. cxxxix), by Alexander III in 1172 (no. clxi), and by Lucius III in 1183 (no. clxxix); and compare the charters of Bishop Charles of Turin in 1165 (no. cxlv), of Bishop Milo in 1172 (no. clxv), and of Bishop James II in 1226 (no. ccliv).

he said that, though on the earlier occasion he had been prepared to deliver judgement in favour of Oulx, nevertheless, in the interest of peace he had thought it better to proceed by way of composition (*per concordiam*) and had therefore enjoined the clergy of Susa thenceforward not to disquiet the provost of Oulx, but to assist him faithfully in the administration of the affairs of the church, which engagement they had promised to fulfil.[1] This amicable agreement does not seem consistent with the definitive sentence which Eugenius had pronounced in 1147. Possibly he desired to make his decision less unpalatable to the clergy of Susa by persuading them to bind themselves to a course of action which would facilitate its practical working without compelling them to go into the question of right. He added some words as to the obligations of the provost towards Susa which may have helped to salve the wounds of the defeated party. As a natural sequel to his settlement of the dependence of Susa, when the Pope on 9 February 1152 granted a general confirmation of the possessions of the abbey of Breme, he placed Novalesa in the diocese of Turin.[2]

Reviewing the history of this long course of documents, it appears to me that, while the rights of Maurienne over the valley of Susa from the sixth century onwards may be accepted as authentic, there was a break in its actual possession caused by the incursions of the Arabs in the tenth century. What is known to have happened to Novalesa[3] must have affected the whole upper region of the valley; and when late in that century it was possible to re-establish the monastery of Novalesa,[4] the settlement of the jurisdiction of the whole area must have had to be begun afresh. There was a void to be filled, and it was filled in the first instance by the pious energy of the ruling house at Turin. The question of the ecclesiastical authority was not so much thought of as the need for providing monastic and capitular foundations as religious centres to which the neighbouring churches might be attached. Thus in the eleventh century arose the monastery of St. Justus at Susa and the capitular houses of St. Mary and of Oulx. As the directing force came from Turin, it was natural that the bishop of that city should be, slowly and by degrees, recognized as the spiritual head of the new group of

---

[1] Collino, no. cxxv.
[2] *Monum. Novalic.* i. 251 ff.
[3] *Chron. Novalic.* v. 5.
[4] *Monum. Novalic.* i. 111.

monasteries. St. Justus's was then exempted from his authority and placed under the immediate jurisdiction of the Holy See. At Oulx Turin found no counter-claimant; but at St. Mary's of Susa the bishop of Maurienne, in spite of repeated pressure, steadily refused to abandon his ancient rights, and the canons were reluctant to accept their subjection to Oulx. In 1123, when the influence of Vienne was powerful, the bishop actually obtained a papal confirmation of all that he desired; but in another quarter of a century his hopes were finally dissipated by the sentence of Eugenius III. The extensive and elaborate use of forgery to secure the end aimed at by Turin is a plain testimony to the strength of the legal position of Maurienne.

It may also be observed that the subjection of the church at Susa to Oulx did not of itself involve a transference from the diocese of Maurienne to that of Turin; a church in one diocese was often annexed to a monastery in another. But it is probable that in this instance Maurienne did in fact lose its Italian dependencies. Only six years after the bull of Calixtus II, Bishop Cono of Maurienne, in confirming the possessions of the monastery of Novalesa within his diocese in 1129, included no properties lying eastward of Mont Cenis;[1] and when on 16 October 1184 Lucius III confirmed the bishop of Maurienne in the lands granted to his see by King Guntchramn 'of blessed memory' and enumerated near a score of properties, he likewise said not a word of any situate beyond the pass.[2] It was no doubt merely as a brave assertion of claims that had long been obsolete that in 1262 Bishop Anselm marched into the valley of Susa and went as far as the bridge of Valgioje near Avigliana, where he caused a formal record to be made that that bridge formed the boundary of his jurisdiction.[3]

[1] *Monum. Novalic.* i. 248 f.
[2] Billiet, *Chartes du Diocèse de Maurienne*, no. xx, pp. 32–35.
[3] Besson, *Mémoires*, preuves, no. 114; *Hist. patr. Monum.*, Chart. i. 1467. The date has been erroneously given as 1208.

PAPAL CHRONOLOGY IN THE ELEVENTH CENTURY[1]

THE precise dates of the pontificates of the first half of the eleventh century are extremely hard to fix. The materials are scanty and not free from textual corruption; and the fact that only one of the Popes of that time—or more strictly, of the Popes between the death of Silvester II in 1003 and the appointment of Leo IX in 1048—occupied a commanding position has led to a neglect even of the materials that are at our disposal. It is agreed that the history is of little moment, and it has not been thought worth while to attempt to reconstruct its chronology. As Monsignor Duchesne remarks in another connexion, *il est juste de proportionner le soin que l'on consacre aux textes à l'importance de ceux-ci.*[2] But there are difficulties even after Leo IX, when the details of the Popes' biographies acquire great historical importance; and although it may not always be possible to settle these difficulties, a step will have been gained if we can establish the principle on which the records of the times during which the Popes held office were drawn up. Hitherto it has been almost universally maintained that the time recorded was that of the pontificate, that is, that it was reckoned from the date when a Pope attained his full powers by ordination or consecration; in some cases enthronement is mentioned. It is, however, certain that the years of Gregory VII are computed in these records not from his consecration on 29 June 1073, but from his election on 22 April. Monsignor Duchesne is of opinion that this was the first time that this mode of calculation was adopted.[3] It is with great hesitation that I venture to differ from the illustrious scholar whose work on the chronology of the early Popes is not the least enduring of his contributions to the establishment of a critical knowledge of the *Liber Pontificalis.* But a careful examination of the durations—I use this word to avoid prejudging what the figures mean—assigned to the seventeen Popes from Silvester II to Alexander II has led me to the conclusion that in only four cases, which can be accounted for by exceptional circumstances, is the strict pontificate recorded, and that in no other case are the figures given

---

[1] Reprinted from the *English Historical Review*, vol. xxxii (1917).
[2] *Liber Pontificalis*, ii (1892), introd., p. lxiv *a*.   [3] *Ibid.*, p. lxxiii *b*.

inconsistent with a computation from the day of election, while many of them conflict with a reckoning from that of ordination or consecration.

The materials on which we have to depend are a series of brief lists, giving the name of each Pope, with perhaps his birth-place and parentage, followed by the years, months, and days of his 'session': *Sedit annos*, &c. The earliest of these lists for the time in which we are interested is the *Catalogus Augiensis*. This is a list which was apparently compiled under Leo IX, and was used by Herman of Reichenau, who died in 1052. The manuscript, however, in which it is preserved was not written until 1165–7, and it cannot be made use of with the same confidence as lists which were transcribed at an earlier time. Moreover, the figures it gives for the duration of each Pope are often stated defectively or in general terms, so that the list is not available for our present purpose.[1]

The oldest list actually written in the eleventh century is perhaps the *Catalogus Farfensis* (now Cod. 2010 in the Biblioteca Casanatense). This has been carefully described by Commenda-tore Giorgi, who prints the text and gives reason for believing that it was written in the Sabine monastery of Farfa in 1087, with a continuation in another hand going on to the time of Paschal II.[2] Signor Giorgi considers it to be the archetype, directly or indirectly, of all the preserved lists written towards the end of the eleventh century or in the early years of the twelfth. In particular he regards it as the archetype from which the *Catalogus Cavensis* (Cod. Vatic. 3764) was transcribed. This latter he believes to have been written at Farfa and carried away to the monastery of La Cava during the disturbances which followed a double election to the abbacy of Farfa in the time of Calixtus II.[3] It was written after the death of Gregory VII in May 1085, but it diverges so markedly from the *Farfensis* in some important points that I cannot regard it as a copy from it.[4]

[1] The same thing is true of the Zwettl *Historia Romanorum Pontificum*, which goes on to the time of Celestine III. It is printed by B. Pez, *Thesaurus Anecdotorum Novissimus*, I. iii. 330–95 (1721).

[2] *Appunti intorno ad alcuni Manoscritti del Liber Pontificalis*, in *Archivio della R. Società Romana di Storia Patria*, xx (1897), 278–312.

[3] p. 272. See *Il Regesto di Farfa*, ed. I. Giorgi and U. Balzani, v (1892), 319 ff.

[4] The list in the *Cavensis* beginning with Pope Lando is printed by Signor Giorgi, pp. 302–12. It must be distinguished from another list which precedes it in the manuscript and was written under Paschal II: Vignoli, who published this text in his edition of the *Liber Pontificalis* (1724), i. pref., calls it *Vaticanus I*.

There were many transcripts of the papal list made about the same time, and the corrections inserted in the *Farfensis* indicate that he or his corrector made use of more than one manuscript. Among these may be mentioned the *Catalogus Estensis* from Pomposa, which ends in 1081–2; the *Catalogus Sublacensis*, written under Gregory VII;[1] the *Codex Vaticanus* 629, written 1095–9;[2] and the *Catalogus Volturnensis*, which is of the time of Honorius II.[3] The list adopted by Monsignor Duchesne as the text of his edition of this part of the *Liber Pontificalis* is one written at the monastery of St. Giles in the diocese of Rheims in 1142 by Peter, surnamed William, librarian of the monastery of St. Giles on the Lower Rhone.

If one makes a table of all the sets of figures given in these various lists—I copied out ten for my own study—the first impression left is one of hopeless confusion. There are between two and five discordant figures given for every Pope but one. But a closer inspection shows that the variants must be weighed, not counted. When, for instance, years only, or years and months only, are recorded, these are manifestly round numbers, which do not conflict with precise figures, with years, months, and days, given in our lists. Conversely, 2 years 9 months and 12 days in two lists are not opposed to 2 years 9 months in one or to 3 years in three; but they are opposed to 3 years 15 days in another. Then there are certain well-known sources of scriptural error to be taken into account, in particular the confusion between *u* and *ii*, and *uiii* and *uiiii*, and even between *ui* and *uii*. In two instances at least there is clear evidence that two distinct records existed, but these instances will not suffice to group the texts into two families. We must, I think, admit a process of selection and combination, as well as of subsequent revision, with the help of more than one of the available lists. But I cannot doubt that all the lists are ultimately traceable to an official record drawn up in Rome.

I now proceed to examine the figures in detail.

The documents of Silvester II begin on 15 April 999. He died on 12 May 1003.[4] The lists assign him a pontificate of 4 years 1 month and 9 or 8 days. These take us back to 3 or

[1] Printed in the *Regesto Sublacense*, pp. 7–10, ed. L. Allodi and G. Levi, 1885; cf. pref., p. vii.
[2] *Catalogus Vaticanus III*, printed by Vignoli.
[3] Printed by Muratori, *Rerum Italicarum Scriptores*, I. ii. 333.
[4] See his epitaph in Duchesne, *Lib. Pontif.* ii. 264 n.

4 April 999, Monday or Tuesday. I infer that that was the date of his election, and that he was consecrated on the following Sunday, the 9th. Monsignor Duchesne[1] proposes the Sunday before; but this gives a duration not of 8 or 9 days, but of 10; and *x* is not easily confounded with *viii* or *viiii*. The two Johns, XVII and XVIII, who succeeded, are vaguely or defectively dated, and may here be left out of account.

The next Pope, Sergius IV, has his record precisely stated on his epitaph, which is still extant: he sat for 2 years 9 months and 12 days, and died on 12 May in the 10th Indiction, A.D. 1012.[2] He was therefore consecrated on 31 July 1009. But one list assigns him 3 years and 15 days,[3] which implies that his election took place on 27 April; and in the *Farfensis* the figures agreeing with those on the epitaph have been changed into *iii*. The interval is unusual, but the times were also unusual; there was another candidate for the Papacy, and Sergius only gained the day after some fighting.

Benedict VIII's pontificate is reckoned in charters as running from 21 May 1012 at least to 7 March 1024. He was probably consecrated on 18 May.[4] His death is assigned in the contemporary obituary of Fulda to 7 April,[5] so that his pontificate lasted 11 years 10 months 20 days. The lists, however, fluctuate as to his duration, giving 11 years 1 month 21 days, 11 years 10 months 21 days, and 11 years 11 months 21 days. Plainly the years and days are accurately given, and the error is in the months. The first variant is too short,[6] as the documents mentioning Benedict as Pope extend beyond the period indicated; and the third is too long, because there is evidence that

---

[1] p. lxxi *b*.

[2] The inscription, *Lib. Pontif.* ii. 267, n. 4, gives the year as 1013, a mistake which may perhaps be explained if the stone was engraved a year later. There is no doubt whatever that 1012 is the true year.

[3] One text, that of the Vatican MS. 629, by an evident slip, gives *annos iiii*.

[4] See Duchesne, *Lib. Pontif.* ii, introd., pp. lxxi, lxxii. Dr. Hartmann, in *Mittheilungen des Instituts für Oesterreichische Geschichtsforschung*, xv (1894), 485, disregarding Sergius IV's epitaph, advocates 20 April. The evidence of the document adduced by Gregorovius, *History of the City of Rome*, iv. 14 n. (Engl. tr., 1896), to show that Benedict was already Pope on 5 May is indecisive, because the Indiction is undoubtedly wrong. The date is given *anno primo mense Madio die vᵃ Indictione iᵃ: Regesto Sublacense*, no. 193, p. 231. The editors propose to emend *Indictione xiᵃ* and date the document 1013.

[5] *Annales, necrologici Fuldenses*, in *Monum. Germ. Hist., Script.* xiii. 211 *a*. The obituary of the monastery of SS. Cyriac and Nicholas at Rome gives the day as the 9th, *v. Id. April.*: Hartmann, *l.c.*

[6] So too is the duration of 11 years and 25 days of the Augiensis.

the years of his successor were counted from a date not later than 1 May 1024. This appears from a document at Monte Cassino, which is dated precisely in the 9th year of John XIX, in the 6th of the Emperor Conrad II, in the 15th Indiction, on 1 May, that is, in 1032.[1] If, with Monsignor Duchesne,[2] we adopt the reading 11 years 10 months 21 days and reckon back from 7 April 1024, we arrive at 17 May 1012 for Benedict's election.

If, then, Tuesday, 7 April 1024, be accepted as the date of Benedict VIII's death, his brother, John XIX, could not have been consecrated before Sunday the 12th. His duration is diversely given. The *Farfensis* apparently at first contained the entry, *Sedit annos viiii menses vi*, but these last two words have been changed into *dies viiii*. The *Cavensis* has 9 years 9 months. But any number beyond nine years would be impossible; *viiii* must be a slip for *viii*; and if we make this correction in the Farfa text and disregard the alteration in the manuscript, we reach a number which agrees with that of the *Sublacensis*, 8½ years. The extreme date would then be October 1032. Supposing we accept the 9 months of the *Cavensis*, we are taken on to January 1033, and it should be noticed that Herman of Reichenau says that John *sedit annis ferme 9* and records the ordination of Benedict IX under the year 1033.[3] There was evidently a lack of certain information, and the omission of the days in all but the redacted Farfa text suggests that the duration is stated roughly. I incline to think that John died between October and January, and note with interest the specific entry of his death in a Roman obituary under the date of 6 November.[4] John's pontificate would then have lasted nearly 8 years and 7 months, and Benedict IX might have been elected in November or December 1032. In agreement with this a Sutri document reckons December in the 8th Indiction, that is in 1039, as falling in Benedict's 8th year.[5]

The dating of private documents by pontifical and Imperial years, in a period of such obscurity as that with which we are

---

[1] Gregorovius, iv. 31, n. 2. According to Dr. Hartmann, p. 483, John XIX may have succeeded any time after 25 March. There is, however, a document in the Subiaco Register, no. 177, p. 221, which places 24 May in the 13th Indiction (1030) in John's 6th year; so that on this reckoning his 1st would have begun after 24 May 1024.

[2] *Lib. Pontif.* ii, introd., p. lxxii *a*.

[3] *Chronicon*, in *Monum. Germ. Hist., Script.* v (1844), p. 121.

[4] Hartmann, p. 485.   [5] *Ibid.*, p. 483.

concerned, must be used with caution as a help to ascertaining the exact chronology. There is a charter to the monastery of Subiaco dated on 11 November in the 3rd year of Benedict IX, the 8th of the Emperor Conrad II, and the 3rd Indiction,[1] that is, in 1034; so that it would appear that Benedict was believed to be already Pope on 11 November 1032. A Farfa document, the dates of which are suspicious, has been cited in confirmation of this:[2] it was granted on 15 November in the 4th year of Benedict, the 8th of Conrad, and the 4th Indiction.[3] The Imperial date must be disregarded; for that would give the year 1034, and as the bulls of John XIX go down to January 1032, it is plain that the 4th year of Benedict cannot begin until at least January 1035. The Indiction points to 1035; for the document was written by Anastasius, a *scriniarius* of the Roman Church, and it was the practice of the Papal chancery down to the accession of Urban II to begin the Indiction in September. The editors of the Farfa Register however incline to place the charter in 1036, assuming that, in spite of the Roman usage, Anastasius dated it by the Indiction which began at Christmas. I should be indisposed to accept this conclusion were it not that the charter contains another indication of date, the bearing of which has escaped notice: it speaks of *Crescentio olim praefecto*. Now there exists a charter granted to the monastery of Subiaco by Crescentius as prefect on 17 June in the 5th year of Benedict, in the 4th Indiction,[4] that is, in 1036. The Farfa document must therefore be later than this,[5] and it affords no support to the date before 11 November 1032 for Benedict's accession implied in the other Subiaco charter mentioned above. A Ravenna document calendared by Marco Fantuzzi[6] is dated on 27 January in Benedict's 5th year, in the 10th of Conrad, and in the 5th Indiction, that is, 1037: these dates are consistent, and show that Benedict was believed to have been Pope at least as early as 27 January 1033.[7]

---

[1] *Regesto Sublacense*, p. 146, no. 101.

[2] Jaffé, *Reg. Pontif. Rom.*, 2nd ed., i (1885), 519; Duchesne, *Lib. Pontif.* ii, introd., p. lxxii *a*.

[3] *Regesto di Farfa*, iii. 292 f., no. 587. It had been previously printed by P. Galletti, *Gabio antica* (Rome, 1757), pp. 134 ff., app. xxiii.

[4] *Reg. Sublacense*, p. 75, no. 36.

[5] It may be observed that the charter in the *Regesto* stands first in a group of four documents, the other three of which undoubtedly belong to 1036.

[6] *Monumenti Ravennati*, ii. 369, no. 43, Venice, 1802.

[7] The Ravenna documents of this time seem to be dated with remarkable

The *Farfensis* gives Benedict IX a pontificate of 14 years 4 months and 20 days; the *Cavensis*, of 14 years and 4 months: in the *Farfensis* the months and days are cancelled. The *Sublacensis* reads 12 years 4 months and 20 days. These variants seem to indicate the adoption of two distinct durations. The scribe of the *Farfensis* had both before him; one indicated simply a rough date of 14 years, and the other recorded precisely 12 years 4 months and 20 days. He copied out the 14, which in his opinion was correct, but accidentally added the months and days of the shorter reckoning. Finding out his mistake, he cancelled these. If this suggestion be right, we have to inquire when the 12 years 4 months and 20 days terminated. Now it seems incredible that Benedict should be considered to have ceased to be Pope when he was driven out of Rome by a riot on 7 January 1045 and an Antipope set up, because on 10 March he went back and resumed his power. The terminal date must be 1 May, when he voluntarily disposed of the Papacy in favour of Gregory VI. If, then, we reckon back 12 years 4 months and 20 days from 1 May 1045, we arrive at 12 December 1032 for his accession. This was a Tuesday. His consecration might take place on the following Sunday, 17 December. The alternative reckoning of 14 years, with no months or days, from this date would carry us almost exactly to the time of the synod of Sutri, 20 December 1046, or that of Rome four days later. I venture therefore to suggest that the apparent discrepancies in the lists represent two different computations: one from his election to his cession on 1 May 1045; the other running on to his deposition (according to the received account) in December 1046.

The Antipope to whom I have referred, Silvester III, was set up on the third day after 7 January 1045; he was deposed on 10 March.[1] The lists reckon his pontificate from his consecra-

accuracy. Fantuzzi calendars six (including that mentioned above) between 27 February 1036 and 28 June 1042, and their dates are uniformly consistent, with the single exception that one (no. 44) begins the 11th year of Conrad II a month too early. They all agree in placing Benedict's 1st year in the 1st Indiction (from 1 September 1032). I note this because Monsignor Duchesne (p. lxxii *b*) speaks of the uncertainty as so great that we can hardly be sure who was Pope in the spring and summer of 1032.

[1] *Annales Romani*, in *Lib. Pontif.* ii. 331. It used to be supposed that the series of events which led to the setting up of Silvester III took place in the winter not of 1044–5 but of 1043–4. This was due to a mistake in the first edition of Jaffé's *Regesta Pontificum* (1851), pp. 361 f. Jaffé read *annum i*, instead of *mensem i, et dies xxi*, in one of the papal lists, though this made havoc of the other figures which are given with precision in those lists. The fact that

tion; but there was evidently a doubt whether this took place on Sunday, 13 January, or the Sunday after. The Farfa list accepts the later date, and gives him a duration of 49 days; the *Cavensis* takes the earlier, and arrives at 56 days. Both equally lead to the same terminal date, 10 March.

The existence of a double form of record, based upon a diversity of opinion as to the date when a pontificate ended, is apparent not only in the case of Benedict IX, but also in that of Gregory VI. Gregory obtained the Papacy, it is known, on 1 May 1045; he could not be consecrated before the following Sunday, the 5th. Now the *Farfensis* gives him a pontificate of 1 year and 8 months, less 11 days. This takes us precisely to 20 December 1046, and is reckoned not from his consecration, but from his accession. Monsignor Duchesne has accidentally missed the word *minus*[1] and therefore rejects the figures given. The *Cavensis* extends Gregory's pontificate to 2 years and 6 months, that is, to 1 November (or, if we will, 5 November) 1047. This likewise Monsignor Duchesne considers inadmissible. It can, however, be easily explained, though the explanation has not, I think, been observed. The writer of that list held Gregory to be the lawful Pope down to the end of his life, and there is evidence that his death took place about the same time as that of Clement II, who died on 9 October 1047.[2]

Clement II was appointed on 24 December 1046 and consecrated on Christmas Day; he died, as I have said, on the 9th of

the *Annales Romani*, after mentioning the beginning of the disturbances at Rome, record an eclipse of the sun on 22 November, which indubitably occurred in 1044, is decisive. Jaffé's dating, however, was accepted without comment by Giesebrecht in the first edition of his *Geschichte der Deutschen Kaiserzeit*, ii (1858), 386 f.; and it was seriously defended by Ernst Steindorff, *Jahrbücher des Deutschen Reichs unter Heinrich III*, i (1874), 489 f. The error was pointed out by G. Grandaur in *Neues Archiv der Gesellschaft für ältere Deutsche Geschichtskunde*, v (1880), 200 f. It was corrected by Giesebrecht in later editions (e.g. in the 5th, 1885, ii. 410 f., 663), and also in the second edition of Jaffé's *Regesta*.

[1] 'Annum i et menses viii minus dies xi.' Monsignor Duchesne, presuming the calculation to be made from Gregory's consecration on 5 May, reckons 1 year 7 months and 14 days to the synod of Sutri (p. lxxii *b*); but these figures are given in none of the lists.

[2] Beno, *Gesta, Romanae Ecclesiae*, ii. 8, in *Lib. de Lite Imper. et Pontif.* ii (1892), 378. In Jaffé, i. 525, it is asserted that Gregory was alive in 1048 on the authority of Anselm's *Gesta Episcoporum Leodiensium*, lxx (*Monum. Germ. Hist., Script.* vi (1846), 228). But Anselm's statement expressly relates to a time before Christmas 1047, and Dr. Tangl maintains with great force that the reference to an unnamed Pope is not to Gregory VI, but to Benedict IX: *Neues Archiv*, xxxi (1906), 172 f.

the following October. These dates are abundantly attested. His duration is given as 9 months and 16 days; it was therefore reckoned from his election. In the *Farfensis*, where the months are written by a slip *viii* instead of *viiii*, the days have been altered from *xvi* into *vii*; and this figure, which may be due to wrong information as to the date of the Pope's death, reappears in the *Cavensis*. The Subiaco list has *xiii*, which is probably an instance of the common misreading of *u* as *ii*.

After a short resumption of power by Benedict IX, three Popes in succession, Damasus II, Leo IX, and Victor II, were elected in Germany; so that it would not be likely, apart from other considerations, that any date but that of consecration would be recorded in the Roman lists. But it is curious that both the discrepant lengths assigned to the pontificate of Victor II, who died on 28 July[1] 1057, in the *Cavensis* and the *Estensis*, namely 2 years 3 months and 13 or 27 days, imply a beginning on Saturday, 1 or 15 April. Monsignor Duchesne rightly suspects the statement of Berthold[2] that the ordination took place on Maundy Thursday, the 13th, and thinks that this refers to his installation at the Lateran, the consecration taking place on Easter Day, the 16th.[3] This may be well accepted, but the lists seem to imply some formal act the day before.

The next Pope, Frederick of Lorraine, Stephen IX, was abbot of Monte Cassino, and the Annals of that monastery give his dates precisely. He was elected on 2 August 1057 and consecrated on the following day; he died on 29 March 1058.[4] His pontificate therefore lasted for 7 months and 26 days. The lists, however, assign him a duration of 7 months and 29 or 28 days, either of which gives a number of days in excess of the period, whether reckoned from election or consecration: a mistake must have therefore been made in writing the figures, or else the information as to the date of the Pope's death was incorrect.[5]

On Stephen's death Benedict X was set up and held the Papacy until 24 January 1059, the date of consecration of

---

[1] '5 Kalend. Aug.': Anonym. Haserensis *de Episcopis Eichstetensibus*, xli (*Monum. Germ. Hist., Script.* vii (1846), 266, from a late transcript).

[2] 'In sequente quadragesima in coena Domini 154us papa ordinatus': *Annales*, a. 1054 (*ibid.* v (1844), 269).

[3] *Lib. Pontif.* ii, introd., p. lxxiii, n. 1.

[4] Leo of Ostia, *Chron. Monasterii Casinensis*, ii. 94 (*Monum. Germ. Hist., Script.* vii. 693 f.); Bernold, *Not. Necrol.* (*ibid., Necrol.* i (1888), 659).

[5] Possibly the *xxviiii* arose from a confusion with the number of the day of the month on which he died.

Nicholas II, who had been elected against him. The lists assign Benedict a duration of 9 months and 20 days, which take us back to 4 April 1058. He is said, however, to have been elected and consecrated on the same day, and that day would be Sunday, 5 April.[1] Leo of Ostia says that the tumultuous irruption which made Benedict Pope took place at night,[2] that is, on Saturday night; so that the election was very possibly on the night before the actual consecration.

The chronology of Nicholas II is complicated by the facts that two different dates, 19 and 27 July 1061, are recorded for his death, and that the lists assign three different periods for his pontificate. It is not disputed that he was elected at Siena at the end of 1058[3] and consecrated between 20 and 28 January, that is almost certainly on Sunday the 24th, 1059. The variations in the lists point to two distinct modes of reckoning, each of which presents a consistent calculation, but agrees with neither of the recorded dates of the Pope's death. The writer of the *Farfensis* wrote, *Sedit annos ii, menses vi, dies*, and did not fill in the days. Evidently there was a doubt about the number. Afterwards *xxv* was inserted, and then the *Cavensis* gave *xxviii*. Another text allowed but one day beyond the two years and six months. This may be taken as computed from the Pope's consecration, 24 January 1059, to his death (*ex hypothesi*) on 25 July 1061. The 28 days of the *Cavensis* take us back to 28 December 1058 for his election, which agrees closely with what we gather from the historical notices. But the *Cavensis* notes a *cessatio* of 2 months and 8 days between Nicholas's death and the election of Alexander II on 30 September, and this implies that Nicholas died on 22 July. The mentions of the *cessatio* are a peculiar feature of this text, and are not necessarily derived from the same source as the other reckonings. If the source be that which supplied the smaller number of 25 days inserted in the *Farfensis*, we have a period computed, like the other, from 28 December 1059, but ending on 22 July 1061. I am inclined to think that this is the correct statement.[4] The date *vi. Kal.*

[1] Duchesne, *Lib. Pontif.* ii. 334, n. 1, and introd., p. lxxii *a*.

[2] *Hist. Monast. Casin.* ii. 99, p. 695.

[3] The record of an act of his as bishop of Florence and Pope elect is dated in 1058 (*Neues Archiv*, iv. 402, 1879), but this may be reckoned in the Florentine style, according to which the year began on 25 March.

[4] After I had written this I found that the same conclusion had been arrived at by Pagi in his *Crit. ad Baronii Annales*, xvii. 182, n. 1 (ed. 1745). It is bluntly rejected in Jaffé, i. 557.

Aug. which is recorded for Nicholas's death in two manuscripts of the Annals of Berthold of Reichenau[1] might easily be mis-written for *xi. Kal. Aug.* The other date, *xiv. Kal. Aug.*, which is found in a twelfth-century obituary at Monte Cassino,[2] is difficult to explain.

If Nicholas II died on 22 July and there was a *cessatio* of 2 months and 8 days, we are led precisely to 30 September for the accession of Alexander II, and this date is accepted by Mon-signor Duchesne as that of his installation.[3] There is, indeed, no positive evidence for it. We have only the statement of Peter Damiani, who did not write with a chronological purpose and whose words need not be understood as fixing a precise date:

> Constat enim tres plus minus menses interim decurrisse ex quo sanc-tae memoriae papa Nicolaus occubuit, usque ad Kalendas Octobris cum iste successit.[4]

The date, 30 September, *pridie Kal. Oct.*, agrees exactly with the statement of Berthold of Reichenau that Cadalus of Parma, the Antipope, was elected *vii. Kal. Nov.*, and that Alexander was elected on the 27th day before. Alexander died on 22 April 1073. The lists give him a duration of 11 years 6 months and 22 or 25 days.[5] The former reckoning is computed correctly from 30 September 1061; the latter may be accounted for by the common misreading of *ii* as *u*. It would be almost impossible to throw back Alexander's election three days before his consecration; and it may be taken that the two acts were performed within twenty-four hours.[6]

We have thus arrived at the accession of Gregory VII and the end of our inquiry. Henceforward, says Monsignor Duchesne, the rule was to reckon from the Pope's election, except in the case of the troubled pontificate of Gregory's successor, Victor III, whose duration is computed from his consecration. To resume the results of the calculations which I have examined, it appears that out of seventeen Popes only four can be said with

[1] *Monum. Germ. Hist., Script.* v (1844), 271 note. Hence it was repeated in the Chronicle of Bernold of Constance: *ibid.*, p. 427.

[2] Muratori, *Script. Rerum Italicarum*, vii. 944.

[3] *Lib. Pontif.* ii. introd., p. lxxiii *b*.

[4] *Disceptatio Synodalis*, in *Opera*, ed. C. Cajetanus, iii. 64 (1783), or in Migne, *Patr. Lat.* cxlv. 79.

[5] The Subiaco list has *xviiii* days, which cannot be correct.

[6] Benzo of Alba, whose statements must always be received with caution, makes the election take place on one day and the enthronement on the night following: *ad Henr. IV*, lib. vii. 2, in *Monum. Germ. Hist., Script.* xi. 672.

confidence to have had their periods reckoned from their consecration. These were the Antipope Silvester III, who was
elected in a tumult, and the three successive pontiffs, Damasus
II, Leo IX, and Victor II, who were chosen in Germany. Of
three, John XVII, XVIII, and XIX, nothing definite can be
said. Ten remain: of these the lists count the periods of five,
Silvester II, Sergius IV, Benedict VIII, Gregory VI, and Clement
II, from their election; and the same may be said, with greater
or less probability, in regard to Benedict IX, Stephen IX, and
Benedict X. In the case of Nicholas II the earlier lists reckon
from election, the later from consecration; in that of Alexander
II it is likely that the two acts took place on the same day. It
seems therefore that there is a considerable balance of probability in favour of the conclusion that, except in unusual circumstances, the papal chronologers were in the habit throughout
the eleventh century of computing the duration of each pontiff
from the day of his election. Whether the principle holds good
for the earlier lists or for the integral part of the *Liber Pontificalis*, I have not examined; but *a priori* one would expect
that this should be the case.

It was the custom that the election should take place at the
church of St. John in the Lateran, or, if it took place elsewhere,
that the Pope should be at once conducted to the Lateran and be
solemnly proclaimed there.[1] According to the account written
by Cencius the Chamberlain, afterwards Pope Honorius III, in
the last years of the twelfth century, the Pope after his election
was handed the keys of the Lateran palace and held a reception
of all the officials.[2] Among them the notaries of the chancery
occupied a conspicuous rank, and it was an appropriate occasion
for making a record of the date and the Pope's name. That this
should be done at the Lateran is rendered the more probable by
the fact that it was there that the papal archives were preserved.
The ordination or consecration at St. Peter's, which commonly
took place on the following Sunday, was a great ceremonial function which did not offer the same opportunity for doing a piece
of formal official business.

[1] See, for instance, the Lives of Popes Conon (A.D. 686), Stephen II (A.D. 752),
and Paschal II (A.D. 1099) in the *Liber Pontificalis*, i. 368, 440, ii. 296; and
Mabillon's *Museum Italicum*, ii (1724), p. cxvi.

[2] *Ordo Romanus xii*, in Mabillon, ii. 211 f.

THE NAMES AND NUMBERS OF MEDIEVAL POPES[1]

EARLY in 1913 it was announced in the newspapers that the Roman Commission of Historical Criticism, of which the late Cardinal Ferrata was president, had struck out four names from the list of Popes.[2] These were Boniface VI, who occupied the Holy See for fifteen days in 896; Boniface VII, who usurped it for a month in 974, was driven out, but returned ten years later and maintained his position for some time in 984 and 985; John XVI, who contested the Papacy against Gregory V in 997–8; and Benedict X, who was set up on the death of Stephen IX in 1058 and held his ground for nine months. It was at once stated in the *Osservatore Romano* that there was nothing new in the correction; the revised order merely went back to a list authorized by Benedict XIV in 1751. I have no means of ascertaining the precise fact, but it is undoubtedly true that not one of the four will be found in the official *Annuario Pontificio* for 1865. The corruption of the list, as we find it, for instance, in the *Gerarchia Cattolica* for 1901,[3] is therefore due to the misplaced industry of a more recent editor.

I

The question thus raised led me to look more closely into the names and numbers of the medieval Popes, and first of all to inquire when it was that they began to adopt new names on election. Towards the end of the twelfth century it was believed that the first Pope who changed his name was Sergius II, who became Pope in 844. According to Godfrey of Viterbo,

Iste Sergius papa vocabatur prius Os Porci, et propter hoc mutavit nomen et vocatus est Sergius in papatu. Ab illo tempore unusquisque in papatu nomen quod habuerat permutavit. Quod ante illud tempus non faciebant.[4]

---

[1] Reprinted from the *English Historical Review*, vol. xxxii (1917).

[2] See *The Times* for 17 February 1913.

[3] I cite this book at second hand through C. Mirbt's *Quellen zur Geschichte des Papsttums* (2nd ed.), pp. 450 ff. [Since this article was printed I have had an opportunity of seeing the *Gerarchia Cattolica* for 1904, issued shortly after the election of Pius X. This differs considerably from the volume for 1901 and has been partially revised with the help of Monsignor Duchesne's introduction to the *Liber Pontificalis*.]

[4] *Pantheon*, in *Monumenta Germaniae Historica, Scriptores*, xxii (1872), 292.

A similar statement appears in the Chronicle of Gilbert, a compilation, as it seems, of Roman origin dating from the early part of the thirteenth century,[1] and also, for instance, in the Lesser Chronicle of Erfurt; in the latter there is added,

> Hic constituit ut mutari debeat nomen pape, ut[2] Dominus Symonem appellavit Petrum, qui fuit primus papa.[3]

The story that Sergius II was first called Os Porci or 'Hog's Snout' is a simple mistake arising from a confusion with Sergius IV, who became Pope in 1009. When Thietmar, who was made bishop of Merseburg in that very same year, had occasion to mention the appointment of Sergius IV, he inserted in his own handwriting the words *qui vocabatur Bucca Porci*;[4] and several papal lists of the eleventh century give him the name of Os Porci.[5] A variant form is found appended to a manuscript of the Chronicle of Otto of Freising, written at Augsburg between 1165 and 1167 and now preserved at Hanover.[6] In this we read,

> Petrus, qui et Sergius, episcopus Albanensis, ex patre Petro, matre Stephania, cognomento Bucca Porca.[7]

Whatever may have been his surname, Sergius's name had been Peter; and this is in fact stated on his epitaph in the church of St. John Lateran:

> Albanum regimen lustro venerabilis uno
> Rexit. Post summum ducitur ad solium,
> In quo mutato permansit nomine presul
> Sergius ex Petro sic vocitatus erat,
> Ductus mente pia.[8]

A natural *pietas* restrained him from calling himself Peter II.

---

[1] *Is vocabatur Os porci, unde ab isto in antea omnis papa proprium nomen mutat*: ibid. xxiv. (1879), 130.   [2] Most manuscripts read *et*.

[3] *Chron. min. Minoritae Erphordensis*, with the date 841, in *Monumenta Erphesfurtensia*, p. 615, ed. O. Holder-Egger, 1899. (In another Erfurt chronicle the change of one numeral placed him five hundred years later, MᵒCCCᵒXLIᵒ: *Chron. S. Petri Erford.*, ibid., p. 385.) See also the Lives of Sergius II in Platina's *Hist. de Vitis Pontif. Roman.* (ed. 1572), p. 100, and Onuphrius Panvinius' *Epitome Pontif. Roman.* (1557), pp. 41 f.

[4] *Chron.* vi. 61 [vii. 40], ed. F. Kurze, 1889.

[5] It is found, for instance, in a catalogue formerly at the monastery of La Cava (Vatic. MS. 3764) and in another which was once preserved at St. Mary's beyond the Tiber (Add. MS. 14801, in the British Museum): see the *Liber Pontificalis*, ed. L. Duchesne, ii (1892), 267.

[6] See R. Wilmans, in *Monum. Germ. Hist., Script.* xx (1868), 102, and A. Hofmeister's preface to the *Chronica*, pp. xxx, xxxi (1912).

[7] Eccard, *Corp. Hist. Medii Aevi*, ii. 1639 b (1723).

[8] Cited by Duchesne, ii. 267, n. 4.

But no statement is made that Sergius IV was the first Pope to adopt a new name: with two such famous examples of this practice as those of Gregory V and Silvester II almost immediately preceding, the compiler of a catalogue could not easily fall into that mistake. It is therefore probable that the supposition that a Pope Sergius was the first to change his name must have arisen after the surname Os Porci had been erroneously attributed to Sergius II.

Can the inventor of the practice be discovered? One turns, as a matter of course, to see what Mabillon has to tell us. But here, by a rare exception, his information is unsatisfactory. After mentioning that from the eleventh century the Popes were in the habit of changing their names on election, he says:

> This indeed had been done near the end of the ninth century in the case of Adrian III who was previously called Agapitus; then in the tenth century in the cases of Sergius III, John XII, and John XIV, Gregory V, and Silvester II. But in the eleventh century it became a practice, at least from Benedict IX onwards, and after that time you will hardly find any Pope who did not change his name, excepting Marcellus II, who kept his own name.[1]

The statement about Adrian III seems to have arisen from some accidental confusion, which I think can be explained;[2] and I find no evidence that Sergius III adopted a new name when he became Pope, but the facts about his history are extremely obscure. I incline to think that Mabillon must have meant Sergius IV.

The first undoubted instance in which a Pope was known by two names is that of John XII, otherwise Octavian. This man, I need not say, is the Pope who crowned Otto the Great Emperor in 962 and who a year later was deposed for many irregularities by a Roman synod. Contemporary evidence as to his name is found in the Chronicle of Benedict, monk of St. Andrew's at the foot of Mount Soracte near Rome. Benedict is an illiterate

---

[1] *Acta Sanctorum O.S.B.*, saec. VI. ii (1701), praef. § xii. 93.

[2] The sixteen months of Adrian III's rule fall in a time when there is a gap of thirteen years, between the death of Adrian II in 872 and the election of Stephen V in 885, in the *Liber Pontificalis*, just before it stops abruptly in 891, and the brief lists of Popes which take its place are too meagre to supply any details about the life of Adrian III. Mabillon's statement as to the name Agapetus may have been due to his eye having strayed to a notice of the following century, where, just as Marinus I was followed by Adrian III, Marinus II was followed by Agapetus.

writer who pays no regard to numbers and cases, and it is not always easy to be sure of his meaning. He says of the Pope's father, Alberic prince of the Romans,

Genuit autem ex his [i.e. apparently from the issue of the king of the Lombards] principem ex concubinam filium; imposuit eis nomen Octabianus.

Then the Romans

omnes promiserunt fide per sacramentum ut Octabianus filium suum post mortem Agapiti pape Octabianus papa eligerent. . . . Inter haec non multum tempus Agapitus papa decessit. Octabianus in sede sanctissima susceptus est, et vocatus est Iohannes duodecimi pape.[1]

Flodoard, canon of Rheims, a most careful annalist, knows only of Pope Octavian;[2] but his information about an undoubtedly confused period in the history of the Papacy was defective, and he calls this Pope's successor John instead of Leo VIII. Richer, who drew much of his material from Flodoard, turns the one Pope into two: when he means John XII he speaks of

domno Iohanne papa, qui iam succedebat Octoviano, domni Agapeti successori.[3]

This mistake is found in later writers who made use of Flodoard. Hugh of Flavigny, writing about 1100, says,

Octavianus autem papa, cum de inreligiositate culparetur, a. 962 Romam exiit, et in locum eius Iohannes XII substitutus est.[4]

Hugh of Fleury, not many years afterwards, errs in a different direction: he says that the Romans deposed 'Otthavianum', who succeeded Agapetus, and set up 'Iohannem quendam';

quod audiens imperator Romam rediit, et prefatum Iohannem iudicio synodali deposuit.[5]

There was a difference of opinion among these writers whether it was Pope Octavian or Pope John who was deposed in 963. Evidently the news which reached France from Rome was incomplete. It told of a Pope named Octavian and of a Pope named John. Flodoard thought that John was the Pope set up after the deposition of Octavian, that is Leo VIII. Richer misunderstood his account and supposed that Octavian was followed

[1] *Chron.* xxxiv, xxxv, *Monum. Germ. Hist., Script.* iii (1839), 717.
[2] 'Octaviano papa': *Annales*, a. 965, ed. P. Lauer, 1905.
[3] *Hist.* iii. 17, ed. G. Waitz, 2nd ed., 1877.
[4] *Chron.*, in *Monum. Germ. Hist., Script.* viii (1848), 364.
[5] *Modern. Reg. Franc. Actus, ibid.* ix (1851), 383 f.

by John XII: what he says of this John certainly refers to John XII.[1]

To go back to Benedict of Soracte, it is possible that what he means is that Alberic prince of the Romans desired that his offspring should be known by a name which would connect them with the historical tradition of the empire.[2] He made inquiries (we may suppose) and learned that the first Emperor bore not the name but the surname of Octavian, and so let his son John be known as Octavian. It is no doubt true that Benedict says that when he was made Pope he was called John. But it is difficult to believe that this particular Pope introduced what after all was a remarkable innovation, still less that he did this from a scruple about the gentile associations of the name Octavian.[3] If he did so, he must have merely intended to make the change from his position as prince to that of Pope, and in this case he adopted the name of his uncle John XI. But it seems much more likely that John was his original name and that Octavian was the surname by which down to that time he was commonly known. Archbishop Adalbert of Magdeburg, the continuator of the Chronicle of Regino, calls him 'Iohannem, qui et Octavianus',[4] which was the usual way of mentioning a name and a surname; and a generation later Gerbert of Rheims, soon to be Pope Silvester II, speaks precisely of 'Iohannem cognomento Octavianum'.[5] The Papal Lists for this period usually do no more than copy out a jejune catalogue of Popes, with their origin and length of session; but the account of John XII forms an exception. It contains a full narrative manifestly taken from an official source. But it makes no mention of the name Octavian.[6] Nor is this name found in any Papal List until soon after the middle of the twelfth century, and then it appears in the Augsburg list already mentioned,

---

[1] Compare Richer, iii. 17, with Flodoard, a. 962.

[2] Monsignor Duchesne says, 'Peut-être Albéric s'était-il flatté qu'un jour cet Octavien deviendrait Auguste et qu'un empire romain vraiment indigène sortirait de sa principauté et de sa famille': *Les Premiers Temps de l'État Pontifical*, 2nd. ed., 1904, p. 335.

[3] See the *Nouveau Traité de Diplomatique*, iv (1759), 566 n.

[4] *Regin. Chron.*, a. 964, ed. F. Kurze, 1890. So too in Herman of Reichenau, *Chron.*, in *Monum. Germ. Hist.*, *Script.* v (1844), 115. Afterwards he speaks of 'Iohanne seu Octaviano'.

[5] *Acta Concil. Remensis* (991), xxviii, *Monum. Germ. Hist.*, *Script.* iii. 672. The words are put into the mouth of a speaker at the council of St. Basle, but the form of the report is plainly due to Gerbert. [6] *Lib. Pontif.* ii. 246 f.

which, though of earlier origin, is known to have received additions from other sources. Here the Pope is entered as 'Iohannes XII qui et Octavianus'.[1] The form agrees with Adalbert, but it is in fact derived from the Chronicle of Herman of Reichenau.[2]

In 983 a vacancy occurred in the Papacy, and Otto II not many weeks before his death secured the election of his arch-chancellor Peter, bishop of Pavia; and Peter took the name of John XIV.[3] This is the earliest example of a change of name which is entirely beyond dispute, and the person elected bore the name of Peter: *qui Petrus antea extiterat*, according to his epitaph as given by Peter Malleus.[4] It seems to me evident that the change was made because the name was Peter. The motive which is said to have actuated Sergius IV in 1009 had already been effective in the case of John XIV. The fact about Sergius IV was erroneously transferred to Sergius II, and the change which was really due to his name being Peter was wrongly attributed to his nickname of Os Porci.

Not long after John XIV two foreigners, a German and a Frenchman, attained the Papacy. Now in the seventh and eighth centuries there had been many Popes who came from regions far distant from Rome; but they all came from the Greek or Oriental sphere, whether from southern Italy or Sicily, Greece or Syria. No Pope had ever been chosen from the west. It may be that Bruno of Carinthia and Gerbert of Aurillac thought their names incongruous to the papal series. At all events they followed the example of Peter of Pavia, and became Gregory V and Silvester II.

II

We may next inquire what was the reason which induced Popes, when they changed their names, to adopt the particular names they chose. I speak designedly of their adopting names, for the theory of Dr. Wilhelm Martens, a dogmatic and uncon-vincing writer, that at least between 1046 and 1100 these names were imposed on Popes by the electing assembly without their

[1] Eccard, ii. 1638 *b*.
[2] Usually the Augsburg list is the source from which Herman takes his details, but here it seems that the words in the Augsburg list are a later insertion.
[3] *Ann. Einsidlenses, sub ann., Monum. Germ. Hist., Script.* iii. 143.
[4] J. B. de Rossi, *Inscriptiones sacrae Urbis Romae*, ii (1888), 216, n. 84.

consultation, cannot be taken seriously.[1] Dr. Martens indeed is more than serious on the point. He is vituperative of any one who holds a different opinion: any contrary statement which we find is 'false and dictated by a contaminated tendency'. Some of Dr. Martens's examples in support of his theory may be quoted. Of Clement II Benzo 'says precisely', *Vocatus est Clemens, et merito, fuit quippe bonus et benignus*; and the *Annales Romani* record the coronation of the Emperor *a suo sancto benignoque pontifice*. Then Poppo bishop of Brixen was made Pope, whom the Romans *alio nomine Damasum vocaverunt*. The like is said of Bruno of Toul, *Leo papa Romano more nuncupatur*; or as Leo of Ostia relates positively, *Romani Leonem papam vocari decernunt*. It is absurd to suppose that Bruno took his name from Leo VIII: the Romans acted with complete independence ('ganz autonom') and called him after Leo I. His biographer, Wibert, says, *Hic Deo devotissimus mores et vitam magni Leonis imitatus, cuius et vocabulo fuerit insignitus.*[2] Hildebrand chose the name Victor II for Gebhard of Eichstädt, and very likely also that of Nicholas II for Gerard of Florence. There can be no doubt that Hildebrand himself was called after Gregory I; his biographer Paul of Bernried speaks of *Gregorius VII super quem vere primi Gregorii requievit spiritus.*[3] Dr. Martens slurs over the statement of Leo of Ostia[4] that Gerard of Florence *Nycholai nomen indeptus est*. Other inconvenient phrases are summarily disposed of. When the Emperor in 1076, addressing Hildebrand, spoke of *beatum Gregorium cuius nomen tibi usurpasti*,[5] 'dies ist einfach unwahr'; and when Hugh of Flavigny said that Desiderius *Victorem se nominavit*,[6] this is 'a lie'. In this way it is easy to get rid of the obvious explanation, which is opposed by none of the evidence cited, that the new Pope made known to the assembly the name by which he intended to be called before he was proclaimed. It is strange that so sober a writer as Dr. Meyer von Knonau should in the case of Gregory VII have given countenance to Dr. Martens's

---

[1] See his article in *Zeitschrift für Kirchenrecht*, xxii (1887), 58–66, and *Gregory VII*, i (1894), 51 f.

[2] *Leonis IX Vita*, ii. 3, in Watterich, *Romanorum Pontificum Vitae*, i. 152, (1862).

[3] *Gregorii VII Vita, ibid.*, p. 474.

[4] *Chron. Monast. Casin.* ii. 12, *Monum. Germ. Hist., Script.* vii. 705.

[5] *Monum. Germ. Hist., Const. et Acta publica*, i. 110.

[6] *Chron. ibid., Script.* vii. 466.

wild hypothesis. He says that the cardinals proclaimed the new Pope as Gregory 'with unmistakable allusion to the similar condition of things when in 590 with complete unanimity the voice of the assembled Roman people chose the first Gregory as Pope'.[1]

I come now to the choice of names. One can hardly doubt that John XIV, the nominee of Otto II, went back intentionally to John XIII, the most imperial of Popes, who was elected after a special embassy had been sent to Otto the Great eighteen years earlier. But it cannot be supposed that when Bruno, the son of Otto III's cousin, Duke Otto of Carinthia, became Pope in 996 and adopted the name of Gregory V, he desired to associate himself with the last Pope of that name, who played a sorry part in the civil war between Lewis the Pious and his sons in 833. He must evidently have taken the name from a representative Pope, the greatest who had down to that time occupied the see, Gregory I. Gerbert no less plainly went back to the Pope who was contemporary with the first Christian Emperor, Silvester I, who was then believed to have baptized Constantine. The Popes who fill the interval between 1003 and 1046 have little but local interest, and need not detain us. The revolution made by the Emperor Henry III in the latter year had effects on the Popes' choice of names which continued for a century. During this time there were eighteen Popes elected, and all but five of them were the second of their name. In other words, they intentionally passed back beyond the period of papal occultation, when the Crescentii or the counts of Tusculum held the mastery, and openly connected themselves with the names of the pontiffs of the earlier church, eleven of them with Popes earlier than the middle of the seventh century, and only two with Popes of the ninth. The five exceptions are Leo IX, Stephen IX, Benedict X, Gregory VII, and Victor III. Of these Benedict is one of the four now finally eliminated from the list. Leo IX, Bishop Bruno of Toul, elected in Germany, may have wished to associate himself with Leo III who crowned Charles the Great, or perhaps with Leo VIII who was set up under Otto the Great,[2] or possibly may have thought of the first Leo.[3] Stephen IX was elected on

---

[1] *Jahrbücher des Deutschen Reichs unter Heinrich IV und Heinrich V.*, ii. (1894), 209.

[2] So Steindorff thought, ii. 71 f.

[3] The latter is suggested by Wibert of Toul, *Leonis IX Vita*, ii. 3, in Watterich, i. 152.

2 August, the day on which Pope St. Stephen I († 257) was venerated, and chose his name for that reason.[1] Gregory VII had personal reasons for attaching himself to Gregory VI.[2] Victor III was in the confidence of Gregory VII, as had been Victor II, and this link perhaps determined his choice of name. But these four are the only exceptions to the rule of reversion to the name of a Pope numbered One.

But Number Two could not be continued for ever. Eugenius III begins a series of Popes numbered Three. The system was apparently not understood at once, for he was followed by Anastasius IV and Adrian IV. But after Adrian in sixty-eight years there were eight Popes, all but one of whom were the third of their name. The one exception is Gregory VIII. After Honorius III there is no such long spell of Popes bearing the same number. Gregory IX is followed by five Popes numbered Four; Gregory X by two Popes numbered Five. But what is remarkable is that with the exceptions of Anastasius IV and Adrian IV there is still no return to the names of the Popes who reigned between Nicholas I († 867) and Clement II (1046): there is no John, Marinus, Theodore, Benedict, Sergius, or Boniface; Leo and Stephen appear but once. It is not until 1276 that any of these names are again used, and then so confused was the tradition that the two Popes who first reverted to them mistook either the number or the name. John who ought to have been the Twentieth called himself the Twenty-first, and Martin who was really the Second was known as the Fourth, because two Popes named Marinus were supposed wrongly to have borne the name of Martinus. Soon afterwards Boniface and Benedict were revived without scruple: the Crescentian and Tusculan days were too far distant for the names to excite suspicion. But with these exceptions the tradition begun in 1046 was steadily maintained until 1458, and since then in more than four centuries and a half only four Popes have departed from it; and these four all went back to the number Two. Aeneas Sylvius by an innocent conceit called himself Pius II. When his successor Pietro Barbo was elected, it is said that he proposed to be the second Formosus or the second Mark before he decided to become Paul II.[3] In 1503 Giuliano della

---

[1] See Leo of Ostia, *Chron. Montis Casini*, ii. 94 (*Monum. Germ. Hist., Script.* vii. 693).   [2] Otto of Freising, *Chron.* vi. 32, p. 300, ed. Hofmeister, 1912.
[3] M. Creighton, *Hist. of the Papacy*, iii (1887), 5.

Rovere, by a slight modification of his baptismal name, assumed that of Julius II. Finally, in 1555 Marcellus II retained his own name: the fact that his pontificate lasted only twenty days may have deterred subsequent Popes from following his example. They have all adopted names which were in use not earlier than 1378. No Pope has borne a lower number than Four; there have been a thirteenth Innocent, a fourteenth Clement, a fifteenth Benedict, and a sixteenth Gregory.

In connexion with the numbering of the Popes, there is one conspicuous difference between the time before and after 1046. In the earlier time Antipopes—I use the word without prejudice, to designate the opponents of Popes whose claims were ultimately accepted—were as a rule counted among the popes. Among these it would be historically untrue to reckon Leo VIII, who was elected after a Roman council in 963 when Otto the Great was in Rome and when John XII was deposed; for in fact no one ever disputed that he was a genuine Pope until Cardinal Baronius on *a priori* grounds excluded him.[1] Platina[2] and Panvinio[3] had no doubts about him; but now his name has long disappeared from the official lists. Nor was Boniface VI, who occupied the Papacy for fifteen days in 896, exactly an Antipope; there was no other Pope at the moment. Two years later a council at Ravenna declared his election null, and this decision, at least since Baronius, has been respected. The Antipopes whom I have in mind are Felix II in the middle of the fourth century, and Boniface VII and John XVI towards the end of the tenth. However questionable their position may have been, their numbers were accepted by subsequent Popes who bore or assumed the same name.[4]

After 1046 no Antipope has been allowed a place in the series. If the Tusculan Benedict X be quoted against this statement, I reply that he may properly be called a usurper and has in modern times been rightly struck out of the list. But an

---

[1] See his long dissertation, *Ann. Eccles.* 963, cc. iii–xl, vol. xvi. 129–38, ed. 1744. He adds: 'Non quia, sicut plerique alii male asserti, inter Romanos Pontifices numeratus reperitur, idcirco vere legitimum dixerimus fuisse Pontificem. Scriptorum error nullum afferre potest veritati praeiudicium, nec numerata Leonum ita nominatorum Pontificum series esse faciet quod non est (c. xxxviii).

[2] *Hist. de Vit. Pontif. Rom.*, p. 119.

[3] *Epit. Pontif. Rom.*, p. 50.

[4] Cf. Duchesne, *Lib. Pontif.* ii, introd., p. lxv.

Antipope he was not until nine months after he invaded the Holy See, when Nicholas II was elected against him. There was, therefore, nothing to prevent a Pope from adopting the number of Benedict XI in 1303. With Antipopes in the strict sense the case was different. In 1061 Alexander II had to withstand an Honorius II; but Honorius II was the style chosen by an acknowledged Pope in 1124. A Clement III was set up in 1084 against Gregory VII and maintained some sort of a position for sixteen years; but this was no obstacle to another Pope taking the name of Clement III in 1187. One of the Antipopes to Alexander III was Calixtus III (1168–78): his name and number were repeated nearly three hundred years later. Another was called Innocent III (1179–80): the great Innocent III was elected only eighteen years later. I need not speak of the confusion caused by the Clement and Benedict of the Great Schism, or of their hardly known successors who carried on an obscure tradition for fifteen years after the deposition of this Benedict XIII by the council of Constance in 1417. The acknowledged Benedict XIII was elected in 1724.

III

I have mentioned how a confusion between the names Martinus and Marinus led to a misnumbering in the case of Martin IV. The error which arose with respect to the Popes named John has been explained by Monsignor Duchesne.[1] It was not, I may notice, due to the inclusion of any one of the several Johns who with varying success usurped the Holy See in the last years of the tenth century. It came from a simple mistake in transcription. Under John XIV the papal catalogue mentions the length of his pontificate, *mens. VIII*, and proceeds to record his imprisonment *per IV menses*. Now in some copies these figures are both given as marking the length of the pontificate, and thus attributed to two successive Popes, each named John. Thus in a shortened list written about 1100 we read:

Iohannes m. VIII.
Iohannes m. IV.[2]

The mistake was the easier to make since John XIV was in fact followed by John XV. The two successive Johns became three.

---

[1] *Lib. Pontif.* ii, p. xviii.
[2] *Monum. Germ. Hist., Script.* xxiv. 84.

But the mistake was not made until there had been Popes John
to the number of Nineteen—the last died in 1032—for they all
reckoned their numbers correctly and had no knowledge of the
supposititious Pope who is nowadays conveniently distinguished
as Pope John 'XIV *bis*'. But by the thirteenth century the
corrupted text was everywhere accepted, and thus when, 244
years later, a Pope once more took the name of John, he called
himself the Twenty-First, though there never had been a
Twentieth. The point is worth going into, because it has been
supposed that the redundant Pope was the fictitious Joan.[1]
But no disturbance of the numbers of the Popes named John
occurred in the lists until the end of the eleventh century, and
the much later legend concerning Pope Joan placed her immediately after Leo IV, who died in 855.[2] John XIV *bis* was not
the only John inserted by mistake among the Popes of the end
of the tenth century. In some late copies of the *Liber Pontificalis*
the notice concerning John XV was repeated and a John XVI
produced who was different from the Antipope of Gregory V.
This purely imaginary Pope finds his place in the *Gerarchia
Cattolica* for 1901.[3]

I need not linger over another imaginary Pope Domnus or
Donus II who was inserted by a scribal error next after Benedict

---

[1] See Duchesne's note, ii. 457; cf. p. xxvi.

[2] Platina, p. 103, inserts the lady under the name of Johannes VIII, so that
he reaches John XXI by 1024.

[3] It may be helpful to give a table of the Popes during this period of confusion, with their numbers in the entire series, as they are given in the Benedictine *Art de vérifier les dates* (ed. 1818), the *Annuario Pontificio* for 1865, the
Gerarchia Cattolica for 1901, and Monsignor Duchesne's edition of the *Liber
Pontificalis*.

Art de vérifier.	Annuario.	Gerarchia.	Lib. Pontif.
136 John XIV.	139 J. XIV.	140 J. XIV.	140 J. XIV.
... J. XV. [=XIV *bis*].		141 Boniface VII.	
137 J. XVI.	140 J. XV.	142 J. XV.	141 J. XV.
138 { Gregory V. / J. XVII. }	141 Gregory V.	{ 143 J. XVI. / 144 Gregory V. }	142 { Gregory V. / J. XVI. }
		145 John XVII.	
139 Silvester II.	142 Silvester II.	146 Silvester II.	143 Silvester II.
140 J. XVII [*sic*].	143 J. XVI vel XVII	147 J. XVIII.	144 J. XVII.
141 J. XVIII.	144 J. XVII vel. XVIII.	148 J. XIX.	145 J. XVIII.
142 Sergius IV.	145 Sergius IV.	149 Sergius IV.	146 Sergius IV.
143 Benedict VIII.	146 Benedict VIII.	150 Benedict VIII.	147 Benedict VIII.
144 J. XIX.	147 J. XVIII, XIX, vel XX.	151 J. XX.	148 J. XIX.

VI in 974.[1] We find in several manuscripts entries of the following type:

> Benedictus sed. ann. I. m. VI.
> Domnus de Suri sed. ann. I. m. VI.

If the words *de Suri* are original, they must refer to Benedict VII, who was of Sutri, and thus indicate a text from which the intruder Boniface VII was omitted. But the years and months certainly belong to Benedict VI, and so we are led to suppose that the writer stopped short, possibly from uncertainty which name to supply, and then through inadvertence repeated the figures indicating the length of Benedict VI's pontificate.

There are two instances in which a series of Popes has been variously numbered, not in consequence of any mistake in transcription or any confusion of name, but through a difference of opinion as to whether one of them was truly Pope or not. The first case is that of the Popes named Felix, and I need only mention it in passing because it belongs to an earlier age in the history of the Church than that with which I am concerned in the present paper. The question of course has arisen from the famous controversy whether the Felix who was set up against Pope Liberius in 355 was to be reckoned a Pope or not, that is, whether he was to be called Felix II. It has only affected two of his successors, Felix II or III in 483, and Felix III or IV in 526. But this variation of number was introduced in modern times. In the middle ages the position of the doubtful Felix in the papal list was not contested, and when the council of Basle in 1439 elected an Antipope to Eugenius IV, he chose the style of Felix V.

The other case is that of the Popes named Stephen. Nearly five hundred years after St. Stephen I, who died in 257, one Stephen was elected Pope in March 752, on the death of Zachary; but he was never consecrated: on the third day after his election he apparently had a fit and died on the day following. The *Liber Pontificalis* speaks of him as *Stephanum quendam*, and does not include him among the Popes.[2] In modern times, however, he has been ranked as Stephen II and even canonized; so that the Stephen II who is famous for his relations with the Frankish king became Stephen III. Monsignor Duchesne says truly that this mode of reckoning is foreign to medieval practice.[3] For

---

[1] Duchesne, ii. 255, 256, n. 4, and introd., p. xviii.
[2] *Lib. Pontif.* i. 440.
[3] *Ibid.*, p. 456, n. 3.

the single example of a later Stephen being called by a number which requires the interpolated Stephen to be included may be fairly dismissed as an error of transcription. It relates to Stephen V, who was Pope from 885 to 891, and is found in the collection of canons of Cardinal Deusdedit,[1] where the Pope is called Stephen VI. That the mistake also appears in the British Museum Additional MS. 8873, the *Collectio Britannica*,[2] can be explained on the supposition, which is on other grounds probable, that the compiler of this book derived some of his materials from Deusdedit.[3] But there is no doubt at all that the canonists Ivo of Chartres and Gratian knew this Pope only as Stephen V.[4] And Stephen IX, who is called X in the official list, inscribed his number in full letters on his leaden seal, STEPHANI NONI PAPÆ.[5] The interpolated Stephen was brought very late into the list. Platina does little more than repeat what the *Liber Pontificalis* says about him and forthwith proceeds to the election of the real *Stephanus secundus*.[6] But Onofrio Panvinio held that he ought to be inserted. He says,

Hunc scriptores gestorum Rom. Pont. in numero Paparum non recensent. Opinor quia consecratus non fuerit, et propter temporis brevitatem, quod haud recte factum est, quâm [=quoniam] et legitimè creatus fuerit, et vir ingentis spiritus et animi semper existimatus sit, eum in Pontificum Rom. numero ponere nobis placuit, notam tamen nominis non addidimus, propter vitandam in sequentibus Pontif. qui Stephani nomen habuere confusionem. Ipsi enim in nominis appellatione et numero huius Stephani rationem non habuere.[7]

He at once contradicts himself by calling his successor Stephen III; but he returns to the correct numbers when he gets to the true Stephen III of 768. This is in the *Epitome Pontificum Romanorum*, published in 1557; his later *Chronicon* appended to Platina's History[8] represents a further stage. Here Stephen II

---

[1] *Die Kanonessammlung des Kardinals Deusdedit*, i. 244 [116], ed. V. Wolf von Glanvell, 1905. An opposite error occurs in ii. 161, where an extract is cited 'Ex sinodo secundi Stephani papę', meaning Stephen III.

[2] P. Ewald, in *Neues Archiv der Gesellschaft für ältere Deutsche Geschichtskunde*, v (1880), 587.   [3] Cf. *ibid.*, p. 582.

[4] See Ewald's references, *ibid.*, p. 399.

[5] J. von Pflugk-Harttung, *Specimina Chartarum Pontif. Rom.* iii (1887), plate vii. 5.

[6] *Hist. de Vit. Pontif.*, p. 87.   [7] *Epit. Pontif. Rom.*, p. 37.

[8] Panvinio's preface is dated September 1567, and the author died in April 1568. But the title-page bears the date 1572.

and his successors are renumbered 'Stephanus iij. dictus ij.' down to 'Stephanus x. dictus ix' in 1057. This method was followed by Baronius,[1] but the emphasis was now more strongly laid on the higher number, which although unknown until the sixteenth century has established itself in the modern official lists. It is still, I think, most generally current among Roman Catholic writers. It was used by Mabillon and by Döllinger, and it will be found in the first edition of Jaffé's *Regesta Pontificum*, which was not of Catholic origin. I am not able to explain how the restoration of the correct medieval numbers came about. It may have been due to the popularity of Platina's History; or perhaps Protestant writers may have adopted it from suspicion of Baronius—at any rate the correct numbering has been long accepted by them, from Mosheim down to Gieseler and Milman, to name no others. They had the powerful support of the later Benedictines of the congregation of St. Maur, who in the *Nouveau Traité de Diplomatique*[2] rejected the opinion of Baronius, and in the *Art de vérifier les Dates* printed the interpolated Stephen in small type and assigned him no number in the series of Popes.[3]

To go back to the point from which I started, if, as I understand, the revised list of 1913 did no more than exclude Boniface VI and Boniface VII, John XVI, and Benedict X, it merely omitted four names which were only added within the last half-century. It did not profess to deal critically with the whole matter of the papal succession. Had it done this, it could not have left standing, for example, the duplicated Cletus near the beginning of the list or the imaginary Donus II. Most likely Boniface VI was canonically ineligible; Boniface VII and Benedict X may be truly said to have invaded the Holy See; and John XVI is admitted to have been an Antipope. But these four were not the only alleged Popes whose position was open to dispute. What are we to say, for instance, of Sergius III on the one hand or of his four predecessors, whom he declared to be no Popes, on the other? Probably it was not desired to open up difficult problems. The commission of 1913 restored a list which went back to the eighteenth century and which represented generally the conclusions of Baronius. It is considerably in advance of Panvinio, who by inserting a number of Antipopes, not to speak of Pope Joan, raised the total by more than a

---

[1] *Ann. Eccles.* 752, c. x, vol. xii. 579, and elsewhere.
[2] v. (1762), 158, n. 1.　　　　　　　　　　[3] II. iii. 293, ed. 1818.

dozen,[1] though he did not admit Donus II nor exclude Leo VIII or Silvester III. But it is far less critical than that constructed by the Benedictine authors of the *Art de vérifier les Dates*. On the other hand, it does not give a list which accords with the series in the *Liber Pontificalis* nor one which would have been recognized in the middle ages.

[1] The excess is in appearance sixteen, because Panvinio numbers the two invasions of Boniface VII and Benedict IX in each case as separate Pontificates.

IMPERIAL INFLUENCES ON THE FORMS OF PAPAL DOCUMENTS[1]

THE relations between the Papacy and the Empire on the one side and the Frankish kings on the other during the eighth century form a large and complicated subject for study. My present purpose is only to show how the changes in those relations are reflected in the forms of documents. I take first the manner of dating bulls. The traditional rule had been to record the regnal year of the Emperor, and it had been the practice that the election of a Pope should be confirmed by the Exarch of Ravenna; when therefore the Exarchate was conquered by the Lombards in 751,[2] it might perhaps have been expected that the Imperial date would disappear from papal documents. But in fact it was maintained, possibly from force of habit, for more than twenty years longer. The last instance in which it has been found is in a solemn bull granted by Adrian I to the monastery of Farfa in 772, which concludes with the words:

Data x. Kalendas Martii, imperantibus domno nostro piissimo Augusto Constantino a Deo coronato magno imperatore anno liii., et post consulatum eius anno xxxiii., sed et Leone magno imperatore eius filio anno xxi., Indictione x.[3]

How much longer the Imperial date continued in use cannot be precisely stated. During the nine years following, though at least twenty-three genuine documents of Pope Adrian are preserved, they are all letters of the simpler type which did not contain an elaborate date.[4] It is not until nearly the end of 781 that in place of the Imperial date we find the year of the Pope's pontificate, prefaced by an entirely different formula. This appears in a letter of 1 December 781 addressed by Adrian to Fulrad the archpriest and Maginar the abbot conferring

---

[1] Reprinted from the *Proceedings of the British Academy*, vol. viii (1917).

[2] The exact date is not recorded: see T. Hodgkin, *Italy and her Invaders*, vii (1899), 163. But the Farfa Chartulary contains a document of King Aistulf dated at Ravenna, 4 July in his third year and the fourth Indiction, that is, in 751: *Regesto di Farfa*, ii (1879), 33, no. 18.

[3] *Ibid.*, p. 85, no. 90.

[4] These, all addressed to Charles the Great, are to be found in the *Liber Carolinus*, last edited by W. Gundlach, in *Monum. Germ. Hist., Epist.* iii (1892), 566–601. The letter to Archbishop Tilpin of Rheims, given by Flodoard, *Hist. Rem. Eccl.* ii. 17, is also without date. Its genuineness has been disputed: see Jaffé, *Regesta Pontificum Romanorum*, 2nd ed., no. 2411.

privileges on the monastery of St. Denis. The final clauses here run as follows:

Scriptum per manum Theodori Notarii et Scriniarii in mense Novembrio, indictione suprascripta quinta. Bene valete. Data Kal. Decembris regnante Domino et salvatore nostro Iesu Christo, qui vivit et regnat cum Deo patre omnipotente et spiritu sancto per immortalia saecula, anno pontificatus nostri in sacratissima beati Apostoli Petri sede[1] Deo propitio decimo, indictione quinta.[2]

If the change was first made in that year, it may be connected with Charles the Great's second visit to Rome at Easter, when two of his sons were baptized by the Pope; but we cannot say for certain that it was not done seven years earlier, when Charles on his first visit to the city also kept Easter there.

For more than one reason, to which I shall turn shortly, it may be taken as certain that the change of the form of dating was adopted under Frankish influences, and therefore most probably when the Frankish king and his attendants were at Rome; but emissaries were passing backwards and forwards all through these years, and it may have been by any one of them that the new form was suggested. The innovation marked a change which was compatible with a closer advance towards the Franks, but it need not be inferred that it was designed to precipitate a breach with the Empire in the East. Indeed, in this very year, 781, a daughter of Charles was betrothed to Constantine VI. Placed as he was in the midst between two great powers, Adrian was no doubt gravitating towards the West; he relied upon Charles for the maintenance and increase of his temporal dominion. But ecclesiastical and other reasons forbade his provoking the enmity of the Emperor. Hence, as it seems to me, he omitted the Imperial date as an element in his documents on the supposition that it had become obsolete when the Imperial authority in Upper Italy was overthrown by the Lombards. No doubt such a theory would be legally untenable: the Exarch was merely the representative of the Emperor, and when he was displaced his authority reverted to his master; but as a fact that authority was never acknowledged by the Popes after 781, and the Imperial date disappeared. Its place was taken not by any words implying a recognition of the

---

[1] Printed *sub die.*

[2] Edited in Baluze's *Miscellanea* (ed. Mansi), iii (1762), 3 *b*, from the Paris MS. Colbert 5034 (now Lat. 2777), assigned to the tenth century.

Frankish power but by the date of the year of the Pontificate. To this was prefixed a formula which has no chronological reference but is a simple statement of the Divine government. It has a long history which deserves examination all the more since it now for the first time is found as a part of the date at the end of a document, using this word in its technical sense.

The formula runs, with some variations in detail, as follows:

regnante domino Deo et Salvatore nostro Iesu Christo cum Deo Patre et Spiritu sancto per infinita secula.

It is in substance identical with the words by which the records of the Acts of Martyrs were habitually closed, and is of high antiquity. We can trace it so early as in the letter of the Church of Smyrna reporting the martyrdom of St. Polycarp in A.D. 155 or 156:

Βασιλεύοντος δὲ εἰς τοὺς αἰῶνας Ἰησοῦ Χριστοῦ· ᾧ ἡ δόξα, τιμή, μεγαλωσύνη, θρόνος αἰώνιος ἀπὸ γενεᾶς εἰς γενεάν· Ἀμήν.[1]

The words are possibly an addition to the original text, but if so they are a very early addition. They were deemed so appropriate, we may almost say so necessary, for the termination of such Acts that we find them added in other narratives. For instance, in the Acts of the Scillitan martyrs, A.D. 180, they are absent from the original Latin but appear in the Greek translation;[2] and in the Greek Acts of St. Apollonius they are considered to be a later insertion.[3] But the wide diffusion of the formula[4] is evidence of its antiquity, and the supposition of several modern scholars that it must have been constructed subsequently to the invention of the reckoning of the year of the Incarnation by Dionysius Exiguus early in the sixth century is based simply on a confusion of ideas, since it has no chronological significance at all.[5]

The derivation of the formula is unquestionable, but how it came to be introduced into documents is obscure. I do not know that it was so used in Italy, but it is found in Anglo-Saxon

---

[1] xxi., in Lightfoot's *Apostolic Fathers*, 2nd ed., II. iii (1889), 400.

[2] See J. Armitage Robinson, 'The Passion of St. Perpetua', in *Texts and Studies*, I. ii. 107 ff. (1891).

[3] Κατὰ δὲ ἡμᾶς Βασιλεύοντος τοῦ Κυρίου ἡμῶν Ἰησοῦ Χριστοῦ, ᾧ ἡ δόξα εἰς τοὺς αἰῶνας; *Acta S. Apollonii*, § 47 b, p. 130, ed. E. T. Klette (1897).

[4] I had copied out a series of specimens from Ruinart's *Acta Sincera Martyrum* (2nd ed., 1717), but need not print them as they are cited by Bishop Lightfoot, *op. cit.*, II. i. 636.

[5] Cf. Lightfoot, p. 635. His remarks on p. 503 about the Acts of the Scillitan martyrs need revision in the light of Dr. Robinson's later work on their text.

charters from the early part of the eighth century, and perhaps very much earlier; and these unquestionably derived their form and structure from Italian models. Here the words

Regnante domino nostro Iesu Christo

are written at the head of the document; they have nothing to do with a date, but serve practically as an alternative to the more usual invocation

In nomine domini nostri Iesu Christi.

In no charter of undoubted genuineness are they combined with any date of time. I cannot therefore think that Pope Adrian I took the phrase from an Italian source, but he may have learned it from the Frankish formulary of Marculf. This book is believed to have been compiled about the year 700; it is more probably a little later, and there is no certain trace of its having been used as a guide for the writing of documents until 741.[1] Here we find the formula introducing a date by the year (apparently of the Incarnation), the Regnal year, and the day, at the head of a will:

Regnante in perpetuo domino nostro Iesu Christo, qualibet[2] anno illo regnante rege illo, sub die illo.[3]

As the collection became current as a manual towards the middle of the eighth century, it is likely that it was from it, directly or indirectly, that Adrian's clerks took the formula. They adopted the whole clause, substituting the Pontifical for the Regnal year, and introduced it at the place in which the Popes had been accustomed to insert the date, namely, at the end of the document.

It is interesting to observe that a century later the formula *Regnante Christo* was the specific mark of an interregnum. It was so used, in the form

Regnante imperatore domno Ihesu Christo,

by Pope John VIII on 3 October 875, during the interval between the death of the Emperor Lewis II on 12 August and the coronation of Charles the Bald at Christmas.[4] This may possibly have arisen from Pope Hadrian's practice being regarded as indicating an interregnum between Byzantine and Frankish

---

[1] See K. Zeumer, *Formulae* (*Monum. Germ. Hist.*, *Leg.* v, 1886), pp. 33 f.
[2] *Sic.*   [3] ii. 17, *ibid.*, p. 86.
[4] *Cod. Diplom. Fuldensis*, ed. E. F. J. Dronke (1850), pp. 279 f., no. 618.

supremacy. In the tenth century the formula appears not infrequently, especially in Burgundy, when the succession was uncertain or disputed. But I cannot believe that it was chosen with any signification of this sort by Adrian. In the Anglo-Saxon charters of the time it is prefixed to a large number of documents granted by kings.

It was not until nearly the end of the eighth century that the Pope abandoned this formula and inserted the Regnal year of the Frankish king in Italy. On 20 April 798 Leo III dated a document

domini Caroli excellentissimi regis Francorum et Langobardorum et patricii Romanorum a quo cepit Italiam anno xxv.[1]

Then after Charles's coronation at Rome on Christmas Day 800 we find the full date in the Imperial style. It runs something like this, though in the absence of originals the form is uncertain ; perhaps at first it was not regular:

imperante nostro domino Carolo piissimo perpetuo Augusto a Deo coronato anno tertio.[2]

This date not only appropriated the form used by the Eastern Emperors, but it also led to a revival of the reckoning *post consulatum* and made it equivalent to the Imperial year, e.g.

Imperante domino nostro piissimo perpetuo Augusto Karulo a Deo coronato magno Imperatore anno primo et post consulatum anno primo.[3]

This was not due to Frankish influence, for the Carolingians did not assume the Consular title:[4] it was simply a mechanical repetition of the formula as it had been in use down to 772 ; and, not understanding the nature of the Consular dignity in the East, the Papal clerks treated the date *post consulatum* as chronologically identical with the Imperial year.

[1] A. Brackmann, *Germania Pontificia*, i (1911), p. 8, no. 7 (Jaffé, *Reg.* 2498) ; from which the date has been inserted by a modern editor in another document of the same date, 'Epist. Karolini Aevi', in *Monum. Germ. Hist., Epist.* v (1899) 59, note *h* (Jaffé, *Reg.* 2495) : see Brackmann, l. c., no. 8.

[2] To Fortunatus, Patriarch of Grado, 21 March 803: set out by Andrea Dandolo, *Chronicon*, VII. xiii. 25, in *Muratori's Rerum Italicarum Scriptores*, xii (1728), 153.

[3] John VIII's bull for Tournus, 876, in J. von Pflugk-Harttung's *Specimina Selecta Chartarum Pontificum Romanorum*, i (1885), 6.

[4] In one single instance Charles the Great used *consulatus* as equivalent to *imperium*. This was in an Italian capitulary of 801, *anno vero regni nostri in Frantia XXXIII, in Italia XXVIII, consulatus autem nostri primo* : *Capitularia Regum Francorum*, ed. A. Boretius (*Monum. Germ. Hist., Leg.* ii), i, 204, no. 98 (1883).

This mode of dating continued, except during two interregna, for a little more than a century. It ceased with the eclipse of the Empire in the time of Lewis III, who was blinded and driven out by Berengar of Friuli in 905;[1] and when Berengar was crowned Emperor ten years later it was not resumed. The restoration of the Empire by Otto the Great in 962 was naturally soon followed by the restoration of the Imperial date, without however the mention of the *Post Consulatum*, in papal documents; we find it under John XIII,[2] but it did not last beyond the reign of Henry II.[3] When the series of German Popes began under Henry III we might have expected that the date would be uniformly admitted. But it was not so. Under Clement II indeed we find two documents in 1047 bearing a simple Imperial date, with no honorific titles;[4] but when Bruno bishop of Toul became Pope in the following year, as Leo IX, he definitely abandoned it. This is all the more remarkable because he was a great organizer of his chancery. But it will be remembered that, though he was elected at Worms, he declined to assume the Pontificate until he had been formally accepted at Rome.

After this time the Imperial year is found only on two occasions. One of these is in a document of the Antipope Guibert of Ravenna, otherwise Clement III, who was set up by

---

[1] The last known instance is found in a document of Sergius III of 904, *Imperante domno piissimo perpetuo Augusto Ludovico a Deo coronato magno imperatore anno IIII, et post consulatum eius anno IIII, Indictione VIII*: Migne, *Patrol. Lat.* cxxxi. 972 (Jaffé, *Reg.* 3533).

[2] It appears in a bull of Leo VIII dated 9 December 964 (a mistake for 963), which is preserved in a late medieval transcript and printed by Dr. von Pflugk-Harttung, *Acta Pontificum Romanorum Inedita*, ii (1884), no. 81. But this document has long been suspected (see Jaffé, *Reg.* 3700), and is now condemned as spurious: Brackmann, *Germania Pontificia*, i. 15, no. 32.

[3] Dr. Bresslau's statement (which I repeated in my *Lectures on the History of the Papal Chancery*, p. 49, 1915) that the Imperial year of Conrad II seems to be used by the Pope only once, and that when the Emperor was in Italy (*Handbuch der Urkundenlehre*, i. 837, ed. 1, 1889), rests on a mistake. The one example cited (Jaffé, Reg. 4080) is a mere abstract of a bull for Cluny (*Chartes de Cluny*, no. 2798, vol. iv, 1 f., 1888). It ends with the following clauses:

Domnus Humbertus episcopus Valentinensis propria manu hoc firmavit
Domnus Wigo frater ipsius similiter propria manu hoc firmavit
Anno primo consecrationis domni Conradi imperatoris.

The date is obviously that of the confirmation by these Burgundians, not that of the bull itself. Dr. Bresslau's error is the more remarkable since he devoted special attention to the document in his *Jahrbücher des Deutschen Reichs unter Konrad II*, ii (1884) 489. [but cf. the 2nd ed., 1931, of Bresslau's *Urkundenlehre* where a second example is given, ii, 421, note 3].

[4] *Anno domni Clementis secundi papae primo, domni Henrici tertii imperatoris similiter primo*: Migne, cxlii. 585 f (Jaffé, *Reg.* 4150).

the agency of the Emperor Henry IV. He is not recognized as a Pope, and the document therefore does not concern us.[1] The other occasion occurred at perhaps the most tragic moment in the history of the Papacy. In IIII, when the violence of Henry V had reduced Paschal II to abject submission and compelled him to perform the coronation in St. Peter's, the Pope retired to an obscure spot on the Island in the Tiber, and there two days later perforce concluded his bulls

Datum Romae in insula Lycaonia per manum Iohannis sanctae Romanae ecclesiae diaconi cardinalis ac bibliothecarii vice domni F[riderici] archicancellarii et Coloniensis archiepiscopi, xvii Kal. Maii, indictione iv, incarnationis dominicae anno mcxi., pontificatus autem domni P[aschalis] secundi papae anno xii, imperio vero H[enrici] quarti imperatoris anno primo.[2]

Before leaving these chronological details, I will mention another point in which Imperial influence is unmistakable. This is the employment of the year of the Incarnation. Though the system of reckoning from the *Annus Domini* was devised as early as 525, it was not until just two hundred years had elapsed that it was brought into currency by the publication of the Venerable Bede's treatise *de Temporum Ratione*. From that time it became an established element in the dating of charters in England, but in England only. It passed to the Continent by the means of Anglo-Saxon missionaries and scholars. St. Boniface took it with him into the Frankish kingdom.[3] But it does not appear to have been regularly employed in the Royal Chancery until the last quarter of the ninth century,[4] from which time it became a fixed element in diplomas. The Popes never adopted it until after the Imperial coronation of Otto the Great in 962. Three years later John bishop of Narni was elected at the Emperor's nomination. This Pope, John XIII, was grievously

---

[1] *Anno dominice incarnationis LXXXVI, imperante Heinrico tertio Romanorum Augusto, anno imperii eius ii,* with no Pontifical year: Mittarelli, *Annales Camaldulenses,* iii (1758), 40.

[2] *Udalrici Codex,* cli (in Jaffé's *Monumenta Bambergensia,* 1869, p. 279), calendared in Jaffé's *Reg.* 6291.

[3] See Carloman's capitulary of 21 April 742: *Capitularia Regum Francorum,* i. 24.

[4] Bresslau, *Handbuch der Urkundenlehre,* i8. 39 (ed. 1) [cf. 2nd ed., (1931) ii. 427-8]: Giry, *Manuel de Diplomatique* (1894), p. 89. An isolated diploma of earlier date is an original of Pippin II, King of Aquitaine, dated 839, which is preserved among the archives of Solignac at Limoges: see the *Bibliothèque de l'École des Chartes,* lxii (1901), 715.

mishandled by the Romans and driven into exile; but in the following year, when it was known that Otto was on his way to Italy, he was hurriedly recalled. Otto took terrible vengeance on John's adversaries in Rome, and for the rest of his pontificate he was unmolested. It was during these years, when the strength of the Empire was most vigorously exercised, that the Pope introduced into his bulls not only, as we have seen, the dating by the Imperial year, but also the dating by the year of the Incarnation in the form which had become established in the Imperial chancery.[1] It was not, however, uniformly inserted in papal documents until Leo IX made a fresh reorganization of his system eighty years later. Here and elsewhere I speak only of the more solemn form of papal document, the Privilegium, for the features on which I comment are not found in simple letters.

I return now to the eighth century and to Adrian I. When this Pope abandoned the Byzantine Imperial date and substituted the year of his pontificate, he made also a great change in the form in which the date was expressed. His object was plainly to distinguish the responsibility of the scribe for the correctness of the text of the document from that of a higher official for the fact that it had the Pope's authority. He therefore introduced a Scriptum at the end of the text, and then, after the Pope had written his Subscriptio, added the Datum of the official. I quote an example of 1 November 782:

Scriptum per manus Iohannis scriniarii in mense Octubrio indictione supradicta sexta. † Bene valete.

Data Kalendas Novembris per manus Anastasii scriniarii regnante domino Deo et Salvatori Iesu Christo cum Deo Patre omnipotenti et Spiritu sancto per infinita secula. Anno Deo propitio pontificatus domni Adriani in apostolica sede undecimo. indictione sexta.[2]

It is not unlikely that this division of the date into two parts was suggested by the double date which was one of the first marks of

---

[1] There is evidence of this between 968 and 970. See an example of 17 December 970, in Muratori's *Antiquitates Italicae*, iii (1740), 235. The insertion of this date has been attributed to Leo VIII. But it is not found in the document (Jaffé, *Reg.* 3702) as printed in Baluze's *Miscellanea* (ed. Mansi), iii. 5, where it breaks off imperfectly in the Scriptum. The date is taken from a modern collection of transcripts in the Bibliothèque Nationale, Lat. 12762.

[2] Recited in a corrupt text in a notarial act of 1053 relating to St. Apollinaris in Classe at Ravenna: Mittarelli, *Ann. Camaldulenses*, i (1755), app. iii (Jaffé, *Reg.* 2437).

orderly method set up by King Pippin in the Frankish chancery. There, it is true, the division rested on a different principle. The Datum, as in the Papal form, certified the authority for the document; and it was followed by the Actum, which registered the place where the business was done. But though the Datum had been used by the Popes for centuries and the Scriptum may now have been introduced from an Italian source, it is under Hadrian, when Frankish influences were coming in, that we first find the combination of the two elements.

But the introduction of the name of the higher official of the chancery gave an opening for the adoption of an organization which was directly borrowed from the system of the Empire. Down to the eighth century the whole business of drafting and executing papal documents had been in the hands of the College of Notaries, a body of men who were entirely bound up with the traditions of their office. It was natural that a Pope who proposed to introduce changes in his system should wish to employ a secretary—for such he really was—who was personally dependent upon him. Adrian took the preliminary step of appointing a Librarian—previously the Library together with the Archives had been in the charge of one of the higher Notaries—but it was not until the first quarter of the ninth century that the Librarian is found to have been employed to add the date to documents. Thenceforward the Librarian was in fact the head of the chancery, though there are a few instances of one of the chief Notaries taking his place.[1] It was he who regulated all the details connected with the production of the Pope's documents. The system, as we might expect in a period when the Papacy rarely exerted itself to go outside the traditional track, was conducted in a conservative spirit, and underwent no marked change until the revival of the Empire by Otto the Great. The documents were still written in the Curial hand-writing, an artificial and highly intricate development of the ancient Cursive. But when Otto secured the election of John XIII, the same Pope who revived the Imperial date and introduced the year of Grace into his bulls, a conspicuous alteration was made in the writing of the Datum. While the entire text of the document continued to be written in the Curial hand, the certificate of the Librarian was written in that beautiful delicate character, the Caroline Minuscule, which had

---

[1] See my *Lectures on the Papal Chancery*, pp. 55 f.

been in use in the North for not far short of two centuries.[1] This distinction of handwriting between the document itself and the Datum was retained until the Curial hand silently died out early in the twelfth century. What is of interest here is that the Minuscule was brought in under a Pope who owed his position specifically to Imperial influence, and to whom was due the adoption of two distinct notes of time, both derived from the Imperial Chancery.

But the Librarian had not yet assumed the Imperial title of Chancellor. Even under Otto III and Silvester II, when great attention was paid to ceremonial forms, there is no trace of a Chancellor. He suddenly emerges for a brief space, two years after Silvester's death. If the adoption of the title was due to Imperial influence, we can only surmise that it was an afterglow of the day of Imperial splendour; for in 1005 there was no Emperor, and the Pope was in the hands of a civic faction at Rome. Nor was the title continued.[2] In 1042, however, Benedict IX, one of the Tusculan Popes, definitely established it; from that time the responsible head of the chancery was styled Librarian and Chancellor of the Holy Apostolic See.[3] The title borrowed from the Empire led to further inroads on the old papal system.

The revolution in the Papacy caused by the masterful intervention of the Emperor Henry III in 1046 was soon followed by a notable change in the whole appearance of the Pope's bull. The first two Popes who were brought in from the Empire lived less than a year, with an interval of Tusculan anarchy between them; but Leo IX, who was elected in 1048, had full range for impressing his personality on the system which he was called upon to administer. Of the importance of his ecclesiastical and political activity this is not the place to speak: I have only to deal with the manner in which Leo, a man of high intellectual cultivation and of an artistic temperament, reformed the aspect of his documents. Down to his time authority was given to them by the Pope's Subscriptio. Now a Subscriptio according to Roman tradition did not mean the signing of his name. It

---

[1] See a facsimile of part of a bull for Bologna, 15 April 967, in Pflugk-Harttung's *Specimina*, i. 8. Mabillon, *de Re Diplomatica* (ed. 1709), p. 444, gives a remarkable specimen from a bull for St. Remigius at Rheims, 23 April 972 (Jaffé, *Reg.* 3763), which is entirely written in Minuscule. This appears to be a unique exception.

[2] *Papal Chancery*, pp. 59 f.   [3] *Ibid.*, pp. 62 f.

consisted of a final greeting, a farewell;[1] and its form had gradually settled down to the words BENE VALETE written in Capitals, and preceded by a Cross. This Subscriptio was, at least in part, written by the Pope's own hand. The effect was clumsy, and the big Capitals made an unpleasing contrast to the Datum written in a shapely minuscule. Almost immediately after his accession Leo determined to reconstruct his Subscriptio.[2] He separated the Cross from the Bene Valete, and placed them on the left and right at the foot of the document. Between the limbs of the Cross he inserted his name; and he surrounded it by a double circle in which was written a text from the Psalter. This is known as the Rota. On the right hand he contracted the Bene Valete into a Monogram, in which the letters of the words were compressed into a rectangular framework. Both Rota and Monogram were written very large and stand out as the conspicuous features of the document. Part of the Rota was written in the Pope's own hand; the rest was completed by a notary.

The Monogram is unquestionably derived from that which reproduced the Emperor's name in his diplomas. It was first used by Charles the Great and assumed various developments as it became necessary to reduce such unmanageable names as Cuonradus and Heinricus into a compact figure. The original basis was certainly a Cross with the letters of the name worked into and round it; but this model was not always observed. The Monogram was matched by the Seal imposed on the face of the document. I cannot say that the two features, the Monogram and the Seal, balanced one another, for the places in which they were inserted were irregular.[3] But there were these two striking features, and Leo IX determined to transplant them in a better form into his documents. He could not take the seal, because his leaden seal was always pendent upon strings or ties. So he invented the Rota, which had the same shape as his seal and like it was surrounded by two circles. The seal on its two faces bore the inscription LEONIS $\begin{vmatrix} \text{IIII} \\ .\text{V.} \end{vmatrix}$ PAPAE; but the Rota was

---

[1] Cf. C. G. Bruns, 'Die Unterschriften in den römischen Rechtsurkunden', in the *Sitzungsberichte der K. Preussischen Akademie der Wissenschaften (philos. und hist. Klasse)*, 1876, pp. 53 ff.   [2] See *Papal Chancery*, pp. 99 ff.

[3] See W. Erben, 'Kaiser- und Königsurkunden', in Erben, Schmitz-Kallenberg, and Redlich's *Urkundenlehre*, i (1907), 155 f. A specimen of Henry III of 1043 is reproduced in *Monumenta Graphica*, v. ii.

a single figure, and so the Pope wrote the words short, LEO P.
Having thus indicated his name on the left hand of his bull,
there was no reason to repeat it on the right hand; besides, the
words BENE VALETE were a time-honoured form which could
not be abandoned. He therefore constructed a Monogram out
of these words. The two pictorial elements, the Rota and the
Monogram, were written of the same size and placed so as to
match exactly on each side of the document below the Scriptum.
Thus he took the whole idea from the Imperial diploma, but
very greatly improved on his model.

Soon afterwards, probably in June 1049, Leo took the important step of appointing the Archbishop of Cologne Arch-
Chancellor of the Apostolic See. The Archbishop was already
by virtue of his office the Imperial Arch-Chancellor of Italy;
he now became Papal Arch-Chancellor of Rome as well.[1] But
though this was a mark of the harmony which subsisted at the
time between Pope and Emperor, it led to no practical consequences; for the Archbishop was content with the new dignity
and with the emoluments which were attached to it, and never
exercised his Roman functions except by deputy. Still, the
formal annexation of the headship of the papal chancery to
the see of Cologne gives the impression that at the beginning
of Leo's pontificate it was intended to unify the administration
of the Empire and Papacy in a way which had hardly been
attempted before, even during the reign of Otto III.

It is easy to exaggerate the significance of these features in
their system which the Popes borrowed from the Empire. Their
source is manifest, but their real meaning is apt to be misunderstood. In the eighth century the Popes were led by the
political conditions of the time to welcome the protection of
Charles the Great and all that it implied; but the Empire on
which they depended crumbled away, and in the tenth and
eleventh centuries they found themselves in an unenviable
situation. Their administrative activity was hampered by the
oligarchy of the College of Notaries. If they sought an escape
from it, they fell into the hands either of a wild city faction or
else of the lawless counts of Tusculum. If they were to gain any
independence, they must be masters in their own house; they
must establish a business office over which they could exert

---

[1] Once before, in 1023, an Archbishop of Cologne had been made Librarian,
but it does not seem that this was more than a personal mark of honour.

personal control. They therefore first set up a Librarian, and then wishing to give him a more imposing title borrowed that of Chancellor from the Empire. The changes made under Otto the Great were no doubt forced upon, rather than originated by, the Papacy. They consisted of new formulae and of a reformed handwriting. But the tradition set on foot by the introduction of the minuscule handwriting enabled the Pope gradually to emancipate himself from his traditional surroundings; for the Roman notaries could not write in that character. The freedom thus acquired was extended when the Pope was no longer permanently established in the city of Rome. Leo IX was the first Pope for ages past who went on his travels.[1] During a pontificate of five years he lived hardly more than six months in the city. Naturally, when he departed the Roman notaries were left behind; the tradition was broken; and even when Leo was resident in Rome he sometimes avoided the employment of the old staff.[2] The former system might reappear from time to time, owing to special circumstances; but it was more and more passing out of use, and with the early part of the twelfth century the Pope is found managing his affairs by means of officials all of whom he appointed himself.

From that time there is no further question of Imperial influence upon the Papal system. What influence there was flowed in the opposite direction. It was the perfect regulation of the Papal Chancery, in all that concerned form and style and legal exactness, that reacted upon the Imperial lands, as upon the rest of Western Europe. When the class of notaries public, a specifically Italian institution, made its way into Germany, it diffused the methods which had been slowly evolved at Rome; and Italy furnished the model from which the Imperial scribes learned the refinement of their art.

---

[1] Since John VIII spent half a year, from May to November 878, in different parts of France and Burgundy, no Pope had quitted Italy, with the exception of Benedict VIII, who was absent for a month in Germany in 1020. The alleged visit of Benedict IX to Marseilles in 1040 is open to suspicion, though it must be admitted, with Delisle (see the *Revue des Sociétés Savantes*, 2nd series, v. 534, 1861), that there is no proof that the Pope did not go to Gaul in that year. The positive evidence is contained in the act of consecration of the church of St. Victor at Marseilles, on 15 October 1140, which is drawn up in the name of Benedict IX, the Archbishop of Arles, and other prelates. It is last printed in *Gallia Christiana novissima*, Marseille, pp. 54-7, 1899, with a defence of its genuineness by J. H. Albanès.   [2] See *Papal Chancery*, p. 66.

BENEDICT IX AND GREGORY VI[1]

I

IT is a famous story that in 1046 King Henry III of Germany went into Italy and held a synod at which three Popes were deposed. It appears in perhaps its most picturesque form in the Bari annals known as the Chronicle of Lupus Protospatharius, an author who wrote about forty years later and who did not so much as know the German king's name. 'In this year', he says, 'Conus', that is Conrad, 'king of the Alemans went to Rome because there were three Popes there: Silvester in St. Peter's Church, Gregory in the Lateran, and Benedict in the Tusculan. They were expelled, and Clement was consecrated by the aforesaid emperor.'[2] Now there is no doubt that at various dates in the preceding two years three men had occupied the Holy See; but whether all the three were claimants to it in 1046 is still disputed.

The three Popes in question were, first, Theophylact or Benedict IX, of the family of the counts of Tusculum, who had succeeded two uncles in the Papacy in 1032; secondly, John Bishop of Sabina, who took the name of Silvester III; and thirdly, John, otherwise known as Gratian, who became Gregory VI. For the purpose of the criticism of our authorities the vital point is that, when this last, Gregory VI, was deposed and banished to Germany, he was accompanied by a young man who rose to the greatest influence in the Church as Archdeacon Hildebrand and who, when he became Pope in 1073, showed his firm attachment to his friend by adopting the name of Gregory VII.[3] It is evident that, whatever may have been the rights and the wrongs of the case, the position of Gregory VI could naturally be regarded in a different way from what it had been before, when Hildebrand openly declared himself a supporter of his canonical rank as Pope. We may therefore expect that a Hildebrandine version of the facts would emerge and

---

[1] Reprinted from the *Proceedings of the British Academy*, vol. viii (1917).

[2] 'Hoc anno venit Conus rex Alemannorum Romam, eo quod erant ibi tres papae, Silvester in ecclesia sancti Petri, in Laterano Gregorius, et Benedictus in Tusculano; quibus eiectis consecratus est Clemens a praedicto imperatore': *Monum. Germ. Hist., Script.*, v (1844), 58 f.

[3] See my paper on the 'Names and Numbers of Medieval Popes', above, pp. 162 ff.; cf. below, p. 210, n. 6.

would become more distinct as the controversy between Pope and Emperor developed. It is thus necessary to separate the accounts which were composed at this later time from those which are more nearly contemporary; and we must bear in mind that more than a quarter of a century elapsed between the proceedings of 1046 and Hildebrand's elevation to the Papacy.

We must also take into consideration the fact that Henry III's action was so remarkable that it could not fail to be summarized in a form which enhanced his majesty and power. At various moments in the two preceding years there had been three claimants to the Apostolic See: on Henry's appearance in Rome not one of them remained; the field was clear, and the German king secured the election of a German bishop as Pope. Could this be more succinctly described than by saying that he deposed three Popes and set up Clement?[1] This is in fact the form in which Clement described his appointment to the church of Bamberg: *cum illud caput mundi, illa Romana sedes, haeretico morbo laboraret*, Henry intervened, and, *explosis tribus illis quibus idem nomen papatus rapina dederat*, the Divine grace caused him to be chosen Pope.[1] There is therefore, besides the Hildebrandine tradition, an Imperial version to reckon with.

Moreover, there was a third strain of tradition which was opposed to the party of reform, but which still less favoured the Imperial intervention. This may be distinguished as the anti-German or local Roman statement of the facts. It grew up slowly, but ended by superseding the others in the late medieval texts of the Lives of the Popes.[2]

One would like first of all to know what account of the matter was given in Rome itself at the time when the events took place.

---

[1] Adalbert, 'Vita Henrici II Imper.', in *Monum. Germ. Hist., Script.*, iv. 800; Jaffé, *Regesta Pontif. Rom.*, 2nd ed., no. 4149.

[2] Steindorff's excursus on the Roman journey of Henry III (*Jahrbücher der Deutschen Geschichte unter Heinrich III*, i. 456–510, 1874) is so excellent a piece of work that later students have for the most part considered themselves dispensed from undertaking a fresh examination of the materials. It is true that, through following an error of Jaffé's, he misled scholars for a generation into placing the disruption of the Papacy in 1044 instead of 1045 (see my paper on 'Papal Chronology in the Eleventh Century', above p. 150, n. 1. But in other respects he is at once thorough and acute, particularly in his discrimination between the authorities which are of contemporary value and those which are affected by the later controversies under Alexander II and Gregory VII. The remarkable thing is that the conclusions arrived at in this excursus have had little influence on the book itself, in which later evidence is constantly cited and accepted on the same terms as that of contemporary writers.

Unfortunately the *Liber Pontificalis*, which may almost be called the official collection of the Lives of the Popes, is not at our disposal. It ends abruptly in the last decade of the ninth century, and is not resumed in a form deserving the name of an historical narrative until 1073. During the interval we have, with rare exceptions, only meagre lists containing the Pope's name and the length of his pontificate, with perhaps a few particulars of his parentage and birthplace. The complicated succession of Popes between 1044 and 1046, however, made a somewhat more extended record necessary; and for these events the lists furnish at least the outline of a narrative. But there is no list preserved in an actually contemporary manuscript, and curiously enough not one of the existing texts was written at Rome. If we follow the careful analysis of them published by Commendatore Giorgi in 1897, the earliest manuscript which contains any details about the time in which we are interested was drawn up in 1087 at the Sabine monastery of Farfa. At Farfa also, he thinks, a transcript of it was made not long afterwards, which passed to the monastery of La Cava and was printed as the received text of the *Liber Pontificalis* for the time in the editions previous to the standard one of Monsignor Duchesne. Other copies, some of them abbreviated, were written during the following thirty or forty years, either in the shape of chronological lists or else embedded in chronicles. The earliest list then was written in a manuscript, which we still possess, more than forty years after the contest of 1044–6. But we may conclude from the slightness of the differences between the texts that they depend upon an earlier source. Commendatore Giorgi is of opinion that that source is the Farfa manuscript; I am inclined to think that at least two different texts were in existence.[1] But the precision with which the dates of each pontificate are recorded—though here, as might be expected, there are various readings—appears to justify the inference that they are based on an official Roman list, in which the succession of the Popes with the exact length of their pontificates was set out.[2] I suggest therefore that,

---

[1] In the following paragraphs I resume the conclusions at which I arrived in a paper on 'Papal Chronology in the Eleventh Century', above, pp. 144 ff.

[2] This view of the strictly Roman origin of the Farfa lists has been supported since Commendatore Giorgi wrote by Monsignor Duchesne, in his paper on 'Serge III et Jean XI' in the *Mélanges d'Archéologie et d'Histoire*, xxxiii (1913), 25–41. [In a more recent discussion of the subject, *Archivio della R. Società Romana di Storia Patria*, xxxix (1916), 513–36, Commendatore Giorgi maintains

though the manuscripts are forty years or more later, they present a record of contemporary value.

The following is the purport of the text preserved at Farfa:

Benedict nephew of the preceding Popes sat fourteen years.[1] And he was cast out of the pontificate, and there was appointed in the apostolic see John the Sabine bishop, to whom they gave the name Silvester; and he wrongfully occupied the pontifical throne for 49 days.[2] And being cast out therefrom, the aforesaid Benedict recovered it and held the pontificate one month and 21 days. Then he himself gave[3] it to John archcanon of St. John at the Latin Gate, his godfather, on the first of May; to whom they gave the name Gregory. And he[4] held the pontificate for one year and eight months less eleven days;[5] and he lost it through the Emperor by process of law and was led by him to the parts beyond the Alps.[6]

This narrative, on the face of it, relates, first, that an Antipope, Silvester, was set up against Benedict but ejected after seven weeks; secondly, that Benedict after another seven weeks handed over his office to Gratian, who held it undisturbed for more than a year and a half. There is no hint that there were three Popes at any one time: there is an Antipope who is promptly expelled and then his rival abdicates. Not a word is said to suggest that the Antipope, Silvester, even afterwards made any claim to reassert his title. The dates make it clear that he was deposed in March 1045.[7]

The Roman lists which I have just quoted have the merit of extreme simplicity: they merely record the succession of the

substantially the opinion which he had formerly expressed. Two points in this article are of special interest: the author thinks first that the Farfa list was written not at the monastery itself but at the cell which it possessed at Rome (pp. 522 f., 526, 535); and secondly he gives reasons for believing that the part down to 1048 was actually compiled not long after July in that very year (pp. 533 f.).]

[1] The MS. originally added '4 months and 20 days', but these words are cancelled. The La Cava MS. has '4 months' only. There were probably two variant durations given in different lists: one of 14 years, the other of 12 years 4 months and 20 days, which is found in the Subiaco list.

[2] The La Cava MS. reads '56 days'.

[3] Gregory of Catino, who worked from this list, altered *dedit* into *vendidit*: *Chron. Farfense*, ii. 244, ed. U. Balzani, 1903.

[4] The La Cava MS. has 'Gregory, who is called Gratian'.

[5] The La Cava MS. reads '2 years and 6 months'.

[6] *Archivio della R. Società Romana di Storia Patria*, xx (1897), 310 f.

[7] Steindorff, i. 258 f., placing Silvester's elevation a year too early, says that in the very next month he attended a synod held by Benedict and subscribed its acts in the style of John bishop of the holy Sabine church (Ughelli, *Italia Sacra*, v. 1115). The date is April, in the 12th Indiction, which is 1044.

Popes and the lengths of their pontificates; they say nothing about the good or the evil character of one Pope or another, or about any malpractices in the manner by which the Papacy was conferred. Only two possible indications of passing judgement appear: one is the statement that Silvester occupied the see *iniuste*, which indeed was self-evident; and the second is the concluding statement that Gregory was deposed *legaliter*, which need not be pressed to mean more than that the act was that of a lawfully constituted body.

The chronological notes call for closer examination.[1] They point to the existence of two variant lists, each consistent with itself, but each drawn up on a different theory as to the dates when the pontificates of Benedict IX and Gregory VI came to their end. The intervals of days are given with minute accuracy and they are in absolute agreement with the days of the month recorded in the *Annales Romani*, the compiler of which, though he wrote long after the time—in the last years of Gregory VII or perhaps a little later,[2]—unquestionably made use of early materials of a documentary character. These Annals tell us more particulars of what happened. Towards the end of 1044,[3] before 22 November, the townsmen of Rome rose up against Benedict IX and drove him out. Then there was a conflict between them and the men beyond Tiber, and they set forth to lay siege to this district on 7 January. A battle took place in which they were beaten. On the third day, Wednesday the 9th, there was an earthquake. Then the Romans elected John bishop of the Sabina, and named him Silvester. He held the Papacy for forty-nine days, when he was deposed and Benedict was restored to his see. But Benedict could not endure the people of Rome, and he resigned his office to Gratian, the archpriest of St. John at the Latin Gate, on 1 May, to whom they gave the name Gregory; and he held the pontificate for 1 year and 8 months, less 11 days.[4] To complete the dates we must add

---

[1] Compare my paper on 'Papal Chronology in the Eleventh Century', above pp. 150 f.

[2] Duchesne, *Lib. Pontif.* ii, introd., p. xxiii *b*. Commendatore Giorgi is of opinion that the writer made direct use of the Farfa catalogue: *Archivio della Società Romana di Storia Patria*, xx. 289 f.

[3] The year is given by an obvious slip as *mxlvi*. The Annals add, in the 13th Indiction, in the 12th year of Benedict IX. The year is fixed by the mention of an eclipse, which occurred on 22 November 1044. This ought to have saved a number of modern historians from carrying back these events to the winter of 1043-4.   [4] Annales Romani, in *Lib. Pontif.* ii. 331.

from the Papal lists that Benedict's period of restoration lasted for 1 month and 21 days.[1] Now it was the rule that the Pope should be ordained on a Sunday. If Silvester III was appointed on 20 January, his 49 days take us to 10 March;[2] that was the day of Benedict's restoration. Then 1 month and 21 days lead exactly to 1 May.

I lay stress upon the minute accuracy of these details, because it furnishes a presumption of the trustworthiness of other chronological data supplied by the lists. Some of these assign to Benedict a pontificate of 12 years 4 months and 20 days; others one of 14 years. The question is, at what point are the periods supposed to terminate. Not surely, as is suggested as a possible alternative by Monsignor Duchesne,[3] in January 1045, when Benedict was driven out for a brief space of time. The shorter duration given for his pontificate must end at his resignation on 1 May, and 12 years 4 months and 20 days would carry us back to 12 December 1032 for his accession. It is not known with certainty when his predecessor John XIX died or when he himself was elected.[4] The time was one of extreme obscurity, and it is possible that the record in the Papal lists is not absolutely correct. But it cannot be very far wrong. The longer period stated in some of these lists is 14 years. This is a round number, which allows of an elastic interpretation; it may be a few days or weeks too long or too short. But if we reckon 14 years from December 1032 we arrive at the time of Henry III's intervention, at the time when he held two synods on 20 and 24 December 1046 and, according to one account of the matter, formally deposed Benedict. Which of the two statements represents the facts I do not at this stage presume to

[1] Similarly Gregory of Catino says 'post mensem 1' (*Chron. Farfense*, ii. 264). Steindorff's proposed emendation of one year and 21 days (i. 489 f.) was rendered necessary by his mistake as to the year in which Benedict was deposed.

[2] Some lists give 56 days, evidently believing that the ordination took place on 13 January. This involves no derangement in the chronology.

[3] *Lib. Pontif.* ii, introd., p. lxxii b.

[4] Signor Fedele has produced evidence from the dating clauses of private charters that John XIX was believed to have died before 13 October 1032 (*Archivio della R. Società Romana di Storia Patria*, xxii. 67, 1899); and Signor Buzzi, that Benedict IX became Pope after 23 August but before 7 September (*ibid.* xxxv. 619, 621 f., 1912). But such dates in the eleventh century are not always safe guides, and for the present I am inclined to accept the recorded obit of Pope John on 6 November: see my paper on Papal Chronology, above, p. 148.

decide; but it may be said that in a Roman list it is more likely
that the date when a Pope resigned would be taken as the end
of his pontificate rather than that when he was deposed, if
deposed he was. On general grounds, therefore, I should be
inclined to think that the longer period recorded indicates
a later revision of the figures. It is worth noticing that the
writer of the Farfa list gives 14 years 4 months and 20 days,
but the months and days are deleted. Evidently he had before
him two lists, one of which read 12 years 4 months and 20 days,
and accidentally conflated the readings. In order to be consistent he ought to have corrected the 14 into 12, for the 14
involves Benedict's deposition in December 1046, and of any
such deposition his narrative is silent. We may, infer, however,
from this textual detail that this deposition had become recognized in some papal lists which were current at the time when
the Farfa writer drew up his.

A similar discrepancy occurs with regard to the length of the
pontificate of Gregory VI. Some lists give 1 year and 8 months
less 11 days; that is, they make it end exactly on 20 December
1046, the date of the synod of Sutri. Others extend it to 2 years
and 6 months, that is, to about 1 November 1047.[1] The meaning
of this computation seems to have escaped notice; but it can
only mean one thing, namely that Gregory was regarded as the
lawful Pope as long as he lived. Incidentally it furnishes the
only evidence for the approximate date of his death, and it
confirms the statement of the scurrilous pamphleteer, Cardinal
Beno, that this took place about the same time as that of
Clement II,[2] who died on 9 October.

These varieties of reading are of value because they point
to a difference of opinion in Roman circles as to the authentic
succession of the Popes. One view held that Benedict ceased to
be Pope on 1 May 1045 and that Gregory who followed him was
the rightful Pope down to his death. The other view terminated
both their pontificates in December 1046, and thus implies that
they were deposed. Of Silvester III after his transient intrusion

---

[1] It is a mere mistake when Desiderius of Monte Cassino says that Gregory VI
had ruled for two years and eight months before Henry entered Italy: 'Dialog.'
iii., in Migne's *Patrol. Lat.* cxlix. 1005. Evidently he confounded the reckonings
in the variant lists.

[2] 'Defuncto autem in exilio sexto illo Gregorio, Hildebrandus perfidiae
simul et pecuniae eius heres extitit. Eodem tempore Clemens papa defunctus
est': 'Gesta Romanae Ecclesiae', ii. 8, in *Monum. Germ. Hist.*, *Libelli de Lite
Imperatorum et Pontificum*, ii (1892), 378.

in 1045 nothing is said.[1] It is in the accounts written by foreigners that three Popes are brought upon the scene when Henry III came into Italy.

II

By a strange chance it appears that our earliest record of the events of 1046 comes from the Westphalian monastery of Corvey. The Annals written in that house are extremely scanty; they are mere insertions in an Easter table: but for a good part of the eleventh century the notices are added from time to time in contemporary hands and are preserved in the original autograph. The order of the entries is not always clear. I follow Jaffé's arrangement in the present instance because he had the manuscript before him and designedly abandoned the order in which Pertz had given the notices.[2] I have unfortunately no means of examining the manuscript, which is preserved at Hanover. Now these notices hardly say a word about any but German affairs until the entry for 1046 is ended. Then comes a fresh entry for the same year, which looks like the production of a man who went into Italy in Henry III's train. He begins by describing an earthquake which occurred in the valley of Trent on 11 November and the obstruction of the river Taro, which was caused by the fall of rocks. This river he would cross on the road between Piacenza and Parma, and as Henry was at Pavia on 28 October, the Corvey annalist or his informant may have been in the neighbourhood at the time. He then proceeds:

A great synod, the first, was held at Pavia, in the presence of Henry, then king; a second, at Sutri, in which in the king's presence according to the appointments of the canons, two Popes, the second and the last, were deposed; a third, at Rome on Tuesday and Wednesday, which was the eve of the Lord's Nativity, in which Pope Benedict was canonically and synodically deposed, and by the unanimous election of the clergy and people Suidger bishop of Bamberg was appointed in his place, and being consecrated next day by the name of Pope Clement he crowned Henry emperor by the choice and full approval of the Roman people.[3]

The annalist next records the death of Clement II in 1047, and there is no further mention of the Papacy until 1111.

---

[1] A document in the *Regesto di Farfa*, no. 1234, vol. v. 220, drawn up in March 1046, is dated 'in the time of Gregory VI and of John the bishop and of Crescentius and John counts of the Sabine territory'.

[2] *Monum. Germ. Hist., Script.* iii (1839), 6.

[3] *Annales Corbeienses, s.a.*, in Jaffé's *Monumenta Corbeiensia*, pp. 39 f. (1864).

It is plain that the writer of these notes was not told very much. He knows only the name of one of the three Popes whose fall he describes. If I may venture upon an hypothesis, I would suggest that he heard talk about three men who were still alive having claimed the Papacy during the past two years, and learned that Benedict was deposed on Christmas Eve. As his removal left the field clear for the election of Clement II, he not unnaturally inferred that two Popes were deposed at Sutri. But it was really the deprivation of Gregory, as simoniacally elected, which made the resignation of Benedict invalid and thus required that he should be deposed. There is no reason to believe that any formal action was taken against Silvester, who had long subsided into obscurity in his Sabine bishopric.

Another very early account of the entire series of transactions at Rome was written in the Suabian monastery of Reichenau on the lower Lake of Constance. The house had long been renowned as the seat of a great learned tradition, and its chronicler at the middle of the eleventh century, Herman the Cripple, is reputed the most conscientious and trustworthy historian of the time. From 1040 to 1052, when he died at the age of forty-one, his work is absolutely contemporary. There are grounds for believing that he made use of a papal list in an earlier and purer form than any of the Italian manuscripts, but this list is only preserved in a copy a century later, and we have to take what Herman gives embodied or paraphrased in his Chronicle. It may be added that the bishop of Constance attended Henry III in his visit to Italy in 1046; and, though he died during his stay there, he no doubt did not journey unattended, and Herman may have learned something of what happened from the bishop's chaplain.

Now Herman tells us that in 1044 Benedict was by many accused (*criminatus*) and was expelled by the Romans from his see. They then set up one Silvester in his place. But a party came to Benedict's support, and he excommunicated and drove out Silvester. But afterwards he abdicated, and contrary to the canons appointed another man out of avarice. According to this account there was no question of three Popes being in existence at the same time. For Silvester had been excommunicated and deposed, and Benedict had voluntarily resigned the Papacy. However improper were the means by which he secured the office, this third man—Herman mentions no name—

was the only claimant. In 1046, he proceeds, Henry III held a synod at Pavia and then went on to Piacenza, where Gratian, whom the Romans had made Pope after the expulsion of the others, came to him and was received with honour. It almost seems as though the information which reached Reichenau distinguished Gratian from the unnamed person to whom Benedict had disposed of the Papacy. Herman then relates that Henry went on to Sutri, where a synod was held and the case of the 'erroneous' Popes diligently examined. Gratian was convicted and deprived of his see. No reason is assigned for his deprivation, but it is clear from the fact that he had had an honourable reception at Piacenza that he was treated on a different footing from Benedict; we may even say, that he was the one man who at that time was considered to have any claim to the Papacy. But before deciding on the validity of his claim it was necessary to inquire into the circumstances in which the Papacy had changed hands so irregularly in 1045. It is not said that either Benedict or Silvester was deprived by the synod: they were treated as having already ceased to be Popes. Only Gratian was deposed.[1]

Two points may be noticed. Herman, as I have observed, does not expressly say that Gratian was the third of the three Popes who came upon the scene in 1044. His words even suggest that all three were deposed and that Gratian was elected in their place. This was certainly the sense in which the statement was understood by Otto of Freising[2] a century later. Secondly, Herman does not say that Gratian assumed the name of Gregory VI. Had he written after Hildebrand had shown his adhesion to Gratian by calling himself Gregory VII, the chronicler's silence would be easy to explain; he might have wished to dissociate Hildebrand from the deposed Pope. But Herman, I have said, died in 1052, more than twenty years before Hildebrand succeeded to the Papacy. I can therefore only infer that the story which reached Reichenau told that a certain Gratian was made Pope, that he was favourably received by Henry III, and that shortly afterwards he was deprived—for what reason is not stated[3]—by

---

[1] No Acts of the synod are now preserved.

[2] *Chron.* vi. 32, p. 299, ed. A. Hofmeister, 1912.

[3] It is hinted at in the *Catalogus Augiensis* (Eccard, *Corpus Historicum*, ii. 1640), which, though only preserved in a later manuscript, is believed to represent the papal list used by Herman: *Gratianus a Romanis constitutus, quem rex Henricus convictum causa erroneorum pastorali baculo privavit.*

the synod of Sutri. An essential fact had been concealed from Herman's knowledge.

If Herman was only partially acquainted with what happened we need not be surprised if the reports which reached Germany later were still less well furnished with accurate information. For example, the Annals of Niederaltaich were written about twenty or twenty-five years after the events in which we are interested; and the monastery, situated on the Danube between Ratisbon and Passau, was in a favourable position for hearing news from Italy. This is the account we there read of the synod of Sutri:

The cause of this assembly was three Popes who were all alike living at that time. For the first of them abandoned the see by reason of an unlawful marriage which he contracted; he retired by his own will rather than by the pressure of any opposition. Wherefore, while he was still living in the flesh, the Romans conspired together and set up another Pope. The first, however, sold his office for money to a third, because in his wrath he refused that one subject to him should have it. To be brief, they were all judged in this synod, and deposed; and Suitger bishop of Bamberg, a man worthy of the see, was chosen by the whole council of clergy and people.[1]

Here we note the suppression of all the names, and this is again the more interesting, because the notice was written before Gregory VII became Pope: it was not influenced by the controversy which followed. It is not, however, essentially inconsistent with the other German accounts which I have quoted. The only new point which it brings in is the story of Pope Benedict's marriage.[2]

III

After Hildebrand became Pope and marked his attachment to Gregory VI in the plainest manner by adopting his name, it was natural, as I said at the beginning, that the events of 1046 should assume a different aspect. This we find well displayed in one of the Dialogues of Desiderius abbot of Monte Cassino,[3] who succeeded Hildebrand as Victor III and very likely learned from him his version of what took place.[4] He draws a strong contrast between the demerits of Benedict IX, whose misdoings he can hardly bring himself to describe, and the high character

---

[1] *Annales Altahenses maiores*, a. 1046, ed. G. H. Pertz, 1868.
[2] The remaining contemporary account, that of Rodulf Glaber, I deal with later on.   [3] 'Dialog.' iii, in Migne's *Patrol. Lat.* cxlix. 1003 ff.
[4] See Steindorff, i. 464.

of the man to whom he resigned the Papacy; but he does not conceal the fact that the transaction was accompanied by a money payment (*non parva ab eo accepta pecunia*). What is more important is the way in which he tells us the circumstances in which Gregory VI ceased to be Pope. Before, he says, the German king entered Rome,

he assembled a council of very many bishops and abbots, clergy and monks in the city of Sutri, and asked John, who was called Gregory, to come to him, sending to him bishops in order that ecclesiastical business and especially the situation of the Roman church, which then appeared to have three Popes, might be discussed under his presidency. But this was done by design, for the king had long determined that with the counsel and authority of the whole council he would rightfully depose those three men who had unrightfully usurped the Apostolic See, and that a man should be appointed by the election of the clergy and people who would devote himself to the charge of the Lord's flock in conformity with the ordinances of the holy Fathers. Therefore the aforesaid pontiff, at the urgent request of the king and the bishops, willingly went to Sutri, where the synod was assembled, in the hope that the other two might be deposed and the Popedom be confirmed to him alone. But when he arrived there, and the matter began to be raised and debated by the synod, he recognized that he was unable rightfully to administer the functions of so great a charge: he rose up from the papal chair, divested himself of his papal raiment, and asking for pardon laid down the dignity of the great high-priesthood.[1]

This account, which I do not doubt Desiderius set down in entire good faith, represents the tradition which had grown up in Hildebrandine circles. The fact that Gregory VI had paid money for the Popedom was too well known to be denied. But the more Benedict was depicted as a monster of wickedness, the more venial did Gregory's offence appear in buying him out. And Gregory was in all the rest of his life so good a man that people could not believe that he was deposed. Consequently the events which took place at Sutri were related in a new form: it was not the synod that deposed Gregory, but Gregory who resigned his office. It is generally agreed that this account is untrue,[2] but we can easily see how the story once stated would be willingly, and very soon honestly, accepted.

---

[1] *Dialog.*, p. 1005.

[2] It must not, however, be concealed that this view has its defenders: see for instance Dr. Hermann Grauert's 'Papstwahlstudien', in the *Historisches Jahrbuch*, xx (1899), 320 f.

This can hardly, I think, be maintained with respect to Bonizo, bishop of Sutri, who wrote his *Liber ad Amicum* in order to gain the protection of the Countess Matilda of Tuscany in 1085. His narrative, however, is so lively, and so much of it has passed down into most current histories, that it will be well to quote its substance. But I may premise that Bonizo was not only one of the most inaccurate of writers and extremely ill informed about the history which he relates, but was quite without scruple in falsifying facts which did not suit his opinions. For example, he more than once tells us that Charles the Great was never crowned Emperor.[1] This is what he has to say about the three Popes of 1045:

Theophylactus, who by inversion of meaning was called Benedictus, fearing neither God nor man, was often guilty of shameful adultery and with his own hands committed many murders. At length he desired to marry his cousin, the daughter of Gerard de Saxo, and Gerard refused to give her unless he would renounce the Papacy. Wherefore he went to a certain priest named John, who was then deemed a man of great merit, and by his advice condemned himself and renounced the pontificate. The advice would have been highly praiseworthy, had it not been followed by a most shameful sin. For the priest whom I have mentioned, seized by wicked ambition and seduced [by the evil one,] took the opportunity [to purchase the Papacy from Theophylact][2] and by immense payments of money compelled all the people of Rome to swear to him: thus he mounted to the Pontifical dignity, and they called him by the name of Gregory. After this Gerard de Saxo with other captains elected for themselves a certain bishop of the Sabines as Pope, and named him Silvester. So Theophylact was defrauded of his bride, and his brothers, hearing what had come to pass, raised him once more to the Papal throne.[3]

It will be seen that Bonizo turns the course of events upside down, and places the election of Silvester III after that of Gregory VI.[4] He implies that they were both Popes at the same time, and does not say what happened to them when Benedict was restored. Moreover, he gives no explanation of the conduct

[1] 'Ad Amicum', lib. v, in Jaffé's *Monumenta Gregoriana*, p. 630, 1865; cf. lib. iii, p. 614.

[2] The words which I have enclosed within brackets represent a lacuna in the manuscript, which I have filled in according to the correction proposed by Jaffé.   [3] 'Ad Amicum', lib. v, pp. 625 f.

[4] This same inversion appears in Cardinal Beno's 'Gesta Romanae Ecclesiae', ii. 8 (*Libelli de Lite Imperatorum et Pontificum*, ii. 378).

of Gerard de Saxo, who after Benedict had fulfilled his condition refused to allow his daughter's marriage. Whether such a marriage was ever proposed, it is impossible to determine. We have seen that it was believed in Bavaria not many years later.[1] But, in view of the spirit of defamation which pervaded that age, we cannot confidently exclude the possibility that the tale was a simple slander.

Bonizo goes on to relate that Peter, the archdeacon of Rome, with a number of cardinals, clergy, and laity, withdrew from the communion of the usurping Popes, and that he crossed the Alps and implored the German king and bishops to come to Italy and convoke a synod. No other writer mentions this action of Archdeacon Peter, and Bonizo's account has not always been accepted.[2] However this may be, King Henry marched into Italy in the autumn of 1046, and Bonizo continues the story as follows:

This intruder (*abusivus*) Gregory was invited by the king to go to meet him, being as the sequel showed conscious of no wrongdoing; and he went to Piacenza and there found the king. He was honourably received by him, as beseemed a Pope; for the bishops who were present did not think it religious to condemn any bishop without judgement, let alone one who appeared to be the pontiff of so great a see. And so advancing together they came to Sutri, and when they had arrived there the king asked him who seemed to be Pope that a synod should be assembled. This he granted and confirmed by decree; for he was an ignorant man (*idiota*) and of wonderful simplicity.

Bonizo says that the synod was held under Gregory's presidency, and he mentions three prelates by name as present, two of whom had long been dead.

When the question about the usurper Silvester was raised, it was adjudged by all that he should be divested of his episcopate and priesthood and be consigned to a monastery for life. They also decided that Theophylact should be passed over (*supersedendum*), especially because the Roman Pontiff himself judged that he should be deposed. But as to what they should do with the third claimant, what course could they take when no liberty of accusing and bearing testimony was granted to them? The bishops therefore begged the president to declare the reason of his election, and, simple as he was, he disclosed the naked fact[3] of his election.

---

[1] See above, p. 195.

[2] For instance, by Steindorff, i. 262. It is, however, defended by Giesebrecht, *Geschichte der Deutschen Kaiserzeit*, i (5th ed., 1881), 413, 664.

[3] Jaffé interprets *puritatem* as *suppurationem*, but this seems unnecessary.

He said that by a life of abstinence he had acquired much riches which he had intended to devote to the good of the church in Rome. But when he meditated on the tyranny of the nobles, how they set up Popes without election by the clergy and people, he determined to use his money for the purpose of restoring to the true electors the right of election of which by this tyranny they had been wrongfully deprived. When the council heard this, they hinted at the devices of the old enemy: nothing, they said, which was venal could be holy.

Judge thyself out of thine own mouth, for it is better for thee to live poor with St. Peter, for whose love thou didst this thing, than to perish with Simon Magus who deceived thee.

Gregory then pronounced his own deposition, and the council confirmed it.

This statement that Gregory was not deposed by the council but deposed himself became an accepted part of the Hildebrandine tradition. It appears in a striking form in the Chronicle of Bernold of Constance, who began by transcribing the work of Herman of Reichenau, and afterwards altered his text so as to emphasize the wickedness of Benedict and suppress the scandalous circumstances in which he parted with the Papacy: Benedict, he says, resigned 'of his own free will', and allowed Gratian to be ordained Pope Gregory VI in his stead. Then he proceeds to add that in 1046 Gregory, whom Herman described as convicted and deposed, 'not unwillingly laid down his pastoral office'; and somewhat inconsistently says that the earthquakes which prevailed under Clement II were attributed to the fact that his predecessor had been 'uncanonically deposed'.[1]

It is unnecessary to accumulate further evidence of the form taken by the developed Hildebrandine account of what happened in 1045 and 1046.[2] The main points were the depravity of Benedict IX which drove Gregory VI to adopt forbidden means in order to oust him, and the substitution of the statement that Gregory voluntarily resigned the Papacy for the earlier statement that he was deposed by process of law.

Before inquiring into the charges made against Benedict, it will not be out of place to remark that it was not only against

[1] *Monum. Germ. Hist.* v. 425.

[2] If I pass over St. Peter Damiani, it is not because I underrate the importance of his contribution to the formation of opinion in his time, but because on the precise points of fact he adds very little, and that little not, I think, until a good many years later.

him that charges of nefarious conduct were made. We must remember that they were made when the conflict between Gregory VII and the Emperor Henry IV was at its height. In a time of acute political hostility accusations, as we know too well, are made and are believed, which in a calmer time would never have been suggested. Let me give a specimen or two of what was said about Gregory VII. Cardinal Beno informs us that he had in his employment an expert by whose help he was said to have poisoned five Popes in thirteen years.[1] The synod of Brixen in 1080 was more moderate; it only stated in its decree that four Popes were proved to have been poisoned by Gregory's means.[2] Of another Imperialist champion, Bishop Benzo of Alba, it will be enough to say that he accuses Alexander II and Gregory VII of almost every vice that can or cannot be named, not to speak of simony, gambling, corruption, sorcery, necromancy, homicide, and other misdoings.[3] Now no one, I suppose, believes these gross calumnies against Gregory VII; and yet a not very different set of statements about Benedict IX has been universally accepted. This has happened, no doubt, because it was considered that in his case they were not improbable. But probability is not the same thing as proof. The history of the Tusculan Popes has in truth been contaminated by the fact that their dynasty was followed by a reaction. I will digress for a moment to inquire how their power was created.

[1] He says (*Gesta Rom. Eccl.* ii. 9, *Libelli de Lite*, ii. 379) that when Hildebrand returned to Rome in 1049, 'in brevi loculos implevit, et cui pecuniam illam committeret, filium cuiusdam Iudei noviter quidem baptizatum sed mores nummulariorum adhuc retinentem, familiarem sibi fecit. Et iam diu conciliaverat sibi quendam alium incomparabilibus maleficiis assuetum, Gerhardum nomine, qui cognominabatur Brazutus, amicum Theophilacti [Benedict IX], qui subdola familiaritate dicitur sex Romanos pontifices infra spacium tredecim annorum veneno suffocasse; quorum nomina haec sunt: Clemens . . . Damasus . . . Leo . . . Victor . . . Stephanus . . . Benedictus . . . Hic non veneno sed vi et dolis Hildebrandi fuit eiectus . . . Nicolaus.'

[2] Jaffé, *Monumenta Bambergensia* (1869), p. 134; also in *Monum. Germ. Hist.*, *Constitutiones*, i. 119, 1893. The agent is here called John Brachiutus or Brachtutus. John Braciuto subscribes a Roman document in 1060: *Regesto di Farfa*, iv (1888), 302. The synod had declared among other things that Hildebrand had been wont 'obscenis theatralibus ludicris ultra laicos insistere, mensas nummulariorum in porticu transigentium turpis lucri gratia publice observare. His itaque questibus pecunia cumulata, abbatiam beati Pauli invasit', etc.

[3] Karl Pertz has collected a number of specimens of the bishop's vile and filthy abuse: *Monum. Germ. Hist.* xi (1854), 593. He misses the point of Benzo's disgusting invective in i. 22, p. 608, in consequence of his not seeing the allusions to Proverbs xxx. 15, 16.

IV

The city of Rome had for ages past been torn by internal discord. There was always one or more parties of the local nobility who sought to strengthen themselves by exciting the lesser people to riot and pillage. One of these parties was headed by the house of Crescentius, whose power was put down for the moment by Otto III. Another great Roman family was represented at that time by Gregory *de Tusculana*, the naval prefect, whose mother was a first cousin of the famous Alberic, the Prince of the Romans, who had ruled the city with firmness for more than twenty years towards the middle of the tenth century.[1] The territorial possessions of the family had been continually growing in the Roman Campagna, and near the end of the century Gregory is found established in authority at Tusculum. It may be that Otto conferred the countship upon him in order to detach a prominent noble from his fellows and, by establishing him in a strong fortress not too far distant for effective control, to set up a power which might keep in check the factions of Rome and assist the Imperial interest. If this was so, Otto's expectations were not unrewarded. The counts of Tusculum soon gained the upper hand in Roman politics, and they were as a rule friendly to the Emperors. Their victory over the house of Crescentius was marked by the successive appointment to the Papacy of two of Gregory's sons,[2] and these were followed by a grandson; so that for thirty-three years the Popedom continued in the family.

It is with the third and last of the dynasty that I am particularly concerned. But before speaking of him I will observe that his evil repute has cast a shadow upon his two predecessors; in modern histories they are all tarred with the same brush. But the first, Benedict VIII, was an able and vigorous pontiff, who not only kept Rome in order but also took a leading part in Italian politics. Besides this he worked in harmony with the Emperor Henry II and supported him in his aims for reforming abuses in the Church. But he was too much occupied by public

---

[1] The details of Gregory's ancestry are discussed below, in the appendix on the Counts of Tusculum.

[2] It is possible, as Gregorovius suggests (*History of the City of Rome*, iv. 11), that the Tusculan ascendancy began three years earlier with the appointment of Sergius IV, for he was bishop of Albano, a place where the Tusculan influence was very strong. See below, pp. 218, 221.

O

affairs to bestow much attention upon ecclesiastical administration. Not many more than seventy rescripts are attributed to him in a pontificate of nearly twelve years.[1] But here it is fair to notice that no Papal Register is preserved between the end of the ninth century and the time of Gregory VII, and that, though parchment came into use in the chancery towards the end of Benedict's pontificate, rescripts continued to be written on papyrus, a far more perishable material, until beyond the middle of the century. Scanty, however, as is the list of Benedict's documents, it is respectable as compared with those of his two successors. The nine years of John XIX produced but forty-seven; the twelve of Benedict IX, only eighteen. John seems to have been a colourless person, timid and inert; he left no mark as an administrator and not a creditable one as a statesman. It is generally said that these Tusculan Popes lived the rough lives of secular nobles, and this is very likely true, though I am not aware of any contemporary evidence to support it. It is certain, however, that Benedict VIII stood high above the Crescentian Popes who preceded him, and I do not know that the two brothers understood their episcopal duties in a very different way from a great many of the French, German, and English prelates of the same century.

I now turn to their nephew, Benedict IX. His character has been blasted at the outset by the statement, which has been repeated by every historian who has written about him, that he was a boy of ten or twelve years of age at the time he was made Pope. Now this statement rests upon the sole, unsupported testimony of a single writer, Rodulf Glaber, at that time a monk of St. Germanus at Auxerre, who made a collection of trifling, largely fabulous, narratives, and called it a history. He wrote entirely for edification and put down anything that served his turn. He is not only the most credulous but the most careless and inaccurate of writers. I will give one example from near the end of his book, where he is relating a fact which he knew from personal observation. After saying something about the year 1045 he proceeds: 'In the following year, that is the forty-sixth after the thousandth, there was a great dearth of wine and vegetables, and after this on the 8th November there

[1] The number of 71 in the second edition of Jaffé's *Regesta Pontificum Romanorum* includes documents which we know only from references to them, as well as documents still preserved. When Dr. Kehr's new Regesta is completed the number may be expected to be somewhat, but not largely, increased.

was an eclipse of the moon which affrighted men exceedingly.'
He gives the calendar notes accurately, the age of the moon, the
epact, and the concurrent; but these belong not to 1046, but to
1044, when the eclipse actually occurred.[1] A writer capable of
so gross a blunder is not to be taken as an authority on matters
of detail. Again, under the year 1033 he describes correctly an
eclipse of the sun which occurred on Friday, 29 June. On that
day, he says, the Feast of the Apostles, certain of the Roman
princes rose against the Pope in the church of St. Peter and
sought to put him to death, but, not succeeding, they drove him
from his see. Howbeit, on account of this thing, as well as for
other malpractices, the Emperor went thither and restored him
to his see.[2] Conrad did not go to Italy until the end of 1036,
three years and a half after Benedict's supposed expulsion; and
there was no need to restore the Pope, since in 1036 he is found
holding a synod to all appearances at Rome. Modern historians
accept the fact that Benedict was expelled, but think that it was
in 1035 or 1036. What, then, becomes of the eclipse so scrupu-
lously recorded?

Rodulf twice mentions Benedict IX's age, and each time
gives it differently. First, in book iv, chapter v,[3] he laments the
degeneracy of the times. All the rulers, whether of church or
state, were boys, *in puerili etate*. The very Pope, a lad of hardly
ten years (*puer ferme decennis*) was elected by the Romans with
the help of money from his treasures. Secondly, in the last
paragraph of his work[4] he says that the Holy See had suffered
from the disease of corruption for twenty-five years; for 'a
certain boy of about twelve years (*puer circiter annorum xii*) was
appointed to it who was recommended only by his wealth in
gold and silver rather than by his age or piety. It were a shame
to mention the baseness of his conversation and life. However,
by the consent of the whole Roman people and by the command
of the Emperor he was expelled from his seat, and in his place
a most religious man and conspicuous for holiness was appointed,
namely Gregory, by race a Roman, by whose good repute that
which the former had defiled was changed for the better.' It
may be presumed that when Rodulf wrote this he was not
aware of the fact that Gregory VI had possessed himself of the
Papacy by the very means which he had just denounced. The

---

[1] *Hist.* v. 1, § 18, ed. M. Prou, 1886, p. 128.   [2] Lib. iv. 9, § 24, p. 112.
[3] § 17, p. 105.   [4] Lib. v. 5, § 26, pp. 134 f.

statement that Gregory's appointment was made after Benedict
had been deposed by the Emperor's command, which inverts
the order of events, may possibly represent a story which was
circulated by Gregory's friends. Whence Rodulf derived the
twenty-five years during which the Papacy had degenerated I
cannot say; if he reckoned from the accession of John XIX,
that would be little more than twenty years. What reason is
there to suppose that he was more accurate when he stated that
Benedict was a boy of about twelve years? I should not be at all
surprised if he simply blundered over a notice of Benedict's life,
which stated that when he had been Pope *for twelve years* he was
expelled by the Romans. This at least is the shape in which his
catastrophe is recorded by writers of the next generation.[1] There
is not much difference between *per ann. xii* and *puer ann. xii.*

It is strange, too, that it has not been observed that Rodulf's
account of Benedict IX's extreme youth can hardly be reconciled
with the known facts of the Pope's pedigree. His grandfather,
Gregory, appears as *vir illustrissimus* in 980, in 986 as senator:
in 999 he held high office. There are indications which lead us to
place his birth not later than 940; he died before 1013. This
date agrees well with those of his two elder sons, Popes Benedict
VIII and John XIX, who died in the course of nature in 1024
and 1032. The youngest son, Alberic, is found acting in a
judicial capacity in 999. Now if the men of those days were not
as a rule long-lived, at any rate those who married married
early. Though not impossible, it is at least unlikely that this
Alberic's son, Benedict IX, would be born when his father was
about fifty. A comparison of ages and generations in a pedigree
about which a great deal is known[2] would lead to the conclusion
that Benedict IX was nearer thirty than ten years old at the
time that he became Pope.

The scanty records of Benedict's earlier years as Pope furnish
no indication of his exceptional youth.[3] Four years after his
accession, in November 1036, we find him holding a synod.[4] In
the following summer he went to Cremona to visit the Emperor,
Conrad II, by whom he was honourably received.[5] A little later

---

[1] Thus Leo of Ostia, under 1044, 'Romae praeterea cum papa Benedictus per
annos 12 sedem apostolicam obsedisset potius quam sedisset, a Romanis expulsus
est': 'Chron. Monast. Casin' ii. 77, in *Monum. Germ. Hist., Script.* vii. 682.

[2] See appendix.   [3] See the summary in Steindorff, i. 256 f.

[4] Mansi, *Concil. Collect. ampliss.* xix. 579.

[5] Wipo, *Gesta Chuonradi Imperatoris*, xxxvi, p. 43, ed. H. Bresslau, 1878.

he made a change in the administration of his chancery, which looks as though he intended to adopt an independent policy. The office of librarian, the titular head of the chancery, had been conferred fourteen years before on Peregrine, archbishop of Cologne, who died in 1036; but instead of appointing the new archbishop, who was actually in Italy, to the office, Benedict determined, in November 1037, that it should be held by one of the bishops of the Roman province, the bishop of Selva Candida and his successors.[1] When we remember that Conrad had made himself unpopular in Italy by introducing Germans into bishoprics there, the significance of Benedict's act can hardly be misunderstood.[2] On the other hand, it may be contended that the Pope was not strong enough to carry matters further, for next spring he supported Conrad by excommunicating his principal opponent, Archbishop Aribert of Milan.[3] In 1040 it is said, though the evidence is not quite satisfactory, that he travelled to Marseilles to take part in the consecration of a church. All these acts fall within a time when we are asked to believe that the Pope was under eighteen or twenty years of age; and yet no one of our authorities betrays the smallest indication that he was canonically incapable of exercising the powers of a Pope.

Benedict was evidently a negligent Pope, very likely a profligate man. We may believe Herman of Reichenau when he says that he was unworthy of his high office.[4] But we have to wait until he had discredited himself by his sale of the Papacy before we hear anything definite about his misdeeds; and the further we go in time and place, the worse his character becomes. At Auxerre very soon he is denounced as a reprobate by Rodulf Glaber.[5] Then, some twenty years after, it was said in Germany that he gave up the Papacy because he had taken a wife.[6] A good deal later, after Hildebrand had become Pope, Benedict's crimes grow in wickedness, and we get the picture which is familiar in all the modern histories. I do not say that the picture

---

[1] Marini, *I Papiri Diplomatici*, p. 83; Jaffé, *Reg.* no. 4110.

[2] Cf. Bresslau, *Jahrbücher des Deutschen Reichs unter Konrad II*, ii (1884), 177–188.

[3] *Ann. Hildesheim.*, a. 1038, p. 42, ed. G. Waitz, 1878. I do not find evidence that Benedict kept Easter at Spello with the Emperor in that year, as Dr. Bresslau says, ii. 285, 286. But the fact is probable.

[4] 'Indignus tanto ordini moribus et factis': *Chron.*, a. 1033, p. 121.

[5] Above, p. 203.   [6] Above, p. 195.

is false: all I say is that it was drawn at a time of acute controversy, when the party opposed to the tradition which he
represented was in the ascendant. He had indeed no friends.
The supporters of the Imperial side would have nothing to say
for a Pope whom they believed to have been removed by Henry
III. The reform party of the school of Hildebrand considered
that the transaction with Gregory VI was proof of Benedict's
infamy: to them Gregory, to the day of his death, continued to
be the lawful Pope. In the version of the Liber Pontificalis
which won currency in later ages both Clement II and Damasus
II were set down as usurpers.[1] So, too, it was said of Clement II:
*Qui ab aliis potius demens quam Clemens dici dignus iudicatur,
cum utique per violentiam Gratiano amoto eum intrusum asserant.*[2]
The true line of Popes was only restored with Leo IX after
Gregory was dead.

V

To this Gregory I now turn. His name was John, but to
distinguish him from many namesakes he was commonly known
as Gratian.[3] He is never styled John Gratian by contemporaries.[4]
He was the head, archcanon or archpriest—the two titles
indicate the same office[5]—of a house of clergy established in the
Church of St. John at the Latin Gate. By universal testimony
he was a man of unblemished character, who was held by all in
the highest regard. When he was already past middle life, for
he was godfather (*patrinus*) to Benedict IX, he appears to have
been so deeply impressed by that Pope's unworthiness for his
office that he took the daring step of buying him out of it.
Whether the act was simoniacal or not, I do not know. Simony
is understood to mean the payment of money for a spiritual

[1] *Lib. Pontif.* ii. 273 f.

[2] See the 'Zwettl Hist. Rom. Pontif.' cliii, in Pez's *Thes. Anecd. Noviss.* i. iii
(1721), 385 *a*.

[3] It is possible that this surname was derived from a kinsman, perhaps an
uncle, who on conversion translated Johanan into Gratianus, just as Baruch
became Benedictus. That Gratian was equivalent to John seems to be indicated
in a letter of John of Salisbury (ep. ccxcii) where he speaks of Gratian, afterwards Cardinal deacon, as *meum cognominem*. See also L. Zunz, 'Namen der
Juden', in *Gesammelte Schriften*, ii (1876) 54.

[4] I notice this because Dr. M. Tangl, in the *Neues Archiv der Gesellschaft für
ältere Deutsche Geschichtskunde*, xxxi (1906), 162, adduces this combination
of names as an argument against Gregory VI's connexion with the family of
Leo son of Benedict, in which the double name does not occur.

[5] See Duchesne, *Lib. Pontif.* ii. 271, n. 3.

office which one desires; whether it includes also the payment
of money in order to remove a scandalous holder of an office by
a person who does not desire it, I leave to those better versed in
canon law than I am to decide. The nature of the transaction
was perhaps not at once made known. Directly Gratian became
Pope St. Peter Damiani wrote him a florid letter of congratula-
tion, in which he specially welcomed the blow which his election
had struck at the evil of simony:

Conteratur iam milleforme caput venenati serpentis; cesset com-
mercium perversae negotiationis; nullam iam monetam falsarius
Simon in ecclesia fabricet.[1]

But the problem is, how a man like Gratian could have been in
the possession of the immense amount of money which he was
reputed to have paid.[2] Bonizo of Sutri, with his accustomed
scurrility, says that he amassed wealth by his abstinence from
profligate courses.[3] This cannot be taken seriously. It is plain
that Gratian must either have inherited great wealth or have
had very rich relations.

It is an old-established statement that he was a member of
the powerful family of Peter Leonis. Ciaconius speaks as though
he were Peter's son,[4] but this is, on chronological grounds,
impossible. From what source the statement is derived I have
been unable to discover. There is an inscription formerly on
Peter's tomb at St. Paul's without the Walls, which asserts
definitely that Gregory VI was his uncle (*patruus*);[5] but the
inscription is unmistakably of late date, and has had the misfortune of having been restored in the seventeenth century.
According to it Gregory was a brother of Peter's father Leo,
the son of Benedict the Christian. Signor Pietro Fedele, with

---

[1] *Epist.* i. i, *Opera*, iii. 2, ed. C. Cajetani, 1783. Dr. Grauert, *op. cit.*, pp. 315,
321–5, argues that Peter was aware of the facts and thought that Gregory's
conduct could be defended.

[2] The sum is variously stated as a thousand pounds of pennies of Pavia (*Lib.
Pontif.* ii. 275) and 1,500 pounds (Beno, *Gest. Rom. Eccl.* ii. 7, p. 378); it grew
in time to 2,000 pounds (Cod. Vat. 1340, *Lib. Pontif.* ii. 270). A thousand
pounds meant a thousand pounds' weight of silver, and this, according to the
twelfth-century ratio of 1 : 9, would mean something not far short of £6,000 in
modern value.

[3] 'Lib. ad Amicum', v, in *Monum. Greg.*, p. 628.

[4] 'Ioannes Gratianus Petri Leonis, eximiae nobilitatis in urbe vir': *Vitae
Pontif. Rom.* i. 781 (ed. A. Oldoinus, 1677).

[5] It is printed by A. Nerini, *de Templo et Coenobio ss. Bonifacii et Alexii*
(1752), app. viii, p. 394 note; and by V. Forcella, *Iscrizioni delle Chiese di Roma*,
xii (1878), 79, no. 31.

his habitual caution, admits that the relationship is not proved; but he thinks that some near relationship is highly probable.[1]

Now Benedict the Christian was a wealthy merchant established, it seems, in the region beyond Tiber which was the Jewish quarter of the city.[2] His name before his conversion was presumably Baruch or Berachiah, and this was translated into Benedictus when he became a Christian. He is said to have been converted during the pontificate of Leo IX and to have called his son after the Pope.[3] This was a not unnatural conjecture for a later writer to make,[4] but it will not suit the dates of Leo's activity. For Leo IX was enthroned in 1048, and in 1051 we have a grant of land made *Leoni, vir magnificus et laudabilis negotiator, filio Benedicti bone memorie Christiani*.[5] In 1060 he was among the principal witnesses to the investiture of the abbot of Farfa by Nicholas II.[6] Moreover, we know from his epitaph that his mother was of noble birth—a member of the nobility of Christian Rome:

> Romae natus, opum dives, probus, et satis alto
> Sanguine materno nobilitatus erat.[7]

Her marriage may have taken place as early as 1010, and

[1] 'Le Famiglie di Anacleto II e di Gelasio II', in the *Arch. della Soc. Rom. di Storia Patria*, xxvii (1904), 409 f.

[2] *Ibid.*, pp. 405 f. Nothing helpful for our purpose will be found in A. Berliner's *Gesch. der Juden in Rom*, II. i (1893); and very little in the work with the same title by H. Vogelstein and P. Rieger, i (1896). These writers are not interested in converted Jews. The latter say (i. 214) that there are no Jewish materials for the history of the Roman Jews at this time.

[3] *Chron. de Morigny*, p. 51, ed. L. Mirot, 2nd ed., 1912. This part of the chronicle was finished about 1132.

[4] It is elaborated in the scurrilous account given by Arnulf, afterwards bishop of Lisieux, of the most famous member of this house of converts, Anacletus II: 'Parcendum tamen est obscoenitati verborum, dum Petri vita narratur, et rerum veritas sermonum pallianda decore, ut honos habitus honestati legentium videatur. Libet igitur praeterire antiquam nativitatis eius originem et ignobilem similem prosapiam, nec Iudaicum nomen arbitror opponendum, de quibus ipse non solum materiam carnis sed etiam quasdam primitias ingeniti contraxit erroris. Ipse enim sufficiens est et copiosa materia, neque quidquam domui eius ipso turpius vel esse vel fuisse coniecto. Cuius avus cum inaestimabilem pecuniam multiplici corrogasset usura, susceptam circumcisionem baptismatis unda dampnavit, etc.': 'In Girardum Engolismensem', iii, in L. d'Achery's *Spicilegium*, i (ed. 1723), 155 a.

[5] 'Carte del Monastero dei SS. Cosma e Damiano in Mica Aurea', ed. P. Fedele, *Arch. della Soc. Rom. di Stor. Patr.* xxii (1899), 97.

[6] *Reg. Farf.*, no. 906, vol. iv. 300 f. He witnesses another document in 1063: *ibid.*, no. 936, p. 329.

[7] The inscription was written by Archbishop Alfanus of Salerno, and is printed by Baronius, *Ann.* xviii. 217.

Benedict was no doubt then already a convert. He was dead in 1051, and his son Leo is no longer mentioned after 1063.

It has been necessary to consider the antecedents of Leo de Benedicto Christiano,[1] because it has been frequently said that the family was one of recent conversion, perhaps as recent as the time of Leo IX.[2] They had in fact been opulent and powerful members of the Christian community in the region beyond Tiber and on the Island for at least a generation; and Leo and his son Peter were pre-eminent among the supporters of the reforming party in Rome. When the Tusculans set up Benedict X, in 1058, Hildebrand obtained money from Leo by means of which he divided the populace, and it was in the Transtiberine district that he succeeded in holding his ground.[3] In 1062, when there was hard fighting on behalf of the Antipope Cadalus (Honorius II), Leo stood by Hildebrand and Alexander II, and distributed money through the city all the night.[4] His wealth was each time an important auxiliary to the Hildebrandine forces. The eminent services performed by Leo's son Peter for Hildebrand after he became Pope, and for Urban II when he too was in trouble, are too well known to need recording.[5] Peter had now removed into the heart of the city, and it was in his house *apud sanctum Nicolaum in Carcere* that Urban died.[6] Peter lived on until between 1124 and 1130.[7] One of his sons, also named Peter, was raised to the Papacy as Anacletus II, but after many fluctuations of fortune he was destined to rank as an Antipope.

The great wealth of the house of Peter Leonis and their unvarying support of Hildebrand and his party are prominently mentioned in the literature of the time both by friends and enemies; and there is a remarkable statement in a chronicle of the twelfth century which claims Hildebrand himself as a member of it. This is found in the Annals of Pegau, near Merseburg—a compilation which contains some kernels of fact mixed up with a great deal of loose and unsupported tradition[8] —according to which Peter Leonis was Hildebrand's *avunculus*;

---

[1] So he is called, under 1058 and 1062 in the *Annales Romani, Lib. Pontif.* ii. 334, 336.

[2] See, for instance, Giesebrecht, *Geschichte der Deutschen Kaiserzeit*, iii (ed. 4, 1876) 16; and compare the allusion in Beno's story, above, p. 200, n. 1.

[3] *Ann. Rom., Lib. Pontif.* ii. 234 f.   [4] *Ibid.*, p. 336.

[5] See Fedele, in *Arch. della Soc. Rom.* xxvii (1904), 411–15.

[6] *Lib. Pontif.* ii. 294.   [7] Fedele, p. 415, n. 5.

[8] There is, however, no need to travesty the narrative in these Annals, as Dr. Tangl does (*Neues Archiv*, xxxi. 179), in order to hold them up to ridicule.

so that Hildebrand's mother was Peter's sister. This relationship is indeed favoured by Signor Fedele, who thinks that the difficulty arising from a consideration of the men's ages—as Hildebrand was born perhaps as early as 1020 and Peter lived until after 1124—is not insuperable.[1] To me this view appears quite out of the question. It is, however, asserted that in the region where the Pegau Annals were written the meanings of *avunculus* and *nepos* were inverted; so that the annalist really described Peter as Hildebrand's nephew.[2] The proof of this strange usage has not yet, to my knowledge, been produced. If it be correct, it is surprising that neither the Lives of Hildebrand nor any contemporary writers give a hint that he had a sister married to a well-known citizen. I incline rather to believe that *avunculus* was used in a general sense to indicate relationship on the mother's side. Now it has lately been discovered that Hildebrand's mother was a Roman lady named Bertha, who lived near the church of St. Mary in Portico.[3] We still await the evidence for this identification; but it is not in itself unlikely. Bertha, I would suggest, was the sister of the wife of Leo, son of Benedict the Christian.

We have seen that Gratian has been asserted to have belonged to this same family of converts; and the close ties which bound him to Hildebrand have naturally led to a speculation whether they were not connected in blood. When Gratian was deposed and exiled beyond the Alps, it was Hildebrand whom he took as his companion.[4] On his death, it is stated, but on suspicious authority, that he made Hildebrand his heir.[5] Nearly twenty years later Hildebrand himself attained the Papacy, and in remembrance of his old friend he adopted his name, Gregory.[6]

---

[1] p. 407 and n. 1.   [2] See Tangl, p. 166, n. 3.

[3] The statement is quoted by Signor Fedele, p. 407, n. 3, from an Italian book to which I have not access. Hugh of Flavigny, who wrote at the end of the century, stands alone in saying that Hildebrand was born in Rome 'parentibus civibus Romanis' (*Monum. Germ. Hist., Script.* viii. 422). His birthplace was a village in the district of Sovana, and his father was of Tuscan race; but Hildebrand speaks of his early Roman associations ('ab infantia', *Reg.* i. 39, *Monum. Greg.* p. 58; iii. 10 *a*, pp. 223 f.: cf. vii. 23 p. 415). If his mother belonged to a Roman family, this might explain Hugh of Flavigny's statement.

[4] *Reg.* vii. 14 *a*, p. 401. Bonizo, p. 630, says that Hildebrand had previously been his chaplain, but it is unlikely that he was yet in holy orders.

[5] Beno, ii. 8, p. 378.

[6] 'Hunc Gratianum Alpes transcendentem secutum fuisse tradunt Hiltibrandum, qui postmodum summus pontifex factus ob eius amorem, quia de catalogo pontificum semotus fuerat, se Gregorium VIIm vocari voluit': Otto of

If there be a grain of truth in the tales which were told against Hildebrand in later years, he was brought up under Gratian's immediate influence. Cardinal Beno has a wonderful story of how Gerbert, Pope Silvester II, who had already acquired the reputation of a necromancer, taught his evil arts to Theophylact (afterwards Benedict IX) and to Lawrence (afterwards archbishop of Amalfi), and how Lawrence lived in the house of John the archpriest, otherwise Gratian, his disciple. From these three Hildebrand learned magic.[1] Now in 1046 Lawrence undoubtedly resided at the monastery of St. Mary on the Aventine; and Hildebrand, according to his biographer, Paul of Bernried, was sent for his education to his uncle (*avunculus*), who was abbot of that house.[2]

The monastery has an interesting history. Alberic the Prince had a palace on the site, which he gave, perhaps in 936, to St. Odo, abbot of Cluny, in order that he might found a monastery there;[3] and from that time St. Mary's was the place where the abbot of Cluny stayed when they visited Rome. St. Odilo was there more than once: his biographer, Jotsald, says,

Habebat autem hospitium in monasterio sacrae puerperae Virginis, quod est situm in Aventino monte, qui, prae caeteris illius urbis montibus aedes decoras habens et suae positionis culmen in altum tollens, aestivos fervores aurarum algore tolerabiles reddit et habilem in se habitationem facit.[4]

But Odilo was not in Rome after 1032 until he returned near the end of his life, in 1046, arriving on the eve of the appointment of Clement II.[5] There is therefore no question of any personal acquaintance between Odilo and Hildebrand. Still, though Odilo was not himself at Rome, it is evident that St. Mary's was always the head-quarters there of the reforming movement which is associated with the famous Burgundian monastery. It was this connexion that drew thither Odilo's friend Lawrence, the expelled archbishop of Amalfi, *vir per omnia sanctissimus, in scripturis*

Freising, *Chron.* vi. 32, pp. 299 f. For Dr. Martens's opinion that the name was *imposed* upon Hildebrand in memory of Gregory the Great (*Zeitschrift für Kirchenrecht*, xxii. 63 f., 1887) see above pp. 162 f.

[1] *Gesta Rom. Eccl.* ii. 3–5, *Libelli de Lite*, ii. 376 f.

[2] Vit. Greg. VII, in Watterich, i. 477. One Peter, abbot of St. Mary's, subscribes the acts of a Roman synod in 1044: Ughelli, v (ed. 1720), 1116; as does also John, the archcanon and archpriest of St. John's.

[3] Hugh of Farfa, 'Destr. Farf.', in *Chron. Farf.* i. 39 f.

[4] *Vit. s. Odilon.* ii. 9, in Migne, cxlii. 923.

[5] This is acutely pointed out by Sackur, *Die Cluniacenser*, ii (1894), 282, n. 2.

utriusque linguae, Graecae videlicet et Latinae, facundissimus;[1] and the same personal ties most naturally explain the favour with which Peter Damiani welcomed the appointment of Gratian to the Papacy as ushering in a new time of purity for the Church.[2]

It would not be wise to make too much of the accusation brought against Hildebrand that he accumulated riches by usury.[3] He was certainly closely associated with Peter Leonis, whose money more than once was of service to his interests;[4] and this may have given rise to the story that he himself engaged in speculation. Peter's constant support suggests, though it does not prove, that he was his kinsman.

Now in what manner can we combine the various uncertain indications about Gratian and Hildebrand in such a way as to build up a tentative pedigree? We find (1) a modern statement that Gratian was of the house of Peter Leonis; (2) an inscription, probably also modern, asserting that he was Peter's uncle; (3) his great wealth, which implies that he belonged to a family of capitalists; (4) his close attachment to Hildebrand, whom by one dubious account he made his heir; (5) that Hildebrand was later on reputed to be connected on his mother's side with Peter Leonis; (6) he was associated with Gratian in a way that suggests relationship; (7) he was reputed to have business relations with Peter Leonis; (8) when active in ecclesiastical affairs he enjoyed the steady adhesion of Peter Leonis. These data, however much they differ among themselves in their value as evidence, tend to a conclusion which I am tempted to set out in a provisional pedigree.

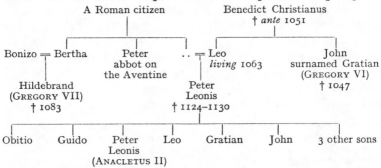

---

[1] *Vit. s. Odilon*, i. 14, p. 909. Compare the additional passages of Jotsald's Life, printed by Sackur, in *Neues Archiv*, xv (1890), 120.

[2] It is not without interest to read that Peter Damiani was staying in Rome on the critical days when Clement II was made Pope and Henry III crowned Emperor: see *Opusc.* xlii. 6, in *Opera*, iii. 698.

[3] Above, p. 200 and notes.   [4] Above, p. 209.

This reconstruction avoids the inference, which Signor Fidele's hypothesis carries with it, that Hildebrand was of Jewish origin. I do not indeed lay the same stress as Dr. Tangl does[1] on the silence on this point of Hildebrand's enemies, who brought every conceivable charge against him. For the family of Benedict the Christian bore so high a character in ecclesiastical Rome, and were converts of such old standing, that no slur on this ground could be plausibly insinuated. I contest the theory of Hildebrand's Jewish extraction simply because it seems to me irreconcilable with such data as we possess relative to Benedict's descendants.

POSTSCRIPT

After this paper was completely written and prepared for publication, I found that its subject had just been discussed with much greater elaboration by Signor G. B. Borino in two articles which fill 228 pages of the thirty-ninth volume of the *Archivio della R. Società Romana di Storia Patria* (1916). I have thought it best to leave my paper exactly as it stood; for it may not be without interest for the student to compare two independent essays produced at almost the same time by two writers belonging to different nations and living in different countries. It is particularly gratifying to me that on many of the controverted points Signor Borino's conclusions agree with mine.[2] He goes indeed far beyond me in his analysis of the political situation, and his remarkable exposition of the reasons which made it necessary for Henry III to get Gregory VI out of the way (see especially pp. 332 f., 370–82) deserves attentive consideration. It is, however, true that, while he balances every detail of evidence in the most thoroughgoing way, he is not free from the fault, which he shares with most writers on this complicated business, of not sufficiently distinguishing between contemporary and later authorities. I should like to avail myself of Signor Borino's ample materials to add a couple of supplementary notes.

1. As to the youth of Benedict IX. Signor Borino quotes from a contemporary Life of Leo IX, published by A. Poncelet in the

---

[1] *Neues Archiv*, xxxi. 174 ff.

[2] For instance, he has arrived at the same conclusion as mine with regard to the name of John *cognomento Gratianus*, and even hazards the same conjecture as I have done, which I have read nowhere else, with regard to Gratianus being a translation of a Jewish name (pp. 229–31).

Analecta Bollandiana, xxv (1906), 275, the statement that Benedict's father Alberic *habebat filium parvulum, nomine Theophilactus, qui succedente Iohannis sanctissimi papae per multa donaria militiae Romanorum sedis apostolicae ordinatus est antistes.* Secondly, he cites the statement of Luke, abbot of Grottaferrata,[1] that Benedict was elected νέος ὤν, ὡς μὴ ὤφελε. Thirdly, the later comment of Desiderius of Monte Cassino, *Adolescens iuxta viam suam.* This evidence indeed does not prove very much. When Otto the Great was told of the misdeeds of John XII seventy years before, he is reported by Liudprand[2] to have said, *Puer est: facile bonorum immutabitur exemplo virorum.* And John was at that time twenty-five years of age. On the other hand, Signor Borino mentions (pp. 144, n. 1, 146 n.) that one of Benedict's brothers was married and had a child in 1030. [This brother, it may be added, was of legal age in 1022.[3]] He relates at length what is known of Benedict's official career down to 1044 (pp. 157–69), and agrees with me that were we not informed of the scandal of his beginning and end *giudicheremmo il pontificato di questo papa presso che normale, e persino d'una certa attività politica e religiosa* (p. 148).[4]

2. Noticing the long interval which passed between the deposition of Benedict IX, which he places as early as the beginning of September 1044 (pp. 180 f.), and the election of Silvester III in January 1045, Signor Borino considers that the former act was the result of a general movement of the Romans, while the latter was effected by the party which represented the old house of Crescentius and defeated the Tusculans. This party had great influence in the Sabina and they set up their Bishop John as Pope Silvester III. Then after a couple of months the Tusculans appeared in force, expelled Silvester, and restored Benedict. Signor Borino examines the position of the Crescentian family with great knowledge of the local circumstances (pp. 188–201): the contest, he thinks, was more between two rival parties than between the individual persons (p. 221). But he considers

---

[1] 'Vita S. Bartholomaei Iun.' x, in Migne, *Patrol. Graec.* cxxvii. 484.

[2] *Hist. Otton.* v.

[3] 'Querimonium Hugonis Abbatis', in *Chron. Farfense*, i. 76.

[4] In his criticism of Rodulf Glaber Signor Borino is wrong in thinking that Rodulf's date 1000 for 1033 is an error of transcription. Rodulf's words are *Anno igitur eodem die dominice passionis Mᵒ, die tercio kalendarum Iuliarum* (*Chron.* iv. 9). Evidently the *dies passionis* could not fall on 29 June. The word *die* should be omitted, and the year (as reference to ch. v shows) is the year not of the Incarnation but of the Passion.

that Silvester was not a man to accept his deposition as final (pp. 204, 206). Here he differs from most scholars who have discussed the subject. The upshot of his argument is that there was in fact no sale of the Papacy by Benedict to Gregory, but an agreement between the two parties in accordance with which the Crescentians recouped Benedict for the money which he had paid for his election twelve years before (p. 221). In support of this view he cites some words from the anonymous tract *de Ordinando Pontifice*,[1] which he takes with Sackur[2] to proceed from Lower Lorraine, and which he is no doubt right in assigning not to 1048, as its editor Dümmler did, but to the last months of 1047 (p. 217, n. 1). The following is this writer's account of the resignation of Benedict and of the mode by which Gregory obtained the Papacy:

Ministerio quod illicite appetierat se carere velle disposuit si quis ei redderet summam pecuniae quam ex appetitu in eo dispendit. Quem sane tenorem arripiens Satanas non defuit, quaerens et cito inveniens qui, repensa (ut a quibusdam dictum est) pecunia, in eadem cathedra pestilentiae resedit. . . . Alii autem excusant eum pecuniam non dedisse sed dantibus amicis et parentibus suis consensisse.

Signor Borino does not, I think, mention the obvious objection to his theory, that if Benedict's resignation was effected by the party of Silvester III one would naturally expect that they would have attempted to restore the latter. He suggests that the party of reform intervened; they united with the Crescentians to get rid of Benedict, and then brought forward Gratian as a candidate for election who would command general approval (pp. 248 f.). But he does not dispute that Gratian consented to the antecedent transaction. Signor Borino's treatment of the question is extremely ingenious, but I cannot say that it appears to me altogether convincing.

APPENDIX

The Counts of Tusculum

The ancestry of the counts of Tusculum who exercised so continuous and powerful an authority over the city of Rome in the eleventh century has been obscured by a number of legendary accretions; but there are sufficient materials contained in a long

---

[1] *Lib. de Lite*, i. 10. [2] *Die Cluniacenser*, ii. 305, n. 2.

series of charters, in the names of grantors and of witnesses, to enable us to arrive at the conclusion that they were derived from the family to which Alberic the Prince of the Romans belonged. The fact has been regarded as doubtful,[1] because one link in the pedigree has been filled up by conjecture. I propose to show that there is definite documentary evidence which almost certainly proves the connexion. The accompanying table, a few details in which may still need verification, sets out the result.[2]

On the face of it, when we consider the persistence of the same names in Italian families in the Middle Ages, one is struck by the recurrence of names like Theophylact, Alberic, Octavian, and Theodora; but the difficulty has been to show the origin of Gregorius de Tusculana, from whom the counts of Tusculum descend. He appears with this surname in the record of a lawsuit at Rome in 999, and he ranks second among the lay judges:

> Residentibus . . . Gerardo gratia Dei inclito comite atque imperialis militiae magistro,
>
> Gregorio excellentissimo viro qui vocatur de Tusculana atque praefecto navali,
>
> Gregorio viro clarissimo qui vocatur Miccinus atque vestarario sacri palatii,
>
> Alberico filio Gregorii atque imperialis palatii magistro . . .[3]

The Alberic here named was brother to the first two Tusculan Popes, Benedict VIII and John XIX. His father Gregory, who in 999 had attained a position of high dignity at Rome, is found as early as 961 witnessing as *consul et dux* a grant of certain vineyards

---

[1] See Wattenbach's preface to the Chronicles of Monte Cassino, in *Monum. Germ. Hist., Script.* vii. 562 f.

[2] The pedigree of the Tusculan house up to Gregorius de Tusculana is given by Wattenbach in the preface above cited. Monsignor Duchesne supplies the higher generations from Theophylact and Theodora downwards (*Lib. Pontif.* ii. 252, n. 2). Tomassetti ('Della Campagna Romana nel medio evo', ii, in *Arch. della Società Romana di Storia Patria*, ix. 81 n., 1886) gives a complete pedigree of the whole family. But he fell into error through following a suggestion of Gregorovius (*Hist. of the City of Rome*, iv. 10) that Gregorius was either the son or grandson of Alberic II, and made his mother, Marozia, Alberic's daughter instead of his first cousin. The insertion of Theodora III is due to a brilliant reconstruction of an inscription by De Rossi (*Bullettino di Archeologia Cristiana*, ii. 65–9, 1864). Monsignor Duchesne, I venture to think wrongly, identifies her with Theodora II. The pedigrees given by Wattenbach and Tomassetti are vitiated in the later generations by the acceptance of statements derived from Peter the Deacon's 'improved' version of his own descent found in the Monte Cassino MS. 257 (see the notes to Muratori, *Rerum Ital. Script.*, iv. 488, and *Biblioth. Casin.* v. 51 a, 1894); they do not appear in his earlier version. It is clear that in order to attach himself to the Tusculan family Peter had recourse to an elaborate system of falsification. See E. Caspar, *Petrus Diaconus und die Monte Cassiner Fälschungen* (1909), pp. 21 ff.

[3] *Regesto di Farfa*, iii (1883), 150, n. 437 [470].

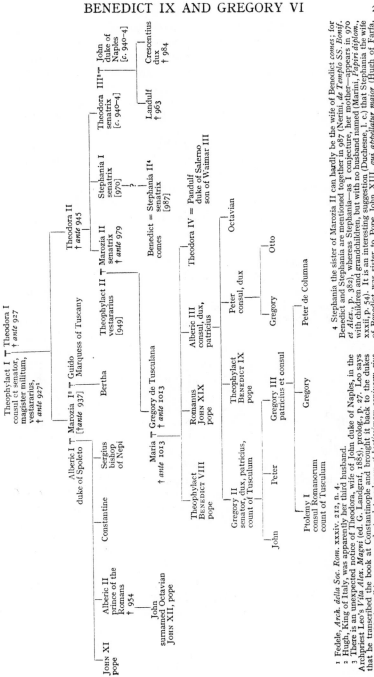

4 Stephania the sister of Marozia II can hardly be the wife of Benedict *comes*; for Benedict and Stephania are mentioned together in 987 (Nerini, *de Templo SS. Bonif. et Alex.*, p. 382), whereas Stephania—as I conjecture, her mother—appears in 970 with children and grandchildren, but with no husband named (Marini, *Papiri diplom.*, xxxii, p. 54). It is an interesting suggestion (Duchesne, l. c.) that Stephania the wife of Benedict was sister to Pope John XIII, *qui appellatur maior* (Hugh of Farfa, *Exceptio Relationum*, in *Chron. Farf.* i. 62); but I am not sure that the reference is not, as the editor, Ugo Balzani, supposed, to John XV.

1 Fedele, *Arch. della Soc. Rom.* xxxiv. 212, n. 4.
2 Hugh, King of Italy, was apparently her third husband.
3 There is an unexpected notice of Theodora, wife of John duke of Naples, in the Archpriest Leo's *Vita Alex. Magni* (ed. G. Landgraf, 1885), prolog., p. 27. Leo says that he transcribed the book at Constantinople and brought it back to the dukes John and Marinus [his young son] *et ad praeclaram et beatissimam coniugem eius* [scil. *Iohannis*], *Theodoram videlicet senatricem Romanorum, quae die noctuque meditabatur sacrae scripturae.* This must have been about 941-4.

in the territory of Albano to the monastery of Subiaco.[1] In 980 or 981 there is an agreement *inter Gregorius illustrissimo viro filius Maroze senatrix . . . rectorem monasterii sancti Andree apostoli et sancte Lucie qui appellatur Renati* and the abbot.[2] Now in 949 we read of a charter of sale *da Maroza nobili femina conius vero Theophilactus eminentissimus bestarario* of land in the territory of Albano called Zizinni.[3] In 979, after the death of *Maroze nobilissime femine*, her uncle Demetrius at her desire gave property at Zizinni to the monastery: this document is witnessed by Gregorius *consul et dux*.[4] The title of *senatrix* given to Maroza in the document of 980 brings us very close to the ruling power at Rome. In 959 Marozia *senatrix omnium Romanorum* makes another grant to Subiaco;[5] in 961 she is mentioned as *excellentissima femina atque senatrix*;[6] and it has not escaped notice that this title is assigned to her soon after the death of the famous Alberic *senator* and Prince of the Romans in 954.[7] It is evident that she stood in the foremost rank of the nobility of the city. Her husband Theophylact held the office of *vestararius*, one of the highest administrative posts which a layman could hold in the papal court, and she herself bore the title of *senatrix*. What relation did she bear to Alberic?

There is a piece of evidence among the Subiaco charters, hidden away unobserved in a record of boundaries, which furnishes nearly positive proof that she was his first cousin. In 985 a church and its appurtenances at Albano were granted to the monastery; the adjacent landowners are enumerated: on three sides were the heirs of the grantor, who had become a monk, *et a quarto latere Gregorius de Maroza de Theodoru*.[8] The absence of honorific titles hardly presents a difficulty, for it was not necessary to insert them in a record of boundaries; and I have no doubt that *Theodoru* is a simple slip of the pen for *Theodora*. It cannot be accounted for on palaeographical grounds, for, whether in the original Lombardic or in the minuscule of the chartulary, *a* and *u* are perfectly distinct. While in the rude Latinity of these documents little regard is paid to the correct use of case-endings, we find that proper names are by preference written in the nominative, no matter what the construction of the sentence may be. In the rare instances in which a name is written with the termination *-u*, it seems always to represent *-us* or *-um*, moving in the direction of the Italian *-o*; I do not think it ever stands for *-a*. Therefore in the present instance Maroza ought to be the daughter of Theodorus. But if this were so it would be difficult to connect her with the family of Alberic or to explain how after his death she came

---

[1] *Regesto Sublacense*, p. 191, no. 139.   [2] *Ibid.*, p. 155, no. 109.
[3] *Ibid.*, p. 176, no. 126.   [4] *Ibid.*, pp. 175 f., n. 125; cf. p. 194, no. 143.
[5] *Ibid.*, pp. 106 f., no. 65.   [6] *Ibid.*, p. 174, no. 124.
[7] Wattenbach, *op. cit.*, p. 562.   [8] *Reg. Sublac.*, p. 189, no. 138.

to bear the title of *senatrix*. These documents, however, are by no means free from textual inaccuracies, and I believe that the scribe accidentally wrote *Theodoru* when he should have written *Theodora*. This Marozia, then, was the daughter of Theodora sister of Marozia I, the mother of Alberic II. Her relationship to him is precisely stated in a document which has been several times printed from a notarial transcript of 1301.[1] It is a grant to the monastery of SS. Andrew and Gregory *quod appellatur Clivuscauri* dated 14 January in the 3rd year of Marinus [miswritten Martinus] II in the 3rd Indiction, that is, in 945. The important sentence for our purpose runs as follows; I divide the names for clearness into paragraphs:

Nos Albericus Domini gratia humilis princeps atque omnium Romanorum senator,

atque Sergius humilis episcopus sancte Nepesine ecclesie,

nec non et Constantinus illustris vir,

atque Bertha nobilissima puella uterina,

et germani fratres Marozze quondam Romanorum senatricis filii,

nec non et Marozza seu [=et] Stephania nobilissima femina,

germane sorores et consobrine eorum Theodore quondam Romanorum senatricis filie.

The subscriptions are arranged in the following order: Alberic, Marozia, Stephania (both the ladies *litteras nescientes*), Bertha, Sergius, Constantine. Marozia thus ranks next after Alberic, and she is expressly described as daughter of Theodora formerly *senatrix Romanorum*. That Alberic's son John, surnamed Octavian, afterwards Pope John XII, is not mentioned is accounted for by the fact that he was a boy at the time: his death in 964 left the inheritance of Alberic's possessions to Marozia.

Marozia *senatrix*, then, the mother of Gregory de Tusculana, was the daughter of Theodora, who, with her sister the elder Marozia, had occupied a position of unequalled influence at Rome in the early part of the tenth century. They were the daughters of Theophylact, who as *vestararius* and *magister militum* held the highest rank among the officials of the Roman state. As early as 901 Theophylact is mentioned second in a list of eleven *iudices*, following next after the bishops and counts, who were present at the decision of a lawsuit at Rome;[2] he soon became beyond question the most important layman in the papal domains.[3]

---

[1] I cite it from Marini, no. c, pp. 155 ff.

[2] Schiaparelli, *Diplomi di Lodovico III*, p. 19 (1910). For the early pedigree of Theophylact's family, see W. Sickel's paper on 'Alberich II und der Kirchenstaat', in *Mitth. des Inst. für Österreichische Geschichtsforschung*, xxiii (1902), 77–81, 87 f.

[3] This is excellently brought out by Monsignor Duchesne, *Les Premiers Temps de l'État Pontifical*, 2nd ed., 1904, pp. 310 f.

The pedigree thus constructed receives an interesting support from the evidence preserved as to the house which the head of the family inhabited at Rome. The Palazzo Colonna, adjoining the Church of the Santissimi Apostoli, bears its name from a descendant in the fifth degree of Gregory de Tusculana. Gregory's son Alberic (III) count of Tusculum is found in 1013 dwelling there: on the occasion of a lawsuit the judges by command of the Pope, Benedict VIII, assembled *intra domum domni Alberici eminentissimi consulis et ducis iuxta sanctos apostolos.*[1] Seventy years before, a suit was in like manner held in the same house, which was then occupied by Alberic (II) the Prince: in 942 the judges assembled by his command *in curte ipsius principi Alberici iuxta basilica sancti apostoli.*[2] The property seems from later indications to have extended up the Quirinal, where the Torre Mesa, destroyed by Innocent XIII, is believed to have been built by the Tusculan counts in the eleventh century.[3] Tomassetti thinks that this Roman house was possessed by the lords of the Via Lata, and that it may even be possible to trace the family back to Pope Adrian I.[4] Into this conjecture I will not enter, for I am at the moment interested only in establishing the pedigree which connects the family of Alberic the Prince with the house of Tusculum in the eleventh century. It is manifest that this Roman property came down from Theophylact and Theodora. They transmitted it to their daughter Marozia, the consort of Alberic (I) duke of Spoleto, and hence it was inherited by their son Alberic the Prince.

There is no sign that the elder Alberic had anything to do with Rome until his alliance with Marozia. According to Benedict of Soracte, this followed the victory which he and Pope John X won over the Saracens at the Garigliano in 915 or 916. On his return he was received with honour by the Roman people and formed an alliance (not, according to Benedict, a marriage) with the daughter of Theophylact.[5] This is the generally received account. But Signor Fedele points out that the date is difficult to reconcile with the fact that in 932 the son of this union, Alberic the Prince, was old enough and strong enough to imprison his mother and drive the Pope from

[1] *Reg. di Farfa*, iv. 35, no. 637 [670].

[2] *Reg. Sublac.*, p. 203, no. 155, where *sancti apostoli* is the nominative plural; as Benedict of Soracte speaks of 'ecclesia sanctorum apostolorum Iacobi et Philippi, que nos vocamus sancti apostoli': *Chron.* xxxi., *Monum. Germ. Hist.*, *Script.* iii. (1839) 715.

[3] See an article by C. Corvisieri in the *Arch. della R. Società Romana di Storia Patria*, x (1887), 636–40.

[4] *Ibid.*, ix. 80.

[5] 'Accepit una de nobilibus Romani ... Theophilacti filia, non quasi uxor sed in consuetudinem malignam': *Chron.* ed. Zucchetti, p. 158. Cf. Duchesne, 'Serge III et Jean XI', in the *Mélanges d'Archéologie et d'Histoire*, xxxiii (1913) 48 ff.

Rome.[1] He thinks, therefore, that Alberic's connexion with Rome began some years earlier,[2] probably at the time when Sergius III succeeded in gaining possession of the Popedom of which he had previously failed to make himself master. Be this as it may, it is necessary to guard against a figment which has come down from the writers who in former times sought to magnify the greatness and antiquity of the counts of Tusculum: this is the assertion that Alberic I was himself count of Tusculum, which is repeated by De Rossi[3] and Tomassetti.[4] It is absolutely unsupported and is rightly described by Gregorovius as absurd.[5]

The family of which Theophylact I and Theodora I are the first proved ancestors was a Roman family which probably had been long established in the city.[6] From the early years of the tenth century it held, as we have seen, a place of great distinction and authority in Rome. Naturally its members acquired property in the neighbouring districts. We find them as landowners in the territory of Albano, and just at the end of the century Gregory, the heir to the main part of the estates, appears for the first time connected with Tusculum, a fortress which for nearly two hundred years continued the head-quarters of his descendants.[7] He died before 1013.[8] The only positive statement that Gregory held the office which in his son's time is described as the countship of Tusculum appears, I think, in the Life of St. Nilus, who settled near Grotta Ferrata in the closing years of the tenth century and died at a great age in 1005. Here we read that 'the ruler of that township, by name Gregory, was notorious for his tyranny and injustice, but exceedingly shrewd and well furnished with intelligence',[9] very much the typical feudal baron of romance. He was, however, a good friend to the saint, to whom he granted a site for the future monastery. As time went on, the counts of Tusculum sought to carry back their lineage to ancient times. It was asserted that Alberic II called his son, the future Pope John XII, Octavian to commemorate his descent from Octavius Mamilius, the

---

[1] *Arch. della Soc. Rom.* xxxiii (1910), 216 f.

[2] So too Gregorovius, *Hist. of the City of Rome*, iii. 256, 271.

[3] *Bullettino di Archeologia Cristiana*, ii (1864), 68.

[4] Marozia 'makes her entry into the Tusculan family by marrying Alberic I count of Tusculum': *Arch della Soc. Rom.* ix. 79 f.

[5] *Hist. of the City of Rome*, iii. 275, n. 2.

[6] Signor Fedele makes some acute suggestions about their ancestry, but admits that they must for the present remain conjectures: *Arch. della Soc. Rom.* xxxiv. 208 f.

[7] Cf. Julius Jung, 'Organisationen Italiens', in the *Mittheilungen des Institutes für Österreichische Geschichtsforschung*, Ergänzungsband v (1896–1903), 50 f.   [8] *Reg. Farf.*, no. 639, vol. iv. 37.

[9] Ὁ δὲ ἄρχων τῆς κώμης ἐκείνης Γρηγόριος τῷ ὀνόματι, περιβόητος ἐν τυραννίδι καὶ ἀδικίᾳ τυγχάνων, λίαν δὲ ἀγχίνους καὶ συνέσει κεκοσμημένος, *Vita S. Nili*, xiv, § 96, *Act. Sanctorum*, Sept. vii (1760) 340 B.

son-in-law of Tarquinius Superbus.[1] In the twelfth century Peter the Deacon, the chronicler of Monte Cassino, who wished to make himself a scion of the Tusculan house, boldly invented a letter in the name of Ptolemy, the count of his day, making him describe himself as *Iulia stirpe progenitus*,[2] and thus claim an ancestry less ancient but more august than that which traced back to Tarquin.

[1] See Gregorovius, iv. 9, n. 1. Livy says (i. 49) that Tarquin *Octavio Mamilio Tusculano* (*is longe princeps Latini nominis erat, si famae credimus, ab Ulixe deaque Circa oriundus*): *ei Mamilio filiam nuptum dat.*

[2] Muratori, *Rerum Italicarum Scriptores*, iv. 488 note.

THE MASTERS OF THE SCHOOLS AT PARIS AND CHARTRES IN JOHN OF SALISBURY'S TIME[1]

I. JOHN OF SALISBURY'S NARRATIVE

THE chapter in the *Metalogicon*[2] in which John of Salisbury describes his studies in France is a famous passage in the history of learning. Into the larger problems raised by it I do not propose to enter in the present paper, but its interest is so great that the notes of time and place and the identification of persons deserve looking into very carefully. These minor questions were the subject of active discussion some thirty years ago, and little new material has been added since. But a good many problems were then left undecided, and it has seemed to me that a fresh examination might lead to the solution of some of them. At least I hope to show that some statements of fact and some identifications of persons which were formerly accepted may be definitely rejected.

John says that he went abroad in the year next after Henry I died. Henry died on 1 December 1135, and the next year began on Christmas Day. It is true that from the middle of the twelfth century the practice of reckoning the year from Lady Day was coming into fashion, but at Canterbury the older rule certainly prevailed long after that time.[3] John first studied under Abailard and then under one Alberic,[4] and Robert of Melun. These masters taught on Mount St. Geneviève in the southern suburb of Paris, and here John continued for near two full years. This brings us towards the end of 1137. Then by the advice of his teachers he resorted to the Grammarian of Conches and heard his teaching by the space of three years. It is evident that these three years are counted from his departure from the Mount, and not, as Hauréau insisted,[5] from the beginning of his residence in France. They run from the winter of 1137-8 and end in 1140-1.

When he has told us of the three years during which he

---

[1] Reprinted from the *English Historical Review*, vol. xxxv (1920).
[2] ii. 10, ed. C. C. J. Webb, 1929, pp. 77–83.
[3] See Gervase of Canterbury, *Opera historica*, i. 90, ed. Stubbs, 1879.
[4] Apparently the same with Alberic surnamed de porta Veneris: John of Salisbury, Epist. cxliii, *Opp.* i. 206.
[5] *Mémoires de l'Académie des Inscriptions*, XXXI. ii (1884), 102, n. 1.

studied under William of Conches, John proceeds to enumerate several teachers whom he attended before and after this time. Afterwards, he says—that is, after the end of 1140—he worked afresh over old subjects under Richard surnamed the Bishop, and entered upon some studies pertaining to the *quadrivium*, on which he had heard some lectures from Hardwin the German, otherwise unknown to us. He also went again through rhetoric, on which he had previously attended Master Theodoric, and afterwards learned more thoroughly from Peter Helias. He took pupils too, and made friends with Adam of the Little Bridge. It is not easy to arrange the sequence of this narrative. John concludes it by saying that he was induced by the narrowness of his means and by the advice of his friends to undertake the office of a teacher; in other words, to obtain a licence giving him authority to teach. But for this a further course of study was requisite. He returned at the end of the three years (*in fine triennii*) and found again Master Gilbert, whom he heard in logic and divinity; but he was too quickly removed. This gives us a fixed date, as Gilbert of La Porrée became bishop of Poitiers in 1142. John then pursued a course of theological study under Robert Pullen and Simon of Poissy; and so nearly twelve years passed. They must have ended not later than 1146 or early in 1147. That John says so little about the second half of his long period of study is accounted for by the fact that the *Metalogicon* is a philosophical treatise. John allows himself a long digression on his studies in the arts, but only mentions his theological course summarily because it was not relevant to his subject.

John does not tell us where he spent the three years, 1137–40, after he quitted Mount St. Geneviève, and it was usually presumed that he simply passed from the suburb into the city of Paris. In 1862, however, Carl Schaarschmidt gave reasons for supposing that he went to Chartres. His arguments are as follows.[1] First, William of Conches was a Norman and became (a good deal later) the instructor of Henry, afterwards Henry II: we should not, therefore, expect to find him at Paris. Secondly, John tells us that Gilbert of La Porrée was wont, when he was chancellor of Chartres, to say certain things. This, Schaarschmidt says, explains why John mentions that 'on my return to Paris [he does not in fact say 'to Paris'] I found Gilbert

---

[1] *Iohannes Saresberiensis*, pp. 22 f.

again '. Thirdly, John's description of the teaching of Bernard of Chartres is so intimate that it can only be based on personal knowledge. Before examining the evidence about William of Conches and Gilbert of La Porrée it is worth while to note that Schaarschmidt introduces an unnecessary complication into the matter by suggesting that John spent part of these three years at Provins and Rheims. He forgets that John lived twelve years in France, and we are now concerned only with the three years beginning with his third year. His visits to these places may have been made in any of the last seven years of his stay in France, which he only just glances at. He introduces this precious bit of autobiography as an episode, to illustrate the way in which philosophical studies were pursued; and it is only as an afterthought that he speaks very briefly of his later years of study.

Schaarschmidt's opinion that the *triennium* was mainly passed at Chartres has been generally accepted. But a good deal of fresh material has accumulated since he wrote, nearly sixty years ago; and one inconspicuous source of evidence which was made public a few years earlier escaped his attention. This is a letter-book which throws light on the schools of Chartres in the first quarter of the twelfth century, and introduces us to Bernard and Gilbert, and perhaps also to William of Conches.

II. THE CHARTRES LETTER-BOOK

A manuscript formerly belonging to the chapter of Chartres and now preserved in the public library of that town (no. 1029) contains at the end of a collection of the letters of Bishop Ivo, the famous canonist, a number of letters and epistolary specimens or *formulae* occupying the last sixteen leaves of the volume. Thirty-six of these letters were printed by Lucien Merlet in the *Bibliothèque de l'École des Chartes* for 1855.[1] The manuscript was at that date assigned to about 1150, but the last catalogue places it at the end of the twelfth century.[2] Not much later it received additions of papal bulls and letters of bishops derived from sources which point to a Venetian origin.[3] But the

---

[1] 4th ser. i. The manuscript was then designated 2nd ser. 19.

[2] *Catalogue général des Manuscrits des Bibliothèques publiques de France*, Départements, xi. Chartres, pp. 319 f (1889).

[3] See M. Omont's remarks in the *Bibliothèque de l'École des Chartes*, l (1889), 566.

manuscript itself is indubitably a Chartres book, and the private letters at the end show that it was in part compiled from the correspondence of a particular family closely connected with some member of the capitular body. That this family was that of Arnold, who was dean from at latest 1087 to 1119,[1] is pretty clear; for the manuscript includes not only letters relating to Arnold's disputes with his bishop, Ivo, but also a number of domestic letters which could not have been of interest outside his immediate circle. As the names are mostly given only in initials, it is not possible to identify them all with absolute certainty; but enough is plain to enable us to fix the date of the collection. Bishop Ivo died on 23 December[2] 1115, and few of the letters are later than that year. It is necessary to state positively that Ivo died in 1115, because the year has been given differently by recent writers. M. Léon Mirot places it in 1116,[3] and Father De Ghellinck in 1117.[4] Both dates are wrong; for Paschal II announced the consecration of Ivo's successor, Geoffrey, in a letter of which the original is still preserved at Chartres, dated from the Lateran on 5 April.[5] This can have been written only in 1116; for in April 1117 the Pope was not at Rome but at Benevento, and in January 1118 he died.

One letter (VIII) is so early as 1087, but most belong to the first fifteen years of the twelfth century. Among them is a group of familiar letters addressed to their mother Letitia by two schoolboys A. and James (IX–XI). Letitia I take to be the sister of Dean Arnold; she is afterwards mentioned as a widow (XXXIV). The editor of the letters would carry the letters back to an earlier generation and make Letitia the dean's mother.[6] But the two brothers were boys together, and they are associated in a letter (XVI) addressed to Geoffrey, dean of Le Mans, when the younger, James, was still a student. Now Geoffrey was dean in 1096, possibly a little earlier, and was made archbishop of

---

[1] He subscribes charters as late as 6 June 1118 (*Gall Christ.* viii, instr. 316 B); his successor Sampson appears on 29 November 1119 (*ibid.* viii. 1199 B). The charter of Bishop Geoffrey, which makes Arnold still dean in 1120 in the third year of his episcopate (*ibid.* instr. 320), contains incompatible dates.

[2] *Cartulaire de Notre-Dame de Chartres*, ed. E. de Lépinois and L. Merlet, iii. 225, 1865.

[3] *Chronique de Morigny*, p. 15, n. 2, 2nd ed., 1912.

[4] *Le Mouvement théologique du douzième Siècle*, p. 297, 1914.

[5] *Cartul. de Notre-Dame de Chartres*, i. 123, 1862; Jaffé, *Reg.* 6518, 2nd ed.

[6] *Bibl. de l'École des Chartes*, 4th ser. i. 469 n. So, too, A. Clerval, *Les Écoles de Chartres au Moyen-Âge*, pp. 194, 217, 1895.

Rouen in 1111. Arnold, however, was already dean of Chartres in 1087, and it is not likely that he had a brother of student's age ten years or more later.[1] That they were Dean Arnold's nephews is a conjecture which I base on the fact that letters of this sort appear in a collection mainly connected with him and his family. Arnold had also a nephew Hugh, who in time became dean himself. A letter which bears no name (xiv) sends messages to the writer's father and uncle (*avunculus*), his mother and grandmother, which perhaps bring together the dean and his sister. From another letter (xvii) it appears that Hugh had a brother Dionysius, to whom letter xviii is addressed. Three other letters (xx–xxii) are written by Dionysius.

By whom the letters were collected must be left doubtful. They may have been by A., by Hugh, or by Dionysius. What is evident is that they come from some member of Arnold's family. Most of them belong to the time of Bishop Ivo, before December 1115. Two refer to Anselm of Laon, who died in 1117 (xxvi, xxvii); the second of these mentions the ruin of the city during the riots of 1112. Another letter (xxxv) is addressed on public affairs to Adela, countess of Blois, who retired to a nunnery in 1117. No letter to which a date can be assigned postulates a later year than 1116;[2] and this being so, it is unlikely that the compilation was made very long afterwards. It is important to establish this, because one letter has been placed with confidence by Hauréau[3] a quarter of a century later.

A good many of the letters bring us into relation with the schools of the time, and three are directly connected with Chartres. In one of these (xviii) a friend at Orleans writes to Dionysius making mention of the brother of Master B.: this is Theodoric, the brother of Bernard of Chartres. He has heard news *de gente nostra*; Bernard and Theodoric were Bretons, and the writer was of the same race. The next letter (xix) is accepted as the composition of Gilbert of La Porrée to Bernard (it bears only the initials G. to B.), and almost every one has taken it as written soon after Gilbert left Paris, *ex hypothesi* in 1141, to

---

[1] Merlet, p. 459, strangely attributes this letter (xvi) to Dean Arnold, at the time when he had resigned the deanery. But this was after 1114, and then Geoffrey was archbishop.

[2] Letter xxxiii, indeed, bears the superscription of Bishop G. and Dean G., but at no time until 1165 did such a bishop and dean coexist. If the bishop be Geoffrey, who succeeded Ivo at the beginning of 1116, the initial of the dean must be miswritten.   [3] *Mém. de l'Acad. des Inscr.* xxxi. ii. 93.

become *scholasticus* at Poitiers. It may be noted that this letter is the only basis for the supposition that Gilbert returned to Poitiers before he was made bishop in 1142.[1] But the letter says nothing of a recent departure; it only expresses regret that his occupation as master of the schools in Aquitaine deprives him of the pleasure of Bernard's company. It is a rhetorical exercise which may have been composed at any time after he ceased to be Bernard's pupil at Chartres; and Clerval[2] very reasonably assigned it to a date not long after Gilbert returned to his home at Poitiers, perhaps in 1116, perhaps a little earlier. The letter in fact helps us to fill in a gap in Gilbert's career. Now Gilbert is known to have studied under Anselm of Laon and Bernard of Chartres. In 1124 he is found as a canon of Chartres[3] and in 1126 as chancellor. It now becomes clear that in the interval he went back to his first home, Poitiers, as master of the schools, and presumably stayed there until he was recalled to Chartres. The third letter which concerns us (XXIII) was written by a monk G. to Master G., recommending his kinsman Geoffrey for admission to his instruction, *in scola vestra docendum*, at Chartres. It is tempting to find in Master G. William of Conches, who was a leading disciple of Bernard: the letter preceding it (XXII) speaks of *tabulae* which had been asked back *a domno Guillelmo*, who may be the same person as *magister G.*

The letter-book thus brings before us several masters living at Chartres about 1118, whom there are reasons for connecting with that place later on, Bernard and his brother and William of Conches; also Gilbert of La Porrée, who had studied at Chartres, but was no longer there.

III. BERNARD OF CHARTRES

The school attached to the cathedral church of Our Lady at Chartres had two officers. Its head was the chancellor, who also conducted the business of the chapter; and under him was the master of the schools, who actually gave the instruction.[4] The inferior office was held by Bernard in 1115,[5] and probably a good

---

[1] See below, p. 333.   [2] p. 164.

[3] *Cartulaire de l'Abbaye de Saint-Père de Chartres*, p. 469, ed. B. Guérard, 1840.

[4] The two officers appear together in a document of about 1121: see R. Merlet and A. Clerval, *Un Manuscrit Chartrain du XIe siècle*, p. 196, Chartres, 1893.

[5] Hauréau, *Mém. de l'Acad. des Inscr.* XXXI. ii. 90; Clerval, *Les Écoles de Chartres au Moyen-Âge*, p. 160.

deal earlier; for Gilbert of La Porrée studied under him before he attended Anselm of Laon,[1] and Anselm died in 1117. The chancellorship was occupied by one Vulgrin from about 1099 to about 1119. There is no reason to doubt that he was succeeded by Bernard, who is named as chancellor in 1124[2] and perhaps a little earlier; but he ceased to be chancellor before November 1126, when Gilbert of La Porrée held the office,[3] and there has been much discussion as to what happened to him afterwards.

John of Salisbury gives so large a description of Bernard's method of teaching that Schaarschmidt and Hauréau[4] were persuaded that he wrote from personal knowledge. I myself shared this opinion in 1884.[5] It was supposed that after his retirement before the latter part of 1126 Bernard still continued to take a friendly interest in the school. It should, however, be observed that, so far from saying that he had learned directly from Bernard, he concluded his account with the words 'Ad huius magistri formam praeceptores mei in grammatica Gulielmus de Conchis et Ricardus cognomento Episcopus . . . suos discipulos aliquandiu informaverunt'.[6] This was the good old method; but now things are changed, and every one wants to get to the end of his studies before he has laid a proper foundation. Thus William and Richard are John's own masters,who carried on the tradition of the *senex Carnotensis*.[7]

We must also note that if John was brought into relations with Bernard it was not before 1138, and evidence has been adduced to show that he was dead before 1130. This is taken from the oldest necrology of the church of Chartres, preserved in the library at St. Étienne, MS. 104. The book was written before April 1028, and received subsequent additions, the last series being inserted between 1090 and 1130. The name of Stephen, abbot of St. John at Chartres and patriarch of Jerusalem, who died 12 June 1130, is absent. There is no obit of any one who died after 1130, with the exception of a few royal names which were subsequently inserted in uncials. The text of this volume was printed with scrupulous distinction of the

---

[1] Otto of Freising, *Gesta Friderici*, i. 50 [52].
[2] *Cartulaire de l'Abbaye de Saint-Père*, p. 469.
[3] *Ibid.*, p. 267.   [4] *Op. cit.*, p. 91.
[5] *Illustrations of the History of Medieval Thought*, pp. 120, 206.
[6] *Metalog.* i. 24, ed. Webb, p. 57.
[7] *Policrat.* vii. 13, vol. ii, p. 145, ed. C. C. J. Webb, 1909.

handwritings by M. R. Merlet and the late Abbé A. Clerval in 1893.[1] Clerval observes[2] that the entry commemorating *Bernardus subdiaconus et cancellarius Sancte Marie* under 2 June states that he bequeathed his books to the church, whereas the necrology which was begun when this one was finished and continued in use down to the fourteenth century specifies the number of the volumes he left as twenty-four. The inference drawn is that Bernard's obit was one of the latest inserted in the old book.

Clerval's argument about the date is indeed not absolutely conclusive. For first, though it may be true that all the obits of persons who can be identified relate to persons who died before 1130, there are many others of people about whom nothing is known. Secondly, it was not the practice to enter up an obituary at a precise date, immediately after the death of the person who died latest. In the third place, the entries in uncials relate to persons who died as late as 1137; and one cannot say for certain that some of the obits of unknown people, and also that of Bernard, belong to these later years. It would be unwise to speak too positively; all I am inclined to assert is that it is improbable that Bernard lived beyond 1130 and therefore that John cannot have been personally acquainted with him.

The chronological point is of importance, because it bears closely on the question whether Bernard of Chartres was the same person as Bernard Silvestris. Before Clerval published his book on the schools of Chartres in 1895,[3] Hauréau in 1884 had brought forward other reasons[4] which make the identification, formerly accepted by almost every one,[5] impossible. This is the more to be regretted since all that John of Salisbury tells us about the opinions of his Bernard corresponds closely with those expressed in the *Cosmographia* of the other Bernard; even the verses quoted by John from the one might easily be believed to be taken from the other. Still, it is the fact that Bernard Silvestris belongs to a younger generation than Bernard of Chartres, and that he was connected not with Chartres but with Tours.

[1] *Un Manuscrit Chartrain du XIᵉ siècle*, pp. 100 ff.

[2] *Ibid.*, pp. 140, 165; *Les Écoles de Chartres*, p. 161.

[3] Clerval first maintained that the two Bernards were different persons in 1882 in a publication which I have not seen.

[4] *Mém. de l'Acad. des Inscr.* XXXI. ii. 99 f.

[5] See *Hist. litt. de la France*, xii (1763), 261.

Matthew of Vendôme informs us that he was a disciple of Magister Silvestris at Tours:

> Me docuit dictare decus Turonense magistri
> Silvestris, studii gemma, scolaris honor.[1]

Many years later he was once more at that place, and dedicated his *Tobias* to Bartholomew who was archbishop from 1174 to 1206.[2] Hauréau sought to extract from this dedication an outline of the chronology of Matthew's life. Suggesting that the poem was finished in 1175 and finding that Matthew says that he had lived ten years at Paris,[3] he inferred that he went to Paris at latest in 1165; but the argument is precarious, since though the dedication raises a presumption that the *Tobias* was completed near the beginning of Bartholomew's episcopate, this does not carry us very far. Matthew, says Hauréau, went to Paris from Orleans, and was there no doubt about 1145. This he infers from the fact that in his *Ars versificatoria*, which he wrote at Orleans, he cites the *Cosmographia* of Bernard Silvestris, and the *Cosmographia* speaks of Eugenius III apparently as recently elected. Now Eugenius became Pope in 1145, and it is natural to suppose that Bernard wrote of him some time during his sojourn in France between 1147 and 1148. Indeed a gloss in one of the manuscripts of the *Cosmographia* definitely states that the book was presented to the Pope at that time.[4] But all that follows from Matthew's citation is that he wrote some time after its publication; it does not tell us whether it was soon or long after. Hauréau then attempts to fix the date of Matthew's residence at Orleans by quoting his statement that he was there *tempore Primatis*. He says:

Le chroniqueur Richard de Poitiers nous atteste que cet illustre farceur Hugues, déjà surnommé le Primat ou Primat, comme ayant eu le premier rang parmi les professeurs d'Orléans, et pour son inconduite dépossédé de sa charge, résidait en 1142 dans la ville de Paris, où sans doute il s'était réfugié après son éclatante disgrâce.[5]

[1] See the verses printed by W. Wattenbach from a Tegernsee MS. of about 1200, now at Munich, in the *Sitzungsberichte der philos.-philol. und hist. Classe der k. B. Akademie der Wissenschaften zu München*, 1872, ii. 581, ll. 69, 70.
[2] Migne, ccv. 933.
[3] Wattenbach, p. 582, l. 85.
[4] 'In cuius presentia liber iste fuit recitatus in Gallia et captat eius benivolentiam': Bodl. Libr., MS. Laud. Misc. 515, fo. 188 b.
[5] *Bibl. de l'École des Chartes*, liv (1893), 794.

Now Richard of Poitiers, in a late redaction of his chronicle,[1] inserts a notice of Hugh after mentioning the death of Fulk of Jerusalem and the succession of Baldwin. Fulk, however, died in November 1143, or more probably 1144,[2] and Baldwin succeeded him at the following Christmas. Richard then writes:

Hiis etenim diebus viguit apud Parisius quidam scolasticus Hugo nomine a conscolasticis Primas cognominatus, persona quidem vilis, vultu deformis. Hic a primaeva aetate litteris secularibus informatus, propter faceciam suam et litterarum noticiam fama sui nominis per diversas provincias divulgata resplenduit. Inter alios vero scolasticis in metris ita facundus atque promtus extitit, ut sequentibus versibus omnibus audientibus cachinum moventibus declaratur, quos de paupere mantello sibi a quodam presule dato declamatorie composuit.

De Hugone lo Primas Aurelianensi

Here follow the verses about the cloak, which are known from other sources.

It is not easy at first sight to understand how so sound a scholar as Hauréau should have built up his story upon this basis. Richard of Poitiers or his interpolator says that Hugh was a popular versifier at Paris at a date which may be placed about 1144 or 1145. He then quotes a poem in which he is described as of Orleans. There is not a word about his dismissal from Orleans, though the scurrility of his preserved compositions would undoubtedly have justified his expulsion from any decent society. The evidence, so far, tells us only that, when resident at Paris, Hugh was known as the Primate of Orleans. The explanation of Hauréau's view is to be found in another work of this learned and entertaining writer. In his *Notices et Extraits de quelques Manuscrits de la Bibliothèque Nationale*, vi (1893), 129–31, he published an improved text of the poem beginning 'Dives eram et dilectus', which is well known from its inclusion among the works of Walter Map.[3] This describes the hard case of Primas, who was driven out, from what cause is not said, from some house apparently of canons. There is no hint that it was at Orleans. But the poem was written when the author was an old man:

> Modo curvat me senectus
> et aetate sum confectus.

We have therefore to inquire what is known of Hugh's age.

<hr>

[1] MS. Reg. 1911, in the Vatican, whence printed in the *Monum. Germ. Hist.* xxvi. 81 n.   [2] See T. A. Archer, *Eng. Hist. Rev.*, iv (1889), 99 f.
[3] *Poems attributed to Walter Mapes*, pp. 64 ff., 1841.

Dr. Wilhelm Meyer of Spires unearthed in 1907 a series of unsavoury compositions by him in the Bodleian MS., Rawlinson G. 109, which he expounded with true Teutonic learning and curiosity.[1] From these we learn that Primas was living at Rheims some time before 1136, and that in 1144 or 1145 he was at Beauvais. At the latter date he was more than fifty years of age; so that his birth may be placed a little before 1095. In another poem he tells how he was kicked downstairs by a Levite on whom he made a claim for some payment. He fled back to Paris, where he was a famous poet. This was written in his old age, Dr. Meyer says after 1140,[2] probably much later. Hugh's residence at Orleans must then be fitted in between his stay at Rheims before 1136 and that at Beauvais in 1144 or 1145. The notice by Richard of Poitiers may indicate his removal to Paris shortly before the latter date. But a man of fifty does not describe himself as worn out with age, and the two poems which inform us of the ill treatment he received on two different occasions must belong to a later time, when the elderly libertine had returned in the one case to Paris, in the other to some place unknown. Beyond this we need not explore his biography.

From these facts it is plain that we cannot follow Hauréau in asserting that, since Matthew of Vendôme says that he lived at Orleans *tempore Primatis*,[3] this must have been before 1142; or that as he had previously been a pupil of Bernard Silvestris at Tours (Hauréau assumes for at least five years), Bernard must have been an established teacher there not later than 1136, so that Bernard cannot be the same person as Bernard of Chartres, because in 1136 the latter was settled at Paris and instructing John of Salisbury. Here again the facts are hopelessly confused. No one ever said that John was Bernard's pupil in 1136, whether at Paris or elsewhere, and John never says that he was Bernard's pupil at all.

I have gone into this matter in detail, because Hauréau more than once repeated his statements as definitely proved. But the evidence tells us no more than that Matthew studied under Bernard Silvestris at Tours, and was afterwards at Orleans at an uncertain date before about 1145 and remained there until perhaps some time after 1147 or 1148. Matthew's biography is

---

[1] *Nachrichten der Gesellschaft der Wissenschaften in Göttingen, philos. Kl.,* 1907, pp. 95 ff.   [2] *Ibid.,* pp. 152 ff.
[3] *Not. et Extr. des Manuscrits de la Bibl. nat.* XXIX. ii (1880), 260.

a blank until he appears at Paris not earlier than 1165 and possibly a good deal later. We learn from it not one single positive date to help us to fix the time when Bernard was engaged in teaching at Tours. The title which Matthew elsewhere gives to Bernard's book, *Cosmographia Turonensis*, furnishes explicit evidence that he was settled there, but we do not know whether that book should be placed in 1145 or about 1147, or 1148. The residuum is sufficient to prove that Bernard Silvestris was connected with Tours at some undefined date, probably many years before 1145, and that he was still active then or a few years later; but it tells us no more.

Bernard Silvestris then lived at Tours, very likely between 1130 and 1140. There is nothing to suggest that he was ever connected with Chartres. It is only a conjecture that brings him to Paris a little after 1140. To this point we shall recur later. At present it is enough to say that the evidence of place and time make it impossible to identify Bernard Silvestris with Bernard of Chartres. To clinch the matter, we may add that the former dedicated the *Cosmographia* to 'the most famous doctor Terricus' in the second person plural, a style which it is incredible that Bernard of Chartres should have used in addressing his brother. This is rightly insisted on by Sir John Sandys in his *History of Classical Scholarship*.[1]

A valiant attempt was made many years ago by M. Charles V. Langlois to reconcile the data concerning Bernard of Chartres and Bernard Silvestris by arguing that when Bernard made his reputation at Tours he was naturally known at that place as *Turonensis*, and that going later to Chartres he was called *Carnotensis*.[2] He took *Silvestris* to indicate the master's Breton origin. The attribute was used elsewhere of Celtic folk: Merlin was called *Merlinus Silvester*, Giraldus Cambrensis was *Giraldus Silvestris*. The 'wild' Welshman had his counterpart in the 'savage' Breton. In the French verse of Henry of Andeli Bernard Silvestris became *Bernardins li Sauvages*.[3] Now it is quite true that the use of surnames in the twelfth century was very various. John of Salisbury almost always calls Abailard the philosopher of Palais (*Palatinus*); and Gilbert bishop of Poitiers was known as of La Porrée (*Porretanus*). These were

[1] i. 534, 2nd ed., 1906. [2] *Bibl. de l'École des Chartes*, liv (1893), 242–7.
[3] *The Battle of the Seven Arts*, l. 328, p. 55, ed. L. J. Paetow, Berkeley, California, 1914.

their birthplaces. But the English or Welsh Robert is always of Melun, and another Englishman, Adam, is of the Petit Pont, because he kept a school there. Simon of Poissy John mentions also as Simon of Paris. John of Salisbury himself was bishop of Chartres only for the last few years of his life, and yet he was known as 'holy Carnotense' as late as the fifteenth century. A surname, therefore, is indecisive. But greatly as I should desire to accept the conclusion which M. Langlois brilliantly maintained, I am afraid that it cannot stand against the evidence of the Chartres necrology and the mention of Eugenius III in the *Cosmographia* of Bernard Silvestris.

IV. GILBERT OF LA PORRÉE

When John of Salisbury studied under Gilbert of La Porrée in 1140 or 1141, he says 'Reperi magistrum Gilbertum', from which we must infer that he had known him before. Since Schaarschmidt wrote, it has been commonly agreed that this acquaintance was made at Chartres, and this opinion is confirmed by the fact that John elsewhere quotes some words which Gilbert used, being 'tunc quidem cancellarius Carnotensis'.[1] We have therefore to inquire whether John could have been known to Gilbert when he held that office. Now Gilbert, we have seen, is mentioned as chancellor in November 1126; he afterwards appears with that designation in February 1133/4[2] and 1136.[3] The charter in which this last notice occurs is dated in the twenty-first year of Bishop Geoffrey, who was consecrated shortly before 5 April 1116, presumably on Easter Day, 2 April.[4] But his years were reckoned from an earlier date than that. There is a charter dated on Wednesday 24 January 1138/9, *luna xx*, in the second year of Louis VII and the twenty-fourth of Bishop Geoffrey.[5] All the chronological elements are in accord, except the weekday, which should be Tuesday. It follows then that the bishop's years were counted from a day not later than 24 January 1116. The reckoning was no doubt from Geoffrey's election, not long before 24 January 1116.[6]

---

[1] *Metalog.* i. 5, ed. Webb, p. 16.
[2] *Cartul. de Notre-Dame de Chartres*, i. 142.
[3] *Cartul. de Saint-Père*, p. 506.
[4] See above, p. 226. Compare the documents cited in *Gallia Christ.* viii (1744), 1135 ff.   [5] *Cartul. de Notre-Dame de Chartres*, i. 148.
[6] It chanced that the bishop died on 24 January (*ibid.* iii. 28), and this day has been accidentally given by Gams, *Series Episcoporum*, as that of his accession.

Hence the record mentioning Gilbert as chancellor in 1136 in the bishop's twenty-first year indicates a date earlier than 24 January 1136/7. But in the course of the year 1137, that is before 25 March 1138, another chancellor, Guy, seems to make his appearance.[1] This, however, cannot be asserted with confidence; for the charter of 24 January 1139 bears the attestation not of *Guido cancellarius* but of *Guido cancellarii*, and this form is found in a document more than fifteen years earlier.[2] According to Clerval, Guy was the nephew of a former chancellor, Vulgrin, and was known as *cancellarii* or even as *cancellarius*. If this be so and Gilbert continued to be chancellor for a year or more later, John would have had ample time to become acquainted with him at Chartres, but even if he ceased before 25 March 1138 it would still have been possible for him to have met him there, for John's two years at Mount St. Geneviève need not be pressed beyond the autumn of 1137. In either case we need not hesitate to accept his quotation of what Gilbert said when he was chancellor as meaning that he heard it himself when he was living at Chartres.

On his return to Paris about 1140 John found Gilbert again, but he was too soon taken away. It has almost everywhere been asserted that Gilbert was made master of the schools at Poitiers in 1141 and was then elected bishop in the following year. This statement has grown up from a series of inaccuracies. Otto of Freising, mentioning Gilbert as bishop of Poitiers, says that, 'ex eadem civitate oriundus, ab adolescentia usque ad ultimam senectutem in diversis Galliae locis phylosophiae studium colens, re et nomine magistri officium administrarat noviterque ante hos dies ad culmen pontificale in prefata civitate sublimatus fuerat'.[3] Mabillon abridged the words as follows: 'Is, Pictavis oriundus, ait Frisingensis, ex discipulo magister, ex magistro tandem eiusdem civitatis episcopus evasit.'[4] In *Gallia Christiana*[5] Gilbert is said to have been canon of Poitiers cathedral when he was made bishop, and to have at that time been engaged in teaching theology there. The *Histoire littéraire de la France*[6] was more precise: it said that Gilbert left Paris in the first months of 1141, having been nominated *à la scholastique* of the church at

[1] *Cartul. de Saint-Père*, p. 384.   [2] *Un Manuscrit Chartrain*, p. 196.
[3] *Gesta Frid.* i. 46 (48).
[4] *Praef. in S. Bernardi Opera*, i, § lviii, Paris, 1690.
[5] ii. 1175.   [6] xii. 467.

Poitiers. Hauréau makes a further improvement; he says that in 1141 Gilbert was sent by his diocesan, the bishop of Chartres, to Poitiers, to govern the abbey of St. Hilary.[1] There is, however, no evidence, outside the letter which we have shown to belong to a much earlier date,[2] that Gilbert had anything to do with Poitiers after about 1124 until he became bishop, probably in 1142.

The exact date of his appointment to the bishopric is uncertain. His predecessor Grimoard was consecrated on 26 January 1141,[3] and according to the Life of St. Gerald de Salis,[4] 'non vixit in cathedra illa per annum'. As, however, he died on 27 July, this would seem to be an error, for an unpublished charter has been cited, which names him as bishop and is dated in 1142.[5]

V. WILLIAM OF CONCHES

From what has been said it appears that John of Salisbury became acquainted with Gilbert in the winter of 1137–8 at Chartres. It was at this time that he became the pupil of William of Conches and of Richard l'Évêque; and it is a probable inference from what John says[6] that they also taught at Chartres. We have seen that there was a Master G., probably the same with *dominus Guillelmus*, dwelling in that city about twenty years earlier;[7] and though it is noticeable that neither William nor Richard appears among the witnesses to documents at Chartres as holding any office in its church, there are grounds for associating them more naturally with that place than with Paris. John of Salisbury indeed speaks expressly of their carrying on the tradition of sound grammatical teaching laid down by Bernard of Chartres.[8] Moreover, William was a Norman, born at Conches near Évreux,[9] some forty miles from

---

[1] *Mém. de l'Acad. des Inscr.* XXXI. ii. 102.　　　[2] See above, p. 228.

[3] 'Chron. Malleac.' in *Recueil des Hist. de la France,* xii. 408.

[4] § 15, in *Acta Sanct., Oct.* x (1861), 257 F.

[5] *Gall. Christ.* ii. 1175, n. *b.*

[6] See above, p. 224.　　　[7] See above, p. 228.

[8] *Metalog.* i. 24, p. 60. This corrects the assertion in the *Hist. litt. de la France,* xii. 455, that there is no proof that William studied under Bernard. Hauréau also denies any connexion between William and the church of Chartres (*Mém. de l'Acad. des Inscr.* XXXI. ii. 101).

[9] The statement in the *Hist. litt. de la France,* xii. 455, which is repeated by Clerval, *Les Écoles de Chartres,* p. 181, that William was born in 1080 is an improbable conjecture. The date should probably be placed at least ten years later.

Chartres and seventy from Paris. He dedicated his *Dragmaticon* to Geoffrey Plantagenet as duke of Normandy, therefore not earlier than 1144; and he lets us see that he was then acting as tutor to his sons, Henry and Geoffrey. Now Henry was living at Bristol as the pupil of a certain Master Matthew[1] from 1142 to the end of 1146, when he went back to Normandy and stayed there until the spring of 1149.[2] William of Conches, therefore, must have been his tutor some time in the years 1147–9. In the same book he says that even then he did not fully understand matters which he had taught 'per viginti annos et eo amplius'. This takes us back to the time when Bernard was chancellor of Chartres, before November 1126. But William is here speaking of an advanced subject, 'de substantiis physicis'; and his statement is compatible with his having been a teacher of more elementary things many years earlier. In 1138 John of Salisbury still looked upon him as in the first place the Grammarian of Conches.

It would seem likely that William remained in that city, after Bernard retired or died, and that it was there that John attended his instruction from about 1138 to 1140. He is not mentioned among the Paris masters in the *Metamorphosis Goliae*, to which we shall immediately turn. Now Chartres was subject to the count of Blois, whose brother became king of England, and it may be conjectured that when Geoffrey Plantagenet acquired the duchy of Normandy William quitted Chartres and returned to his native country, where his reputation as a scholar gave him employment in the duke's household. Of Richard l'Évêque's origin nothing is recorded, but as he was in time made archdeacon of Coutances and bishop of Avranches he may be presumed to have been like William a Norman. He, too, does not appear in the *Metamorphosis Goliae*. Thus the negative as well as the positive evidence, defective as it is, points to Chartres rather than Paris as the place where John of Salisbury studied from 1138 to 1140.

There is nothing in John of Salisbury's narrative which is

[1] Gervase of Canterbury, i. 125.
[2] See Round, *Geoffrey de Mandeville*, pp. 405–8, 1892; Haskins, *Norman Institutions*, pp. 128 ff., 1918. [Since this article was written evidence has been adduced to prove that Henry's stay at Bristol was shorter than has been supposed and that he was back in Normandy early in 1144. See A. L. Poole, 'Henry Plantagenet's Early Visits to England', in *Eng. Hist. Rev.* xlvii (1932), pp. 449 ff.]

irreconcilable with this view. The only difficulty is that he mentions his acquaintance with Adam of the Petit Pont before he informs us of his return (as we understand it) to Paris. But this passage is really of the nature of an appendix to his account of his studies at Chartres, and in it he speaks of the masters and friends with whom he came into relations both earlier and later. Among the earlier are Theodoric and the obscure Hardwin; among the later, Adam of the Petit Pont and William of Soissons. After this interlude John reverts to the strict order of events and speaks of the masters whom he attended at Paris.

VI. JOHN'S LATER STUDIES AT PARIS

As John of Salisbury in the *Metalogicon* was writing a treatise concerned with logic, it is natural that he should pass rapidly over the seven years of his student life in which he was chiefly engaged in theology. He says that he first attended Gilbert of La Porrée in logic and theology, and then from 1142 Robert Pullen and Simon of Poissy in succession. But Robert, who was archdeacon of Rochester, did not remain long at Paris; he departed to Rome, where after a time he was made chancellor. The date of his removal has been variously stated, but it can be fixed pretty closely. It appears from a letter of St. Bernard[1] that he was living at Paris at a time when Cistercian monks had already been sent to Ireland. This was in 1141.[2] It has been generally said that Robert received his call to Rome from Innocent II, who died in September 1143, and that he was created cardinal by Celestine II, who held the papal see only until 8 March following. The Annals of Oseney, however, state positively that it was the next Pope, Lucius II, who called him to Rome and made him chancellor;[3] and this is confirmed by a letter from Bishop Ascelin of Rochester to Eugenius III, in which it is expressly said that Robert was still engaged in teaching in France after Lucius became Pope.[4] Lucius died on 15 February 1145, and Robert acted as chancellor under his successor, Eugenius III, until September 1146, after which

---

[1] Epist. ccv: see Mabillon's note *ad loc.*

[2] The sending of the monks was arranged when St. Malachy was at Clairvaux in 1140. Dr. Lawlor dates the saint's visits to that place about January and June in that year; see the *Proceedings of the Royal Irish Academy*, xxxv. c. 247 (1919).   [3] *Ann. Monast.* iv. 20, ed. Luard.

[4] J. Thorpe, *Registrum Roffense*, pp. 39 ff., 1769. Mr. Round called attention to this evidence in the *Athenaeum* journal, 3601, 31 October 1896.

nothing is heard of him. On Robert's departure then in 1144 John passed under the instruction of Simon of Poissy, of whom little is known, and continued his theological studies. Schaarschmidt thought he could not have spent all the remainder of his twelve years under Simon, for we cannot suppose that he studied 'five or six years from 1142 or 1143 to 1148' under one master.[1] The establishment of the fact that Robert did not leave Paris until 1144 removes part of the objection, and it is evident that 'nearly twelve years' reckoned from a year beginning at Christmas 1135 do not necessarily extend into 1147. But it seems on the whole most probable that John's last years of study were not spent wholly at Paris but in part at Provins with his friend Peter of La Celle, and perhaps also at Rheims. It is not, however, my purpose here to carry the narrative of John's biography further.

VII. THE METAMORPHOSIS GOLIAE EPISCOPI

John of Salisbury's account of his studies in France has often been brought into relation with a poem entitled the *Metamorphosis Goliae Episcopi*. This is found in a single manuscript transcribed about 1240 by a monk, as is supposed, of Reading Abbey.[2] It was printed in 1841 by Thomas Wright among the *Latin Poems commonly attributed to Walter Mapes*,[3] but it is certainly a production of at least a generation earlier than Walter Map's time. In this the poet recounts a dream in which the sleeper beholds the divinities of the classical pantheon. Then appear the philosophers, poets, and others, who still pursue their old arts,

> Totum dicunt lepide, nihil rusticantes.

Their company is immediately followed by a band of divines and philosophers of the writer's own day:

Theodoric.	Ibi doctor cernitur ille Carnotensis,
	cuius lingua vehemens truncat velud ensis;
Gilbert of	et hic praesul praesulum stat Pictaviensis,
La Porrée.	prius et nubentium miles et castrensis.[4]

---

[1] p. 25.

[2] Harl. MS. 978, fo. 121*b* (now numbered 100*b*) ff. I have inserted one or two corrections from the manuscript. See the Palaeographical Society *Facsimiles*, i, plate 125. In H. L. D. Ward's *Catalogue of Romances*, i (1883), 407 ff., the manuscript is dated a little later. [3] pp. 21–30.

[4] 'Il était né chevalier, dit le rimeur, et seigneur châtelain,' is Hauréau's exposition (*Mém. de l'Acad. des Inscr.* XXVIII. ii (1876), 227).

Adam of the Petit Pont	Inter hos et alios in parte remota Parvi pontis incola, non loquor ignota, disputabat digitis directis in jota, et quaecumque dixerat erant per se nota.
Peter Lombard Ivo, Peter Helias Bernard	Celebrem theologum vidimus Lumbardum, [1]cum Yvone, Helyam[2] Petrum, et Bernardum quorum opobalsamum spirat os et nardum et professi plurimi sunt Abaielardum.
Reynold	Reginaldus monachus clamose contendit et obliquis singulos verbis comprehendit; hos et hos redarguit, nec in se descendit, qui nostrum Porphyrium laqueo suspendit.
Robert of Melun Manerius	Robertus theologus corde vivens mundo adest, et Manerius quem nullis secundo; alto loquens spiritu et ore profundo, quo quidem subtilior nullus est in mundo.
Bartholomew Robert Pullen	Hinc et Bartholomaeus faciem acutus, retor, dialecticus, sermone astutus; et Robertus Amiclas simile secutus, cum hiis quos praetereo, populus minutus.
Heloissa and Abailard	Nupta quaerit ubi sit suus Palatinus, cuius totus extitit spiritus divinus; quaerit cur se subtrahat quasi peregrinus, quem ad sua ubera foverat et sinus. Clamant a philosopho plures[3] educati, cucullatus populi primas cucullati, et, ut cepe, tunicis tribus tunicati, imponi silencium fecit tanto vati. Grex est hic nequicie, grex perdicionis, impius et pessimus heres Pharaonis, speciem exterius dans religionis, sed subest scintillula superstitionis.[4]

The names included in this most interesting assembly were identified at random by the editor, Thomas Wright; but they have almost all been assigned to the proper persons by Hauréau.[5] They include all the masters mentioned by John of Salisbury, except Alberic and Hardwin who belong to his earliest period, the two Chartres masters William of Conches and Richard l'Évêque, and Simon of Poissy who comes at the end of John's list. It is particularly interesting that the poem mentions Abailard, for the fact that he was once more on Mount St.

---

[1] col. 2.   [2] The manuscript has a full point after *Helyam*.
[3] Wright prints *proles*.   [4] Wright, pp. 28 ff.   [5] *Op. cit.*, pp. 226–38.

Geneviève in 1139 was entirely unknown until John of Salisbury's *Historia Pontificalis* was discovered (though its authorship was not yet divined) and published in 1868.[1] The dream, therefore, describes a state of things at some time between 1139 and 1144. Denifle would place its composition a little later, because he thinks that Peter Lombard did not write his *Sentences* until between 1145 and 1150;[2] but the production of such a work implies that its author had been active as a teacher for some years earlier, and I do not think we need hesitate to assign the *Metamorphosis* to a date not much later than 1142.

It will be well to add some notes about the masters of whom we have as yet said little.

1. The *doctor Carnotensis* is certainly Theodoric, the brother of Bernard of Chartres. Otto of Freising, in his account of Abailard, mentions Brittany as fertile in clerks of acute intelligence and of minds skilled in the arts, but stupid in matters of business—men, we may take it, with speculative rather than practical gifts—such as were the two brothers, Bernard and Theodoric, men of great learning.[3] The order in which he names them implies that Bernard was the elder; and, indeed, we have seen that Bernard is not heard of after 1124, while Theodoric was active twenty-five years later. Theodoric was most likely the *Terricus quidam scholarum magister* who is credited by Abailard with a remarkable interruption in the course of his trial before the synod of Soissons in 1121. Abailard was charged with asserting that God the Father alone was Almighty; whereupon the legate observed with astonishment that one could not believe that even a child could fall into such an error: 'cum communis, inquit, fides et teneat et profiteatur tres Omnipotentes esse.' Then was heard the voice of Terric who 'subridendo subintulit illud Athanasii, *Et tamen non tres Omnipotentes, sed unus Omnipotens*'.[4]

It is natural to believe that Theodoric was master of the schools at Chartres, but Hauréau's conjecture[5] that he was chancellor of that church in 1122 is unsupported. He is next found at Paris, where he made a great name as a teacher. His praises are sung in the metrical life of Archbishop Adalbert II

---

[1] *Hist. pontif.* xxxi, ed. Poole, 1927, p. 64.
[2] *Arch. für Liter. und Kirchengesch.* i (1885), 605–11.
[3] *Gesta Friderici*, i. 47 (49).   [4] Abaelardi, Epist. i.
[5] *Mémoires de l'Acad. des Inscr.* xxxi. ii. 80.

of Mainz. Adalbert's studies were pursued at Hildesheim, Rheims (under Alberic), Paris (under Theodoric), and Montpellier. He was a noble who lived, according to his biographer, in opulence and ostentation. It is not likely that his course of study was as prolonged as that of a more serious student. It may have begun in 1132; it certainly ended before June 1137. During this time, perhaps in 1134, he attended Theodoric's teaching at Paris in rhetoric and logic.[1] Not long after this John of Salisbury also studied rhetoric under Master Theodoric.[2] He does not say where this was or when; but it was no doubt at Paris and before 1141. In 1148 Theodoric attended the council of Rheims as a witness on behalf of Gilbert of La Porrée, the old chancellor of Chartres. In the following year, when Archbishop Auberon of Treves went to attend the diet held by Conrad III at Frankfort on 15 August 1149, he took with him Master Jarland of Besançon and Master Theodoric of Chartres: 'magistrum quoque Iarlandum Bisintinum et magistrum Teodericum Carnotensem . . . secum in sua ducens navali camerata, in illorum disputatione . . . valde delectatus est.'[3] Theodoric is here definitely *Carnotensis*, and we need not doubt that he is the chancellor and archdeacon of the church of Chartres who was commemorated under 5 November.[4]

2. Reserving the two Roberts, Manerius, and Bernard, we may pass over the remaining names briefly. Of the *praesul Pictaviensis* Gilbert of La Porrée, we have already spoken. Concerning the *parvi pontis incola*, the Englishman Adam of the Petit Pont, it need only be added that he was made bishop of St. Asaph in 1175. *Lumbardus* is Peter, the famous author of the Sentences, who became bishop of Paris in 1158–9. Ivo, like Bernard and Theodoric, was a Breton. He is the Master Ivo of Chartres who in 1148 attended the council of Rheims as a witness for his teacher Gilbert of La Porrée.[5] From charters assigned to the years 1155–9 we learn that he was then dean of Chartres;[6] his obituary describes him as 'vir multa scientia et

---

[1] *Monumenta Moguntina*, ed. Jaffé, pp. 589 f., 1866.
[2] *Metalog*. ii. 10. ed. Webb. p. 80.
[3] See the lively description in Baldric's *Gesta Alberonis Trevirorum archiepiscopi*, xxvi, in *Monum. Germ. Hist.* viii. 257. For the date see W. Bernhardi, *Konrad III* (1883), p. 920, n. 32; cf. pp. 765 f.
[4] He bequeathed fifty-five volumes in the cathedral library; see the *Cartulaire de Notre-Dame de Chartres*, iii. 206.
[5] Mansi, *Concil.* xxi. 729.
[6] *Cartul. de Notre-Dame*, i. 161 f., 164.

honestate praeditus'.[1] Peter Helias we have found as one of John of Salisbury's teachers; John mentions him again in a letter written in 1166.[2] Abailard needs no note. Reynold, the jealous monk, is unidentified: Prantl[3] ingeniously suggested that he was the opponent of sound methods of study whom John of Salisbury disguises under the name of *Cornificius*. Bartholomew was a Breton who was made bishop of Exeter in 1162; he is said to have been distinguished as a learned writer. Walter Map, writing between 1181 and 1192–3, calls him 'vir senex et facundus'.[4]

3. It is not easy to say with confidence whether *Robertus theologus* and *Robertus Amiclas* are Robert of Melun and Robert Pullen, or vice versa; for both were famous theologians. But I incline to think that Robert Pullen is designated by *Amiclas* for the following reasons. *Pullus* (Pullen) may indeed be the adjective, 'brown'; but almost certainly it is the substantive, meaning the young of any animal, as a colt or a cockerel, because very early his surname appears as *Pullanus*, the French *poulain*. This form is given by John of Hexham, who wrote soon after 1153.[5] It is not unlikely that *pullanus* had a depreciative implication and was used to mean a poor sort of person. If so, this is just what *Amiclas* had come to mean: it was the opposite of *Croesus*.[6] But the fact has not been generally understood. Hauréau, expert palaeographer as he was, actually proposed to emend *Amictus*, a translation of *Pallain*, of which *Pullanus* might be a corruption. This need not be considered. *Amiclas* has a definite meaning which can be illustrated from more than one writer of the twelfth century. Matthew of Vendôme, who

---

[1] *Gallia Christ.* viii. 1200*b*.   [2] *Epist.* clxviii.

[3] *Gesch. der Logik im Abendlande*, ii. 230, 1861.

[4] *De Nugis Curialium*, i. 12, p. 18, ed. M. R. James, 1914.

[5] Contin. of Symeon of Durham, *Opp.* ii. 319, ed. T. Arnold, 1885.

[6] It was not, I think, until a later time that the word *pullanus* came to mean a person of mixed breed. Ducange, indeed, quotes 'Pullani dicuntur qui de patre Syriano et matre Francigena generantur' from the *Vie de Louys le Gros*, ch. 24 (*Observations* on Joinville's *Vie du Roy Saint Louys*, p. 84, 1668); and this is reprinted in the later editions of his *Glossarium*, vii. 356, ed. 1850. But the passage in fact, as reproduced with a corrected reference in the *Glossarium*, s.v., is taken from the life not of Louis the Fat but of Louis VII; and this work, usually cited as the *Gesta Ludovici VII* (Duchesne, *Hist. Francorum, Script.* iv. 408, 1641), is merely a Latin version of part of the *Grandes Chroniques* of the thirteenth century. There seems to be no evidence to carry back this meaning of the word to the twelfth. If it could be proved, it might suit Robert; for John of Hexham says that *Rodbertus Pullanus* was *Britannia oriundus*. But this interpretation of the name is highly improbable.

wrote not very many years later, wrote in the dedication of his
Tobias:

> Vos, vos, vestra precor plantatio, vester Amiclas,
> portus intimidum confoveatis iter.[1]

Caspar Barth, commenting on this passage, thought at first that
amiclas was a mistake for *amiclus*, that is *amiculus*; but then
he remembered *pauper Amyclas* in Lucan's *Pharsalia*, v. 539,
where Amyclas is the poor boatman whose craft Caesar made
use of in a famous adventure; and he noted that the manuscript
of Matthew had the gloss *Amiclas, servus*.[2] Then he found some
verses by Nicholas of Rievaux on Henry, the Young King:

> Floruit Henricus quasi Carolus; alter Ulisses
> Sensu: Croesus erat opibus; post, pauper Amiclas.[3]

It is evident, therefore, that in the twelfth century, when Lucan
was a regular school-book, the term *pauper Amyclas* had come
to be used as a synonym for a poor man.[4]   Robertus Amiclas

---

[1] The lines are printed corruptly by Jo. Heringius, 1641 (Migne, ccv. 934 B), as

> Vos, vos vestra precor plantatio, vester Amiclas
> poscit me timidum confoveatis iter.

But *poscit* is found neither in the undated Rouen text of Robinet Macé nor in
any of the four Bodleian manuscripts which I have consulted. They read,
Portuus ut timidum confoveatis iter (MS. Auct. F. 5. 6, fo. 116*b*, late
thirteenth century).
Partus in tumidum [Portus intimidum, MS. Laud. Misc. 242, fo. 109 A,
early thirteenth century] confoveatis inops (MS. Laud. Misc. 515, fo. 39*b*, early
thirteenth century, and Auct. F. 1. 17, fourteenth century). *Inops* is evidently
a gloss on *Amiclas* which has been taken into the following line and has
extruded *iter*.

[2] *Advers.* xxxi. 16, p. 1461 (1648). In Bodl. MS. Auct. F. 5. 6, the gloss is
serviens.

[3] Quoted by J. Picard, note to William of Newburgh, ii. 27, in Hearne's
edition, vol. iii. 643. Nicholas of Rievaulx, who is known only from the extracts
printed by Picard, has escaped all the literary historians. But Picard was a
canon of St. Victor, and one would therefore first look for his manuscript in
the collection of that abbey. Now the MS. 1030 of St. Victor, which has now
become MS. Lat. 15127 in the Bibliothèque Nationale, contains the Tobias of
Matthew of Vendôme and other pieces, among which are verses on some abbots
of Rievaulx (fo. 43*b*) and letters of N. monk of Rievaulx (fo. 85*b*). See Delisle's
Inventaire des Manuscrits de l'Abbaye de Saint-Victor (1869). From this manuscript Hauréau quotes two lines, which he says are by 'un anonyme, poète
très fécond, que nous supposons avoir été moine de Riévaux' (*Les Mélanges
poétiques d'Hildebert de Lavardin*, p. 207, n. 1, 1882): these lines are to be found
among the extracts from Nicholas printed by Picard. Dr. H. H. E. Craster
kindly directed my attention to this last reference.

[4] This was observed by Forcellini, *Lex*, s.v. Cf. also Gervase, ed. Stubbs,
1879, i. 87. 'Sedet historicus "inter magniloquos et grandia verba serentes",
at cronicus sub pauperis Amiclae pausat tugurio ne sit pugna pro paupere
tecto.'

in our poem simply means poor Robert. According to John of Hexham, Robert Pullen refused a bishopric offered him by Henry I; 'victum et vestitum habens, his contentus fuit': he had no care for riches.

4. Manerius has hitherto been unexplained. It has been conjectured that the name has been misread for Maurice of Sully, who was made bishop of Paris in 1160.[1] But Mainerius or Meinerius is twice mentioned by Giraldus Cambrensis, who says that 'magistrum Meinerium, principalem Petri Abalardi discipulum et rhetorem incomparabiliter eximium, in auditorio suo Parisius coram multitudine scholarium recitantem audivimus'.[2] Mainerius held a prebend at Paris as late as 1174.[3]

5. We have now seen that, with the exception of the problematic Reynold, every one of the thirteen men named in the *Metamorphosis Goliae* is a known person; most of them are very well known. Now this list includes a certain Bernard. Who was he? The opinion which was formerly entertained that he was Bernard of Chartres must be abandoned. But we have to discover a Bernard who can be identified. He must, I think, probably be Bernard Silvestris. It is true that this Bernard is only associated with Tours; but Paris was the focus to which scholars of his time gravitated, and if it be the fact, as was reputed,[4] that Bernard's *Cosmographia* was presented to Eugenius III, this most naturally points to his residence at Paris, for the Pope's travels did not extend to Tours and he was at Paris in the spring of 1147. It may also be noticed that, though John of Salisbury never mentions the name of Bernard Silvestris, he made considerable use of his commentary on the *Aeneid*, with which he may have become acquainted when both scholars were living at Paris; but this is only a surmise. Nor can we exclude the possibility that Bernard is the Bernard who appears as chancellor of Chartres about 1156,[5] and whose obit is recorded under 4 August in the necrology of that church.[6] He is named

---

[1] *Hist. litt. de la France*, xv (1820), 155.

[2] *Speculum Ecclesiae*, i. prooem., *Opp.* iv. 7, ed. J. S. Brewer, 1873; cf. *Gemma ecclesiastica*, ii. 37; *ibid.* ii. 349, 1862. The former passage was quoted by Anthony Wood, *Hist. and Antiq. of the Univ. of Oxford*, i. 157 (ed. J. Gutch, Oxford, 1792), under the year 1160; but he gave the master's name as *Menervius*.

[3] Denifle and Chatelain, *Chartul. Univers. Paris*, i (1889), no. 6, pp. 6 f. For this reference I am indebted to the kindness of M. Langlois.

[4] See above, p. 231.

[5] Clerval, *Écoles de Chartres*, p. 173.

[6] *Cartulaire de Notre-Dame de Chartres*, iii. 148.

from his birthplace Bernard of Moëlan, and was made bishop of Quimper in 1159. He died in 1167.[1] This last identification involves no chronological difficulty, but at present it must remain a conjecture.

In reviewing the list of scholars one is struck by the wide range from which Paris drew. Among the thirteen named in the *Metamorphosis* five were of Breton origin, three English, and one Lombard. John of Salisbury does not mention all of them, but he adds, besides the Frenchman Alberic, two Normans and one German, of whom nothing is recorded elsewhere. The comparative youth of some of the company is also noticeable; of the two who became bishops in England Adam of the Petit Pont lived until 1181 and Bartholomew until 1184.

[1] See Hauréau, in *Mém. de l'Acad. des Inscr.* XXXI. ii. 86 f.

JOHN OF SALISBURY AT THE PAPAL COURT[1]

OF John of Salisbury's life down to the completion of his twelve years' course of study in France we possess a full account in an often-quoted chapter of his *Metalogicon* (ii. 10). The last sixteen years of his life, from the time when he was compelled to leave England, shortly before the breach between Henry II and Archbishop Thomas, are also abundantly illustrated by a large correspondence and by the many writers who were concerned in the long controversy which followed. But for the intervening period, from 1147 to the end of 1163, our information is partial and defective.

Carl Schaarschmidt, whose invaluable life of John was published in 1862, thought that at the conclusion of his studies in France he passed at once into the employment of Archbishop Theobald of Canterbury,[2] and continued in his service until he quitted England in 1163. This was a warrantable inference from a passage in the prologue to the *Policraticus*, written in 1159, in which John says that he has been engaged in official life for more than twelve years (*iam enim annis fere duodecim nugatum esse taedet*), and these years of service, in default of other evidence, it was natural to place at Canterbury. But, some time after Schaarschmidt wrote, a precious fragment known as the *Historia Pontificalis*, which had hitherto entirely escaped notice, was published in the *Monumenta Germaniae*.[3] Its editor, Wilhelm Arndt, had no inkling of its authorship, but five years later Giesebrecht proved conclusively that it was written by John of Salisbury.[4] But it was not until 1881 that Reinhold Pauli pointed out the value of the work for John's biography.[5] It includes in fact a series of notices relative to the personal history of the Pope which are not written at all in the manner of the medieval chronicler. They are so vivid and incisive that Pauli decided at once that they are the observations of an eyewitness. This hypothesis is confirmed by several references in John's other works which it had previously been difficult to put

[1] Reprinted after revision from the *English Historical Review*, vol. xxxviii (1923). [2] *Iohannes Saresberiensis*, p. 27. [3] *Scriptores*, xx. 517–45, 1868.

[4] 'Ueber Arnold von Brescia', in the *Sitzungsberichte* of the Munich Academy for 1873, pp. 122–54.

[5] 'Über die kirchenpolitische Wirksamkeit des Iohannes Saresberiensis', in the *Zeitschr. für Kirchenrecht*, xvi (1881), 265–87.

into their places. Once it has been suggested, it carries conviction; and it has been my good fortune to discover positive evidence of its truth. We may take it, then, as settled that at least from the time of the council of Rheims, in the spring of 1148, John of Salisbury was attached to the Pope's household, and we cannot doubt that he was there in the capacity of a clerk.[1] But as he attended the council we may presume that he was already in the Pope's employment, and I propose to show that there is a high probability that he came with Eugenius III from Italy. For this it is necessary to go back a little.

The chapter in the *Metalogicon* is a digression in a treatise concerned with logic. Hence, while John describes the five years of his dialectical studies with copious illustrations, he says very little about the theological course which began in 1140–1 and must have occupied nearly six years. He attended in succession Gilbert of La Porrée, Robert Pullen, and Simon of Poissy. There has been some trouble about fixing the dates of these courses, because it used to be supposed that Gilbert left Paris in 1141 and that Robert was made cardinal by Innocent II, who died in September 1143. It has now, however, been established that there is nothing to show that Gilbert quitted Paris until he was made bishop of Poitiers in 1142,[2] and Robert was undoubtedly still at Paris after Lucius II was made Pope in 1144; it was Lucius who called him to Rome as cardinal some time before 4 January 1145.[3] So the tedious lectures of Simon need not be extended beyond 1146 or 1147. Schaarschmidt, supposing erroneously that Robert was appointed cardinal in 1141, had difficulty in making out the 'near twelve years', beginning with 1136, during which John studied in France. He therefore proposed an hypothesis that he spent at least two years with his friend Peter, abbot of Montier-la-Celle, in the suburbs of Troyes.[4] This supposition is devoid of foundation.

---

[1] He mentions that he was present both in ch. ix (*quod vidi, loquor et scribo*) and xi (*qui presens aderam*). Cf. *Policrat.* ii. 22, vol. i. 124, ed. Webb.

[2] Above, p. 237.

[3] Above, pp. 239 f. Robert subscribes a bull dated 4 January 1145 as cardinal priest of St. Martin's (Kehr, 'Papsturkunden in Parma und Piacenza', in the *Nachrichten* of the Göttingen Gesellschaft der Wissenschaften for 1900, p. 40); on the 31st he dates as chancellor (Bresslau, *Urkundenlehre*, i. 241, ed. 2, 1912). The two appointments are carefully distinguished by the Oseney annalist (*Ann. Monast.*, ed. Luard, iv. 20 'a papa Lucio secundo vocatus et in cancellarium sanctae Romanae ecclesiae promotus est').

[4] p. 27.

Though Peter certainly held the abbacy as early as 1146,[1] there is nothing to show that John enjoyed his hospitality, at any rate for more than a short time, until a number of years later.

Now Cardinal Robert Pullen was active as chancellor of the Roman church until 2 September 1146, after which date his name is not found in bulls. Possibly he died soon afterwards; the next cardinal of his title appears to have been nominated in 1150. I am inclined to conjecture that it was through his instrumentality that John was invited to enter the Pope's service. John was his pupil and doubtless his most brilliant pupil, and he needed to earn his living. English scholars were beginning to tend towards Rome to gain experience and other advantages. In 1146 we find Hilary, as clerk in the papal chancery, acquiring that reputation for learning and discretion which led him to the see of Chichester.[2] When Nicholas, the future Pope Adrian IV, was made cardinal bishop of Albano, probably in 1149, the pace was increased. Like him, it appears to me probable that John was brought to Rome by Cardinal Robert.

Besides the fact to which I have adverted, that John was in the Pope's service at the time of the council of Rheims, there is a passage in the *Historia Pontificalis* which impresses one, not less surely than those on which Pauli has commented, as written by a man who was in Italy at or near the time of the events he describes. This is the chapter relating to Arnold of Brescia. Giesebrecht has shown how large a number of particulars concerning this stimulating and meteoric personage have been added to our knowledge by the *Historia Pontificalis*. Here I limit myself to the evidence as to the time and circumstances of Arnold's return to Italy. Arnold, we know, was driven out of France not long after the condemnation of his master, Abailard, at the council of Sens in 1140 or 1141—the date is disputed—and took refuge first at Zurich and then probably in Bavaria. The time at which he went back to Italy has been assigned by Otto of Freising to two discrepant dates. He says[3] that when Arnold heard of the death of Innocent II, in September 1143, he returned to Rome about the beginning of the pontificate of Eugenius III. But there were two Popes, Celestine II and

---

[1] C. Lalore, *Cartul. de Montier-la-Celle*, no. 260, Troyes, 1882.
[2] See a paper by Mr. Round in the *Athenaeum* journal, 3613, pp. 115 f., 23 January 1897.   [3] *Gesta Friderici*, ii. 20 [27].

Lucius II, in the interval. Then, after describing the revolution which Arnold instigated in Rome, Otto says that these convulsions went on from the death of Celestine II, in March 1144. It is plain that Otto was not well informed about the details of what happened, and we must observe that in his chronicle,[1] in which he treats at large about the movements at Rome down to the early part of 1146, he says not a word about Arnold. When, however, we turn to the *Historia Pontificalis*, ch. xxxi, we find a precise statement as to the circumstances of Arnold's return to Italy.

When Arnold after the death of Pope Innocent went back to Italy, he promised to make satisfaction and submission to the Roman Church, and was received back to communion by Pope Eugenius at Viterbo. Penance was enjoined to him, which he promised to perform by fasts, vigils, and prayers in the holy places at Rome; and he took a solemn oath of obedience to the Church. But while he lived in works of penance at Rome, he acquired favour in the city, and when the Pope set out on his journey towards France, he began to preach more freely and to gain a following, which was known as the sect of the Lombards.

This notice enables us to reconcile the apparent discrepancies in Otto's account. Arnold returned to Italy some time after September 1143, but was not reconciled with the Church until he made his submission to Eugenius at Viterbo. Now this Pope resided at Viterbo in 1145 from April to November, except for an interval between 18 August and 22 September. He was also at Viterbo from 23 May 1146 to the end of the year. Giesebrecht takes it for granted that Arnold became reconciled in the former year, but the silence of Otto of Freising in his account of what happened in the early part of 1146 disposes me to believe that it was in that year that the submission was made. John of Salisbury's description has all the appearance of having been written with fresh knowledge at first hand, and if Arnold had his interview with the Pope towards the end of 1146 and John entered his service about the same time, the matter is completely explained.

Here it may naturally be objected that this arrangement of the dates does violence to John's statement that he was engaged in divers studies, as distinguished from official business, for near twelve years, since he went to France in the year following

[1] vii. 27, 31, 34, ed. A. Hofmeister, 1912.

the death of Henry I, on 1 December 1135. Even if he left England in January 1136 his twelfth year would not begin until January 1147. But this is not the only instance of his reckonings of time being stated a little inexactly.[1] If we wish to save his accuracy, we may suppose John to have entered the service of Pope Eugenius during the course of his journey through France, perhaps during his stay at Paris between April and June 1147. In this case his account of Arnold of Brescia at Viterbo will not have been, as I have presumed, written with knowledge at first hand. On the whole, it seems to me more likely that John's *paene duodennium* is an accidental exaggeration, and that he was in fact in Italy towards the end of 1146. In any event I do not doubt that John was the Pope's clerk before the council met at Rheims in March 1148.[2]

From this point, if we follow Pauli's guidance, the course taken by John is plain. He attended the Pope on his journey back to Italy, travelled by way of the Great St. Bernard, and reached Cremona by 7 July. On the 15th the Pope was at Brescia, where he stayed until October. John, whose plan was not to relate events strictly in the order of time, speaks first of the reception of the envoys of the archbishop of Canterbury at Brescia (ch. xviii), and later on of the council held at Cremona (ch. xxi). But the council was certainly in July. John says that the Pope was then on his way to Rome (*iturus Romam*); he may have made another short visit to Cremona before going on to Pisa. From this place he travelled southwards and was at Viterbo on 30 December. His documents are dated from that place down to 25 March 1149. After this there is a gap, and his next letters are from Tusculum on 8 April. Now John states precisely (ch. xxi) that Eugenius entered Rome and was received with honour by the nobles, who were soothed by the rich presents which he brought with him from France. But he found his position there intolerable on account of the claims to jurisdiction made by the newly established senate. Therefore he went on to Tusculum (ch. xxvii). This statement in the *Historia Pontificalis* has been generally discredited; it has been supposed that John is describing what took place a year

---

[1] Compare my *Illustrations of the History of Medieval Thought and Learning*, p. 181, n. 7, 2nd ed., 1920.

[2] Cf. my preface to the *Hist. Pontif.*, pp. lxxii–lxxiii; also C. C. J. Webb, *John of Salisbury*, 1932, pp. 10–12.

later.[1] But I see no good reason to doubt the facts as John related them.

In 1149 Palm Sunday fell on 27 March. The distance from Rome to Viterbo was reckoned as two days' journey,[2] which the Pope may well have performed in the early days of Holy Week. Then he could keep Easter, 3 April, at Rome. He was able to obtain admission with the help of large gifts to the nobles in authority, but he could not remain there on account of the worthlessness of the Romans, the claims to jurisdiction, and other demands made on him (ch. xxvii). He therefore proceeded to Tusculum. This must have been in Easter week, for his chancery was again at work on the Friday, 8 April. John's notices fit in exactly with the dates of the church year, and account for the interval in the Pope's documents in the fortnight after 25 March.

When he was established in safety at Tusculum, Pope Eugenius made preparations for an attack on the unruly Romans. He equipped a force which he placed under the command of Cardinal Guy Puella, and received military support from the king of Sicily. But the operations, though very costly, had little success (ch. xxvii). It was not until late in November that the Pope was able to take up his residence in the Lateran palace, where he stayed until the summer of 1150. During this time I believe, though the evidence is perplexed, Henry of Blois, bishop of Winchester, visited Rome. John tells us that Archbishop Theobald had released the English prelates from the suspension which they had incurred by failure to attend the council of Rheims, but had excepted Bishop Henry, who went to Rome to make satisfaction in person (ch. xl) ; he was required to do this within six months—that is, before September 1148 (ch. iv). That he paid his visit to Rome so early is more than doubtful. Pauli suggested that it was during the Pope's residence in the city from November 1149 to June 1150, and this date is supported by John's statement that he was received into favour through Guy de Summa, bishop of Ostia ; for Guy died before 1152.

[1] See Giesebrecht, *Gesch. der Deutschen Kaiserzeit*, iv (1875), 485. Cardinal Boso's words *ad urbem suam et commissum sibi populum ductore Domino incolumis remeavit* (*Lib. Pontif.* ii. 387) cannot fairly be pressed to refer to this one journey. Muratori cautiously remarks, *O non entrò, o pure non si fermò in Roma* (*Ann. d'Italia*, vi. 489).

[2] See the itinerary in Matthew Paris, Cotton MS. Nero D. i, printed by Palgrave, *English Commonwealth*, ii. 21 note, ed. 1921.

Some light is thrown on the bishop's movements by the chronicle of John of Hexham. There had been a long dispute about the succession to the see of York. William fitz Herbert, known as St. William, had been consecrated by Bishop Henry of Winchester on 26 September 1143 ;[1] but the appointment was not approved by the party which opposed King Stephen, and Pope Eugenius, on 7 December 1147, consecrated Henry Murdac, abbot of Fountains, in his place. When the new archbishop attempted to occupy his diocese, he met with strong resistance, especially from Hugh of Puiset, the treasurer of York, nephew of the bishop of Winchester, whom he placed under excommunication. The Hexham chronicler adds, 'About this time' (*his temporibus*) Henry, bishop of Winchester, went to Rome,[2] and persuaded the Pope to write to Archbishop Henry urging him to deal more gently with Hugh. Hugh, he tells us, was in charge of the bishop's lands and had military command of his castles. This notice, therefore, refers to a time subsequent to that in which Hugh was actively engaged in opposing Archbishop Henry in Yorkshire. John of Hexham relates that Hugh was released from his excommunication at Yarm at the end of his entries for the year 1150,[3] but Hugh the Chantor of York, with more probability, mentions the fact under 1151.[4] If we take Hugh's reconciliation to have been effected early in 1151, it follows that Bishop Henry was at the papal court in the latter part of 1150 at latest.

The date of this visit has been disputed because the Annals of Winchester expressly say that the bishop quitted England in 1151. In 1151 the Pope was not for a single day in Rome; he was at Ferentino and Segni. But this does not really cause difficulty. An Englishman visiting the Pope would naturally be said to be going to Rome, though the Pope might at the time be somewhere else. In the *Historia Pontificalis* Bishop Henry's visit to Rome is related after events of 1151.

The truth is that Henry went to Italy both in 1148 and 1151. In his earlier visit, he obtained his absolution; in the later one

---

[1] Stubbs, *Reg. sacr. Anglic.*, p. 46, 2nd ed., 1897; John of Hexham, under 1144 (*Symeon of Durham*, ii. 315, ed. Arnold, 1885): from 1141 onwards his dates are a year too late.

[2] He enters this under 1149, p. 322, but the year must be corrected as above.

[3] According to his reckoning 1151, p. 325.

[4] *Hist. of the Church of York*, ii. 225, ed. Raine, 1886.

he sought in vain to be made archbishop of the west of England[1] with legatine authority. From the earlier visit he returned homewards in 1149, and we find him at Cluny (*rediens a Roma Cluniacum*), where he lent the monastery a large sum of money. On the later occasion he betook himself to buying ancient statues at Rome, which he sent to Winchester. Whereupon a certain grammarian mocked at him in the words of Horace:

Insanit veteres statuas Damasippus emendo[2]

After a time Bishop Henry returned to England, sailing to Spain and visiting the shrine of St. James on his way. His residence in Italy and his journey home detained him from duties at home for two or three years. He excused his absence from the consecration at Canterbury of Bishop Richard Belmeis II of London on 28 September 1152 on various grounds, including the danger of travelling and bodily ailment; but he may indeed have been then still out of England.[3] We must not forget that from the day when Bishop Henry was superseded as legate by Archbishop Theobald under Eugenius III the relations between the two were strained, and Henry avoided intercourse in England by long visits to the Continent. Having gone abroad in 1155,[4] if we follow the chroniclers, he had not returned home in 1161.[5] In 1157 Theobald wrote urgently begging him to come back.[6] It is only an incidental notice that informs us of his presence in England in the spring of 1159.[7] There is, therefore, nothing surprising if he protracted his foreign travels from 1149–50 to 1152.

The description of the bishop buying ancient statues is unmistakably written by one who was in Rome at the time, and probably, as Pauli suggests, *grammaticus quidam* is a disguise under which John of Salisbury cloaks his own comments on the bishop's doings. In the summer of 1150 the court left Rome and went by way of Anagni to Ceprano on the southern frontier of the papal dominions. Here Eugenius had an interview with King Roger of Sicily, and an agreement was made about certain

---

[1] The Winchester Annalist, *a.* 1143, places the bishop's attempt to get his see raised to an archbishopric in the time of Innocent II; but he candidly adds, *Quo anno profectus fuerit non affirmo.*

[2] *Hist. Pontif.* cap. 40, ed. Poole, pp. 81–2.

[3] Rad. de Diceto, 'Ymagines Historiarum', in *Hist. Works*, i. 296, ed. Stubbs.

[4] Rob. of Torigny, *s.a.* (*Chron. of Stephen*, &c., ed. Howlett, iv. 186).

[5] Rad. de Diceto, *s.a.*, p. 304.   [6] John of Salisbury, Epist. xcviii.

[7] Richard of Anesty's journal, in Palgrave, *Engl. Commonwealth*, ii. 14.

questions of ecclesiastical policy (ch. xxxii). The situation of
the town made it convenient for dealing with other matters in
the Norman kingdom; and when John gives a long description
of a suit for divorce brought before the Pope by a certain
Apulian Count Hugh, the hearing of which he attended (*hiis
presens interfui*), we may well suppose that this took place on
the same occasion. The chancellor of Sicily was then Robert
of Salesby, an Englishman, whose official career extended from
1140, or even earlier,[1] until October 1151.[2] It may have been
at Ceprano that Robert entertained the visitors with wine from
Palermo and Greece, whose injurious effects John remembered
long afterwards (*quo me Siculus cancellarius ad pernitiem salu-
tisque dispendium potare consueverat*);[3] at least we know of no
other time during the period of Robert's chancellorship at which
John was brought into relation with the Sicilian court.

In November 1150 the Pope went to Ferentino, where he
resided until the following summer. That John was with him
is known from an express statement in the *Policraticus* (vi. 24).
He also mentions in one of his letters that he was present at
Rome when envoys arrived announcing the election of Frederick
Barbarossa in the spring of 1152.[4] The Pope was then at
Segni, and John must have been commissioned to attend their
reception, presumably in the suite of one or more cardinals. If
further confirmation be needed of John's familiarity with the
papal court at this time, we may observe that, when writing
many years later about the high personal integrity of the
cardinals, the examples he cites are those of cardinals who were
in office in these years, Guarinus, bishop of Palestrina (1144–54),
Guy, cardinal of St. Pudentiana (1145–57), and Bernard, cardinal
of SS. Cosmas and Damianus (1152–3);[5] just as in the *Historia
Pontificalis* (ch. xxix) he gives a pointed characterization of the
two cardinals, Octavian and Jordan, who were sent to Germany
in 1151, such as could hardly have been written by one who had
not known them well. It is not without interest to notice that
Cardinal Nicholas of Albano, the future Pope Adrian IV and
one of John's closest friends, was in attendance at the court

---

[1] Caspar, *Roger II*, p. 431, 1904.

[2] K. A. Kehr, *Die Urkunden der Normannisch-Sicilischen Könige*, p. 49, 1902.

[3] Epist. lxxxv.   [4] Epist. lix., pp. 64 f.

[5] *Policrat.* v. 15; vi. 24. The account of Cardinal Martin, who died before
1144, in the former passage does not conflict with this statement, for John is
careful to say that he is quoting from St. Bernard, *de Consideratione*, iv.5.

both at Ferentino and Segni; and that the Pope's documents at that time were 'dated' by another Englishman, Boso, afterwards cardinal and the biographer of Pope Adrian.[1]

Pauli was unable to find evidence that John continued in the Pope's service after the death of Eugenius III in July 1153. He was, however, at Rome until some time after the election of Anastasius IV. This we learn from a letter of Peter, abbot of La Celle, the testimony of which has not hitherto been quoted.[2] The abbot, writing to John, mentions that an appeal had been made at Rome in defence of the rights of his house over the cemetery of St. Serenus at Chantemerle, which the abbot and canons regular of that monastery had attempted to impugn, in violation of a bull of Anastasius IV, 'which bull', he adds, 'you yourself have seen and had a hand in drawing up' (*contra privilegium Anastasii papae, quod tu ipse vidisti et partim fabricasti*).[3] No more welcome confirmation of a long series of plausible surmises could be desired. We now know that John was a clerk in the papal chancery employed in the composition of the Pope's rescripts. It is not unlikely that he then acquired practice in the beautiful style of writing used in the chancery, for there still exists a document of Archbishop Theobald, produced most likely while John was in his service, which displays many of the characteristics of the Roman handwriting and which may possibly be in John's own hand.[4]

But though it is now established that John was still in Rome after the election of Anastasius IV, he probably contemplated a return to England some time earlier. St. Bernard wrote a letter[5] recommending him to Archbishop Theobald, in which he says that he had introduced him in person, no doubt at the council of Rheims, and now testifies to his merits by letter. As Bernard died on 20 August 1153, if the letter was obtained to assist John's prospects in England, it must be one of the latest

---

[1] Pflugk-Harttung, *Acta Romanorum Pontificum inedita*, iii (1886), 101–11.

[2] Epist. iv. 9, ed. Sirmond, 1613. The letter is numbered 72 in Janvier's edition, reprinted in Migne, ccii.

[3] The bull, dated 13 December 1153, is still preserved in the departmental archives at Troyes, from which it is printed by Pflugk-Harttung, i (1881), 214. It has also been published from two chartularies by Lalore, *Cartulaire de Montier-la-Celle*, no. 195.

[4] This document, which is reproduced in *Facsimiles of Charters in the British Museum*, i, plate 28 (1903), is later than the death of Queen Matilda (3 May 1152) and before the death of Stephen (25 October 1154); for it omits the mention of the queen which appeared in the charter which the archbishop confirmed.   [5] Epist. ccclxi.

of the saint's compositions. But it is not impossible that John secured the letter a good deal earlier and kept it for use when the occasion arose. When the saint asks Theobald to make provision for him that he may get a respectable, or even a distinguished living, and adds, 'Do this speedily, for he has not whither to turn' (*Providete ei unde honeste, immo honorabiliter, vivere possit; sed et hoc velociter, quia non habet quo se vertat*), we may suspect an element of rhetorical exaggeration from which letters testimonial are seldom free. For John was still, as we have seen, in the Pope's employment as late as the beginning of the winter of 1153; so that, as the journey from Rome to England was reckoned to occupy seven weeks, we cannot be far wrong in believing that he did not enter the archbishop's service at Canterbury until the beginning of 1154.

THE EARLY CORRESPONDENCE OF
JOHN OF SALISBURY[1]

I

THE chief materials for the biography of John of Salisbury from the beginning of 1154, when he found employment at the court of Canterbury, to the winter of 1163–4, when he quitted England to share the exile of Archbishop Thomas, are contained in his letters. It should be premised that what we know as the Letters of John of Salisbury, in number 327, is a book made up of two entirely distinct collections. They are not known to be combined in any manuscript. The first collection (epp. 1–133) is found in two manuscripts, one preserved at Paris, the other, imperfect, at Cambridge. Of the second there are many copies, in none of which are the letters numbered in continuation of the first; and very many of them are incorporated with letters of other writers in the immense Becket correspondence. It was Jean Masson who in his edition of 1611[2] ranged the two collections in a single series and gave them a single numeration. This has given the impression of a unity which is in fact spurious. The later series is one of great historical importance, while the earlier collection contains merely the official correspondence of the archbishop and John's private letters, interesting chiefly for the writer's personal biography. They have, therefore, had less attention paid them by historians. In the present paper, when I speak of John's letters, I refer exclusively to the first hundred and thirty-three letters.

This collection looks in some ways like a formulary compiled for use in the court of Canterbury.[3] Nearly three-quarters of the letters consist of directions, decisions, and mandates in cases brought before the archbishop, which might be preserved either as models of composition or else as precedents to govern decisions in similar cases. The remainder is made up of John's own letters, some of them written in connexion with the archbishop's business, but most forming his private correspondence

---

[1] Reprinted from the *Proceedings of the British Academy*, vol. xi (1924).

[2] *Epistolae Gerberti, Ioannis Saresberiensis, Stephani Tornacensis nunc primum in lucem editae.*

[3] This is markedly brought out in the Cambridge manuscript, where proper names, especially of places, are often represented by the letter *N*.

with friends. There is seldom any difficulty in distinguishing between the two main classes. When the writer speaks in the plural number or mentions a bishop as *venerabilis frater*, the letter is beyond question written for and in the name of the archbishop, who only occasionally in a familiar letter to a prelate descends to the singular number. John, on the other hand, adheres strictly to the singular. Writing, indeed, to the treasurer of York he may speak of the province of Canterbury as *provincia nostra*,[1] but that is a natural form of expression which cannot mislead us. The collection, however, is so completely devoid of arrangement that it is impossible that it should have been transcribed from a register. For a register in the twelfth century was a volume in which letters were entered as they were sent out. Most commonly the drafts of the letters were copied on quires of parchment which were afterwards bound up. The chronological order was often disturbed, when business was heavy and the letters accumulated; sometimes a quire might be misplaced. But no such theory will account for the appearance of some of the latest letters near the beginning and of some of the earliest near the end. The probable explanation is that, when John went into exile at the beginning of 1164, he took with him all the drafts which he had preserved, and caused them to be transcribed without any attempt at arrangement.

In this form we have them in the Paris MS. Lat. 8625, which was written in the fourteenth century and which has served as the basis for the editions of Masson and Giles. The manuscript is to this extent defective, that the inscriptions or addresses which should have been prefixed to the letters were left blank with a view to their insertion by the rubricator, and he never performed his task. There were, however, abbreviated indications of the addresses in the margin, but many of these were partly cut off by the binder. Most of the addresses now found in the manuscript and printed from it in the editions are insertions by a modern hand, which is identified with Masson's, and most of them are derived from the truncated marginal notes. A serious confusion which has arisen from this expansion of the notes is that a number of letters addressed to Pope *A*, meaning *Adriano*, have been printed by the editors as written

---

[1] Ep. 34. In Ep. 27 the context shows that *mandatum nostrum* is a misreading for *mandatum vestrum*.

to Alexander III. It would, however, be a mistake to suppose, as Brial[1] did, that all the letters to the Pope were addressed to Adrian. The difficulty of assigning the letters to the right Pope is increased by the fact that the arrangement of the collection is in complete disorder. This may be shown from a single example. On 26 December 1898 the late Dr. Jessopp wrote to me about Ep. 33 reflecting on the character and morals of William Turbe, bishop of Norwich, 'which', he said, 'I am strongly persuaded does not apply to him. If it really does mean to describe his ways of going on I am equally persuaded it was nothing better than a malignant calumny.' I replied that the explanation appeared to be that Ep. 33 was an enclosure in Ep. 93 and not addressed to the bishop at all. In Ep. 93 the bishop is required to summon R. archdeacon of Norwich to answer before the archbishop in respect of certain charges made against him by Richard of Drayton and A. his brother. Ep. 33 is the form of mandate to the archdeacon ordering him to appear before the archbishop to make answer to the charges brought against him by Alexander of Drayton and R. his brother. The two documents were naturally sent together to the bishop, so that he might forward the mandate; but they came to be separated when the whole correspondence was shuffled, and were placed sixty numbers apart. Dr. Jessopp was quite right in disbelieving the supposed charges against the bishop's character: they rest simply on a blunder of the editor. In the manuscript Ep. 33 bears no address.

It was said in 1813 that the Paris MS. Lat. 8625 is the only copy of John of Salisbury's letters 1–133 existing in France,[2] and no other has been brought to light since. In England also but one single manuscript is known to be preserved. This is in the University Library at Cambridge, MS. Ii. ii. 31. It was written in the fourteenth century, all by the same hand, and contains the Metalogicus, the Policraticus, and the Letters, ending defectively near the end of Ep. 18.[3] The remainder of the volume is occupied by Alexander Neckam's Commentary on Canticles. The letters in this manuscript are entirely rearranged. They are copied out in the order of dignity; letters to Popes, to cardinals,

[1] 'Notice de deux Manuscrits latins de la Bibliothèque Impériale contenant les Lettres de Jean de Salisbury', in *Notices et Extraits des Manuscrits*, ix. ii (1813), 96.   [2] *Ibid.*, p. 94.
[3] Numbered 75 in this MS. The last words are *non admiserunt nec* (p. 20, line 18, in Giles's edition).

to King Henry, and lastly to bishops, abbots, and other clergy. That in thus distributing them the transcriber made a few mistakes does not affect the principle of his system. It would appear that he worked from an exemplar in two volumes and arranged the contents of each separately. The first volume contained sixty-three letters,[1] and the second, if complete, seventy; but owing to the mutilation of the manuscript no more than eleven of these are preserved.[2] It is evident, however, from what remains that all the letters which John wrote in his own person, all his private correspondence, were reserved for the second volume; so that the collection must have passed through a process of classification at an earlier stage than that represented by the Cambridge redactor.

II

The correspondence with which we deal is that of John of Salisbury when he was clerk to Archbishop Theobald. A statement, often repeated, that he was chancellor[3] to the primate can be easily refuted. A covenant of 28 March 1155 is witnessed by William, subprior, and Felix, Arnold, Symon, and Hervey, monks; Philip chancellor; and John of Salisbury, Randolph of St. Albans, and Peter the writer, the archbishop's clerks.[4] Shortly before he died in 1161, Theobald named as administrators of his will Walter bishop of Rochester, Philip his chancellor, Mr. Ralph of Lisieux, and John of Salisbury (Ep. 57). Philip is the archbishop's chancellor throughout; John was simply his clerk, but a highly-trusted clerk who soon came to

---

[1] Epist. 64 in the Paris manuscript is here divided into three, of which two bear separate numbers (24*, 25, and 31). Hence the total in the Cambridge manuscript is increased by one. The numerals prefixed to the letters, it may be added, are in a modern hand.

[2] In the *Catalogue of the Manuscripts in the Library of the University of Cambridge*, iii (1858), 401, it is said that all the letters in the Cambridge MS. will be found in Masson's edition with the exception of six; but these six are in fact there too: no. 25 [= Masson's no. 64, part 3], 31 [= 64, part 2], 32 [= 65], 55 [= 36], 60 [= 43], 51 [= 45]. I noted the addresses of most of the letters in order to discover whether the manuscript supplied any material of independent origin from the exemplar of the Paris manuscript. The results are unimportant and not worth recording here.

[3] Still less did he act, as the late Mr. A. F. Leach imagined, 'as Official Principal of the Prerogative Court of the Archbishop of Canterbury' (*The Schools of Medieval England*, p. 133, 1915).

[4] Madox, *Formulare Anglicanum*, cxxxviii.

take charge of most of the primate's correspondence. The great majority of the letters in this collection were written in this capacity. All were no doubt his composition, but of 133 letters 98 were written in the archbishop's name and on his official business. As my purpose in the present paper is to study the letters with a view to throwing light on John's biography, I limit myself almost entirely to the thirty-five letters which he wrote on his own account. But the attempt to arrange these letters in the order of time is beset by difficulties. In many instances they bear no address, and none of them, according to the practice of the age, are furnished with any date. We can only deduce the time when they were written from the comparison of one letter with others and from internal evidence, the mention of events recently past or expected in the near future.

Much of the correspondence has to do with news received from Rome and with journeys to and from that city. It will therefore be well to begin by constructing a time-table. Here we have to distinguish between the length of time which an urgent message from Rome might take in reaching England and that which would be allowed to an ordinary traveller for the journey. The two reckonings are widely different. As an example of the former we may cite the mandate of Pope Clement III for the excommunication of the persons who had broken into the monastery of Christ Church, Canterbury. This was issued from the Lateran on 17 March 1188, and received at Canterbury on 15 April.[1] The interval of 29 days may be taken as representing the journey of a courier riding at express speed; it is equivalent to $30\frac{1}{2}$ days from Rome to London. But the itinerary given in a manuscript of Matthew Paris assumes that at least 48 days will be spent on the road from London to Rome.[2] A traveller, however, could hardly ever accomplish the journey without interruption; either the horses broke down or one of the party fell sick. There is a good deal of evidence to show that seven weeks were as a rule spent between Canterbury and Rome. A few examples will illustrate this.

---

[1] *Epist. Cantuar.* ccxiii, ccxix, ed. Stubbs, 1865.

[2] Cotton MS. Nero D. i, fo. 182*b*, printed by Palgrave, *English Commonwealth*, ii. 21 note, ed. 1921. The itinerary enumerates $45\frac{1}{2}$ stages, but it makes no allowance for the Channel passage, and gives only two stages between Saint-Michel-de-Maurienne and Susa. At some seasons the crossing of the pass of Mont Cenis required more time.

1. Abbot Reynold of Evesham, after taking part in the funeral of Walter, abbot of Gloucester, on 8 February 1139[1], set out for Rome in order to attend the Lateran Council at Mid-Lent.[2] Mid-Lent Sunday fell on 2 April, and Abbot Reynold would desire to arrive at least a day earlier. This leaves an interval of 52 days. If the abbot started immediately after the funeral—especially if he travelled by way of Evesham—he would hardly reach Canterbury in less than three days.

2. At the beginning of March 1157 the abbot of St. Albans sent messengers to Rome, and they were back on 21 June.[3] If we reckon from Monday, 4 March, the expedition occupied 109 days. The double journey between St. Albans and Canterbury required five days and we must allow at least six for the messenger's stay in Rome. This leaves 98 days for the journey both ways, or 49 for the single journey.

3. Immediately after 9 January 1188 monks from Canterbury departed for Rome and reached the city on 27 February.[4] If they started on the 10th, their journey took exactly 49 days.

4. Late in October 1198 monks left Canterbury and arrived in Rome on 11 December.[5] Their journey must have occupied very nearly the same time.

All these indications lead us to believe that in the twelfth century, while it was possible that news should be brought from Rome in 29 days in a matter of extreme urgency, the usual time allowed for the journey was very nearly seven weeks. In estimating times, when we have no precise evidence, we shall not be far wrong if we lay down that a message from Rome might reach Canterbury in a little less than five weeks, and that a traveller, as distinguished from an express courier, was expected to spend about seven weeks on the journey.[6] It may be added that the routes by the Mont Cenis and the Great St. Bernard were hardly, if at all, different in their length.

---

[1] *Hist. Monast. S. Petri Gloucestr.* i. 17, ed. W. H. Hart, 1863.

[2] *Chron. of John of Worcester,* p. 54, ed. J. R. H. Weaver, 1908.

[3] *Gest. Abbat. Monast. S. Albani,* i. 132 f., ed. H. T. Riley, 1867.

[4] *Epist. Cantuar.* clxv, ccv; see Stubbs's introduction, p. lxiii.

[5] *Ibid.,* Epp. cccclxxxix–ccccxcii, dx, dxi; cf. intr., p. clxii.

[6] To avoid any misunderstanding it may be well to mention that I supplied Dr. H. J. Lawlor with some of the data given above, which he used skilfully in tracing the itinerary of St. Malachy. See the *Proceedings of the Royal Irish Academy,* xxxv C. 6, pp. 240–3, 1919.

III

As a first step towards fixing the chronology of John's letters, I take his correspondence with his life-long friend, Peter of Celle.[1] Peter was undoubtedly a member of a noble family in Champagne, though his parentage has not been discovered. He was a kinsman of the countess of Dreux.[2] This lady was Agnes of Braine, daughter of Guy of Dampierre, who married a daughter of Andrew of Baudement, seneschal of Champagne. She married in 1152 Robert, count of Dreux, a younger son of King Louis VI, and Robert's brother Henry was made Archbishop of Rheims in 1161. This relationship explains the reference in a letter of John's[3] written in 1165, in which he speaks of *comitem Robertum, cuius uxor abbatis mei cognata cum aliis munusculis trecentas ulnas telarum Remensium regi nuper transmisit ad camisias faciendas.* The countess had been first married to Miles, count of Bar-sur-Seine, who died in October 1151.[4] Her second husband also had been married before, first to Agnes of Garlande, and secondly (before 1145) to Harvise (probably Hawise), daughter of Walter of Salisbury and sister of Patrick first earl of Salisbury.

As a youth Peter spent some time at the Cluniac monastery of St. Martinus de Campis, near Paris.[5] It may be that he was one of the nobles whom John of Salisbury took as pupils,[6] and it is not unlikely that he entered on the monastic life at Provins. For, many years later, when John was established at Canterbury, he writes to Peter, 'I am much better off than you and I were at Provins.'[7] This cannot very well refer to a time when Peter

---

[1] I cite Peter's letters from the edition of Jacques Sirmond, Paris, 1613; but have added within brackets the numbers they bear in Janvier's edition as reprinted in Migne's *Patrologia Latina*, ccii. These numbers, it should be noted, differ from the continuous numeration given in Sirmond's margin.

[2] In his Ep. v. 1 [97] Peter makes mention of her as *dominae et cognatae nostrae.*

[3] Ep. 138. Schaarschmidt, *Johannes Saresberiensis*, p. 25, note (1862), misread the text and inferred from it that Peter was related to the counts of Champagne.

[4] For particulars of the family connexions of the countess and of her two husbands see the Chronicle of Alberic in *Monum. Germ. Hist.* xxiii. 845 f., 909; André du Chèsne, *Hist. généal. de la Maison Royale de Dreux*, pp. 18 f., Paris, 1631; Père Anselme, *Hist. de la Maison Royale de France*, i. 424 (ed. 1726); *Art de vérifier les Dates*, xi. 293, 462 (ed. 1818).

[5] 'Ego ipse apud sanctum Martinum de Campis adolescentulus verissimis experimentis quod dico gustavi et vidi ubi erat auro locus in quo conflabatur': Ep. viii. 23 [159].   [6] *Metalog.* ii. 10, ed. Webb, pp. 80–1.   [7] Epist 82.

was in possession of an important abbacy. No doubt his distinguished family connexions raised him to this position at an unusually early age. Already in 1146 he was abbot of Montier-la-Celle,[1] one of the most considerable houses in the diocese of Troyes. This monastery, which has now disappeared, was situate in a place known as the Insula Germanica, in the parish of St. Andrew les Troyes, a short half-league to the south-west of the city.[2] Dependent upon it was the priory of St. Aigulf at Provins, a dozen miles westward, of which we hear a great deal in Peter's time. The secular clerks here had been removed before the middle of the eleventh century by Count Theobald I of Champagne, and thirty monks had been brought in from Celle. The priory at Provins was the object of peculiar interest to Abbot Peter. He devoted himself to its welfare in a time when it had suffered a calamitous conflagration, and was unceasing in the care with which he watched over it. But Provins had also attractions of another sort. It was a pleasant place to resort to when the abbot wished to be free from the business of his monastery, and, moreover, it was on the high road which led from Paris to Rome, and was a centre of news and, it may be, of gossip.

Peter continued to be abbot of Celle from at least 1146 to 1162, when he was promoted to the still more important abbacy of St. Remigius at Rheims. John's correspondence with him, as we have it in the collection now before us, belongs entirely to the time when he was at Celle. Eight, or perhaps nine, of John's letters are preserved, and nine of Peter's. John's letters are numbered 75, 76, 81, 82, 85, 96, 97, 115, and perhaps 73; Peter's are iv. 4–12 in Sirmond's edition, or 67–75 in Migne's reprint. We start with a sure date. John, Ep. 97, mentions that Henry II had opened his campaign in North Wales: this was in July 1157. He expresses his grief at the news that the priory of St. Aigulf at Provins was consumed by fire. The letter is a reply to Peter's iv. 5 [68]. Peter is sending round reliques of St. Aigulf in order to collect contributions for the rebuilding of the monastery. The fire then was in the early summer of 1157. In iv. 11 [74] Peter excuses himself for not having sent John the reliques. He now

---

[1] Lalore, *Cartul. de Montier-la-Celle*, no. 220. In writing the name shortly as Celle I follow the *Histoire Littéraire de la France*, xiv (1817), 236. The form Moûtier often given is erroneous.

[2] See Courtalon-Delaistre, *Topographie hist. de Troyes*, iii. 24–34, Troyes, 1784.

sends one of his monks, Brother W. John replies, Ep. 76,
mentioning the arrival of Brother W. These two letters may be
placed late in 1157; John's was written after Christmas, probably
at the beginning of 1158. In this letter John has much to say
about Brother Thomas, who had come to Canterbury some time
before, and who he feared might get into trouble. John therefore
urged him to return, we presume to Troyes; and he reluctantly
obeyed. That John only secured his object with difficulty may
be inferred from Ep. 75, written after 1 October, apparently in
1156, in which he speaks as though Brother Thomas was on the
point of going back to Troyes. This letter stands in close relationship with Ep. 85, in which John speaks of the 'vile apostate'
Ralph as having behaved disgracefully to Brother Thomas, and
having been on this account excommunicated; these facts and
others are recounted also in Ep. 75.

Ep. 85 may be dated with probability in the last months of
1156. It begins by thanking Peter for his goodness in helping
him when he was in trouble and saving him from a 'perpetual
exile'. The phrase no doubt is an exaggeration, of a type not
uncommon in medieval letters. But it naturally leads one to
think that John was writing after his return to England in
1153–4 from an absence of eighteen years. Later on, however,
he makes the reference to Brother Thomas quoted above and
speaks of having written on the subject to Peter on an earlier
occasion.[1] Evidently, therefore, John did not write this after
an absence of many years. I take it that the 'exile' which might
have been perpetual refers to the time between the autumn of
1155 and the spring following, during which John spent 'near
three months' with Pope Adrian at Benevento.[2] But Adrian,
before going on to Benevento, spent some weeks at Ferentino
(certainly from 30 September to 17 October), and John was
with him there. It was at this time that the Pope handed to him
the emerald ring conferring the investiture of Ireland on Henry
II,[3] and the gift was no doubt made on a solemn occasion with
a full company of cardinals present. On 30 September the papal
court was attended by twelve cardinals, and about that day
we may presume the investiture to have taken place. John,

---

[1] If this letter is Ep. 75, Ep. 85 must have been written very near the end
of 1156.   [2] *Policrat.* vi. 24.

[3] *Metalog.* iv. 42, ed. Webb, p. 218. That the grant was made at Ferentino
appears from Ep. 42.

therefore, was with the Pope from the end of September at Ferentino, and then from some time after 20 November for near three months at Benevento. This brings us to the middle of February, and if John travelled straight back to England he might be home by the middle of April; but there are indications, to which we shall refer immediately, that his journey was delayed at Paris, so that it is likely that he was not again at Canterbury until the summer. If, therefore, he left England in August 1155 or a little earlier, his absence on the Continent extended to some ten months, and this might without undue licence be spoken of as an exile. From Peter's reply, Ep. iv. 10 [73], it appears that John had found himself in difficulties at Paris, when Peter came to his assistance; for Peter expresses his surprise that John should have called Paris, that place of delights, an exile, and proceeds to harp on the phrase.

John's Ep. 76 we have assigned to the beginning of 1158. After this a letter of his is missing, to which Peter's iv. 7 [70] appears to be a reply. Peter is now about to reinter the remains of St. Aigulf in a new shrine. Then there is a gap. In iv. 9 [72] Peter complains of John's silence. One may guess that this letter was written late in the year, when John was travelling abroad. My reasons for believing that John paid a visit to Rome in the winter of 1158–9 are as follow. In Ep. 115 he tells Peter that he has fallen under the king's displeasure. In Ep. 96, which can be dated, as we shall see, in the summer of 1160, he says that he fell out of favour in the preceding year. But it is certain that he was in England in the autumn of 1159, for before that time he had been deprived of some of his employment in the archbishop's court and found leisure to complete his two most considerable works. The *Policraticus* was finished while the siege of Toulouse was in progress;[1] and this lasted from July until the end of September, but the news that it was broken up would not be known in England until the middle of October. John also speaks of Adrian IV as living;[2] he died on 31 August, and the fact would hardly be reported in England until the very end of September. The book then may have been completed in August or September, and soon afterwards the author sent it to Peter (Ep. 81). The *Metalogicon* was finished a little later, when John had heard of the Pope's death[3] but believed

---

[1] *Prol.*, sub fin.; viii. 25.   [2] *Ibid.* viii. 23.
[3] iv. 42, ed. Webb, p. 217.

that the siege of Toulouse was still going on. I should date this concluding chapter in October. Not much later John wrote to Peter telling him that after his return from Rome he had fallen into disgrace, and was in such trouble that he proposed to leave England before the beginning of January (Ep. 115).

John does not say when he came back from this visit to Rome of which we have no other information, nor how long after his return the king's wrath was kindled against him. But it is evident that he was again in England at least as early as mid-summer 1159, because we have to allow time for the completion and revision of two large books by August or September and October. Now the journey from Canterbury to Rome and back occupied, as we have seen, more than three months, and we have to allow an uncertain time for the stay at Rome and for inter-ruptions on the road. It will hardly be excessive if we suppose John to have been absent from England on this occasion for five months, and therefore to have started quite at the beginning of 1159, if not a little earlier. He may have received the first hint of impending troubles from a postscript to a letter of Peter's, iv. 4 [67], in which he writes:

Quia vero minus iacula feriunt quae praevidentur, mando et moneo ut caveas tibi a labiis iniquis et a lingua dolosa. Apud nos enim quaedam de te disseminata sunt, quibus forte, nisi clypeum cautae provisionis opposueris, laedi in curia poteris. Summi nempe quidam viri cuidam de curia qui apud nos est, ut ipse audivi, insusurraverunt te de curia dixisse quaedam inhonesta et te falsum legatum domini papae in his partibus gessisse. Quae nescio utrum sint magis falsa quam maligna, vel e converso. Sapiens es; esto in his sapiens.

Some one connected with the papal court has brought news that John is charged by important persons with not conducting his business in an honourable way. We shall see later on that the story mentioned by Peter was brought by Arnulf bishop of Lisieux. Peter's letters may be dated early in 1159. In the summer we may place his letter iv. 12 [75]. It is composed in a spirit of edification, but the way in which the writer dwells on the advantages of solitude suggests that it was intended to reconcile John to his situation and to persuade him that a life free from official cares has also its merits. Towards the end of the year John wrote his Ep. 115 declaring his resolve to quit England before the end of the year. With this was probably enclosed Ep. 116, a little note to Thomas, provost of Celle.

Not much later, perhaps, he wrote to Peter again imploring to be consoled; for Peter in iv. 8 [71] answers a letter of this purport. John's letter is not certainly preserved, but it may be the unaddressed letter 73; we know from what he wrote about the same time to Thomas the chancellor that others of his letters never reached their destination, having been lost at sea or taken by robbers.[1] About the middle of 1160 he acknowledges (Ep. 96) a letter from Peter which he had received at Eastertide. He had written, he says, about going to Troyes, but was detained by many anxieties since his misfortune of the previous year. He had intended to seek an interview with the king to clear himself of any charge brought against him; but he was assured that this could not be arranged in the absence of the archbishop, without whose mediation he could not recover favour. He is expecting the king's return every day. This anticipation was a mistake: Henry was not again in England until the beginning of 1163. Nor is the mention of the archbishop's absence helpful. Theobald was at his manor of Mortlake in the late summer of 1159, but went early in the winter to Canterbury,[2] where he fell into his last illness. John proceeds to say that he has kept the messenger for some days awaiting the arrival of the queen and the chancellor. Thomas is not recorded as being in England until May 1162, and the queen is only known to have crossed the channel at New Year, 1160, some months before John's letter was written. This difficulty is solved by entries in the pipe roll of 6 Henry II, which distinguish between payments *de passagio regine* and payments *in passagio regine extremo*.[3] *Passagium* on the roll, be it noted, means a crossing to England; the outward voyage is *transfretatio*. The earlier 'passage' was that of New Year; the 'last passage', unnoticed by the chroniclers, may be placed towards midsummer.

John's correspondence with Peter appears to end with the summer of 1160, and if our arrangement of the letters, which is in part admittedly conjectural, be approved, it will be seen that we have found no letters earlier than the last months of 1156. There are, however, two letters not yet mentioned, which may possibly belong to some time in 1154 or 1155. These are John's 82 and Peter's iv. 6 [69], which seems to be an answer

[1] Ep. 113.
[2] Richard Anesty's diary, in Palgrave's *English Commonwealth*, ii. 17.
[3] *Pipe Roll*, 6 Hen. II, pp. 22 f., 47 (1884).

to it. That many other letters passed between the two friends is more than probable. The fact that only seventeen or eighteen in all are preserved is due to the accident that their drafts were kept, and were in course of time made up into the respective collections in which we have them.

IV

We have now to retrace our steps in order to attempt to rearrange John of Salisbury's other letters. Of these the earliest to which we can assign a date is Ep. 34, addressed to John, treasurer of York. This was John of Canterbury, who succeeded Hugh of Puiset in the treasurership when Hugh was appointed bishop of Durham in 1153. Hugh was consecrated at Rome on 20 December, and John can hardly have received his office much before April 1154. The letter ends with a warning against the archbishop of York attempting to crown the king. Now Roger of Pontigny was consecrated archbishop of York on 10 October, and Henry was crowned on 19 December. The letter therefore lies between these two dates. In it John of Salisbury mentions that the bishop of Norwich was in mortal conflict with his archdeacon.[1] The archdeacon was Walkelin, a nephew of a preceding bishop, and he was supported by a family interest at Norwich. His conduct, however, was so bad that Pope Adrian issued more than one mandate for proceedings to be taken against him. It seems that he went to Italy, presumably to pursue an appeal to the Holy See. But, says John in Ep. 27, the wretch added to his crimes by a contemptuous affront to it. He had a mistress who bore him a son; this he named after the Pope Adrian, and proposed to call a second child not yet born Adriana if she was a girl, or Beneventus if a boy, because it was to Benevento that he was going. Now Pope Adrian was at Benevento between November 1155 and May 1156, and the archdeacon went thither during these months. John was also at Benevento for part of the time, and the letter was written after his return, probably in the late summer of 1156. John adds that the proceedings against the archdeacon were committed to the charge of the bishop of Worcester, John of Pagham, but he

---

[1] Archdeacons at this time were frequently styled by the name of the diocese to which they belonged, and not by that of the particular archdeaconry. The list of archdeacons in the diocese of Norwich is defective and confused, but Walkelin is believed to have been Archdeacon of Suffolk.

was slack in carrying out his commission and was about to leave England. The bishop in fact died at Rome on 31 March 1157.[1]

These dates are consistent with a letter of Archbishop Theobald to Adrian IV (Ep. 118), wrongly printed as to Alexander III, in which we read that the charges against the archdeacon had been heard at a council held by the archbishop at London, but no decision was made on account of the absence of the bishop of Worcester. The council was held in the first week of June 1156. We learn this from the Lives of the Abbots of St. Albans. Abbot Robert started for Italy on 9 October 1155, and found the Pope at Benevento, presumably about Christmas. He was home again on the octave of the Ascension, 31 May 1156, and the council at London was a few days later.[2]

It was very likely the same archdeacon, though we must remember that there were four archdeacons in the diocese of Norwich, of whom John speaks as *vir malitia, dolositate, et arte mentiendi conspicuus* in Ep. 107. This letter was written before the death of Earl William of Warenne, about October 1159; it may have been a good deal earlier; in any case we need not doubt that it was addressed to Adrian IV and not, as printed, to Alexander III.

Returning to the year 1156, it was probably in the summer of this year that we may place Ep. 42 to Adrian (erroneously addressed by the editors to Alexander) in which, in recommending a suitor, he calls to mind the Pope's bounty to him at Ferentino. In the course of this summer also John wrote a letter (Ep. 128) to the bishop of Norwich, which is famous on account of its mention of the levy of scutage. The king, he says, is desirous to yield to the archbishop's counsel and to promote the advantage of the church, but nevertheless he is unable to remit the scutage and other exactions because he has not come to terms with his brother Geoffrey. John therefore wrote before peace was made in July.[3]

Three letters, 30–2, relate to the affair of Bishop Neal of Ely. On 22 February 1156 Adrian IV issued a mandate to this bishop requiring him under pain of suspension to make restitution within three months of the possessions he had taken from the church of Ely.[4] The rescript is dated at Benevento, at a time

---

[1] *Annals of Tewkesbury*, in Luard's *Ann. Monast.* i. 48 (1864).
[2] *Gest. Abbat. Monast. S. Albani*, i. 126–9.
[3] Robert of Torigny, in Howlett's *Chron. of Stephen*, iv. 189 f. (1889).
[4] *Chartul. Eliense*, in *Acta Sanctorum Iulii*, iv. 581.

when John was most likely on the spot. A year later, on 17 March 1157, the Pope, then at the Lateran, extended the term owing to King Henry's absence on the Continent; but it was not until 16 January 1159 that the sentence was relaxed, at the prayer of the king and the bishops, on condition of Neal taking oath before Archbishop Theobald to restore the property.[1] In Ep. 30, John, writing to the Pope, says that the bishop was in hopes of being assisted by the testimony of the faithful, and desired the assistance of John, who was conducting the Pope's business. John therefore asked for letters of relaxation. This evidently has to do not with the extension of March 1157, but with the relaxation of January 1159. But at this latter date John was already on his way to Rome, and his letter must have been written some time earlier. In it John speaks of remembering what the Pope had enjoined upon him when he was returning from the papal court. Now John came home from Italy in the summer of 1156, but this is too early, and his return in the summer of 1159 is evidently too late. I therefore infer that he made another visit to Italy which has not been observed. John's correspondence gives no indication of his movements between the last months of 1156 and July 1157, nor between the beginning and end of 1158. But I have found reason to believe that he went to Rome at the beginning of 1159, and it is improbable that he made the journey twice within twelve months. I therefore incline to place this unrecorded visit in the winter of 1156–7, and suggest that he was then instrumental in procuring the extension of Bishop Neal's leave which was granted in March 1157. On his return he petitioned in Ep. 30 for a full relaxation, which was not conceded until January 1159. I therefore place this letter in the summer or autumn of 1157. Ep. 32 is addressed to *Ioanni thesaurario Cantuariensi*. These words, which are added in an early hand in the Paris MS., indicate John of Canterbury, who had been made treasurer of York early in 1154 but continued to be spoken of under his old name; there was no officer styled treasurer of Canterbury. The letter reports progress in Bishop Neal's business.[2] Ep. 31, which

---

[1] *Chron. Eliense, ibid.*, p. 578; cf. Wharton, *Anglia Sacra*, i. 627.

[2] This letter contains a message from Bishop Robert of St. Andrews, who was troubled by the attempt of the abbot of Kelso to obtain exemption from his jurisdiction. We possess a bull addressed to the bishop by Adrian IV, 11 August 1156 (wrongly dated 1154, in *Scotichronicon*, i. 124, ed. J. F. S. Gordon, 1867), from which it appears that he was suffering from age and infirmity, but

bears no address, was evidently written to the same person and deals with the bishop's affair a little earlier, about the same time as Ep. 30.

We have already noted John's letter 97 as written in July 1157. I am inclined to attribute to the autumn of this year a document which Mr. Round discovered among the duke of Rutland's muniments at Belvoir Castle[1] and which presents the remarkable interest of bearing the witness of two famous chroniclers, Henry archdeacon of Huntingdon and Ralph de Diceto archdeacon of London,[2] side by side with that of John of Salisbury. On it Mr. Round observed[3] that it could not be earlier than 1155, while on the other hand it could not be much later, because of the appearance in it of Henry of Huntingdon. The later limit of date has, however, no sure testimony. It rests on the entry in Le Neve's *Fasti* of Henry's successor, Nicholas de Sigillo, as archdeacon of Huntingdon 'about 1155';[4] whence Dr. Liebermann inferred that, as Henry mentions the election of Robert Warelwast to the bishopric of Exeter in June 1155, he must have died between the summer and the end of that year.[5] But Le Neve's date is derived from a charter contained in the chartulary of St. Neot's (Cotton MS., Faustina A. iv, fo. 41), and this charter has no list of witnesses and cannot be assigned to any precise year.[6] It is therefore no argument for placing the death of Archdeacon Henry in 1155. The Belvoir document may very likely have been drawn up in 1157. This I conjecture from the fact that the bishops of London and Lincoln were present with the archbishop on that occasion. We know of two deeds made on 19 and 28 October 1157, the one presumably at Salisbury,[7] the other at St. Neot's in Huntingdonshire.[8] The latter we read of only in a narrative. I would place the Belvoir

he lived until 1159: see the *Chron. de Mailros*, and the *Annals of Holyrood* (*Chron. Anglo-Scot.*, ed. C. W. Bouterwek, Elberfeld, 1863), s.a.

[1] The *Manuscripts of the Duke of Rutland* (Hist. MSS. Comm.), iv. 159 f., 1905.

[2] That is, of Middlesex: see Stubbs's Pref. to Ralph de Diceto, i, pp. xxxv, xxxvi.   [3] The *Manuscripts of the Duke of Rutland*, p. 105.

[4] *Fasti Eccl. Angl.*, ed. Hardy, ii. 48. In the Bodleian copy of this book the date is corrected in pencil to 1165, a year which is supported by John's Ep. 166.

[5] *Forsch. zur Deutschen Geschichte*, xviii (1878), 270.

[6] I am indebted to the kindness of Mr. J. P. Gilson, the keeper of manuscripts at the British Museum, for information on this point.

[7] *Sarum Charters*, pp. 29 ff., ed. W. D. Macray, 1891.

[8] *Gest. Abbat. Monast. S. Albani*, i. 131.

charter in the interval between them. The following are the names of the persons recorded to have been present:

Salisbury, 19 Oct.	Belvoir Charter.	St. Neot's, 28 Oct.
Abp. Theobald	Abp. Theobald	Bp. of Durham
Bp. of Salisbury	Bp. of London	Bp. of London
Abp. of York	Bp. of Lincoln	Bp. of Lincoln
Bp. of Lincoln	Bp. of Exeter	Bp. of Hereford
Bp. of Chichester	Bp. of Chester	
	Abb. of Westminster	Abb. of St. Albans
	Abb. of Peterborough	
	Archdeacons of	
	Huntingdon	
	Middlesex	
	Buckingham	
	Salisbury	

The meeting at which the Belvoir charter was passed—the place is not stated—was evidently one of exceptional importance, though we hear of it in connexion with a very small piece of business, a composition relative to tithes in Suffolk. My supposition is that the archbishop and bishop of Lincoln left Salisbury to reinforce a larger gathering, where three other bishops and two great abbots joined them together with four archdeacons; the archdeacon of Salisbury presumably accompanying the party from that city. I offer this merely as an hypothesis for consideration.

We find no letters by John in 1158, but there are a number by the archbishop which probably belong to this year and which help us to arrange John's subsequent correspondence. Four of these letters mention a claim made by the monks of St. Bertin at Saint-Omer to the church of Chilham near Canterbury, of which they complained that they were wrongfully despoiled. It appears from documents preserved in transcripts at Saint-Omer that the churches of Chilham and Throwley were granted to the monastery of St. Bertin by William of Ypres, whom King Stephen had placed in a position of ascendancy in Kent. This grant was confirmed by Archbishop Theobald, by the king, and by Pope Anastasius IV on 17 November 1153.[1] The archbishop afterwards declared that his confirmation was extorted under compulsion, *vi et metu supradicti tyranni* (Ep. 127). It was also asserted that William of Ypres, instead of handing over the

---

[1] Round, *Calendar of Documents preserved in France*, nos. 1329–32 (1899). The papal rescript is dated at the Lateran where Anastasius was both in 1153 and 1154, but the sequel shows that it belongs to the earlier year.

property to St. Bertin, had given it to an adherent named Odo, who had gone shares with the monks in its profits.[1] The transaction was deemed simoniacal and was brought before Roger, archdeacon of Canterbury, therefore, some time before October 1154 (Ep. 126). When Henry II came to the throne, according to the St. Bertin chronicler, he annulled the grants made by William of Ypres;[2] and the properties seem to have reverted to the lords of the two churches. But it was not long before the monks of St. Bertin obtained Throwley, for Hamon of Throwley's grant of the church to them was confirmed by Henry II in the summer of 1155.[3] Chilham, on account of the intrusion of Odo, presented greater difficulty. It had passed into the hand of the lord, Hugh of Dover; and the monks of St. Bertin were inhibited by a papal mandate from enjoying the profits of the benefice. The archbishop was forced, as he says (Ep. 127), to defer taking action because the days were evil. Until William of Ypres was expelled he had to dissimulate.

Now the pipe roll of 2 Henry II accounts for William's lands in Kent for a full year, as property which he then held (*habet*); but the roll for the next year gives the charge only for half a year, as land which he formerly held (*habuit*).[4] His tenure therefore ended at Easter 1157. A papal mandate was obtained requiring Hugh of Dover to restore the church of Chilham to the monks of St. Bertin. Hugh protested that he could not restore property which had never been conveyed, and he sent messengers to Rome to establish his claim; but before they arrived a second mandate had been issued to compel his restitution of the church. The archbishop meanwhile had summoned the monks to lay their case before him, but they declined to appear unless the property was first restored to them. He therefore asked for a fresh mandate to enable him to proceed (Ep. 126). In Ep. 127 he rehearses the earlier stages of the case and explains that, while Hugh declared himself desirous of paying obedience to the Pope's orders, the monks still refused to risk the result of a trial. The archbishop therefore sequestrated the church until the rights of the claimants could be determined. That an agreement was come to before long was

---

[1] In the sentence in Ep. 126, *ut eis praefatam ecclesiam cederent*, this last word must be corrected into *cederet*.

[2] See the continuation of Simon of St. Bertin's *Chartularium Sithiense*, iii. 7, ed. B. Guérard, 1840.   [3] Round, no. 1333.

[4] *Pipe Rolls of 2, 3, and 4 Hen. II*, pp. 65, 101, (1844).

proved by two charters, in one of which Hugh grants the church
of Chilham to the monks of St. Bertin[1] and in the other this
grant is confirmed by Archbishop Theobald.[2]

If we suppose that the question about the right to Chilham
was not raised until William of Ypres was finally deprived of his
English possessions in the spring of 1157, the repeated missions
to Rome would necessarily protract the proceedings for a long
time, as every such mission required a delay of three months.
For this reason I am inclined to believe that the matter was
opened a little before 1157. Petitions to the Pope were usually
sent in the autumn or winter, and two petitions with their
answers are not often found within the space of two years. To
date the archbishop's letter 127 about the summer of 1158 would
be consonant with this limit and also with the indications
supplied by two other letters.

When Theobald wrote Epp. 110 and 111 he was still occupied
by the case of the monks of St. Bertin and also by that of
Archdeacon Osbert of York, who was charged with having
poisoned Archbishop William in 1154[3] and whose trial had been
long protracted. Theobald expresses his delight that the Pope
was about to cross the Alps and his disappointment that he had
decided to go to Rome. No other record is known of Adrian's
intention to visit France. He was at Sutri until October 1158,
and thence established himself at Rome for the winter. Theobald's two letters were written towards the end of the year. The
expectation of the Pope's journey to France is also mentioned
in a postscript to Ep. 103,[4] addressed to Roland the chancellor,
afterwards Pope Alexander III. These letters, 103, 110, and
111, belong to the summer of 1158.

Ep. 103 shows that Archbishop Theobald was troubled by
hearing that he had incurred the censure of some of the cardinals.
Earnestly protesting his devotion to the Roman church, he
desires, if in anything he has offended, to make satisfaction; if

[1] Round, *Calendar*, no. 1327.
[2] *Ibid.*, no. 1328. This charter is witnessed by John of Salisbury and therefore cannot be placed so early as 1150–3, as given in the Calendar. The two
churches were confirmed to St. Bertin by Lucius III, on 22 December 1184:
Chartularium Sithiense, iii. 50. In later times Chilham belonged to Throwley,
which was a cell of St. Bertin's.
[3] See Ep. 122, from which it appears that the archdeacon proposed to present
himself before the Pope in January 1159. Gilbert Foliot wrote on this matter
to the Pope a letter of which only part is preserved (Gilbert, Ep. 114).
[4] This postscript is omitted in the Cambridge manuscript.

he has not, he prays to be restored to favour; he asks Roland to lay his request before the cardinals. He also wrote to John, cardinal of SS. John and Paul,[1] more briefly but to the same effect. We may naturally suppose that this friction should lead the archbishop to send John of Salisbury to Rome in order to bring about a reconciliation, and we have on other grounds inferred that John paid a visit to Rome in the winter of 1158–9. He found on his return that he was attacked for his conduct of his mission. This we have already learned from a letter of Peter of Celle.[2] In the summer of 1159 John wrote to the Pope informing him that the author of the accusations against him was Bishop Arnulf of Lisieux. The letter (121) is wrongly addressed by modern editors to Alexander III. It was sent out with a letter of Archbishop Theobald relative to an appeal to the papal court (Ep. 120). In Ep. 121 John says:

Episcopus Lexoviensis malleus iniquitatis est ad conterendam ecclesiam Dei. Hic in me pauperem tantam regis coacervavit indignationem ut domino Cantuariensi et cancellario suo rex ipse denuntiaverit me maiestatem regiam minuisse et ob hoc ab amicorum et fidelium numero excludendum. Auditis etiam litteris quibus innocentiam meam vestra benignitas excusavit, mendosus ille et mendax dicere ausus est, *Dominus papa scripsit quod voluit; ergo domino regi refero quod uerum novi.* Provideat igitur mihi pietas vestra et regis gratiam studeat reformare.

The Pope's letter in his favour was presumably obtained during John's visit to Rome in the spring of 1159; whether he lived to receive John's letter just quoted must be left doubtful.

Bishop Arnulf, an influential councillor of Henry II, had been in his court down to the spring of 1157; he does not reappear there until the first months of 1159. It is likely that between these dates he had been in Rome and had made mischief against John, who was the working spirit of Archbishop Theobald's administration. King Henry had been abroad since August 1158, and it was in Normandy that Arnulf was in attendance on him in 1159. John, writing to an unknown correspondent at Lisieux—perhaps Ralph of Sarr—in July of this year (Ep. 60), speaks of the English troops going to Poitiers on their march to Toulouse. They were ordered to be at Poitiers on midsummer

---

[1] *Ioanni Sanctorum I. et Pauli*, in the margin of the Paris manuscript. Giles prints *Ioanni Scor. et Paul. Card.*

[2] Above, pp. 269 f.

day,[1] and the siege of Toulouse began not long after. By this time, we have seen, John had fallen under the king's displeasure. In Ep. 114 he writes to a member of the capitular body at Sens; the letter is addressed in the margin of the Paris manuscript to Matthew the precentor, but its contents prove that it was written to one of his brethren, though it related to business in which the precentor also was concerned. This man had failed in a suit at the papal court, which had been remitted for trial by delegates in France. John advises him to submit to this procedure, but adds that, if he prefers to take his cause in person to Rome, he is ready to offer his assistance, and sends by the same messenger a letter to the Pope. This letter is preserved as Ep. 108, which recommends the bearer and also the precentor to the Pope's favourable hearing.[2] John then passes to his own affairs and ironically begs Adrian to offer his thanks to the bishop of Lisieux for having so greatly kindled the wrath of the English king against him that it was not safe for him to remain in England, while to depart was either impossible or extremely difficult.[3] We have found reason to believe that Bishop Arnulf's hostile report was laid before the king in the early part of 1159 and that John returned from Rome in the course of the spring. His Ep. 108 may have been written a little later.

John spared no labour in obtaining letters on his behalf from the Pope and the archbishop. This he mentions in a letter to Thomas the chancellor (Ep. 113), in which he implores him to use his influence to moderate the king's anger against him, so that he might be allowed the opportunity of escaping from his troubles in literary studies or in some other occupation. As the chancellor was still abroad, he sent this letter through one Master Ernulf (Ep. 112). In another letter (Ep. 91), which bears no address, John writes to thank a person of eminence, whose dignity he marks by the terms *sublimitas* and *sanctitas vestra*, for transmitting to him *per tot terrarum et marium spatia* a letter of consolation in his troubles. The correspondent, whom we presume to have been at Rome, may possibly be Cardinal Boso, the devoted friend of Adrian IV, and the letter may be placed

---

[1] Robert of Torigny, *Continuatio Beccensis*, p. 322.

[2] As usual, the editors have addressed the letter to Alexander III.

[3] The statement at the end that Archdeacon Osbert had failed to make his purgation—that is, had declined to accept this mode of proof—connects this letter with Archbishop Theobald's account of the proceedings (Ep. 122). Cf., above p. 277 n. 3.

late in 1159 before the news of the Pope's death on 1 September had reached England.

The archbishop's testimonial to John's integrity is embedded in a letter to the king (Ep. 64).[1] But this was not written until the end of the year; for Theobald already knew that a schism had been brought to pass by the election of Cardinal Octavian, the Antipope Victor IV, against Alexander III in the first week of September, and had convened a synod to consider the situation. That synod was probably held late in November 1159. In order to fix the date we must bear in mind that on 28 October, during the siege of Crema, the Emperor Frederick sent a letter to Henry II inviting him to send churchmen to assist at an ecclesiastical assembly to be held at Pavia on 13 January 1160.[2] The interval allowed was thus 77 days. It is not easy to calculate how long a courier would take in carrying his message to King Henry, who was in Normandy, or to Archbishop Theobald at Canterbury. If the latter received a missive direct, it may have reached him by the third week in November. But the archbishop needed time for the summons of his synod, and it had to meet early enough to enable envoys to reach Pavia by 13 January, if it was decided to send any. Now the journey from London to Pavia was reckoned at about 34 days,[3] and the English envoys would have to start early in December. I infer therefore that the London synod was held at the very end of November. That in fact the archbishop secured the acceptance of Alexander and no envoys were sent to Pavia does not disturb our calculation.

The council at Pavia did not meet until 5 February 1160; it closed on the 13th. After the news reached England, about the middle of March, John wrote his long and important letter to Ralph of Sarr, Ep. 59, in which he treats of the questions about the double election debated at that assembly. He mentions how the archbishop was carried in a litter to his synod in London, and he also refers to the tendencies of public opinion on the dispute. The bishops of Winchester and Durham were thought to incline towards Victor IV, but the archbishop of York and the treasurer, Richard fitz Neal, strongly supported Alexander. There is evidence that Bishop Henry of Winchester was at

---

[1] This appears in the Cambridge manuscript as three letters, no. 24*, 31, and 24.   [2] *Constit. et Acta Publica*, i. 254 f., in the *Monum. Germ. Hist.*
[3] Matthew Paris, in Palgrave's *English Commonwealth*, ii. 21 note.

Fareham in Hampshire in March,[1] and that Bishop Hugh of Durham was in Normandy in May.[2] John's information about their views was probably obtained while both were in England, and I should therefore date John's letter in April. In it he says that the archbishop is very ill, and that he himself is burthened with debt and pressed by his creditors.

In attempting to arrange John's letters of the following months we have to consider also some of the archbishop's letters. They all belong to a time when a vacancy had been caused in the see of Exeter by the death of Bishop Warelwast on 22 March 1160. The earliest appears to be one (Ep. 70) in which Theobald begs the king to send his archdeacon home as soon as possible. He speaks of Thomas in the first place not as chancellor but as his archdeacon in order to mark that, unless the king's service rendered attendance on him necessary, his absence from his duties in England was an act of canonical disobedience. In Ep. 78 John, writing to the chancellor, reports that by the archbishop's authority he had drafted letters to the king and also to Thomas, urging upon the latter the need of hastening his return to England under pain of anathema and loss of the emoluments which he held from the church of Canterbury. This letter was written before peace was concluded with France in May.[3] In it he states that the monition to the archdeacon was not expedited; he is writing, he says, without Theobald's knowledge—the archbishop was lying on a bed of sickness—to explain the circumstances and sends a less peremptory message.[4] In Ep. 63 the archbishop, in a letter to

[1] Richard of Anesty's diary, *ibid.*, ii. 18.

[2] Eyton, *Itinerary of Henry II*, p. 50 (1878).

[3] In it John mentions that three sees were vacant. These were Exeter, Worcester, and Coventry. The death of Bishop Walter Durdent of Coventry on 17 December is assigned by Stubbs (*Registrum Sacrum Anglicanum*, p. 47, ed. 2) to 1160; but Robert of Torigny, a careful writer, places the event in 1159. It is unexampled, as Eyton observed (Le Neve's *Fasti*, i. 544 note), that at that time a bishop would be consecrated after an interval so short as four months from the death of his predecessor; and to suppose that Bishop Walter lived until near the end of 1160 would introduce havoc into the chronology of John of Salisbury's letters.

[4] The letter to Thomas which was not dispatched was possibly Ep. 71. This in the Paris manuscript is addressed simply *Archidiacono*; but Masson, seeing that part of the letter related to the election to the see of Exeter, thought it was addressed to Bartholomew, and so prefixed *B.* and added *Exoniensi*. Giles increased the confusion by printing *R.* instead of *B.* In the Cambridge manuscript the letter is correctly addressed to Thomas. Cf. J. C. Robertson, note to *Materials for the History of Thomas Becket*, v (1881), 11.

the king, gives thanks for the restoration of peace, and mentions a rumour that the Emperor had sent his chancellor, Archbishop Reynold of Cologne, to win support for Victor IV. This mission was a sequel to the assembly at Pavia in February. Ep. 63 then may have been written between May and midsummer. All this time Theobald was very ill. In Ep. 64** he speaks of his earnest desire to see the king once more before he departs, and repeats his request that his archdeacon may be allowed to return to him. This can hardly have been composed until about the end of 1160. Ep. 54 was written when he was very near his end, probably not long before his death on 17 or 18 April 1161.

Two of John's letters belong to the interval between the vacancy in the see of Exeter in March 1160 and the election of Bartholomew a year later. These two, Epp. 80 and 90, may be noticed together. Ep. 90 was written about the same time as Ep. 78 and addressed to Bartholomew, archdeacon of Exeter, when his election to that see was being discussed and another candidate, Robert[1] fitz Harding was also advocated. John invites Bartholomew to come to advise the archbishop and to bring others with him, particularly *magister B. filius Reinfredi Peccator, fraterculus meus*. The see of Exeter, as we have seen, became vacant on 22 March 1160, and was not filled until May 1161. The letter may be placed near the beginning of 1161. Ep. 80 bears no address, but I have no doubt that it was also written to Bartholomew, perhaps a little earlier. It begins in a formal style addressed in the plural number (*prudentia vestra*). John is here communicating a commission to his correspondent to do justice to a poor man, who has suffered wrong from one of his rural deans; the aggrieved person was a citizen of London who was on his way to his birthplace in Cornwall.[2] When the official business is finished John goes on to speak about domestic affairs, and falls into the singular number and a familiar strain. He ends with greetings to the brethren, *fratribus nostris*, and desires that this name may be taken in a wide sense, *ut non modo*

---

[1] The Christian name is given in Ep. 78.

[2] This letter has been given an accidental importance because John calls the man his *concivis*, and it has therefore been supposed that John was a native of London. This inference is, I think, mistaken. The archbishop possessed churches in London, and would naturally endow his clerks with them or with pensions charged upon them. The holding of such a benefice would entitle John to rank as a citizen of London. When he went into exile some of his ecclesiastical revenues were placed in charge of the bishop of London (Ep. 140); these lay no doubt in his diocese.

ad magistrum extendatur et Peccatorem sed et filium Remfredi et alios, where the reference seems to be to three persons named Richard.[1] The mention of 'our brethren' and a similar expression in Ep. 90 may lead us to think that John already held a place in the chapter of Exeter, of which he is known to have been treasurer in 1172.

Six letters remain to which I am unable to assign any probable date. Ep. 51 is an intimate letter to a friend who was suffering from a grievance. Ep. 94 was written to John's kinsman Master Geoffrey; it appears from a letter in the later collection (Ep. 160) that Master Geoffrey was a monk of Bury St. Edmunds. Two others were written to Pope Adrian: one, Ep. 28, brings before him a complaint of the canons of Merton against the interference of the bishop of Winchester in the patronage of two of their churches; the other, Ep. 29, also relates to an appeal. Ep. 77 was addressed to an unknown suitor, communicating the archbishop's rejection of his petition. Lastly, Ep. 26, which bears no address, was written, apparently to the bishop of Ely, on a matter of business which our materials do not enable us to elucidate.

Our examination of John's letters leads to the conclusion that the materials from which the collection was made up consisted of letters written between 1154 and the archbishop's death in April 1161. A study of Theobald's letters included in the series is much to be desired, but I doubt whether it will alter this conclusion. The collection does not seem to contain any letters of Archbishop Thomas. I add a list of John's letters in the order of time to which it seems to me that they probably belong. It is only a tentative list, and I print it in the hope of inviting criticism and correction.

						Epist.
1154, after October .	.	.	.	.	.	34
1155 ? .	.	.	.	.	.	82
[Sept. 30 *at Ferentino*;						
c. Dec. *to c.* Feb., 1156, *at Benevento.*]						
1156, before July	.	.	.	.	.	128
summer?	.	.	.	.	.	27
						42
autumn .	.	.	.	.	.	85
after October 1	.	.	.	.	.	75
[Winter, 1156–7, *Visit to Rome.*]						

[1] Master Richard, Richard Peccator, and Richard son of Reinfrid witness Exeter documents of about this time: Hist. MSS. Comm., *Report on Various Collections*, iv (1907), 48–51.

								Epist.
1157, spring .	.	.	.	.	.	.	.	30, 31, 32
July	.	.	.	.	.	.	.	97
1158, beginning	.	.	.	.	.	.	.	76
?	.	.	.	.	.	.	.	107
[c. Dec., *Visit to Rome to c.* May, 1159.]								
1159, summer	.	.	.	.	.	.	.	121
July	.	.	.	.	.	.	.	60
summer	.	.	.	.	.	.	.	108, 114
								112, 113
autumn	.	.	.	.	.	.	.	81
								91
late .	.	.	.	.	.	.	.	115, 116
1160, beginning	.	.	.	.	.	.	.	73
April ?	.	.	.	.	.	.	.	59
								80
before May	.	.	.	.	.	.	.	78
								90
summer	.	.	.	.	.	.	.	96
Not placed .	.	.	.	.	.	.	26, 28, 29, 51, 77, 94	

This arrangement of the letters has led me to suppose that John paid two visits to Rome, in the winters of 1156–7 and 1158–9 which have not hitherto been noticed. This hypothesis is welcome, because in the autumn of 1159 John said that he had ten times crossed the Alps since he first left England,[1] and only two journeys into Italy have until lately been discovered; those, namely, after the council of Rheims in 1148, and from the autumn of 1155 to the beginning of 1156. I have recently found reason to believe that he was attached to the papal court before Eugenius set out for France in 1147.[2] This makes a third journey to Italy, and the two proposed in the present paper complete the number of five.

APPENDIX

A comparison of the addresses prefixed to the letters in the collection of John's early correspondence as we find them in the complete Paris manuscript and the imperfect copy at Cambridge, which I shall cite as *C*, shows that the modern editors have assumed a great liberty of conjecture in the forms in which they have presented them. Masson inserted most of the addresses in the Paris manuscript itself, and did not alter them much when he published his edition.

[1] Many years ago I understood *egressus Anglia* to mean 'on my outward journey' (*Illustrations of the History of Medieval Thought*, p. 213, 1884), and I carelessly omitted to correct this in the second edition (1920). It is clear, as Pauli pointed out in the *Zeitschr. für Kirchenrecht*, xvi (1881), 274, that John's meaning is that given above in the text.

[2] See my article on 'John of Salisbury at the Papal Court', above, pp. 251–3.

It would hardly be worth while to print the variations between the addresses which he wrote in the manuscript and those which appear in his edition. These are only stages in the process. For our purpose it will be sufficient to note the main divergences in this point between the addresses given in the original hand of the manuscripts and those in the latest edition by Giles. In the first place we must observe that the name of the Pope is seldom given in full in the manuscripts. We read generally, in an abbreviated form, *domino pape* in the margin. *Adriano* or *Alexandro* is a conjectural addition by one or the other editor. Only in Epp. 27, 28, 30, 38 does the name of Adrian appear. Ep. 36 has the full address given in the edition, but the Pope's name is indicated only by the initial *A*. This initial is found also in Ep. 42. Ep. 41 alone is addressed *Alexandro pape*. In *C*, Ep. 110 (there numbered 10) is addressed [*Ad Alex.*] *iii^m papam*. This copy frequently repeats *Idem eidem* in consecutive letters which were in fact written to different people.[1]

Ep. 23 is addressed *prima manu* to Alfred bishop of Worcester.[2]

Ep. 24 likewise, to the king.

Ep. 25 in an early hand to H. bishop of Durham.

Ep. 26 bears no address; it was written by John, possibly to the bishop of Rochester.

Ep. 32 is inscribed in an early hand to John, treasurer of Canterbury, which I take to be a mistake for John of Canterbury, treasurer [of York].[3]

Ep. 34 to John treasurer of York.

Ep. 37. *Eveshame[n]si conventu[i] pro abbate eligendo* omitted by Giles.

Ep. 43. The long address in the printed text is taken from the manuscript.

Ep. 45, headed by Giles *Ad abbates Wauliae*, is an information by the archbishop to the Cistercian abbots of a mandate he has issued in the business of the abbey of Waverley (*Wau'lie*).

Ep. 46. *Hilario episcopo Cistrensi.*

Ep. 54. *Regi.*

Ep. 56 bears no address. In *C*, Ep. 47, it is headed *Nigillo Eliensi episcopo*.[4]

---

[1] There are many other blunders; for instance, Ep. 87 (*C*, Ep. 51), a letter to the Pope relative to a dispute between the priest of Ginga, that is Ingatestone, and the abbess of Barking, is headed *Grigius pape eidem*, though the preceding letter is addressed to Bishop Alexander of Lincoln (see below, p. 286, note 6).

[2] In *C*, Ep. 55, it is inscribed *Lundoniensi episcopo*.

[3] See above, pp. 271, 273.

[4] That this address is a mistake I have pointed out in the *Eng. Hist. Rev.* xxxviii, 62 f. (1923). Dr. William Hunt has since persuaded me that it was written to Gilbert Foliot, bishop of Hereford.

Ep. 59. *De electione Romani pontificis* A.

Ep. 61. *Domino regi.*

Ep. 62–4. *Regi.*

Ep. 65. Fully addressed as in ed.

Ep. 71. *Ad B. archidiaconum.*[1]

Ep. 76. *Cellensi.*

Ep. 78. *Cancellario.*

Ep. 79. *De quodam eligendo* in an early hand.

Ep. 81, 82, 85. *Cellensi.*

Ep. 90. *M⁰ B. Archid. Exoñ.*

Ep. 92. *[M]onachis de [ ]ocleia?*

Ep. 94. *Magistro Gaufr.*

Ep. 95. *Ep̄o. Sar.*

Ep. 97. *Ad eundem.*

Ep. 98. *[Episcop]o Winton.*

Ep. 99. *Ad eundem.*

Ep. 101. *Ep̄o W[into]niensi.*

Ep. 103. *R. cancellario.*

Ep. 104. *Ioanni Sanctorum I. et Pauli.*

Ep. 105. *Bosoni camerario.*[2]

Ep. 113. *Cancellario Regis.*

Ep. 114. *Matheo precentori Seonnensi.*

Ep. 115. *Cellensi abbati.*

Ep. 116. *Thome preposito [Cel]lensi.*

Ep. 128. *Episcopo Norwicensi.*

Ep. 130. *Abbatisse Bercingi.*

The following letters bear no address in the Paris MS.: 4–22, 26, 31, 33,[2] 35, 39, 40, 44, 47–52,[3] 55–8,[4] 60, 66–70,[5] 72–5, 77, 80, 83,[6] 84, 86–9, 91, 96, 112, 133.

---

[1] This letter in *C* (Ep. 27) is rightly addressed *Thome cancellario.*

[2] The address is written in full, *prima manu*, in the Paris MS. *Cancellario* is a simple misreading in the editions.

[3] In *C*, Ep. 49 (there Ep. 36) is addressed *Cancellario regis.* Ep. 50 (there Ep. 7) is included among letters to the Pope. It relates to a dispute between the canons of Marton in Cleveland and the monks of Meaux, and was apparently written to the archbishop of York. The fact that it transmits the purport of a papal mandate may have led to its careless arrangement among letters addressed to the Pope. Ep. 52 (there Ep. 37) is addressed *Clero Exoniensis ecclesie.*

[4] In *C*, Ep. 68 (there Ep. 43) is headed *Theobaldus archiepiscopus Hylario Cistrensi episcopo*; and Ep. 69 (there Ep. 45) *Episcopo Cestrensi.*

[5] In *C*, Ep. 58 (there Ep. 46) is addressed *Dom. Ricardo Londoniensi episcopo.*

[6] In *C* (Ep. 50) this letter is addressed *Lincolniensi episcopo Alexandro.* But Bishop Alexander died in 1148, more than five years before this correspondence begins. The inscription is therefore probably erroneous, unless an old letter was copied out as a model for a mandate of excommunication.

THE EARLY LIVES OF ROBERT PULLEN
AND NICHOLAS BREAKSPEAR[1]

WITH NOTES ON OTHER ENGLISHMEN AT THE PAPAL COURT
ABOUT THE MIDDLE OF THE TWELFTH CENTURY

THE visit of five bishops and four abbots from England to the Lateran Council of 1139 might have been expected to lead to closer and more frequent relations between the Church in England and Rome. But if this was the result, it did not immediately take effect; for the first Englishman to be given office in the Roman Church was not appointed until 1144, and he was called to Rome, not from England, but from Paris.

1. This was Robert Pullen, of whom John of Hexham[2] speaks under the year 1146 as eminent in the Roman Church. After referring to his wisdom and learning, he says that Robert refused a bishopric offered to him by Henry I, being content with having enough to live upon (*victum et vestitum habens*). A rhymester who wrote about 1140 calls him, in distinction from a namesake, Robertus Amyclas, a favourite term in those days to indicate a poor man.[3] As Robert was without influential connexions, we may presume that he was not offered a bishopric at an early age and may therefore place his birth in the last quarter of the eleventh century. Not long before the end of Henry's reign we have a definite record of his activity as a teacher. In the Annals of Oseney Abbey, just outside the walls of Oxford, we read under the year 1133:

Magister Rob' pulein scripturas divinas que in Anglia obsoluerant aput Oxoñ legere cepit. Qui postea, cum ex doctrina eius ecclesia tam Anglicana quam Gallicana plurimum profecisset, a papa Lucio secundo vocatus et in cancellarium sancte Romane ecclesie promotus est.[4]

Of this there is an expanded version in a manuscript known as the *Continuatio Bedae*, which was written for Robert Wyvill, bishop of Salisbury, 1330–1375. This book, Bodl. MS. 712, contains a compilation chiefly from Walter of Hemingburgh but

---

[1] Reprinted from *Essays in Medieval History presented to Thomas Frederick Tout*, Manchester, 1925.

[2] *Contin. of Simeon of Durham*, ii. 319, ed. T. Arnold, 1885.

[3] See above pp. 224 ff.

[4] Cotton MS., Tiberius A. 9, fo. 54 A.

including a number of notices relative to Oxford and Oseney manifestly derived from the Oseney Annals. Here it is said that—

Eodem anno [1133] venit magister Robertus cognomento pullus de civitate Exonia Oxenfordiam ibique scripturas divinas, que per idem tempus in Anglia[1] absolute erant et scolasticis quippe necglecte fuerant, per quinquennium legit. Omnique die dominico verbum Dei populo predicavit; ex cuius doctrina plurimum profecerunt. Qui postea ob eximiam doctrinam et religiosam famam a papa Lucio vocatus et in cancellarium Romane ecclesie promotus est.[2]

Dr. Rashdall, who quotes this passage,[3] rightly calls attention to the suspicious resemblance to the forged Continuation of Ingulf bearing the name of Peter of Blois, in which we hear of one Master Gilbert *omnibus dominicis diebus . . . verbum Dei ad populum praedicans.*[4] But it is not certain which of the two writers was the borrower. What seems plain from the Bodleian manuscript is that the compiler was here putting together his information from two sources, one of which spoke of Oxford and the other of Exeter, and that he endeavoured to reconcile them by making Robert come from Exeter to Oxford.

Now in the Oseney Annals, the words *oxoñ* and *exon* are written extremely alike. In two instances *oxoñ* is certainly a mistake: the siege in 1135 was of Exeter not Oxford Castle, and there were no bishops of Oxford (fo. 32*b*) in the Middle Ages. It may be observed that the form *Oxonia* given in Luard's *Annales Monastici* is due to the editor. In the fourteen places in which the word occurs between 1133 and 1209 we find *oxoñ* or *oxeñ* nine times, *oxon'* (under 1135, meaning Exeter) once, and *oxeneford'* or *oxenf'* four times. The manuscript from which the edition is printed is a copy made in the fourteenth century from an older book, Vitellius E. 15, which was destroyed in the fire at the Cottonian library in 1731. Of this only a few fragments are preserved; but from these we may be certain that Robert's teaching was in it placed *ap. ox.*, and the erroneous entry of 1135 is correctly assigned to *exonie* (written in full). Still *exon* and *oxon* were very similar, and an Oseney scribe would almost automatically presume that a word so written really meant Oxford.

---

[1] MS. *Angliam.*   [2] Bodl. MS. 712, fo. 275.
[3] *The Universities of Europe,* ii. 335, note, Oxford, 1895.
[4] *Rerum Anglic. Script.* i. 114 [ed. W. Fulman], 1684.

Whether Robert in fact taught at Oxford or Exeter involves a balance of probabilities. On the one hand there is no well-attested instance of any teaching or of any literary activity at Oxford between the isolated appearance of Theobald of Étampes, probably in the first decade of the twelfth century, and some time after 1167.[1] Exeter, on the other hand, about the time that Robert taught, must have been a centre of learned study. The pupils of 1133 would be mature masters twenty years afterwards, and charters drawn up under Bishop Robert Warelwast (1155–60) contain the witness of not a few. In one of them we read of Master Bartholomew the archdeacon, of Master Peter the bishop's brother, and of Master Joseph.[2] In another dated on 1 March 1159/1160 there is a larger list. Among the bishop's clerks are Master Ralph, Master Baldwin, Master Richard. The clerks of the choir include one *magister*, Algar, and there are nine *scholares*.[3] Archdeacon Bartholomew won renown as a divine and was made bishop of Exeter in 1161. Master Baldwin had a greater career before him, for he rose to the archbishopric of Canterbury. Master Joseph became famous as a Latin poet. No one can read the earlier letters of John of Salisbury without the persuasion that Exeter about 1160 was a place of studious activity. Exeter had also a literary tradition. From the time at least of Bishop Leofric books were written there, and of the eighty-one manuscripts which the dean and chapter presented to the Bodleian library in 1602 not a few belong to the twelfth century, and some of them are unquestionably written by English hands. If then there is to be a choice between Exeter and Oxford as the place where Robert Pullen taught, I should not hesitate to support Exeter.

According to the *Continuatio Bedae*, Robert pursued his teaching for five years, that is, until about 1138. He is next found as archdeacon of Rochester. The date of his appointment cannot be fixed, for there is no notice of any preceding archdeacon after 1123. It is unlikely that he was appointed by Bishop John of Rochester, who died in June 1137, and there is no certain record of any bishop having been consecrated to that see until 1142. Most scholars suppose that during the interval

[1] The statement of Gervase of Canterbury that Vacarius taught law at Oxford may be dismissed as an excusable mistake in a chronicler who wrote at the very end of the century.

[2] Hist. MSS. Comm., *Report on Various Collections*, iv (1907), 47.

[3] *Ibid.*, p. 49.

the diocese was administered by Bishop John of Séez; but the Profession Rolls at Canterbury are defective, and there are some traces of a namesake, also of Séez, having held the bishopric until Ascelin was consecrated in 1142. In either event Rochester was brought into relations with the Norman see, and it was a Norman prelate who made Robert archdeacon, and by whose permission Robert left England and established himself as a teacher of theology at Paris. He was certainly there in 1142, when John of Salisbury attended his lectures.

That same year a new bishop, Ascelin, was appointed at Rochester, and a dispute arose between him and Archdeacon Robert about certain rights, into the particulars of which we need not enter.[1] That it was also connected with Robert's continued non-residence may be gathered from the fact that St. Bernard wrote to the bishop urging that the archdeacon might be allowed to remain at Paris.[2] Bishop Ascelin brought his suit before the Pope and Robert failed to appear. This was in November 1143. Sentence was therefore given against him in default, and the bishop was directed to summon Robert to appear next Whitsuntide and to order him to reside. Now it so chanced that while the suit was in process a new Pope was elected, in September 1143. Had Innocent II been still alive, he would probably have followed the counsels of St. Bernard, and Robert would have been left at Paris. But the change of Pope meant a change of policy. Robert was a conservative divine, while Celestine II was reputed to favour the views of Abailard. Hence it was natural that he should wish to remove Robert from his position as a teacher at Paris and send him back to the obscurity of his archdeaconry.[3] Celestine, however, died in a few months, and one of the first acts of his successor, Lucius II, was to call Robert to Rome as cardinal. Lucius was elected in March 1144, and by the following November Robert was engaged in doing business at Rome; he was almost immediately appointed chancellor.[4] From this time down to 2 September 1146 he was active at his post; but from the 18th his duties at the chancery were performed by a subdeacon. No chancellor appears until 17 December. We may therefore presume that Robert either

---

[1] See a letter by Mr. J. H. Round in the *Athenaeum*, 31 October 1896.
[2] Ep. 205.   [3] J. Thorpe, *Registrum Roffense* (1769), pp. 39 f.
[4] Here and elsewhere I take the dates of cardinals' subscriptions from the second edition of Jaffé's *Regesta Pontificum Romanorum*.

died or his health failed early in September. He certainly did not accompany Pope Eugenius III on his journey to France in 1147.

2. I come next to Nicholas Breakspear, afterwards Pope Adrian IV. What little is known of his early life is recorded by Cardinal Boso and William, canon of Newburgh, who both wrote rather more than thirty years after his death. Boso, an Englishman, who was his devoted friend, wrote his life as Pope and passed by his earlier career briefly. Nicholas, he says,[1] was by nation an Englishman, *de castro sancti Albani*, who left his country as a youth in order to improve himself in the study of letters. He went to Arles, where, while he was still engaged in the schools, it was the Lord's will that he should go to the church of St. Rufus and there make his profession as a canon. He advanced to the dignity of prior and then of abbot. Afterwards it happened that he went to Rome on business connected with the church, and having accomplished his task prepared to return. But Pope Eugenius kept him with him and made him bishop of Albano. Here we have only to note that Nicholas was not born at St. Albans but at a village belonging to the abbey, and that he did not go to the city of Arles but to Avignon which lay in its province.

William of Newburgh, as an Austin canon, was careful to collect all the information he could find about a member of his order who became famous. He tells us[2] that Nicholas's father was a clerk of moderate estate who became a monk at St. Alban's. The boy was too poor to become a scholar and sought for subsistence from the monastery; but his father drove him away, and he went to seek his fortune abroad. He found little success in France, and passed on beyond the Rhone into Provence, where he was admitted to a minster of regular clerks known as that of St. Rufus. This was on the outskirts of Avignon: in 1158 it was removed to Valence,[3] a fact which explains some discrepancies in later accounts.

To fill in the details omitted by our early witnesses we have to rely on the materials collected by Matthew Paris about the middle of the thirteenth century. He says that Nicholas, *de quodam viculo abbatis, scilicet Langele oriundus, cognomento Brekespere*, besought Abbot Robert to admit him

[1] *Lib. Pontif.* ii. 388.   [2] *Hist.* ii. 6.
[3] *Gallia Christ.* xvi (1865), 355.

to the monastery;[1] but he was rejected on account of his insufficient learning. In the hamlet of Bedmond in Abbot's Langley, Hertfordshire, there is a farmhouse called Breakspear's, which may have borne its name from Nicholas's family.[2] But a confusion has arisen from the fact that there is another Breakspear, not far off, in the parish of Harefield on the northern border of Middlesex, and this place has been conjectured to be the place from which Nicholas's family came. For this supposition there is no foundation. In another notice Matthew adds the information that Nicholas was the son of Robert de Camera, who, *honeste vivens in saeculo, litteratus aliquantulum*, became a monk at St. Alban's.[3] The father was thus a clerk in the king's chamber, a department of finance which was becoming overshadowed by the exchequer. Matthew's statement that Nicholas was refused admission to St. Alban's by Abbot Robert is a manifest mistake, for Robert was not elected until 1151. The further statement that Nicholas went to Paris, where he worked so strenuously that he surpassed all his fellows and was made a canon of St. Rufus, looks like the account which a writer of the thirteenth century would take to be natural and obvious. But Matthew alone mentions Paris. William of Newburgh says that it was after prospering ill in France that the poor young man went on to St. Rufus, where he obtained means for his subsistence. This is not what one would expect of a scholar who had won laurels at Paris; he would rather have gone on to a place where he could find a famous master to sit under. St. Rufus was not such a place. It seems to me much more probable that he was sent to the Austin canons there by a house of the same order to which he was attached in some humble capacity in England. That he had not risen high may be inferred from the later Life of Adrian IV by Bernard Guidonis,[4] where we read that he was first a poor clerk—*pauper clericus sive clericus pauperculus*—in the church of St. James at Melgueil in the diocese of Maguelonne, and at length (*tandem*) a brother

---

[1] *Gesta Abbat.* i. 112 f.; cf. *Chron. Maj.* ii. 204. The statement in Onuphrius Panvinius' *Epitome Pontificum Romanorum* (Venice, 1557), p. 121, that Nicholas came from Malmesbury, a town of St. Alban's in the diocese of Bath, was repeated in Ciaconius' *Vitae Pontificum*, with various misspellings, and the additional information that Langley is the same as Malmesbury, in the edition of 1601, pp. 443, 453; in that of 1630, pp. 542, 555; and in that revised by Oldoinus in 1677, i. 1044, 1057.

[2] *Victoria Hist. of Hertfordshire*, ii (1908), 325.

[3] *Gesta Abbat.* i. 124 f.   [4] Muratori, *Scriptores*, iii. i. 440b.

at St. Rufus. This church had been confirmed to the abbot and canons of St. Rufus by Urban II, 19 September 1095.[1] It would seem, therefore, that the canons sent him for a time to serve in the church at Melgueil.[2]

I believe it is possible to identify the English house from which Nicholas was sent beyond seas. There is a letter of John of Salisbury,[3] in which he brings a petition of the canons of Merton in Surrey before this same Nicholas when he had become Pope Adrian IV. He ends with the words, *May it be of advantage to the men of Merton that when you were in the church of St. Rufus their sweet savour reached you, and that your worship was wont to speak [of it] in conversation with me your servant.* The priory of Merton was a young foundation, and like other newly founded houses in that age it rapidly grew in favour. From about 1120 one Bernard, a writer in the king's court, was acquiring lands which he bequeathed to Merton;[4] and we may well suppose that official association led Robert, a clerk in the chamber, to send his son there. Merton had a school which was attended by Thomas Becket about 1128;[5] and the priory was in such good repute that Archbishop William of Canterbury, who was himself an Austin canon, shortly before his death in 1136, directed the bishops of Rochester and St. David's to reconstitute the secular house of St. Martin's at Dover on its pattern.[6]

A great difficulty in tracing the biography of Nicholas arises from the total absence of any dates to guide us until he became Pope. We do not know when he was born or when he went to St. Rufus, when he was elected abbot or when he was made a cardinal. All that can be said is that the dates commonly given are in every instance wrong.[7] William of Newburgh is not helpful in this matter. He says that Nicholas quitted England when he was growing up (*adolescentiam ingressus*), and that

[1] The bull is printed by Jacques Petit, *Poenitentiale Theodori Archiepiscopi* (Paris, 1677), p. 615, where the date is wrongly given as 1096.

[2] It is possible that he had recommendations from northern parts, for Bishop Walter of Maguelonne, who is known as a poet, came from Lille (Devic and Vaissete, *Hist. de Languedoc*, iii. 575): he died in 1129.   [3] Ep. 28.

[4] Round, 'Bernard, the King's Scribe', in the *Eng. Hist. Rev.* xiv (1899), 417-30.   [5] W. FitzStephen in Robertson's *Materials*, iii. 14.

[6] Gervase of Canterbury, i. 97, ed. W. Stubbs, 1879.

[7] In A. H. Tarleton's *Nicholas Breakspear* (1896) the future Pope is supposed to have been born about 1100 (p. 18), to have gone abroad about 1120 (p. 19), and to have been made abbot in 1137 (p. 40) and cardinal towards the end of 1146 (p. 45). The *Dictionary of National Biography*, *s.v.* Adrian IV, also dates this last appointment in 1146.

after failing to find a home in France he went on to Provence,
where he was given maintenance at the monastery of St. Rufus
and afterwards made a canon of the house. Thus he lived for
very many years (*annis plurimis*) and was in time elected abbot.
Now one William is mentioned as abbot about 1133;[1] but
Nicholas did not succeed him for many years if we are right in
identifying him with the Nicholas, canon of St. Rufus, who in
1140 wrote a charter at Barcelona which is still preserved.[2] Our
first definite notice of him as abbot occurs at the beginning of
1147, when Eugenius III travelling towards France granted at
Vico[3] in the Val d'Elsa, between Poggibonsi and San Miniato,
a bull addressed to N. abbot of St. Rufus, conferring a privilege
on his monastery.[4] According to William of Newburgh, after
Nicholas had been abbot for some time (*aliquandiu*), his canons
rose up against him and brought a petition to Pope Eugenius
III, no doubt for his removal. The Pope succeeded in arranging
a reconciliation, but peace was not long preserved (*non diu
quievit nescia quietis malitia*). The canons soon renewed their
appeal, and the Pope heard their allegations. The issue was
unexpected. Eugenius calmly said, *I know, brethren, where is
the seat of Satan; I know what has roused this storm among you.
Go forth: elect you a father with whom ye can or will live in peace;
for he shall no longer be a burthen to you.* And he forthwith
consecrated Nicholas to the bishopric of Albano, and thus made
him not only a cardinal but also a member of his intimate
council. This was the form in which the story reached Newburgh.
The discreet Cardinal Boso speaks only of the ability with which
Nicholas conducted the business of his house at the papal court,
and Matthew Paris says that he thrice had occasion to repair
thither, each time with more conspicuous success. Whichever
account be true, it is evident that two or three suits at the papal
court require a considerable length of time. We have no information when they began, except that it was when Eugenius was
Pope, and therefore not earlier than 1145. His absence from
Italy for fifteen months from the beginning of 1147 must have
delayed business at his court. He did not take up his residence

---

[1] Hauréau, in *Gallia Christ*. xvi. 359.
[2] Villanueva, *Viage literario a las Iglesias de España*, xi (1850), 199 f.
Nicholas probably accompanied Archbishop William of Arles, who went as
legate to Barcelona late in 1139: *ibid*. xvii. 317.
[3] Not Vienne in Dauphiny, as Hauréau supposed.
[4] Jaffé, *Regesta Pontif*. 8998, ed. 2.

at the Lateran until the end of November 1149, and Nicholas
first makes his appearance as cardinal on the 30th January 1150.
It would seem, therefore, likely that he was nominated at
Christmas 1149.

But the question remains to be considered, how it was that
an abbot of a comparatively obscure monastery in Provence,
coming to the papal court to answer accusations made against
him by his canons, or possibly merely in connexion with some
title to lands, was at once preferred to one of the highest and
most desirable posts in the Pope's gift. Here we are left to
conjecture, and I propose only an hypothesis. The see of Albano
had been vacant since the spring or summer of 1145, and the
chancellor of the Roman Church was then the Englishman,
Cardinal Robert Pullen. Robert is understood to have been
appointed archdeacon of Rochester about 1137 by Bishop John
of Séez, who a year before had been actively engaged in treating
Merton as a model priory.[1] There are indications that Bishop
John was well acquainted with Merton long before. I suggest
that in this way he knew of Nicholas's merits, and recommended
him to the archdeacon for future advancement. When he became
cardinal Robert found his opportunity, and through him, though
after his death, Nicholas was made cardinal bishop of Albano.

If this hypothesis is favourably regarded, the dates in Nicholas's
biography need reconsideration. He was sent on his long mission
to Scandinavia in 1152, and did not return until late in 1154.
So onerous a task would hardly be imposed on a man past middle
life. I incline to think that Nicholas was born much later than is
generally supposed, and that he went abroad some time after
1130. He would then be well remembered at Merton seven years
later, and the interest of Bishop John might well have been
employed in bringing his name before Archdeacon Robert.
When Robert was made cardinal and chancellor, he would have
a natural desire to promote a fellow countryman, and I think
it likely that he recommended Nicholas for high preferment so
soon as an opportunity presented itself. The distractions of the
time and the Pope's long visit to France sufficiently explain the
fact that the appointment was not made until several years
after Robert's retirement or death.

3. I can here add only a few brief notes about some other
Englishmen who appear at the papal court under Eugenius III.

[1] See above, p. 293.

(a) There can be little doubt that it was Cardinal Robert who brought John of Salisbury thither, as I believe towards the end of 1146.[1] John continued to be the Pope's clerk until after the death of Eugenius in 1154.

(b) Another man owed his advancement to Bishop Henry of Winchester. This was his clerk Hilary, who was dean of Christ Church at Twynham in Hampshire—the name of the church has now supplanted that of the town—about 1140.[2] He went to Rome, that is, to the papal court, probably at Viterbo, and acquired a great reputation for his ability in dealing with litigious business.[3] He came to England at the beginning of 1145, presumably in attendance on the legate Cardinal Imar, and took part in a suit of the monks of Rochester against Bishop Ascelin.[4] It was Eugenius himself who directed Hilary's appointment to the see of Chichester in August 1147. The learning which he had acquired in Italy made him an important accession to Henry II's strength in his later contest with Archbishop Thomas.

(c) Boso, said, on what authority I cannot discover, to have been a nephew of Nicholas Breakspear, became personally acquainted with Thomas Becket from the time of Guido Pisanus.[5] Now this cardinal succeeded Robert Pullen as chancellor at the end of 1146, and Boso had probably belonged to Robert's staff. When Guido ceased to hold the office in the spring of 1149, Boso was employed in the chancery until May 1152. After this, in 1156, he was sent on business into England;[6] and it was then probably that Thomas introduced him to Archbishop Theobald.[7] On his return he was made cardinal deacon of SS. Cosmas and Damianus by Adrian IV before 4 January 1157, and promoted cardinal priest of the title of St. Pudentiana by Alexander III in 1166. He was chamberlain of the Roman see. To him we owe important biographies of these two Popes, and probably a revised edition of the Roman Provinciale.

(d) Baldwin, the future archbishop of Canterbury, we have

---

[1] See my article on 'John of Salisbury at the Papal Court' above pp. 248 ff.

[2] See Mr. Round's paper in the *Athenaeum*, 23 January 1897.

[3] John of Hexham, ii. 321.

[4] Thorpe, *Reg. Roff.*, p. 41.

[5] See the archbishop's letter in Robertson's *Materials*, vi. 58.

[6] See John of Salisbury, Ep. 31. In my paper on *The Early Correspondence of John of Salisbury* (1924), above 273–4, I inclined to date this letter in 1157, but I now think it was probably written in the autumn of 1156.

[7] *Materials, l.c.*

mentioned as clerk to the bishop of Exeter in 1160.[1] It has not, I think, been noticed that nearly ten years earlier his learning must have been well known, because when he was presented to Eugenius III at Ferentino the Pope appointed him as instructor (*institutor*) to Gratian,[2] a nephew of Innocent II. Eugenius was at Ferentino from November 1150 to the following summer. Among the Englishmen who then attended his court were Cardinal Nicholas of Albano and the two clerks, John of Salisbury and Boso. When Baldwin returned to Exeter he became clerk, as I have said, to Bishop Robert Warelwast; and the next bishop, Bartholomew, who was consecrated in 1162, made him archdeacon, an office which he held at least as late as 1168.[3] That he afterwards entered the Cistercian order and became abbot of Ford, and many years later was made bishop of Worcester and then archbishop, are facts which lie beyond the range of the present notice.

(e) From John of Salisbury's words it might appear that another contemporary at the papal court, Gratian, was also an Englishman. John says:

Desiderabam autem revera meum videre cognominem et (quod magis est) compatriotam et quodammodo fratrem Gratianum. . . . Illum fratrem dixerim confidenter, cum quo mihi fidei et societatis sunt iura communia; et, licet nos non ediderit una civitas, patriam tamen nobis unam esse non ambigit, qui patriam fortium, quae nobis individua est et quam ostendit Carmentis, reducit ad mentem.

One might suppose that Gratian's mother, a sister of Innocent II, married into England. But on closer inspection we see that John is amusing himself with elaborate allusions. Gratian is his namesake, because John, that is Johanan, means *gratia Domini*.[4] He is a compatriot, because all brave men are of one country; as Carmentis said to her son Evander,

Omne solum forti patria est.[5]

In 1169 Gratian was sent on a mission to appease the controversy between Henry II and Archbishop Thomas, and was made cardinal deacon of SS. Cosmas and Damianus in 1178. Twenty years later he aspired to the Papacy when Innocent III was elected.

---

[1] See above, p. 289.   [2] John of Salisbury, Ep. 292.
[3] Hist. MSS. Comm., *Report on Various Collections*, iv. 51.
[4] Cf. Ep. 291.   [5] Ovid, *Fasti*, i. 493.

TWO DOCUMENTS CONCERNING ARCHBISHOP ROGER OF YORK[1]

AFTER the murder of Archbishop Thomas Becket on 29 December 1170 his opponents were for a long time in great trouble. It was not indeed suggested that they were in any sense accomplices in the act, but it was held that their previous doings were indirectly the cause of it. Among these opponents the highest in position was Roger, the archbishop of York. He had just before taken part in the coronation of Henry II's son in spite of the Pope's prohibition, and he had therefore been suspended from his office by Alexander III. Not until October 1171 did the Pope give authority for his restoration, and this was only to be effected on definite conditions. He was required to swear before the archbishop of Rouen and other ecclesiastical officers that he had not maintained the Constitutions of Clarendon, that he had never by word or act done anything that led Archbishop Thomas to his death, that he was ignorant that the Pope had forbidden the coronation of the young king, and that at that coronation all things were duly performed.[2] It is stated that the terms of Roger's purgation were properly carried out,[3] and in December the archbishop issued a rescript to the clergy and people of his province notifying the fact. In this document the address is correctly given, but the terms on which his absolution was granted are discreetly omitted. More than this, about two-thirds of the rescript are occupied by a vehement denunciation of his opponents. This part is so remarkable that it is necessary to print it in full.

Fecerunt hoc qui jampridem sederunt mihi in insidiis. Et quidem primo paraverunt laqueum suspensionis, quo dominus papa, plus eorum falsas suggestiones quam juris ordinem secutus, me innodavit. Deinde, ne quoquomodo solvi posset, iniquitatem iniquitati addentes, hinc maximorum virorum libellos arte multiplici, sicut jam a pluribus retro annis instructi fuerant, conquirebant; inde peregrinorum et qui me numquam viderant multitudinem subornabant, ut ea quae non noverant mentientes, apud summum pontificem et curiam

---

[1] Reprinted from *Speculum*, vol. iii (1928).

[2] J. C. Robertson, *Materials for the History of Thomas Becket, Archbishop of Canterbury* vii (1885), 500.

[3] *Ibid.*, p. 502. So too Arnulf of Lisieux, Ep. 57 (misplaced by Robertson. vii. 495).

Romanam quocunque modo famam onerarent. Absens eram, et qui ex parte mea in curia pauci tantae multitudini vix resistere poterant, tam exquisitis pressi mendaciis, maxime cum quidam, solo habitu religiosi, videntes illos prosperari in iniquitatibus suis, cum illis currebant, et neglecto Dei timore ad eversionem dignitatis ecclesiae nostrae, una cum meretricibus suis quas secum duxerant, ne quis sexus persecutioni meae deesset, multa dixerunt. Hi omnes in unum convenientes proposuerunt in cordibus suis gigantes imitari, parietem ex maximis quasi quibusdam lapidibus et multis mendaciis, fictis ad tempus suspiriis et gemitibus, non solum domos, sed et plateas replentes diurno et nocturno ululatu, eundemque ipsum parietem tanquam quodam indissolubili bitumine, vim naturae facientes, simulatis lacrimis linierunt, sperantes hoc modo coelum claudere se posse, et veritatem perpetuo carceri deputare. Quid plura? Idem Pharao illorum, ille spiritualis, cujus ipsi membra sunt, in tali equitatu incedere videbatur cum corona, et ego, miserae cophini servituti deputatus, respiciebam ad auxilium hominum, et non erat. Cuti enim meae, consumptis carnibus, os meum adhaeserat.[1]

This whole passage seems to be an interpolation, an invention composed with the design of showing that the oath taken by the archbishop was, to say the least of it, insincere. I will notice only two points. There is mention of a suit at the papal court where Roger's adversaries appear *cum meretricibus suis*: this is a manifest travesty. Secondly, Becket is spoken of as 'Pharaoh'. Now at that time few works were more familiar than St. Bernard's sermons on the Canticles, and there in serm. xxxix the name Pharaoh is treated as almost convertible with *diabolus*. This then was the language in which Roger was represented to have spoken of the martyred archbishop in a document notifying his absolution.

The use of the name Pharaoh infuriated the Canterbury clerks, and they determined on reprisals. This appears from a letter which is preserved in the immense Becket correspondence and which J. A. Giles included among John of Salisbury's letters as Ep. 305. This letter is addressed to the archbishop of Sens, nephew to Bishop Henry of Winchester, in the name of *miseri illi qui quondam fuere Cantuarienses*.[2] It begins with a sober lamentation over the murder, but soon breaks out into invective

[1] Robertson, vii. 504 f.

[2] According to Bréal, *Recueil*, xvi. 619, one manuscript contains the rubric, *Epistola Johannis Saresberiensis et clericorum beati Thomae*. If John wrote any part of the letter he certainly wrote no more than the opening paragraph.

against Archbishop Roger and his friends, and charges Roger with grave immorality. I proceed to quote the following passage.

Sedent de regione blasphemi, qui sub nomine et honore sacerdotali, sacerdotium persequuntur, principibus adulantes, persecutorum ecclesiae justificantes causam, exultantes in rebus pessimis, scilicet quod potestatibus astiterunt adversus Dominum et adversus christum ejus, cujus sanguis, per eos effusus[1] militum ministerio, de terra clamat ad Dominum magis quam sanguis Abel justi, quem frater ipsius interemit.

Horum caput est ille Eboracensis, quem vidistis et audistis palam in curia archiepiscopum persequentem, et qui indignus fuerat, ore sacrilego, quo necem martyris procuravit, ipsius proferre nomen: eum plane mendosus et mendax, jam inauditis coruscantem miraculis adhuc, sicut ex litteris ejus patet, nominat Pharaonem. Sed non movemur, si flagitiosa bellua martyrem non honorat, quae, sicut opera manifesta convincunt, Deum utique non veretur. Dicitur tamen quod parat ad curiam proficisci, ut purget vitae sordidae notam, quasi homo qui justiciam fecerit, et non deliquerit judicium Dei sui. Et ne ipsius purgatio valeat impediri, procuravit ut nulli nostratum liceat transfretare nisi domini regis impetrata licentia; quae quidem obtineri non potest, nisi praestetur cautio nihil quod queretur contra martyris persecutores. Quid ergo facient miseri zelantes legem, videntes justitiam opprimi, et sibi exitum denegari? Sed certe verbum Dei non est alligatum, et vobis libertas est, et os patens ad ecclesiam Romanam, et notissima veritas.

Novistis enim martyrem in vita sua, novistis causam ejus, novistis et nos qui coexsulavimus ei: novistis et istum Caipham temporis nostri, qui sub specie conquerentis persuasit expedire, et unus moreretur aut caperetur, ne tota gens periret. Eratis in Anglia cum patruo vestro domino Wintoniensi, quando idem nunc Caïphas, tunc archidiabolus, Walterum illum, cujus adolescentis admodum venusta facie ne dicatur[2] nefario concubitu) nimis consueverat delectari, hispidum et procaciori lingua evomentem probra, quae in contumeliam naturae perpessus fuerat, oculis orbari fecit, et postmodum scelus arguentem idem archidiabolus, judicibus qui saecularia negotia exercebant corruptis, adegit suspendio. Sic vir ille, non minus benignus quam pudicus, columbi sui acceptavit affectum. Sic veteris amasii diu exhibitum obsequium remuneravit, ut primo stuprum inferret misero, deinde miseriori, quia de consensu tam sordidae immunditiae poenitebat, capulationem et oculorum avulsionem infli-

---

[1] After *effusus* Giles's text of Joh. Saresb. Ep. cccv adds *licet*.

[2] The words *ne dicatur* which are inserted in several manuscripts, are in one marked for omission.

geret, et tandem miserrimum, quia clamore, ut poterat, suas pro-
testabatur angustias, suspensum in patibulo fecerit jugulari.[1]

The letter goes on to say that it was through the instrumentality of Becket himself that Pope Eugenius III was persuaded
by the bishops of Chichester and Worcester to admit Roger to
purgation. The alleged offence therefore belongs to some time
between 1151 and 1153. It is not worth while to discuss the
impossible caricature of judicial proceedings which the letter
contains—it was part of the furniture of the lowest type of
medieval controversy;—I will only note that no hint of the
charge against Archbishop Roger is contained in any of the
chronicles and correspondence of the time. Had such a scandal
been known it is scarcely conceivable that Roger could have
been made archbishop of York in October 1154. Nevertheless
this fiction has survived as a stain on Roger's character ever
since.

[1] Robertson, *Materials for the History of Thomas Becket*, vii. 527 f.

THE DATES OF HENRY II'S CHARTERS[1]

THE fact that the charters of the kings of England from the Norman Conquest to the accession of Richard I are normally devoid of any date of year is well known. The date of place, indeed, combined with the list of witnesses, may often fix the time of issue within probable and definite limits; but until we are in the possession of a full calendar of the documents of the period, such as Jaffé and Boehmer and their redactors have compiled for those of the Popes and Emperors, a large proportion of these important materials for history must remain in disorder. Robert William Eyton's *Court, Household, and Itinerary of King Henry II* (1878) was an admirable pioneer work, but, like all pioneer works, it is rather a model of what can be done and of the way of doing it than a final settlement of the facts. The most recent investigation into the chronology of Henry's charters is that of the illustrious scholar M. Léopold Delisle, to whom for more than half a century all students of manuscripts and most students of medieval history are under immeasurable obligations. The results of his inquiry have appeared in two articles published in the *Bibliothèque de l'École des Chartes*,[2] in which he has attempted to establish a fixed division between two periods in the king's reign. This division he holds to be marked by the appearance of the formula *Dei gratia* in the royal title. The suggestion itself, M. Delisle admits, is not new. It has been agreed, at least in England, since the days of Sir Thomas Duffus Hardy and Sir Harris Nicolas, that the formula is indicative of the latter part of Henry's reign. What is new in M. Delisle's theory is that the formula was introduced at a definite date, between 1172 and 1173, and that consequently any document in which it is not found is earlier than that date, and any document in which it appears is later. The theory however is deprived of some of its practical value by two limitations which have to be carefully borne in mind. First, it is only on originals that we can rely in testing the date by the formula. Secondly, the rule does not always hold good in respect of charters drawn up by persons unconnected with the king's chancery. There are, therefore, three points to be considered—(1) the date of change,

[1] Reprinted from the *English Historical Review*, vol. xxiii (1908).
[2] Vol. lxvii, pp. 361–401 (1906), lxviii. 272–314 (1907).

1172–1173; (2) the restriction of the rule to originals drawn up in the chancery; and (3) the exceptions caused by certain documents having been produced elsewhere, what may be called irregular originals.

1. As to the date of the introduction of the grace, M. Delisle's theory has not been controverted on the basis of any original charter drawn up in the king's chancery. Mr. Round has indeed published a criticism of M. Delisle's first paper on the subject,[1] but he has been less concerned with the theory itself than with certain inconsistencies in M. Delisle's presentment of his evidence and especially with his application of the hypothesis to the dating of documents preserved only in transcripts. It may be admitted that M. Delisle weakened his case by quoting transcripts side by side with originals, and also that he fell into some errors in matters of detail which have not escaped Mr. Round's vigilance.[2] Until however an original product of Henry II's chancery is brought to light, bearing the formula *Dei gratia*, which can be proved to be earlier than May 1172, M. Delisle's theory may be said to hold the field. The date before which the change of style cannot have been made is arrived at as follows: There is a document of Bishop Richard of Coutances, dated in full on the 6th of the Ides of March 1172, which was confirmed by Henry at Caen. In this confirmation the king uses no grace. Now he is known to have left England in May, and to have been at or near Caen on several days between the 17th and 22nd. On the other hand, the charter must be earlier than 17 May 1173, on which day one of the witnesses, Richard, archdeacon of Poitiers, was elected bishop of Winchester.[3] It may therefore be assigned with confidence to May 1172.[4] The earliest charter which bears the formula of grace is a confirmation to the abbey of Fontevrault which was granted during Henry's stay at that place on 23 February 1173.[5]

[1] *Archaeological Journal*, no. 254 (1907).

[2] I do not attach the importance that Mr. Round does to his criticism of M. Delisle's observations relative to the charter concerning the bakery of Rouen (*Calendar of Documents, France*, pp. 465 f., no. 1280), because, though I have no doubt that Mr. Round is now right in assigning it to the last years of the reign of Henry I, in his *Calendar* he expressed himself in terms which were susceptible of two contradictory interpretations.   [3] *Bibl.* lxvii. 386.

[4] Henry was again in Normandy in the autumn, but there is no evidence connecting him with Caen at that time.

[5] *Les Formules 'Rex Anglorum' et 'Dei gratia Rex Anglorum'*; *Lettre à M. J. Horace Round*, pp. 6 f. (Chantilly: privately printed, 1907).

M. Delisle therefore concludes that the formula was introduced at some time between May 1172 and February 1173. It may however be urged that here at the very opening of the argument he is breaking his first rule, for neither of the documents cited is preserved in the original. That is true, but the originals existed until the last years of the seventeenth century and were transcribed under the direction of Gaignières, whose fidelity is beyond dispute. A transcript of this sort stands on quite a different footing from copies made for business purposes by medieval scribes. However, these two limits, May 1172 to February 1173, form only the basis for a working hypothesis. If we assume it for a moment we may connect the adoption of the new formula either, as M. Delisle hints, with Henry's reconciliation with the Church on 21 May 1172 or, according to Mr. Round's suggestion, with a change of chancellor, though this would not occur until after Geoffrey Ridel's election as bishop of Ely in May 1173.[1]

2. With regard to charters preserved only in medieval transcripts it may be laid down generally that it would not be safe to draw any argument from the presence or absence of the formula. So soon as the grace became established in the royal style the copyists of the charter rolls by force of habit inserted it in transcripts where it cannot be proved to have been in the original. Occasionally they omitted it in cases where we have good reason to believe that the original contained it. The same thing may be said of copies preserved in chartularies. I venture to think that these transcripts are best left out of account in dealing with the question of formulae.

3. Far more interesting is the problem raised by what I have called the irregular class of charters. In his second article M. Delisle deals with seventy-two originals[2] preserved in the Public Record Office and in the British Museum. Among these he finds only four which do not conform to his rule, and three of them can be accounted for on the hypothesis that they were drawn up by some member of the religious houses to which the grants they contain were made.

(1) One is a letter of protection for the abbey of Westminster,

---

[1] In his second paper M. Delisle writes guardedly, 'au cours de l'année 1173, peut-être même à la fin de 1172, ou tout au commencement de 1174, probablement à l'arrivée d'un nouveau chancelier' (*Bibl.* lxviii. 272).

[2] He calendars 74, but two of these are not formal royal charters.

assigned to 1155–57,[1] which bears the title *Henricus Dei gratia rex*, &c., in elongated capitals. Now the use of capitals in the king's title is quite foreign to Henry's chancery. The only other instance known to M. Delisle occurs in a Foucarmont charter, written at Rouen not by a chancery official but *per manum Stephani de Fulgeris scriptoris*.[2] Secondly, the writing of the king's name in full, instead of *H.* or *.H.*, appears in only one other of the seventy-two charters here described. That charters were sometimes drawn up, not merely by representatives of the religious houses concerned, but actually in those houses before the document was submitted for the king's approval, is shown by a charter of which M. Delisle gives a facsimile, and in which the text is written in a set book hand and the witnesses' names added in quite a different writing, presenting features of the chancery hand of the period.[3] It is a peculiarity of such documents that they sometimes, following the ecclesiastical pattern, include a precise date, such as, *Facta est autem ista mea confirmatio anno ab incarnatione Domini Mº Cº LXIIº*.[4]

(2) A charter to Newhouse abbey, assigned to 1175, begins *H. rex Anglie*, instead of *Anglorum*, and omits the grace.[5] M. Delisle points out that, apart from a few changes in the terms of the grant, the document is textually copied from one placed between 1155 and 1164. Both charters, and indeed a third, also for Newhouse,[6] bear marks of being written by the same hand: all have the irregular *Anglie*, and all have the unusual *Testibus* (instead of *T.*) before the list of witnesses. I may cite a parallel, which I owe to the kindness of my friend the Rev. H. E. Salter, in three charters confirming Takeley, in Essex, and other property to the monastery of St. Valéry, and now in the possession of the warden and fellows of New College, Oxford. Two of them are of Henry I, one early and the other late in the reign; the third was granted by Henry II between 1162 and 1164: except in the witnesses and in matters of orthography they appear to be identical.[7] The documents begin respectively as follows:

Henricus Dei gratia Rex Anglie.
Henricus Rex Anglie Archepiscopis Episcopis Abbatibus, &c.
Henricus Dei gratia Rex Anglie Dux Normannie et Aquitanie, &c.

---

[1] Probably January 1156; cf. Eyton, p. 15. [2] Round, *Calendar*, p. 64.
[3] *Les Formules*, postscript. [4] Cf. *ibid.*, pp. 7–9.
[5] No. 51, *Bibl.* lxviii. 288. [6] No. 25, *ibid.*, p. 281.
[7] Two of the three certainly bore a seal; in the third the photograph does not enable me to form any opinion.

A comparison of the orthography leads to the conclusion that the third is a copy not of the second but of the first, and this fact explains the *Dei gratia*. The writing of *Henricus* in full and the use of *Anglie* in place of *Anglorum*, which are found in all three, are perhaps accounted for by the scribe's acquaintance with the usage of the kings of France. The capitals in the second document are unmistakably modelled upon the forms of a papal privilege. The comparison of the three shows how naturally a copyist deputed by his monastery might reproduce the text of what he had before him, only adding in the case of Henry II the extension of his territorial title.[1] The reason for such grants simply repeating former grants M. Delisle sees in the need which the religious houses had for obtaining duplicate or multiple copies of their most important title-deeds in the days before the vidimus or inspeximus or exemplification had come into existence.[2]

(3) A charter confirming the privileges of Rochester Cathedral, which belongs to a date subsequent to May 1173, presents various anomalies.[3] The terms of the address are irregular and the greeting is unexampled. The document opens without any grace, but in its course the king twice resumes his royal style, *ego H. Dei gratia rex Angl.*, contrary to all usage. If the charter is genuine it looks as though a local scribe had taken the *ego* from a French model. In any case no one will attribute it to the royal chancery.

(4) There is a charter to the abbey of Bordesley, issued between 1155 and 1158, and written in a bold court hand, which contains the formula *Dei gratia*.[4] M. Delisle suggests that the scribe may by inadvertence have copied the grace from the seal, on which it is well known it always appeared. This is possible, but I think we must allow a margin of error even in the most strictly regulated chancery. If, as may well be the fact, the document belongs to January 1155, three months after Henry's coronation, we need not be surprised to find a foreign clerk introducing into it a feature with which he was familiar on the continent. Another charter which M. Delisle does not include among his irregular specimens is one granted at Winchester to

---

[1] And in this he had to write *Normannie, Aquitanie,* &c., instead of *Normannorum* &c., in order to suit the *Anglie* with which he started.

[2] *Bibl.* lxviii. 304–7.   [3] No. 53, *ibid.*, pp. 289, 307 f.

[4] No. 11, *ibid.*, pp. 277, 298 f., and facsimile.

Hugh Esturmi, which omits the grace and yet clearly belongs to some date not earlier than 1173, to which M. Delisle doubtfully assigns it.[1] But there is no evidence that the king was at Winchester in 1173, and Eyton placed the document so late as 1181,[2] a date which is favoured by the appearance of Hugh of Morwich among the witnesses. But another witness is given in the form *Gaufrido Ridello Eliensi episcopo*, and this arouses suspicion of the genuineness of the charter, unless *electo* has accidentally slipped out. But a clerk who committed this mistake can hardly be trusted on a point of technical correctness.

---

[1] No. 70, *bid.*, p. 295.   [2] Eyton, p. 245.

THE PUBLICATION OF GREAT CHARTERS
BY THE ENGLISH KINGS[1]

THE royal charter of liberties is an expansion of the oath made by the king at his coronation, to protect the Church and the people committed to his charge, to rule justly and give good laws, and to put down evil customs. In some of the coronation charters granted by the English kings it was deemed sufficient merely to confirm in general terms the liberties and good laws which the people had received from their predecessors. This was the form taken by the coronation charters of Stephen and Henry II. But on one occasion the charter took a more elaborate form. This was when Henry I assumed the throne under a doubtful title. His example was followed by Stephen when it became certain that his tenure was not unchallenged. It was followed again by John when in circumstances which are familiar he was constrained to issue his great charter. These three charters stand by themselves. The last remains for all time the Great Charter, and the first also was given that name in the thirteenth century.[2] That the second charter of Stephen is not so designated is probably to be accounted for by the fact as related by Henry of Huntingdon: 'These things he vowed, but none of them he kept'.[3]

The charter of Henry I has been the subject of a minute study by Professor Liebermann.[4] He examined twenty-eight transcripts, but no original could be discovered. By a comparison, however, of these copies he was able to arrive at the conclusion that, when the charter was first drawn up, one original was deposited in the treasury at Winchester,[5] which he thinks bore a general address. A large number of other originals were sent out to all the counties of England. We have the text of one transcript addressed by the king to the bishop and sheriff, 'to Samson the bishop and Urso of Abetot the sheriff and all his barons and faithful men, as well French as English born, of Worcestershire'; and we have one copy addressed to a sheriff

---

[1] Reprinted from the *English Historical Review*, vol. xxviii, (1913). This paper was read at the International Congress of Historical Studies at London on 3 April.

[2] *Transactions of the Royal Historical Society*, New Series, viii. 21, 1894.

[3] *Hist. Angl.* viii. 3, p. 258, ed. T. Arnold, 1879.

[4] *Transactions*, as above, pp. 21–48.

[5] Richard of Hexham, in *Chronicles of Stephen*, &c., ed. R. Howlett, iii. 142.

alone, 'to Hugh of Buckland the sheriff and to all his faithful men, as well French as English, in Hertfordshire.' These charters were no doubt preserved in the cathedral church of Worcester and in the abbey of St. Albans. There are, further, indications more or less definite which point to originals once existing at Canterbury, Rochester, Malmesbury, Bury St. Edmunds, Peterborough, York, and Hexham, and presumably representing charters sent to the counties of Kent, Wiltshire, Suffolk, Northamptonshire, Yorkshire, and Northumberland. The statement, therefore, of Roger of Wendover that 'as many charters were made as there are counties in England, and by the king's command they were deposited in the abbeys of every county as a memorial,'[1] is confirmed by the copies preserved. Matthew Paris, who repeats the words of Wendover with some interpolations, goes on to say that after a time the king regretted his grant of the charter and by various artifices (*diversis viribus vel fallaciis*) recovered all the specimens, leaving them only at Canterbury, St. Albans, and York.[2] Whether there is any vestige of foundation for this statement we have no means of knowing; but it is clear that the shape which it has taken represents a local tradition or fiction subserving the interests of the dignity of the abbey of St. Albans. The form of the address in the two instances in which it appears may be taken as evidence that the originals were addressed to the bishop and sheriff, if the county had a cathedral city, and if it had not to the sheriff alone. The example of Malmesbury may point to the fact that a county like Wiltshire, which possessed not only a bishop's see but also a monastery of the first importance like Malmesbury, would receive more than one original. Whether all these charters were separately attested it is difficult to say. The transcripts show some differences in the order of the names of the witnesses; the Worcester text has two names which are not found elsewhere, and the Rochester text has at least one.[3] Dr. Liebermann inclines to the opinion that 'only one series of witnesses was authentic'. But it is possible that an examination of the charter of Stephen may lead to another conclusion.

The preservation of what I take leave to call the 'great

---

[1] *Flores Historiarum*, ii. 164, ed. H. O. Coxe, 1841.

[2] *Hist. Anglorum*, i. 180 f., ed. F. Madden, 1866.

[3] I think with Dr. Liebermann, p. 25, that the name of Bishop Gundulf is an interpolation in the Rochester copy; nor can I doubt that Gilbert Crispin has been foisted into the corrupt text traceable to Westminster.

charter' of Stephen granted at Oxford early in April 1136[1] is very different from that of Henry I's coronation charter. Two originals of it exist, and these originals still remain in the places where they were deposited at the beginning, in the cathedral churches of Exeter and Salisbury.[2] The Exeter charter may be seen in an engraved facsimile prefixed to the first volume of the *Statutes of the Realm* published by the Record Commission in 1810, and it was this text which was taken as the basis of the edition.[3] The Salisbury original seems to have escaped the editor's attention; it has been briefly described in a Report of the Historical Manuscripts Commission.[4] Besides these two it has long been known that a third original was once in the possession of Thomas Hearne, the Oxford antiquary, who printed it in an appendix to his edition of William of Newburgh;[5] but, as Sir William Blackstone remarked in 1759, 'what is now become of it is uncertain'.[6] It is, however, mentioned in Hearne's own catalogue of his manuscripts now in the Rawlinson collection in the Bodleian library,[7] and is there described as '17. An old Charter of King *Stephen's* (dated at Oxford an. 1136) by which he grants and confirms divers Privileges to the Church of Hereford'. But the charter itself is not in the Bodleian. It was brought to light three or four years ago, when, on the death of Dr. James Bellamy, President of St. John's College, Oxford, his library came to be examined. Among his books was a portfolio of twenty-nine documents of various dates, entitled in Hearne's handwriting 'Things relating to Hereford', and no. 17 in the series, exactly as stated in Hearne's manuscript catalogue, is the charter of King Stephen. It bears the endorsement *De libertate Her[efordensis] ecclesie*; and this explains why Hearne

[1] See J. H. Round, *Geoffrey de Mandeville*, pp. 23 f., 1892.

[2] The fact that the site of the church at Salisbury was removed in the thirteenth century from the hill to the plain involves no break in the historical continuity of the custody of the document.

[3] The Exeter original is exhibited in the cathedral library with a label describing it as 'the only authentick copy known to be now subsisting'. It is endorsed 'Carta Stephani Regis de Libertatibus Ecclesie Angl' et Regni'. Compare my note on it in the Hist. MSS. Comm., *Report on Manuscripts in Various Collections*, iv (1907) 43.

[4] See my account in the *Report on Manuscripts in Various Collections*, i (1901), 384 f. The document is exhibited in a glass case in the cathedral muniment room.

[5] p. 711, 'charta quaedam antiqua et authentica penes me.'

[6] *The Great Charter and Charter of the Forest*, introd., p. iv, note c, Oxford 1759.

[7] Rawlinson MS., D. 1168, pp. 143–6.

should have stitched it into a volume of Hereford documents, and also why he described it as granting privileges to the church of Hereford. But it is in fact a third original of Stephen's great charter, the exemplar which was deposited for custody in the church of Hereford.[1]

Now it must be admitted that while the preservation of three originals of this charter, two of them in the places to which they were at first entrusted, is a remarkable fact, the charter does not present the same interesting features of Henry I's charter. It is not addressed differently according to the persons who were to take charge of it. And the explanation of this is that it is not addressed at all. It is in fact a very peculiar document. It looks as though a scribe familiar with the style of French charters had attempted to produce a diploma in the Old English form. Anyhow, the address is absent: the king starts at once by declaring what he promises to do; he does not notify this to any one. Nevertheless, the charter was manifestly circulated; and the originals at Exeter and Salisbury and that once at Hereford are no doubt specimens of similar charters preserved at least in all cathedral churches, and, it may be assumed, deposited there on behalf of the counties: so that it is a natural inference that the same procedure was adopted in the case of Stephen's great charter as in that of Henry I's. There are also signs of the charter having been accessible at Canterbury[2] and Malmesbury.[3]

A comparison of the three originals leads to the conclusion that no attempt was made at uniformity in their execution. As for size, the Salisbury document measures $11\frac{1}{2}$ by $7\frac{3}{4}$ inches, the Hereford one 10 by $8\frac{1}{2}$, and that at Exeter $10\frac{1}{2}$ by $4\frac{3}{4}$. Then the text of the charter at Exeter is written continuously: at Salisbury it is marked for division into ten paragraphs. The Salisbury document is written in a more handsome shape than that at Exeter; and the Hereford document is much more contracted. Again, the titles of the witnesses are described in different forms: at Exeter the bishops place the adjective of their see before the word *episcopo*, at Salisbury and Hereford

[1] It has since been presented by St. John's College to the Bodleian Library where it is catalogued Rawl. Q. a. 1 (*Summary Catalogue*, no. 37443).

[2] It is cited in the *Statutes of the Realm*, Table of Charters, from two registers there, v and ix: these indications, however, do not correspond to any existing press-marks of Registers at Canterbury.

[3] William of Malmesbury, *Hist. novella*, § 464, vol. ii. 541 f., ed. W. Stubbs, 1889, gives the text of the charter, adding 'Nomina testium, qui multi fuerunt, apponere fastidio'.

they place it after it; there are several variations in detail in the witnesses of the earls, and in the Salisbury document the order is in one case transposed. The Hereford original disagrees with the others in inserting the name of Roger of Fécamp immediately after the chancellor and Henry the king's nephew, and before the earls. Now Roger of Fécamp appears as a witness to Stephan's grant to Winchester of the church of Sutton,[1] which was made at Easter in the same year 1136,[2] and then he signed between the chancellor and the king's nephew and was designated *capellanus*.[3] We must therefore conclude either that his name has been accidentally omitted in the Exeter and Salisbury originals, or else that even in charters of a specially solemn kind uniformity in the list of witnesses was not invariably preserved.[4] A discrepancy of greater interest occurs in the date, where, after the year of the incarnation, the Exeter and Salisbury texts read 'sed regni mei primo', but the Hereford manuscript has 'in communi concilio'. Finally, while the Hereford document retains a portion of the great seal and that at Exeter has green and yellow silk strings to which a very small fragment is attached, the Salisbury document shows no signs of ever having had a seal at all.

It may be remarked that though the charter was certainly sent out to three cathedral churches and was no doubt published in every county, its provisions did not become well known. Indeed, the account of them given by Henry of Huntingdon states rather what people may have wished the king to do than what he in fact said he would do. Henry says[5] that the king vowed, first, not to hold back the temporalities of sees in his hands (which is substantially correct); secondly, that he would not retain the forests of clerk or layman as King Henry had done (which is quite different from what Stephen promised); and

---

[1] Hearne, *Liber niger Scaccarii*, p. 810.   [2] Round, pp. 18 ff., 263.

[3] The order in Hearne's text is violently distorted. Apparently in the original there were three columns: the bishops and chaplains were given in the middle, the earls and the officials on the left hand, and the barons on the right. The transcriber wrote out these columns continuously, and hence placed the archbishops after the stewards. Cf. Round, p. 264, n. 1. Hearne took his text from an original in the duchy of Lancaster, which, however, does not appear in the calendar appended to the 31st *Report of the Deputy Keeper of the Public Records* (1870), and which I have not been able to trace.

[4] It is by a scribal error that the Salisbury document mentions William de Albin' fourth from the last, in place of William de Albamarla. William de Albiniaco has already appeared higher up in the list.

[5] *Hist. Angl.* viii. 3, p. 258.

thirdly, that he would never again levy Danegeld (about which there is not a word in the charter). It is possible that Stephen's inability to observe his engagements led to their terms being forgotten, so that a legend grew up as to what he might be presumed to have promised.

Passing now to our third Great Charter, that of John, we need hardly mention that the mode of its promulgation was quite anomalous. Although in terms a grant by the king to the church and people, its execution was entrusted to a commission of nine prelates and Master Pandulf: 'We have caused to be made for them [the clergy and lay folk] the letters testimonial patent of the Lord Stephen archbishop of Canterbury, of the Lord Henry archbishop of Dublin, and of the bishops aforesaid, and of Master Pandulf, as touching this security [that is, the appointment under clause 61 of twenty-five barons for safeguarding the provisions in the charter] and the concessions aforesaid.' These letters testimonial are transcribed in the Red Book of the Exchequer,[1] and contain the text of the charter interposed between the opening and concluding formulae. But no original specimen of them is known to exist. The charter, however, is found in a separate form in four originals, and it may be doubted whether the letters testimonial as sent out did not accompany the full solemn text of the charter, instead of (as recorded in the Red Book) merely incorporating a transcript. Otherwise it would be difficult to account for the total disappearance of all the texts said to have been recited in the letters. Two of these originals of the charter are still preserved in the cathedral churches in which, we may believe, they were deposited in 1215, at Lincoln and Salisbury. The *provenance* of the two others, now in the Cottonian collection at the British Museum, cannot be traced. One of them was irreparably damaged in the fire of 23 October 1731; but before this calamity John Pine who made an engraving of it, had examined the seal, which is now a shapeless lump of wax, and certified that it was the great seal of John.[2] The other has slits for three seals, but none remains.[3]

---

[1] Fo. 234: see the *Statutes of the Realm*, i, Table of Charters.

[2] The engraved facsimile [1733] may be seen in the Bodleian Library, Gough Maps 41 n, p. 23. The twenty-five coats of arms on each side of the plate are Pine's own ornamentation, and do not represent seals, as M. Bémont states (*Chartes des Libertés Anglaises*, 1892, p. 25).

[3] See the facsimile published by the trustees of the British Museum.

The originals at Lincoln and Salisbury show no trace of any seal at all. It may perhaps be conjectured that the great seal was attached to the original kept in the exchequer. The chroniclers of the time also speak of the charter having been dispatched throughout the land: Ralph Coggeshall says, to every county 'so that each county of all England should have its charter in the same terms confirmed by the king's seal';[1] and the Annals of Dunstaple, 'deposited in every see in a safe place'.[2] There is here no real discrepancy: the charter, like Henry I's, was to be entrusted to the cathedral church, if there was any in the county; if there was none it would, according to analogy, be kept in a monastery. But Coggeshall's assertion that the king's seal was attached to every specimen cannot be substantiated.

The charter was not merely circulated; it was proclaimed. On 19 June the king issued letters patent to the sheriff and other royal officers in every county ordering that the charter should be read publicly throughout their bailiwicks.[3] The procedure with regard to preceding charters suggests that what was sent to the sheriff was an original of the charter itself. But on no previous occasion was it commanded that the charter should be publicly proclaimed in the county court or in any other court. We have difficulty in believing that so long and technical a document as Magna Charta could have been actually read aloud in Latin in the county courts; and when we follow the text of the document which orders this reading, we may infer that its essential purpose was to enjoin obedience to the twenty-five guardians of the charter and to provide for the election of persons to inquire into and to abolish the evil customs practised by the royal officers. No such conclusion, however, can be drawn from the mode in which Henry III ordered his first confirmation of the charter, dated on 11 November 1216, to be proclaimed; for the writ which he issued to the sheriffs seven months later, on 23 June 1217, contained only a command to cause the charter to be read in the county court and the liberties contained therein to be firmly observed.[4]

---

[1] *Chron. Anglic.*, p. 172, ed. J. Stevenson, 1875. Walter of Coventry says 'Deferebatur interim exemplar illius cartae per civitates et vicos, et iuratum est ab omnibus quod eam observarent,' *Memoriale*, ii. 222, ed. W. Stubbs, 1873.

[2] *Annales monastici*, iii. 43, ed. H. R. Luard, 1866.

[3] *Rotuli Patentes*, i. 180b.

[4] *Rotuli Litterarum Clausarum*, i. 336a, from the roll of Henry's first year, m. 15d. Blackstone, p. xxxiii, n. b, erroneously gives m. 10d, and reads *cartas*

Still, it is possible that the procedure actually contemplated was not unlike that which we know to have been adopted in regard to the Provisions of Oxford in 1258. On that occasion, it is true, no attempt was made to rehearse the lengthy text of the document; but a proclamation was issued on 18 October, declaring the king's will that whatsoever the elected council did should be established for ever, that all persons should maintain the same, and that any one who opposed it should be accounted his enemy: to which end letters patent were sent to every county, and these were drawn up in Latin, French, and English.[1] Of the Latin text I do not know that any copy is preserved, but the French and English are recorded on the Patent Rolls.[2] The English letters as enrolled are those addressed to Huntingdon-shire; an original addressed to Oxfordshire is preserved among the muniments of the city of Oxford.[3] In the enrolment a note is added stating that the document was sent in the same words into every shire in England and also into Ireland. Although there is here no mention of any public reading of it, still the fact that the letters were circulated in more than one language can hardly imply anything but that they were designed to be so read. In the absence of direct evidence we cannot assert that a similar method of publication was adopted in the case of the Great Charter of John, but it seems on the whole not improbable, though I would not venture to express an opinion as to the language in which the proclamation was made.

The first two confirmations of the Charter by Henry III were dispatched through the country in the accustomed manner. An original of that of 1216 is preserved at Durham.[4] From 1217 onwards we have to do not with the single Charter, but with the Charters, because the articles dealing with the forest were removed and expanded into a separate charter; but it need not be doubted that the two were sent out together, although they have now in most cases parted company. Indeed, of the Charter of the Forest only one specimen, a damaged parchment

where the roll itself has *cartam*. But the construction of the clauses following is evidently faulty, as *cartam libertatum* continues first with *quas* and afterwards with *quam*.

[1] Burton Annals, in *Annales monastici*, i. 453, 1864.

[2] Rymer's *Foedera*, i. 377 f., ed. 1816.

[3] See a facsimile prefixed to O. Ogle's *Royal Letters addressed to Oxford*, 1892. The text was printed by the late Dr. W. W. Skeat in *The Academy*, xxi. 338, 13 May 1882.

[4] *Statutes of the Realm*, ii, Charters of Liberties, p. 14, and Table of Charters.

at Durham, is known,[1] and of the Charter of Liberties but one original has been hitherto noticed. This is a beautiful charter, still retaining the seals both of the legate and of the earl marshal, preserved in the Bodleian Library and believed on insufficient grounds to have come from the abbey of Gloucester.[2] The same library, however, possesses two other originals, which are traceable to Oseney Abbey; one of them still bears the seal of the earl marshal, and the other that of the legate.[3] They show at least one variation from the text printed from the supposed Gloucester original.[4]

In 1225 we have the charter, very slightly altered from that of 1217, which became the definitive one; and in all subsequent years, as is well known, where we read of the confirmation of the charters, it is to 1225 that we have to go back. The two charters of that year are preserved at Durham, and the Charter of Liberties is also still kept at Lacock Abbey in Wiltshire.[5] This latter is endorsed *Ex deposito militum Wiltisir*:[6] that is to say, after it had been received by the sheriff and communicated to the county court, it was entrusted to the abbey of Lacock for safe custody. When the charters were confirmed in January 1237 they were not recited;[7] but in February 1252 they were set out at length. In March 1265 the Charters were confirmed by

---

[1] *Ibid.*, Charters of Liberties, p. 20, and Table of Charters.

[2] The main reason for thus attributing this charter (Gloucester charter 8) is that it was bequeathed to the library in 1753 by Archdeacon Richard Furney, who had been for five years master of the crypt school at Gloucester a generation earlier.

[3] They are now marked Oseney Charters 142*, and 142**; their older marks were Oseney 13 and 14.

[4] In the sealing clause they differ from the printed text in the *Statutes of the Realm*, i, Charters of Liberties, p. 17, but agree substantially with that of the London Liber Custumarum, of which Blackstone gives a collation, p. 46.

Furney Charter	*Oseney* 142*
'Quia vero nondum habuimus sigillum hanc [ ] sigillis domini legati predicti et comitis Willelmi Marescalli rectoris et regni nostri fecimus sigillari.'	'Quia vero sigillum non dum habuimus presentem cartam sigillis venerabilis patris nostri domini Gual' tituli sancti Martini presbiteri cardinalis et Willelmi Ma[ ]oc rectoris nostri et regni nostri fecimus sigillari. Testibus prenominatis et aliis multis.'

In the Furney Charter a blank space is left after *hanc*, and *nostri* is omitted after *rectoris*. The gap in the marshal's name in the Oseney Charter 142* is due to a hole in the parchment; 142** has 'Maresc. com. Pembroc' undefaced.

[5] *Statutes of the Realm*, Charters of Liberties, pp. 22, 26, and Table of Charters.

[6] Blackstone, introd., p. xlvii.

[7] *Statutes of the Realm*, i, Charters of Liberties, p. 28.

letters patent which included a number of supplementary provisions necessitated by the circumstances of the time, when the king was not a free agent. This document recites that the two charters had lately been transmitted under the king's seal to all the counties: these were sent out in the form of Inspeximus, and transcripts of the originals addressed to Middlesex and to Somerset and Dorset are still in existence.[1] The letters of confirmation state that the charters and ordinances were dispatched to every county 'to be kept for a record in the charge of trustworthy men chosen for the purpose'.[2] No doubt they deposited them in the cathedral or in some abbey church of their shire. It was ordered that they should be published in the county court next after Easter and Michaelmas, and so year after year.

The famous confirmation of the Charters by Edward I in 1297 was made in several stages. It was executed by his son on 12 October by two charters of Inspeximus, which were circulated and were enrolled on the Statute Roll.[3] An original of the Charter of Liberties, with the order to the sheriffs of London for its publication, is preserved at the Guildhall.[4] Then the king himself at Ghent on 5 November issued letters patent ordering that the charters should be dispatched to all his officers and to all towns throughout the country, and that they should be sent to the cathedral cities and read before the people twice a year.[5] On 28 March 1300 another Inspeximus was issued, of which three originals are preserved;[6] and on the same day writs were sent out to all the sheriffs requiring them to have the charters read in full county court four times a year and publicly proclaimed.[7] On 14 February 1301 Edward I again confirmed the charters by letters patent, but he did not recite them, nor was there any order for their publication.[8] The function of the county courts was in fact now transferred to parliament; and from the beginning of the reign of Edward III the Statute Roll of each session normally opened with an express confirmation of the Great Charter of Liberties and of the Charter of the Forest.

---

[1] *Ibid.*, Table of Charters.   [2] *Ibid.*, Charters of Liberties, p. 32.
[3] *Ibid.*, i. 25 Edward I, pp. 114–22.
[4] *Ibid.*, Charters of Liberties, pp. 33–6; cf. Blackstone, introd., pp. lxi, lxii.
[5] *Statutes*, Charters of Liberties, p. 37.
[6] Blackstone, introd., p. lxx.   [7] *Ibid.*, pp. 85 f.
[8] Prynne's *Records*, iii. 648, 1670; *Calendar of Close Rolls*, 1296–1302, p. 396, 1906.

This continued to be the usual, though not the invariable, custom down to the end of the reign of Henry IV. Under Henry VI, in his second year, the form is changed to a general confirmation of 'liberties and franchises', but after this the practice, which had become a matter of common form, was abandoned. At the same time, it was still customary to send out exemplifications of statutes under the great seal to the sheriffs, with writs annexed ordering their proclamation and publication, and sometimes also directing copies to be made and distributed;[1] but this was the publication not of the king's charters but of Acts of Parliament.

---

[1] *Statutes of the Realm*, i, introd., p. xlv. 'Sometimes', it is added in a note, 'the knights, citizens, and burgesses were simply charged upon their return into the country to shew and publish to the people the matters agreed on in parliament.' A reference is given to the Parliament Roll of 37 Edw. III, no. 38.

HENRY SYMEONIS[1]

IT has often been quoted as an example of the persistence of university customs that down to 1827 every member of the university of Oxford was required, before admission to the degree of bachelor of arts, to swear that he would not lecture nor attend lectures at Stamford, *tanquam in universitate, studio, vel collegio generali,*[2] although the secession to that town of the northern party in Oxford ended in 1335. It is also well known that down to the same year in the nineteenth century all bachelors before inception made oath that they would never consent to the reconciliation of Henry Symeonis; but it has never been established who Henry Symeonis was. The terms of the statute are,

Singuli eciam bachilarii quum responderint in vesperiis fidem prebeant quod nunquam consencient in reconciliacionem Henrici Symeonis nec statum bachilarii iterum assument.[3]

Brian Twyne, in his *Antiquitatis Academiae Oxoniensis Apologia,* § 342 (p. 376, Oxford, 1608), connected the two declarations mentioned in the passage quoted, and speaks of the

iuramentis Magistrorum de non resumendis (non dico Henrici Simeonis gradibus quem in artibus Oxoniae Regentem imperante Ioanne, ut apud exteros in monasterium cooptaretur, baccalaureum se finxisse ferunt) lectionibus alibi in hoc regno, quàm hic Oxoniae et Cantabrigiae.

But the statute does not say that the reconciliation of Henry Simeon and the resumption by a master of a bachelor's degree have reference to the same class of offence. The last clause may be epexegetic, but it cannot be proved to be so unless we have evidence as to what Henry Simeon actually did. Twyne's interpretation is embodied in the Laudian Code of Statutes,[4] in which the form of oath is prefaced by the words *de non resumendo Gradum Simeonis*; but this is no proof that it is correct. A few years later it was admitted that the meaning was a matter of conjecture. In a convocation held on 13 June 1651 it was

---

[1] Reprinted from the *English Historical Review*, vol. xxvii (1912).

[2] Laudian Code, tit. ix, sect. vi, § 1. The oath is found in the Junior Proctor's Book (Arch. Univ. Oxon., Reg. C., fo. 2b); it also appears as an insertion in the Senior Proctor's Book (Reg. B., fo. 37).

[3] Reg. C., fo. 20 [olim 14].　　　　[4] Tit. vii, sect. i, § 6, cf. § 15.

proposed by the delegacy for the reform of the statutes that the
oath 'de non resumendo gradum Simeonis' should cease:

Causa est quod cum ante secula aliquot ex causa nobis vel incognita
vel incerta ortum habuerit, vtcunque pro eorum temporum ratione
rationabili tanti tamen non videtur ut posteri omnes in eandem sub
vinculo Iuramenti astringantur.[1]

But the recommendation does not appear to have been approved.[2]

There was in Oxford one Henry, son of Symeon, who is mentioned in the pipe roll of 1177[3] and appears as a witness to
a charter in the last decade of the twelfth century;[4] he was
perhaps one of the reeves of the town in the time of John,[5] and
was alive in 1226.[6] He had a son, Henry son of Henry son of
Simeon, who appears in 1225.[7] In the next generation 'son of
Simeon' or 'fitz Simeon' or perhaps 'Simmonds', seems to
have become a surname. On 22 May 1242 Henry son of Henry
son of Simeon and Robert Oweyn made fine with the king for
£80 in respite of the outlawry which should have been proclaimed against them *pro morte scolarium Oxoñ*, so that they
might stay at Northampton or further north, but not approach
nearer Oxford until the king's return from Aquitaine.[8] The king
was back in England in the autumn, and in the following spring
Henry Simeonis seems to have been again in Oxford.[9] In 1245
Henry III granted to the friars minor an island which he had
bought from Henry son of Henry Simeon.[10] Many years later
many of the Oxford scholars seceded to Northampton: on 12
March 1264, the king suspended the university during the
session of his council at Oxford,[11] and on the 25th he issued
letters patent reciting that, whereas he had ordered

that if it should appear . . . that the chancellor and university would
be content that Henry son of Henry Simeonis, who withdrew for the
death of a man, would return to Oxford and stay there, so that the

---

[1] Reg. T, p. 142, in the University Archives.

[2] Anthony Wood, who records this decision, assigns it in error to 13 January,
i.e. 1651/2: *Life*, i. 173, ed. A. Clark, 1891.

[3] *Roll of 23 Henry II*, p. 16, 1905. For this and several other references I am
indebted to the kindness of my friend the Rev. H. E. Salter.

[4] *Eynsham Cartulary*, ed. Salter, 1907, i. 129, no. 172; Wood, *City of Oxford*,
ed. Clark, ii. 534, 1890.   [5] *Ibid*. iii. 4, 1899.

[6] *Rotuli Litterarum Clausarum*, ii. 151, 1844.

[7] *Patent Roll*, 9 Henry III, m. 1 (p. 556, 1901).

[8] *Excerpta e Rotulis Finium*, i (1835), 379.

[9] *Red Book of the Exchequer*, p. 1076, 1896.

[10] 22 April a. 29, *Calendar of Patent Rolls*, 1232–47, p. 451, 1906.

[11] *Cal. of Patent Rolls*, 1258–66, p. 307, 1910.

university should not retire from the said town on account of his staying there; then they should permit him to return without impediment and have the king's peace; the king ... has pardoned the said Henry the said death, on condition that he stand his trial if any will proceed against him, and has granted that he may return and dwell there so long as he be of good behaviour and that the university do not withdraw from the town on account of his return and the death of the said Henry.[1]

From this it appears that Henry son of Henry Simeonis was charged with homicide, and that his alleged crime was a cause of the secession of the university to Northampton. When it returned to Oxford, the king was a prisoner and the country was in the hands of his enemies.[2] It was not to be expected that the scholars would pay attention to the order of 25 March requiring them to permit Henry the son of Henry Simeonis to come back peaceably to Oxford. Naturally they resumed their former attitude of hostility to him: they would never consent to his reconciliation. This, it seems to me, was the origin of the oath, which was maintained until 1827.

[1] *Ibid.*, p. 309.
[2] The order for the return is dated 30 May (*ibid.*, p. 320).

INDEX

DUE